The Underclass

The Underclass

Ken Auletta

Vintage Books
A Division of Random House
New York

*Grateful acknowledgment is made to the following for permission
to reprint previously published material:*
Harper & Row, Publishers, Inc.: Extracts from pp. *172, 175, 221–222* in *Black
Boy* by Richard Wright. Copyright 1937, 1942, 1944, 1945 by Richard Wright.
Reprinted by permission of Harper & Row, Publishers, Inc.
Little, Brown and Company: Excerpts from *The Unheavenly City Revisited: A
Revision of "The Unheavenly City"* by Edward C. Banfield. Copyright © 1968,
1970, 1974 by Edward C. Banfield. Reprinted by permission of Little, Brown
and Company.
Longman, Inc: Excerpts from *Race and Economics*, 1st edition, by Thomas
Sowell. Copyright © 1975 by Thomas Sowell. Reprinted by permission of
Longman, Inc., New York.
The Washington Post: Excerpts from an editorial by William Raspberry,
© 1976, The Washington Post Company. Reprinted by permission. Excerpts
from editorials by Herbert Denton, Juan Williams, and Nicholas Lemann.
© 1976, 1980, The Washington Post. Reprinted by permission.

Library of Congress Cataloging in Publication Data
Auletta, Ken.
The underclass.
Bibliography: p.
Includes index.
1. Socially handicapped—United States.
2. Poor—United States. I. Title.
HV4045.A9 1983   362.8   82-40433
ISBN 0-394-71388-5

Manufactured in the United States of America

For Howard Smith, who made it,
and Willy Joe, who didn't

Acknowledgments

This book grew out of a discussion with William Whitworth, then my editor at *The New Yorker* magazine. Bill agreed that a portrait of the underclass could be a good piece, and suggested I talk it over with William Shawn, the editor of *The New Yorker.* Mr. Shawn offered words of encouragement, and caution. The idea was a fine one, he said, but unless I found a "vehicle" through which to write about the underclass I might write what he called "a sociological yak piece."

The vehicle I finally came upon was the Manpower Demonstration Research Corporation (MDRC) and the Wildcat Service Corporation. Without their cooperation, I might not have found my vehicle. Their cooperation was gained with an assist from Mitchell Sviridoff, then the vice-president for urban affairs at the Ford Foundation, and a pioneer in exploring the mysteries of the underclass. Sviridoff's colleague at Ford, Robert Schrank, generated ideas the way a power plant generates electricity. The openness of life-skills teacher Howard Smith, the members of BT-27, and the other poor people who exposed their lives to me made my task easier.

Over the course of two and a half years, my piece expanded into a 90,000 word, three-part series, and into a 150,000-word manuscript. Before the *Atlantic Monthly* was lucky enough to lure him as their editor, Bill Whitworth nurtured my idea as if it were one of his offspring. All that was missing was the chicken soup. Mr. Shawn, who by my count read the manuscript, galleys, and page proofs no fewer than seven times, as usual saw things others missed. He is a great and wise teacher. *The New Yorker* series was edited and shaped by Pat Crow, a skilled surgeon who saved me from more than one mixed metaphor. *The New Yorker* is a collegial enterprise, and a number of individuals there helped improve this work, including: Martin Baron, the tenacious fact-checker who does not permit evenings, weekends, or honeymoons to stand in his way; Peter Canby, who capably fact-checked part II; Eleanor Gould Packard, the legendary proofreader and arbiter of style; and readers Ann Goldstein and Elizabeth Macklin.

A word of thanks to two Brown University journalism students—Suzanne Gluck and Eileen Gilligan—each of whom dedicated a summer as volunteer researchers and fact-checkers. The *New York Daily News,* which thankfully has not tired of granting me leave of absences from my weekly column to write books, was again generous.

I am particularly grateful to Jason Epstein, my editor at Random House. I know writers who moan about how their book editors are high-priced clerks, focusing more on syntax and chapter headings than ideas. Jason, thankfully, devoted his time, energy, and brilliance to this book. When I thought my task complete, he prodded me to think some more. At times I wanted to strangle him. Now I'd like to thank him. Others offered valuable assistance: Erroll McDonald, an editor at Random House, carefully read the manuscript and offered astute advice; Nancy Inglis is both a professional and a pleasant copy editor; Esther Newberg, my agent, is a valued critic and friend. Finally, I'd like to thank my wife, Amanda, who somehow understands and supports my compulsions.

Ultimate responsibility or blame for this book is, of course, mine.

Contents

Contents

Introduction

In *Butch Cassidy and the Sundance Kid,* Redford and Newman scrambled to shake a coldly efficient posse that chased them up mountains and across rivers. Repeatedly, an exasperated Butch Cassidy would turn to his partner and exclaim, *"Who are those guys?"*

This book began with a similar question. I wondered: who are those people behind the bulging crime, welfare, and drug statistics —and the all-too-visible rise in antisocial behavior—that afflicts most American cities? I wondered what effect the Great Society and other government initiatives had had, and why antisocial behavior grew as government efforts to relieve poverty also grew. I wondered whether white and rural poverty differed much from black, Hispanic, and urban poverty. And since most poor people are not criminals or welfare cheats, I wondered whether there was a distinct underclass, a hard-core group of Americans hidden among the statistical generalizations. I did not know the answers. And more crucial for a journalist, I did not know most of the questions.

I began somewhat timorously. As a white journalist, I worried about the racial freight the subject carried. What was the proper racial etiquette? What were the correct code words? At first I used the word *underclass* gingerly, fearful that it was somehow racist. I worried whether a focus on crime, welfare, and pathological behavior might present a distorted picture of the American poor.

I started by asking simple questions: Was there an underclass? If there was, who comprised it? How big was it? What were its characteristics? What were its origins? How did the underclass affect the rest of society? And was there anything the American people and their government could do in the long term to assist the underclass, and in the short term to protect itself?

I quickly learned that among students of poverty there is little disagreement that a fairly distinct black and white underclass does exist; that this underclass generally feels excluded from society, rejects commonly accepted values, suffers from *behavioral* as well as *income* deficiencies. They don't just tend to be poor; to most Americans their behavior seems aberrant. There is some dispute over whether the term underclass is the right word to describe this group of Americans. Two issues are raised. First, critics of the phrase say it leaves the impression that the problem is intractable. That criticism would carry more weight if the phrase was the *permanent* underclass. This book demonstrates that individuals can be helped. Second, there is concern that the phrase sounds cold. Most abbreviations—derelict, drunk, obese—do sound cold. I came to believe that whether one refers to the underclass, as the National Urban League and some civil-rights leaders do, or to the hard-core unemployed, as many in the sixties did, matters little. The problem is more important than the phrase. And the problem is real.

I then asked the experts: What is the most interesting government or private anti-poverty program through which I could learn about the underclass? Answers varied, but a surprising number of people I respected said that the most significant work with the underclass was being conducted with no fanfare by a Manhattan-based non-profit corporation with a clumsy name: the Manpower Demonstration Research Corporation, or MDRC. This organization, I discovered, blended several attractive elements. To begin with, its efforts were targeted on those hardest to reach—long-term welfare recipients, ex-convicts, ex-addicts, delinquent youths. Furthermore, the MDRC funded and supervised experiments among the underclass not only in cities but in rural communities across the nation; it focused on whites, as well as blacks and Hispanics. Run by professional managers and trained academics, the MDRC was relatively free of "politics"—that is to say it was research-oriented and interested in discovering what worked rather than what assisted a particular interest group or ideology. Through the MDRC and its local affiliates, I could meet members of the underclass and those who worked with them, as well as gain access to national data about what works, what doesn't, and why. Finally, and not incidentally, the MDRC interested me because it had yet to be "discovered" by other journalists.

After the MDRC officials agreed to cooperate, I began wondering whether their enrollees would cooperate. Would they talk freely to a stranger armed with a pad and pencil? Would black and Hispanic members of the underclass speak to a white reporter? These doubts soon faded. Over the course of more than two years I found that people who had never been interviewed before except by welfare workers and parole officers were eager to talk about their lives—their hopes, their anger, their fears—to be understood.

After visiting various MDRC programs, I decided to concentrate on what was called its supported-work program. This effort, which at one time or another functioned in twenty-one locations across the country, provided supportive counseling and training and a one-year job to ex-convicts, ex-addicts, long-term welfare recipients, school dropouts, and delinquent youths—the core of the underclass. At some of the twenty-one locations, these supported workers attended training school for seven of their twelve months in the program. A group of twenty-six trainees attending the Wildcat Skills Training Center in Manhattan from December 1979 to June 1980 became the narrative spine for this book. After working on a supervised job in the private or government sector for five months, the members of this class—called Basic Typing-27—came to the West 37th Street training center to learn not just English, math, and typing but how to use an alarm clock and telephone, follow dress codes, cash checks, say please and thank you, tell the truth about their pasts, write letters, conduct job interviews.

From the first day of class, I was introduced as a reporter. I sat among the members of the class for seven months, my notepad or tape recorder visible. Members of BT-27 consented to have their real names used—some, eager to see their name in print for the first time, insisted on it. It was my decision to alter their names and the names of all other trainees in this book. I came to fear that the trainees, unlike public figures, might not fully comprehend the implications of saying something was "on the record" or "not for attribution." Over a period of time, many came to trust me, and spoke of crimes and private matters. Even though I took notes, I think they often thought they were speaking to a friend. Additionally, Wildcat officials would open their records only on condition that I not use real names. I came to believe that by changing the trainees' names (but no other details) I was best serving the twin and sometimes contradictory interests of privacy and truth. At first it may be as difficult for the reader to sort through the blizzard of names and biographies of these people as it was for me. Please bear with them, and me.

Unavoidably, since there were few public records of their lives, I became dependent on what those I interviewed said. And since exaggeration observes no class boundaries, a word of caution is necessary. It is possible that Leon Harris of BT-27 was jiving me when he boasted of once having earned $1,500 to $3,000 a day as a stickup man and of writing "sorry notes" to the loved ones of those he shot. Was Michael Mathews really free of drugs? Or was he trying to impress me? Did Jean Madison really have eight children by the time she was fourteen, and twenty-nine by the age of thirty-eight? Ultimately, like any reporter, I had to rely on my sniffer. Mine told me that these people were generally pretty straight, certainly a lot straighter than many politicians I interview.

I learned a lot from the twenty-six members of BT-27 and the roughly two hundred and fifty other members of the underclass I interviewed. I learned that neither traditional left- or right-wing dogma fully explains the growth of what threatens to become, perhaps for the first time in American life, an intergenerational underclass. Neither the domestic Marshall Plan schemes favored by liberals nor President Reagan's supply-side economic nostrums will by themselves solve the problems of this hard-to-reach group. A guaranteed job, as we shall see, may not lure a hostile or fearful person back into the mainstream of society. A tax break or suspension of government regulations, as we shall also see, may not induce private businesses to locate in the South Bronx or to hire unskilled or belligerent people.

I learned that for most of the 25 to 29 million Americans officially classified as poor, poverty is not a permanent condition. Like earlier immigrant groups, most of these people overcome poverty after a generation or two. There are no precise numbers on this, but an estimated 9 million Americans do not assimilate. They are the underclass. Generally speaking, they can be grouped into four distinct categories: (a) the *passive poor,* usually long-term welfare recipients; (b) the *hostile* street criminals who terrorize most cities, and who are often school dropouts and drug addicts; (c) the *hustlers,* who, like street criminals, may not be poor and who earn their livelihood in an underground economy, but rarely commit violent crimes; (d) the *traumatized* drunks, drifters, homeless shopping-bag ladies and released mental patients who frequently roam or collapse on city streets.

While I believe these categories are a useful shorthand, I also learned how hard it is to generalize about real people. It is true, for instance, that the underclass is drawn disproportionately from single-parent homes and from welfare-dependent families. But it is also true that there are members of the underclass who were raised in two-parent homes where welfare was unknown. I witnessed among the underclass the so-called culture of poverty often ascribed to them. But I also witnessed such presumably middle-class values as patriotism, moderation, frugality, loyalty to friends and extended family, devotion to church and the Good Lord. It does not take long to learn that too many poverty experts—including many of the seventy-five or so I consulted—generalize about people they barely know.

I learned that there is often a political or ideological reason for this. Liberals have a stake in blaming society for creating an underclass, and therefore urge government intervention. Conservatives have a stake in blaming individuals for their poverty, and therefore strive to keep government small. The gap between the two is wide, for each usually starts with very different assumptions about human nature. As George Orwell once observed, the left asks, "How can you improve human nature until you have changed the system?" The right asks, "What is the use of changing the system before you have changed human nature?"

This leads to still another lesson: what each of us thinks about the underclass depends at least in part on judgment, as well as facts. In truth, there are ample "facts" to support most contentions. Some readers may think that the MDRC's five-year national supported-work experiment was a *failure* because two-thirds of the 10,000 enrollees did not complete the program and go on to unsubsidized jobs. Such readers may claim that little can be done for the underclass, and that government must therefore concentrate on controlling rather than transforming it. Other readers will think the program a *success* because this group is so difficult to reach yet one-third managed to enter the world of work. Thus, they claim, there are solutions, reasons to retain hope and not surrender to despair.

There have been a good number of valuable books about the lives of the poor by important authors—Henry Mayhew, Charles Dickens, Jacob Riis, Michael Harrington, Robert Coles, Oscar Lewis, John Fetterman, among others. This book does not seek to duplicate their achievements. Although I visited the homes of many of the people you will meet, I do not dwell on their home and street lives. Instead I follow them mostly through their encounters with organized society, with instructors and counselors and training programs that seek to instill the habit of work and to expunge bad habits. A major aim of mine is to investigate the underclass in order to illuminate public policy—what can and should be done about the underclass?

The subject of the underclass is like a political battle zone. I have tried to weave my way through it free of ideological baggage. To get combatants to listen, it is helpful if they respect your fairness. So I set out trying not to take sides, neither to portentously prick the nation's conscience nor to cheerlead for America. I consider myself neither a "liberal" nor a "conservative." Not because I am truly neutral, but because I don't fit in either box.

"But every writer," as Orwell also said, ". . . has a 'message,' whether he admits it or not, and the minutest details of his work are influenced by it." My own bias (and judgment) is that the supported-work program was a *success,* and that the federal government should support it. I don't believe in pink pills and panaceas, but I do believe in trying. I came to believe members of the underclass could not succeed without practicing self-help, but I also believe they usually need a government helping hand.

Because of federal budget economies, as I write this, many of

MDRC's experiments among the underclass have been forced to close. The supported-work program, where I spent much of my time, lost all its federal funding on December 31, 1981. Many of the twenty-one sites around the nation have already shut down. Due to declining federal support, in June of 1981 the MDRC was compelled to sever almost half its staff, and in early 1982 officials there said that without support from the Reagan administration they may go out of business. There is grand irony in all this, for the Reagan administration would be depriving itself of the kind of low-cost community-based, research-oriented programs their press releases extol. And while these experiments are little known, they may represent the most productive effort ever undertaken to reach the underclass and help lift them into the mainstream of society and the world of work.

I had a vague sense when I began reporting this book back in mid-1979, that next to war and peace and the state of the economy, the underclass might be the most momentous story in America. Today that vague sense has hardened into a conviction. For to study the underclass is to understand a little more clearly the epidemic of violent crime that sweeps America; to understand why welfare rose even while poverty and unemployment declined; to better comprehend the insecurities of the unemployed, the reasons for school dropouts, arson, vandalism, for the escape into drugs, drink, and the hostile, antisocial behavior of some Americans. A study of the underclass provides clues as to what went wrong—and right—with the Great Society; whether the "war on poverty" made any progress; whether racism or class, the society or the individual—or both—are to blame for the creation of an American underclass.

Finally, I learned that the underclass, as Thomas Jefferson said of the Missouri Compromise, is "like a firebell in the night." It is both America's peril, and shame.

The Underclass

1

The BT-27 Class

The life-skills class convenes on Tuesday and Friday mornings, and among the twenty-two students registered for it are people who have been murderers, muggers, stickup men, chain snatchers, pimps, burglars, heroin addicts, drug pushers, alcoholics, welfare mothers, and swindlers. Their teacher, Howard Smith, is a former heroin addict, drug peddler, welfare cheat, and near alcoholic, and has spent several of his thirty-nine years behind bars. Beginning in December 1979, I joined these students and rode a creaking elevator to the tenth floor of the Wildcat Skills Training Center, on West 37th Street, for the first meeting of the class known as basic typing 27, which would continue for ten weeks and, for those who successfully completed that hurdle, would be followed by a twenty-week course called advanced office practices. Five afternoons and three mornings each week, in dreary, unheated classrooms with windows caked with dirt and naked pipes crisscrossing the ceiling, they would partake of standard training fare—English, math, and clerical and typing instruction. The remaining six hours would be devoted to life skills—the course that Howard Smith teaches.

Life skills is not a typical academic offering, but then this is not a typical class. Most of the students are high school dropouts; few have ever held a regular job. To be eligible for BT-27 and the other classes at Wildcat, which are part of a national experiment, a person must satisfy one of four sets of criteria: be an ex-offender who has been released from prison within the past six months; be an ex-addict who has recently been or is currently in a treatment program; be a female who has been unemployed and on welfare for thirty of the preceding thirty-six months, and has no children under the age of six; or be a youth between the ages of seventeen and twenty who has dropped out of school (half of the dropouts must be delinquents). In the sixties, such people were referred to as the hard-core or structurally unemployed; today they are sometimes referred to as the underclass. Whatever they are called, they constitute a group that few training or jobs programs reach. This experiment, called supported work by its founders, tried to test whether in the course of one year, with special counseling and training, such people could be lured into the world of work. Each participant was provided private or government employment at an initial salary of $105 a week. Unlike most supported workers in the United States, the Wildcat recruits who qualify also attend school for seven months of their year's enrollment. The experiment was designed by a New York–based nonprofit corporation, the Manpower Demonstration Research Corporation (MDRC), which attracted money from the federal government, the Ford Foundation, and other sources to help finance the program.

In the first several weeks of the training regimen, the enrollment of BT-27 dwindled from twenty-two to sixteen. Ronald Brooks was arrested; Phillip Rivers, Earl Billings, Larry Pearl, and Stanley Lawrence were dismissed from the program for excessive absences and lateness; Liza Lance quit, because, Smith said, "she doesn't feel she can make it—she feels that everyone in the class is smarter than she is." (The names of all the trainees in this book have been changed.) With the orientation period over, Smith was ready to begin in earnest the life-skills process; his aim is to help each of the students confront the reality of his life, accept responsibility for it, and learn to communicate with others. Smith is a lean, lanky black man with a goatee, a mustache that rims his mouth, and a closely cropped Afro. He has the long arms of a basketball player, which he might have been if a birth defect had not deformed his right shoulder. He smiles easily, speaks softly, moves languidly, usually dresses casually, in a blazer and an open-necked shirt, and achieves an instant rapport with most students, because, he says, "I've been where they've been."

On this December day, Howard Smith circles the formica-topped tables at which the class sits, and dispenses crayons and large sheets of white paper. He asks the students to sketch "anything significant in your life."

After several minutes, he invites William (Akim) Penn to step to a lectern at the front of the room, put his drawing on an easel, and share an account of his life with BT-27. Penn, a wiry, muscular man with jet-black skin and a short Afro, begins haltingly, almost shyly.

Pointing to a line of capital letters he has written across the top of the paper—"LOVE AND PEACE AND HAPPINESS"—Penn explains, "I had a close family. My mother and father were very close. That's why I put 'love and peace and happiness' there. In the eighties, I want to give them what they gave me." So far, he feels, he has given them heartache. He has been in and out of state prison frequently between 1974 and 1979, the last time for armed robbery. He has used pills, marijuana, cocaine, and alcohol, and has committed acts he would like to forget. Though he is only twenty-three, numerous scars mar his skin. A tiny bald spot in the middle of his head is from a knife that gouged a piece of his scalp. Two weeks after he was released from prison in 1979, four toughs leered at his date on a subway platform. Penn lunged at them, and they left him lying on the platform with a broken jaw and a gash that went from one side of his chin to the other. "After that incident, I was ready to put a pistol back in my hand," he says. "But I used my intelligence." It didn't help. Employers were wary of an ex-convict. Penn offered few skills, no job references, and a rather menacing look. Unable to find work, he turned to alcohol and welfare. Still, he says that the 1980s—he has written the numbers in bold black on his sheet of paper—are going to be good years, because supported work will "teach me I can be a person, allow me to recognize my abilities." He adds, "It also gets me off the street and puts money in my pocket." He boasts of his four-year-old son; of plans to marry the boy's mother, a twenty-three-year-old domestic worker who is on welfare; of his ambition to lead a new life. The members of BT-27 applaud Penn, and several slap his palm as he returns to his seat.

Next, William Mason ambles to the front of the room and attaches to the easel a drawing of a house surrounded by stick figures. At thirty-seven, Mason is the senior male member of BT-27, and in time he will become the dominant member of the class. A thin beard hugs his jawline, reaching up and around his mouth; he has a slightly waved Afro, with a red tint; he usually wears mirrored sunglasses, a bright flowered shirt, and gold chains. The house he has drawn, Mason explains, was in Salt Lake City, where he was born. When he was nine, the family moved to Brooklyn. "My mother had nineteen children, fifteen of them with my natural father," he says. He saw little of his father, and grew up with a man he called his stepfather. "My brothers and I were all right for a while," he says. "I looked after my baby sisters—there were four girls and fifteen boys. But I wanted to cut loose. I was the lead singer of a group called the Jesters. There were other things I wanted to do. I was a hell of a softball center fielder. And I idolized three people on the pool table. I became a good pool player. But I always wanted to be a fighter. So I walked away from sports and pool and became a fighter. I was good with my hands, but my hands got me put away." Mason explains that he had earned several karate belts, and while working as a bouncer in a bar he got into a fight with three men, which led to two months in jail. This was one of several collisions he had with the law, the most serious of which led to his spending thirteen months in prison for narcotics possession. "Now I want to be a success at Wildcat," he says. He tells the class that he has nine children, the oldest of them twenty-one, and eleven grandchildren. He is divorced, and currently lives with another woman and the youngest of his nine children, an eleven-year-old daughter.

A member of the class asks, "Are your brothers and sisters alive?"

"All but one sister," he replies. "She was murdered a month before I got out of prison."

Mason is the substitute father for his brothers and sisters. When a brother was mugged and stabbed, Mason sped to the hospital and spent the night there. When a sister was arrested, he accompanied her to court. In a fatherless home, he became the family rudder, as he later became the rudder for several members of BT-27.

Willy Joe is called upon, and he comes to the front of the room and puts his sketch on the easel. A thin twenty-four-year-old who jams his hands into the pockets of a black leather jacket, Joe moves lethargically, speaks slowly, and has a good-natured smile for everyone. The combination of kindness and vulnerability makes him appealing. He is not given to swagger or showboating, as some of the others are; he eagerly shares a backgammon game he brings to class every day, and he still possesses an innocence that allows him to open his life to strangers. Yet in depressed moments Willy Joe will sigh and say, "I just feel crushed." He has a passive personality; where a Mason will create and shape his opportunities, Joe waits for his. Joe starts by explaining that his family was from the South and moved to New York when his father abandoned them. "I think I'd remember his face," he says, noting that he was only a year old when his father left. There were five children, and the family struggled. "My mother made sure we did good," he says. "She did domestic work." When she couldn't find work, they survived on welfare. "Me and my mom had a lot of arguments, but I loved her. We'd go places together more than anybody else in the family." Written on Joe's paper are the word "Love" and several dates, including "1972"—the year his mother died of cancer. The children were raised by a stepfather. "I had a personal problem," Joe says. "I was unhappy in my family." He dropped out of school. At sixteen, he was arrested for stealing a car.

He started smoking marijuana, graduated to heroin, and eventually entered a rehabilitation program for addicts. He straightened out, and went to cooking school by day and worked as a porter at night, finally latching onto a job as a cook at a fast-food restaurant in Manhattan. He was happy, but after a month he forged a company check and was fired. He bounced from part-time job to part-time job, once going a whole year without regular employment and making do by selling grass and working off the books for his older brother, who organizes disco dances. Of the part-time employment, he says, "I had no interest after a while. There were all these rules and pressure. So I got into disco. I met a lot of girls. That's why I put 'Love' here." He points to the word on the drawing. Joe also returned to crime, and not long afterward he was convicted and sentenced to five years on Rikers Island for sticking up a store. While he was in prison, a girl he had dated for two months bore him a son, whom he has never seen, and who, he says, lives somewhere—he does not know where—in Trenton. After ten months Joe was released from prison. Today he lives in his brother's house "with my old lady" and their year-old daughter, in the devastated East New York section of Brooklyn. In the early weeks of class, Joe regularly showed off their snapshots, which he kept in his wallet. "Now I'm in Wildcat trying to get it back together," he concludes.

Gladys Miller declines Howard Smith's invitation to share her drawing, saying that she's too nervous. Carlos Rodriguez accepts, but steps to the front of the room only after receiving encouragement from Pearl Dawson, an older woman he insists on sitting beside each day. Rodriguez is a slender, effeminate-looking young man who shields his eyes with dark sunglasses and grips the lectern to steady his trembling hands. His skin is chalk-colored and is speckled with pimples, betraying his age—nineteen. Rodriguez tells the class that he is one of five children and was born in Spanish Harlem. He qualified for BT-27 as a school dropout and delinquent youth. His fondest childhood memory, he says, is of helping teachers direct school plays. Other memories are not so bright. When he was eight, his father and his mother split up, he says. Life seemed to go downhill from there. After two years, his mother and the children moved to Puerto Rico, where he lived with an aunt. Spanish vexed him, and he was demoted from the fifth grade to the second. A month later, he was shuffled to the fourth grade. He felt lost. His aunt, with whom he continued to live even after his mother got her own house, died after a prolonged illness. Finally, in 1978, he returned to New York. "I couldn't find a job, because I had no experience in the city," he says. Eventually, he received a job under the federal Comprehensive Employment and Training Act (CETA). "I made three thousand police barriers for the Pope's visit to New York in 1979," he says. Rodriguez hopes to go to college and become an airline flight attendant and, one day, a pilot. "You travel to a lot of places and meet a lot of interesting people," he says.

Pearl Dawson prefers to keep part of her résumé private. A woman with high cheekbones, narrow eyes, and an Afro, she dresses as if she worked in a fashionable Manhattan office, which sets her apart from the others in the class. She has on a herringbone-tweed jacket, a long-collared fire-engine-red silk shirt, and dark tapered slacks. She does not volunteer her age—forty-five—or the fact that she was convicted of manslaughter in 1976. She keeps to herself, quietly performs her assigned tasks, and demonstrates a fierce determination to land a good job—a goal that she knows is compromised by her age and her criminal record. Pearl Dawson says that she was the next to youngest of eight children and was born in Newport News, Virginia. Although her father died when she was two, "we were never hungry," she says. "We were never unclothed. We were never on welfare. We grew up normally." There were piano lessons, a procession of pet dogs, a fling as a tomboy, a stint as a soloist in the high school choir, and the honor of being selected class valedictorian. "But due to unforeseen circumstances"—the birth of a boy—"I never graduated."

At seventeen, she became a mother and a housewife. A second son was born the following year. Her husband was in the Army, and her life seemed to be going well, but in 1962 he divorced her. She remarried in 1969 but began to drink heavily. Pointing to "1976," highlighted on her drawing, she says, "In 1976, he went that way. Then I had a drinking problem and got help from A.A." (In a drunken rage during this period, she knifed a woman fatally, and she served eighteen months in prison.) In 1978 (when she left prison) her health was frail, she could not find a job, and she wound up living alone on welfare in Jamaica, Queens. She resented the prying forms and the nosy social workers and the degrading waits at the welfare office. She tried a CETA job, but it led to a dead end. Then in late 1979 she was introduced to Wildcat by her probation officer. "My main aim is for a secure job, so I can get off this welfare, 'cause this welfare is bugging me to death," she says.

At twenty-two, John Hicks could pass for one of Pearl Dawson's children. He is a handsome cocoa-colored man with flared, bushy sideburns and a manner that mixes pride and defiance. His sketch reveals the same qualities. It features a road that twists and turns, with a house and what he identifies as apple trees at one end, and the word "Hell" at the other. "I had my first encounter with the law in 1975," he says. "I was placed on probation for four years. In 1979, I violated parole and was incarcerated for six months. I got out on September 6, 1979. My daughter was born on September twenty-sixth. Then I went into Wildcat. Now I plan to take the civil-service test on January 12th. Wildcat is not the only option I have. I plan to go to college in Jamaica, Queens, and study social science. I want to forget about the rat race, have a nice family. It may not be in New York. That's what I want to do in life."

"What does the 'Hell' road mean?" Howard Smith asks.

"An idle mind is a playground for the devil," Hicks responds. "I may or may not finish Wildcat. But if I don't it's not because I don't have options." He tells the class that he once managed a Nedick's, and that he received a high-school-equivalency certificate—a General Education Diploma, or G.E.D. He complains about Wildcat's "rules and regulations" and meager pay. With an almost tenth-grade reading level—high for Wildcat—Hicks wonders whether he's not already ahead of what Wildcat can offer. He is the only currently married member of BT-27; his wife attends York College. He's proud of that and confident that he can pass the civil-service test, and thinks constantly about whether he wouldn't be better off elsewhere. But he has doubts, and concludes, "I benefit from being here. It's getting me ready for college."

Jerome Patterson, who goes by the name Mohammed, is next. His head is shaved, and he wears a small Black Muslim cap. Mohammed is attired in a black vest, a black shirt, and black pants; he has ebony skin and is missing his front teeth. "I was born in '57," he says, pointing to a sketch showing an assortment of dates and numbers. "As you can see here, I have a question mark about my sister and myself, because I don't know who our father was." In all, four children were born to his mother, in Macon, Georgia, but one of them died at birth. Before he was a teenager, their mother bundled them off to Brooklyn's Bedford-Stuyvesant section. The family became dependent on welfare, and he remembers how welfare weakened his mother's self-confidence, led her to say, "I can't do no better." Mohammed remembers liking to draw, but his most persistent memory is of being consumed by anger—initially at white racism, then at society. He became a street criminal, and was first arrested at the age of twelve, for snatching an elderly woman's pocketbook. He later became a warlord in a youth gang. "My mother, she tried to play the role of my father," he says. "We didn't listen." As a juvenile he was convicted ten times; he has lost count of the number of arrests. He was sent to three reform schools and to a mental institution. He joined the Black Panthers. "I was very limited and very racist," he recalls. By his late teens Mohammed had advanced to heroin and a conviction for attempted murder. When he got out of prison for that crime, he went right back in, for armed robbery. "I was going a hundred and twenty miles an hour in a fifty-five-mile-an-hour speed zone." In prison he became a convert to the Nation of Islam. After Mohammed was released, finding a job proved difficult, and he went on welfare. "It doesn't motivate you at all," he says of welfare. "It makes you a lazy being." But he was inspired by religion, he says. "I stopped using drugs. I stopped jumping on my sister. I learned respect. The Lord blessed me. He blessed me great. He gave me internal peace." At twenty-two, Mohammed was recruited by the Wildcat program. Now, Mohammed tells his classmates, he wants to become an architectural draftsman.

Like Mohammed, William Block favors dark clothes, and in class he is generally subdued. Born on the lower East Side, he was abandoned to the care of a grandmother when he was an infant. They moved to Harlem when he was twelve. His grandmother tried to discipline him for poor school attendance, but he ignored her. Dropping out of school, Block got married at seventeen and had a son. He moved his family to Baltimore, entered and completed a technical training course, and landed a decent job. But bad luck intervened. Block's house was destroyed by fire; soon thereafter, his son died of a congenital heart defect. Seeking to start anew, the Blocks moved to Georgia. Life was never the same, however, and in 1970 the marriage dissolved. He began to drink, and wandered back to New York, where, in 1972, he says, "I got into an argument and shot and killed somebody." Block was never apprehended, and he returned to Georgia. In 1976, under circumstances that go unexplained, he was shot twice—the bullets lodged near his heart—and was subsequently arrested and sentenced to three years in prison. "I did two years, and it was a good two years," he says. "It gave me time to think. I'm twenty-eight now, I've been working since fourteen." When he got out, he went to live in Bedford-Stuyvesant. His health was bad, he still drank, and job doors were slammed in his face because he was an ex-convict, so welfare became his only lifeline. Pointing to a "1980" at the top of his drawing, Block says, "Nineteen-eighty is a year of peace for me. I won't let nothing affect me. When I was in jail, I let nothing affect me. I had no fights."

Hicks asks, "Can't you get a job as a technician that pays more than Wildcat?"

"They want job experience," Block answers in a shy, solemn voice. "But how do you get on-the-job experience unless you have a job?

Man, you go two, three years not working and hanging around and smoking reefer or drinking and then you get a job—you can't handle it. You do two, three years of idleness and after the first two, three weeks of working, you feel people are pushing you. You say, 'I don't want to get up in the morning, get pushed and shoved. I'm gonna get on welfare.' Unless a man sits down and gives it good thought, he's not gonna figure out how he got there. He's gonna fall into the same cycle. I'm twenty-eight, and have been working for fourteen years. Never the same job more than one year." Eventually, Block tells the class, he hopes to flee crowded Bedford-Stuyvesant and resettle in the rural South.

John Painter, who is as gregarious as Block is subdued, also has a year penciled in at the top of his drawing—"1960." An apple and the year signify where and when he was born. A stick figure in the drawing is "my mother taking me home," he says. His mother died during an abortion when he was less than a year old; he does not know who his father was. He was adopted by his mother's brother, who lived in Brooklyn. Painter says, "The people I call my mother and father—they stuck by me." But he was a troubled youth; at fourteen, he was frequenting bars and drinking heavily. Attempting to steer him away from a street gang, his adoptive parents, who are not poor—Mr. Painter is a superintendent in the Postal Service—moved from Brooklyn to Queens. Moving didn't help. John didn't listen, added marijuana to his alcohol habit, and was soon suspended from school. Desperate, the parents talked him into joining the Army, in 1977. That didn't help, either. During basic training, he was arrested for robbing a Holiday Inn in Virginia at gunpoint. The next seventeen months he spent in prison. "I said when I got out I'd rip off everything I see," he goes on. "I was lucky to have a parole officer who talked to me on my level. He introduced me to Wildcat. In 1979, I seen a rainbow"—he points to an arc in his drawing—"and the rainbow was Wildcat." Still, he is ambivalent. Although he is twenty, Painter still fantasizes about going to St. John's University and becoming a basketball star. He is a tall, athletic, and good-looking light-skinned black man. In class, he will often browse through a newspaper or ponder a book of crossword puzzles he keeps in a hip pocket. "At the age of twenty, it would be a crime for a man who knows as much as I know not to be famous," he boasts. "I can't take orders. I can't have no one telling me what to do. I can't take no job for nineteen years. I got to be my own boss. But I know that for five years I got to be an employee."

Timothy Wilson, who just turned nineteen, is the youngest member of BT-27. He usually comes to class lugging an attaché case, which contains samples of poetry he writes and books dealing with black subjects, like Alex Haley's *Roots*. Wilson has perfect teeth, and he smiles frequently. He is six feet tall and wears an untamed Afro that makes him appear half a foot taller. And, like Painter, he begins by speaking of a broken home. He points to a heart cut in two, in his sketch. "My mother was sixteen when she had me," he says. "My father was young. They couldn't handle it. They shipped me to all these homes." He lived in four foster homes. The experience left scars, as it has on many of the children who have been in foster care. "You had a few people who were homosexuals try to molest guys. I had to take care of myself. It affected me in a lot of ways that I was not with my family." At thirteen he left Chicago, where he was born, and moved to Philadelphia. He lost track of his parents. "I felt inadequate. I knew nobody. The only way to know anybody was to hang out. I was really out of it. I started using drugs to be accepted. So I just grew in this environment." He says that after a while "the only way I could express my feelings was with a baseball bat and hitting someone on the side of the head." He became a heroin addict and stole for "necessities." In December of 1978, he was arrested for mugging a woman outside a check-cashing store at Sumner Avenue and Fulton Street, in Brooklyn, and served forty-five days on Rikers Island. He was released to a rehabilitation center in Queens, where "I found out I had a lot of talent." He began to compose verses, to play the piano, and to realize that he was a good talker, a natural salesman. He boasts of being interviewed with other ex-addicts on the Stanley Siegel TV show; he tells of falling in love with a young girl at the drug center and of how he intends to marry her; and he tells of his reconciliation with his mother, with whom he now lives and whom he helps support, in Bedford-Stuyvesant.

"How important is it to love yourself?" Howard Smith asks.

"I'm not talking about loving myself. I'm talking about self-respect," Wilson says.

Ramon Lopez has none of Wilson's ostensible self-confidence. His drawing proceeds from a house surrounded by trees to an airplane and from there to a box with bars in front and with "P.S. 141" penciled in. "I was born in a house in Puerto Rico," says Lopez, who has short, curly hair, a thin mustache, and a friendly smile, which he nervously flashes to fill the pauses between his words. "There was lots of grass and trees. I went to school there. I got on a plane and came here." He entered public school in the Bronx, but he couldn't keep up with English and was demoted two grades. He tried another school, but eventually he quit. "I got out," he says. "I figured I was dumb enough. I was eighteen. It was time to get out of school. I figured I wasn't gonna make it. I started spending time on the street. After five days my mother found out I wasn't in school. She said, 'Son, if you don't want to go to school, go to work.' I did." Now thirty-two years old, Lopez has never held a job for more than seven months. Initially, after working at a number of jobs, he tried to go back to school to improve his reading skills, but he soon dropped out again, to join the Army. After two years in the Army, he returned to New York; he took it easy, began smoking marijuana, learned to hustle to make money, and eventually began to use heroin. "I bought a gun. I no shoot nobody, but I got caught with it." Lopez went to jail for three years, came out, searched vainly for steady work, and then went on welfare. Suddenly Lopez stops talking, glares down at the lectern, gripping its sides, and blurts, "Friends are a lot of crap!" Just as suddenly, his smile returns, and Lopez repeats information about his pleasant childhood house.

Denise Brown also grew up in a nice house. An attractive black woman with copper-tinted hair and rouged cheeks, wearing a pastel suit and with two gold chains looped around her neck, she tells her classmates she was born into a "well-to-do" Montreal family twenty-eight years ago. There were ten children in all, and as the eldest, she was often assigned to do the shopping and the babysitting. "I was like a second mother in the house—which I couldn't handle, because I was so young," she says. "I had a lot of family problems. My parents split. I had to take on more responsibility. I lost my childhood. Then, later, there was another man in the house. He was a child molester. Violent. And my mother didn't believe it. As I got older, my mother got threatened by my presence in the house." Denise then lived with a succession of relatives, finally fleeing with a boyfriend to New York City, where she got a job at a Waldbaum's supermarket. "It was my first opportunity around large numbers of people. It was not so good, because I wasn't used to dealing with so many people." She took and passed a Postal Service examination, and worked for four years as a distribution clerk. "All day, all I did was sit down and place things in this machine." Bored and deeply in love, she agreed to store a package that her boyfriend, who also worked at the Postal Service, gave her to hold. It contained stolen money. "I wound up here"—she points to her rendering of a court bench—"looking at the big, bad judge. I lost my job." The boyfriend was sent to jail for embezzlement. She was placed on probation for three years, but she couldn't find a job, and was stranded on welfare for two years. "By laying up so long, I became a dead individual. I lost all my skills at the post office. I was disgusted with the whole system, disgusted with the United States of America." Fortunately, she says, a probation officer

13

introduced her to Wildcat's supported-work program. Denise feels better about herself, and now regularly visits her family in Montreal. "In my stay at Wildcat, I hope to complete the course, get my G.E.D., and become a communicator"—an air-traffic controller—"at airports."

Leon Harris, a burly, barrel-chested twenty-nine-year-old black man with a splotchy beard and a round face, takes a ruler in hand and bangs the lectern. "Order in court. I'm up here now." He tells of being the youngest of eleven children, born in San Francisco. "What I remember about childhood most is California girls," he says, lowering his voice and stretching out the last word. "As a child, I had a lot of trouble. I was hardheaded. Black sheep of the family." Harris felt that he was in competition with his father. The family moved to Brooklyn when he was fifteen. The competition at home grew. The sense of authority he now has with a ruler he got then with a gun. He says he earned a living as a "stickup kid," adding, "I bought a pistol for those dudes stronger than me. That pistol put me here." He points to prison bars in his sketch. Leon Harris remembers shooting people and sending unsigned "sorry letters" to the relatives. He was not apprehended for these crimes. At twenty-two he was arrested for armed robbery and convicted. "For five years, I cried," he says. When he got out, at twenty-seven, he began to lean on alcohol, marijuana, cocaine, and heroin. "I started hanging out with older people, gambling. I was good at that." He was, he says, also a good stickup man, earning sometimes three thousand dollars a day when he was very young. "I made enough money to buy my mother a house." He wound up back behind bars, this time for narcotics possession. When Harris was released in 1979, a parole officer introduced him to supported work. "Getting into Wildcat, at first I didn't dig it. Didn't dig taking orders. It was a sissy job." With the ruler, he taps a large question mark at the bottom of his drawing. "The question mark is not only on me but on Wildcat. Wildcat has federal funding, and it's not clear how long they'll have that." From the question mark, he has drawn two roads leading in opposite directions, with a door at the end of each. "There are two roads and two doors. One leading to a closed door, and the other to the graveyard."

Gladys Miller, who earlier refused to speak, now volunteers. "I'm kind of nervous," she admits, adjusting a black stocking cap with a pom-pom. At twenty-eight, Gladys Miller is a heavy-set woman with a clipped Afro who lumbers about and has scars around both eyes. The youngest of three children, she was born in Salem, New Jersey, and her family moved to New York when she was still an infant. She toyed with drugs in high school, got hooked on heroin, and dropped out in the eleventh grade. She was in an automobile accident in 1970 —the year is noted on her sketch—and received five thousand dollars in an insurance-company settlement. She used the money not to get married and resettle in the South, as she had planned, but to buy drugs. She exhausted it all in two and a half weeks. Broke, in 1972 she entered a methadone-maintenance program. Over the next several years, she says, she moved in with three different women on welfare. "I got into being gay by messing with drugs. I want nobody to misunderstand this—we're all ladies."

The students focus respectfully on their classmate. The silence is broken by a question about her future goals.

She responds, "I would like to go into the military service."

When Gladys Miller returns to her seat, Howard Smith goes to the front of the room, scans and ponders the various faces, and then invites Henry Rivera and Hope Parker, both ex-addicts, to explain their drawings. Rivera is a goateed man of thirty-six who has never held a regular job and has left the mother of his child to the support of welfare. He speaks to few classmates, perhaps because his English is rudimentary; dreamy eyes and a swaying manner after the class's morning break suggest that it is optimistic to say he is an ex-addict. Hope Parker is black and twenty-eight and lives in Coney Island with her grandfather, who raised her while her parents pursued their own lives. Her hair is braided, and she wears thick eyeglasses in brown frames. Despite her poor eyesight, she will become the best typist in BT-27. But she is painfully shy—reflexively she lifts a hand to hide a gap where two front teeth are missing—and for as yet unexplained reasons she is hostile to Smith. Both Rivera and Miss Parker refuse to speak. Smith does not press the matter.

Denise Brown asks Howard Smith why the class members have been put through this exercise of explaining their past.

"Because in real life you're going to be forced to talk," he says. Job interviewers will probe, and so will personnel officers and co-workers. Lie about what is unavoidably a part of your personnel file, he tells them, and you risk losing a good job opportunity. Besides, he says, it's important that the class members get to know one another. (The first week in class, he had them go around the room and recite the name of every one of their classmates each morning.) Later on in life skills, he says, he will put them through simulated job interviews, videotape their performances, and let them study the videotape, to sharpen their social skills for the world of work. "What did you think of it?" he asks the class.

"We all have something in common," Ramon Lopez says.

Later, in his office, a cramped space down the hall from his classroom, Smith offers me a sketch of his own life. In many respects, his background parallels his students'. The oldest of three children, he was told when he was very young that his father might be dead. Recently, he has learned that his father may still be alive, but he does not know where he is. In any case, Smith does not remember him. What he does remember is that when he was five another man joined the household, and within a few years his mother had four more boys. The family of nine lived in Philadelphia and attended church, went on outings together, and observed regular mealtimes, and the children were punished if their grades were not sufficiently high. "My mother always insisted that I had to do best—or, at least, better," Smith recalls. He says that he never felt close to his stepfather. "He wasn't like a father to me. I missed that. He was close to my half brothers but not to me." Smith's deformed right shoulder kept him out of sports competition with friends. "And I stammered a lot," he continues. "Between the physical defect and the stammering problem and the isolation I felt from my stepfather, I was a very insecure kid. Never really expressing what I thought. Always conscious of how people treated me. Always looking for ridicule and mocking, almost to the point of being paranoid about friends and their motives. Yet at the same time always wanting close relationships. Outside my family, I wouldn't talk." He remained attached to his mother but resented being called a "sissy" for it. He began to resent her and withdrew further. At thirteen he gravitated to Jehovah's Witnesses. They encouraged him to open up, to talk freely, to be less self-conscious. He began to make friends, learned to dance, gained self-confidence. He began to think of himself as a ladies' man. But a new conflict arose: his friends were doing things that were frowned upon by Jehovah's Witnesses. He had to choose. "My friends won out," he says.

Just weeks before graduation, Smith abandoned high school and Philadelphia, going to live with his mother's father, on West 130th Street in Harlem. He became a member of a local Jehovah's Witness congregation, and tried to mix alcohol and sex with his religion. The congregation excommunicated him, and that, he says, had a "traumatic effect." He drank incessantly, and by 1965 "I was ripe for heroin," he says. "Most of my friends among Jehovah's Witnesses I had cut loose from. When I was at a New Year's Eve party with some new friends, they kept going into the back room. I followed, and there was a guy with blood trickling from his arm and another guy just finished with a hypodermic needle. In those few seconds, I experienced quite a few things—surprise, shock. Here were these two nice guys, with families, dressed well—they were doing it. I also resented the fact that we were supposed to be friends and yet they had never included me in it. I said, 'I want some, too.' They tried to argue me out of it—for about five minutes. Then they said okay. I overdosed. I was out. I woke up with ice cubes on my testicles, and they were pouring milk down my throat." After that, Smith kept away from drugs for three or four months. He had a decent job, as a clerk at the New York State Athletic Commission. But he remained depressed and felt estranged from his family and from Jehovah's Witnesses, so he returned to heroin. "I liked it," he recalls. "I stopped caring about Jehovah's Witnesses. Everything was mellower. I had a good job. I wasn't robbing or snatching pocketbooks. Heroin was in then. I went to a friend's house six months later and said, 'I have the flu.' He said, 'No, you've got a habit.' I got a shot and my nose stopped running; the chills went. Then I knew. But I thought I still didn't have to be a mugger. I thought I'd be different."

Smith continues, "I remember one day sitting in my office and needing a shot. I went off into a deep sleep at the desk." The commission's medical director, who happened to be passing his desk, shook him awake and instructed him to appear the next day for a physical examination. Panicked, Smith put it off. He was desperate to hide the needle tracks on his arms, which he always covered with long-sleeved shirts. At home, he took a razor and slashed his left arm to camouflage the needle marks. To erase traces of heroin from his urine, he followed the advice of a friend and swallowed half a bottle of vinegar. Now he was ready for the examination.

The next day, however, the doctor merely shone a light into one eye and said, "Howard, how long have you been on drugs?" Smith offered to resign. The commission said that it would not accept his resignation. Instead, it arranged for him to enter a Long Island drug-treatment center. He was there only thirty days and then fled to Philadelphia. At first he felt a new warmth with his family and stayed away from drugs, but the secure feeling soon subsided, and he returned to New York City. "As soon as I got back, I went 'cop'—go buy some drugs," he says. He was arrested several times for drug use, but he never spent more than one night in jail. He supported his growing habit by registering at half a dozen or more welfare offices simultaneously, giving a false date of birth, a fictitious address, and spurious parental names at each office—successfully scheming to receive six semi-monthly welfare checks. He could have faced a felony charge for this crime, but he was never caught. His day of reckoning came on August 29, 1969, when he was arrested for selling heroin to an undercover policeman. Smith was convicted and sentenced to three years at Great Meadow, a prison in Comstock, about two hundred miles north of New York City. He was promised treatment. "I was in prison, side by side with hard-core convicts," he says. "The therapy was almost nonexistent." Smith studied, and received his high-school-equivalency diploma.

After serving most of his sentence, Smith was released to a halfway house. "There I learned that addiction is not a matter of sticking a needle in your arm," he says. "Addiction is up here, in my head. And I was still addicted. As soon as the train pulled into Grand Central, I was anxious to get to Fox Street in the Bronx and some dope." His parole officer spotted fresh needle marks within six months. "But he was a typical bleeding-heart liberal," Smith says. "I used to play on him a lot. Every once in a while I was sincere. He wanted to send me back to prison. I said, 'Surely there must be a way to help me other than sending me back to a cell and locking me up.' He said, 'We have something new now—methadone.' I did it—but I took heroin, too. When the methadone blocked the heroin high, I shot cocaine. Here I am taking methadone every day, shooting cocaine, and everyone is telling you how great you're doing because you're not taking heroin."

Cocaine was expensive. In 1972 he got a job at the Pioneer Messenger Service, which was an innovator in the employment of ex-addicts and ex-offenders. He tried to perform his tasks conscientiously, and attracted the notice of Joseph Moskowitz, the assistant director of the Melrose Community Rehabilitation Center, a state-operated narcotics-rehabilitation facility in the Bronx. Moskowitz asked Smith to become a drug-abuse counselor there. "I was afraid," he says. "It would mean being no longer a client but a staff member." But Smith accepted the job and the responsibility. Over the coming months, he quit methadone and, more important, kicked the mental addiction. In 1975, he was invited to speak at a seminar on unemployment among ex-addicts and ex-offenders. A member of the staff of the Wildcat Service Corporation heard Smith speak and asked him if he was interested in a job as an instructor in a new supported-work experiment that Wildcat was conducting.

Smith said that he was, and for the past six years he has been living in the Bronx and commuting to the Wildcat Skills Training Center. His task, as he sees it, is to prepare people for the real world, concentrating on the development of social skills and work habits among a group of people who often operate outside society, who have often lost self-confidence, have frequently grown up with few positive role models, have had scant exposure to the world of work, have low frustration thresholds, and are generally unacquainted with being on time, following orders, saying "Thank you" and "Please." Smith is trying to nurture an attitude of self-reliance among people who often see themselves as victims, just as he once did. "Some people are beyond hope," he says. "And yet I'm put in a position where I have an obligation to help people. And who am I—who is anyone—to make such a final judgment?"

2

Profile of the Underclass: Its Size, Causes and Effects

In and around the classroom the members of BT-27 were, with several exceptions, immensely likable. They cared about and often tried to help one another. They could be humorous, curious, compassionate, vulnerable, and wise. Although cash-poor, they often displayed traditional middle-class values—some were God-fearing and church-going. Many were loyal to family, country, and success. None dared curse in front of Mohammed. Hope Parker, who was uncooperative in the life-skills class, selflessly sacrificed her own social life to stay home and nurse her ailing grandfather. Pearl Dawson despised welfare as intensely as any conservative does. Timothy Wilson was unfailingly polite; Willy Joe generous. During the seven months I attended their class, the members of BT-27 were usually open, kind, and appealing human beings.

It is easy to forget what many of these people have done: Leon Harris was a professional stickup man who says he earned $1,500 to $3,000 a day, and implies that he shot and killed more than a few people; William Block and Pearl Dawson were convicted for manslaughter; Timothy Wilson, shunted off to foster homes, used to stalk the streets, belting strangers with a baseball bat; Gladys Miller still cheats on food stamps and sells her methadone dosage for $120 a week, which is a felony under state law; Howard Smith, their instructor, once committed a felony by forging records and collecting at least six separate bimonthly welfare checks. These are the real faces behind the crime and welfare statistics that concern most Americans. Getting to know the members of Wildcat's BT-27 class may help explain why violence, arson, hostility and welfare dependency rose during a time when unemployment dropped, official racial barriers were lowered, and government assistance to the poor escalated. Getting to know BT-27 is one way to explore the largely uncharted universe of the underclass.

Wildcat was one of fifteen original participants in a five-year, $82 million nationwide supported-work experiment that officially began in 1975. The experiment provides a one-year job for members of the underclass, who are given special assistance—individual counseling, special training, support from their peers, slow, graduated exposure to stress at work. The national experiment was first conceived by two Ford Foundation officials, Vice-President Mitchell Sviridoff and program officer William Grinker, and by Herbert Sturz, the president and director of New York's Vera Institute of Justice, which pioneered a program of supported work for ex-addicts back in 1972. The public-benefit corporation that coordinated that effort among ex-addicts was Wildcat. Looking to build on this model, and convinced that few federal training or jobs programs touched the hardest to reach, Sturz traveled to Holland to study supported work there; Sviridoff and Grinker studied the work of the Wildcat Corporation and the Vera Institute of Justice. Then Sviridoff and Sturz met in Washington with representatives of five federal agencies and presented a draft plan for joint financing of a supported-work experiment. The federal officials, naturally, inundated them with queries. Who would run the program? Who would recruit the students? Who would be eligible? The federal government preferred that the effort be coordinated by a public benefit corporation outside government; it was no coincidence that Sviridoff, Sturz and Grinker had already drawn up incorporation papers for such an outfit.

In November 1974, Grinker left the Ford Foundation to become president of the new Manpower Demonstration Research Corporation (hereafter called the MDRC). The Manhattan-based MDRC selected the combination of urban and rural sites, funneled funds to the community-based organizations like Wildcat which operated them, supervised their management, set goals, audited their performance, and treated each site as a research laboratory for one of the most extensive social experiments ever launched in America. In 1979, with a staff of a hundred people spread over two floors of a Park Avenue skyscraper, and direct or oversight responsibility for an annual budget of $130 million in 1980,* the MDRC supervised sup-

---

*Of this sum, a total of $7.8 million was expended by the MDRC for central operations, personnel, research and overhead; another $16.1 million flowed through the corpora-

ported work and several other innovative experiments designed to test various ways to reach the underclass.

Through December 1980, 18,000 people had been enrolled in supported work. Unlike most organizations that run social programs, the MDRC tries to measure the long-term benefits of its experiments; in 1980 alone, the corporation apportioned $3.5 million for research. And unlike most training or jobs programs, supported-work programs seek to recruit the hardest to reach. Among the four groups eligible to participate, for instance, MDRC surveys have turned up these statistics: the average mother on welfare has been on public assistance more than eight and a half years; ex-offenders have been arrested an average of more than nine times and have served almost 200 weeks in jail, and a third have been regular heroin users; just over three-quarters of the ex-addicts have been in prison, averaging 129 weeks behind bars; virtually none of the youths has completed high school, and more than half have been arrested. Nearly all participants have had incomes below the federally defined poverty level, 30 percent have never worked, three-quarters have not completed high school, and 90 percent have been black or Hispanic.

Although Wildcat recruits often spend seven of their twelve supported-work months in the classroom, recruits at the other locations usually spend the full year at a private or public job. But whether the time is spent in class or at work, this is an unusual program. Gary Walker, the MDRC's senior vice-president, told a Senate subcommittee in 1980:

> While supported work shares many features with other subsidized work efforts, such as public-service employment and sheltered workshops, it is chiefly distinguished from other work-experience programs by its high degree of structure and its reliance on three programmatic techniques designed to make participants initially comfortable with the world of work, and to gradually increase their ability to succeed in that world: peer-group support, graduated stress, and close supervision. The first of these, peer support, is based on the theory that most participants in a new activity feel less anxious about their performance in the presence of people with similar disadvantages or fears, and that a significant proportion of what one needs to know about a job is learned through peer interaction. Gradua-

---

tion and out to community-based organizations; the remaining $106.2 million went directly to community-based organizations to operate experiments supervised by the MDRC.

ted stress stems from the idea that getting and keeping a regular job is too difficult for certain people because they cannot, at least initially, meet the ordinary demands of the labor market. Through gradually increasing performance and productivity standards, it attempts to bridge the gap between what supported workers can do and what a job ordinarily requires. Supervision, finally, represents the key link between the participant and the program, and is chiefly responsible for the development of technical skills, for instilling positive work habits and attitudes, and for providing advice on work and personal problems.

In 1979, the program paid $105 a week—barely more than the minimum wage—and good performance was rewarded with small bonuses. Unlike sheltered workshops in England and elsewhere in Western Europe, where a permanent support net is usually provided for those hardest to employ, poor attendance or behavior in Wildcat and other supported-work programs is supposed to lead to termination; supported work lasts just one year, the assumption being that this is an adequate period in which to effect entrance into the world of work.

Through 1980, the MDRC tested three other social ideas as well. One is represented by the Youth Incentive Entitlement Pilot Projects. Although this program is little known, it was the nation's first guaranteed-job program, and was designed for poor young people living in sections of seventeen designated cities or rural areas across the country. From the spring of 1978 to September 1980, 80,000 youths between the ages of sixteen and nineteen were given, in exchange for returning to or remaining in high school, a part-time job during the school year and full-time summer employment. The purpose of the program was to learn what techniques might curb the twin problems of increasing numbers of dropouts and youth unemployment. A second experiment is the National Tenant Management Demonstration, whose purpose is to stem the decline of public housing. Under the MDRC's aegis, 19,000 tenants at six inner-city projects were granted significant policymaking and operating authority over their housing. The test market question: Would tenant control produce better results—lower costs and improved living conditions, for example—than government management? The third experiment is the WIN Research Laboratory Project. WIN, the Work Incentive Program, was mandated by Congress in 1967 to help welfare recipients enter the job market. In early 1978, the MDRC was asked to help select four WIN sites as research laboratories to test what combination of training, placement, and support services succeeds best in ending welfare dependency.

Early in 1980, as the results from the four tests accumulated, the MDRC began trying to spin off some of these early efforts and concentrate on new social experiments—learning how to assist teenage mothers, providing education and employment services to youngsters in poverty, lessening school truancy, and offering supported work to the mentally retarded. "We're in the business of testing out ideas," says Grinker, the wry and sometimes gruff MDRC president. "Most programs—they're more in the advocacy business. We're not. We're above that—or below that. We have no constituency."

With the coming of the Reagan administration in 1981, the fact that MDRC had no constituency in the White House threatened its very existence. The Republican administration of Gerald Ford and the Democratic administration of Jimmy Carter supported MDRC's targeted approaches to the underclass. But the Reagan administration, committed to across-the-board cuts in domestic spending and instinctively suspicious of most government-funded antipoverty efforts, exhibited little awareness of MDRC's targeted approach, or even of its existence. MDRC's generally liberal board of directors probably complicated matters. They had few ties to the conservative Reagan administration.* By mid-1981, Grinker did what most corporate presidents do in Washington: he hired a law firm with close ties to the new administration. The firm—Anderson, Hibey, Nauheim & Blair, several of whose partners and associates worked for the election of Reagan or on his transition team—acted as social secretary, introducing Grinker and other MDRC officials to the Reagan people. But by late 1981 MDRC officials worried aloud that declining federal support would compel them to abandon their experiments among the underclass. In June 1981, for instance, MDRC handed pink slips to almost half its hundred employees.

*The chairman was economist Eli Ginsberg, director of the Conservation of Human Resources Project at Columbia University. The vice-chairman is Robert Solow, Institute Professor at MIT. Other members are: Richard P. Nathan, professor of public and international affairs, Princeton University; Bernard E. Anderson, director, Social Sciences Division, the Rockefeller Foundation (Anderson is one of three board members who are black); Alan Kistler, director of Organization and Field Services, the AFL-CIO; M. Carl Holman, president of the National Urban Coalition; Nan Waterman, former chairwoman of Common Cause; Gilbert Steiner, Senior Fellow at the Brookings Institution; Phyllis A. Wallace, professor at the Alfred P. Sloan School of Management, MIT; and David Schulte, a vice-president of the Wall Street investment banking firm of Salomon Brothers. With the possible exception of Nathan, a Rockefeller Republican who served in the Nixon administration, the MDRC had few to run interference for them with the new administration. In late 1981, Nathan replaced Ginsberg as chairman.

Although its efforts are almost a state secret, a surprising number of people cite the MDRC as perhaps the nation's single most successful government-funded and research-oriented antipoverty effort to date. "I've always got a sense from the MDRC that's different from the sense I got from other programs we fund," says Dr. Charles Knapp, who was deputy assistant secretary of labor for employment and training in the Carter administration and now teaches at George Washington University. "The others, I often get the sense, are in it for the bucks and the contracts. The fact that the MDRC is encouraging moving the operational part of supported work out of its shop is impressive. As far as I know, it is a unique organization. In making decisions in manpower—and I think this is true throughout government—the thing that is most often missing is solid information. Often you're reduced to anecdotes. The debate takes place at that level. Too few people have an institutional memory. And even when they have results, those results are often arguable. It makes a difference in making public policy. Each idea put into a piece of legislation may be a good one, but the cumulative weight is negative. Some mornings you feel as if you were shooting a cannon into a mountain of Jell-O."

MDRC takes aim not at the poor in general but at those considered the hardest-to-reach. In 1980 an MDRC report concluded that "the nation faces few problems as formidable as the presence of a group of people, largely concentrated in its principal cities, who live at the margin of society. Whether because of distortions in the economy, lack of training or motivation, or the attitudes of employers, these people have been excluded from the regular labor market and find, at most, sporadic employment. Though relatively few in number, they have become a considerable burden to themselves and the public—as long-term recipients of welfare, and as the source of much violent crime and drug addiction. They are simultaneously the source and the victims of urban decay."

There is nothing new about such a social class. There have always been pirates, beggars, vagrants, paupers, illiterates, street criminals and helplessly, sometimes hopelessly, damaged individuals. Probably the first systematic account of this class of "nonworkers" and their culture was Henry Mayhew's four-volume nineteenth-century classic, *London Labour and the London Poor.* Mayhew estimated that at midcentury in all of England and Wales there were about 150,000 members of a criminal class and about 110,000 "habitual vagrants." Despite his sympathy for the downtrodden, Mayhew wrote that some of these people were simply more "beast" than "man"; others "have lived on charity so long, that the habits of wandering and mendicancy have eradicated their former habits of industry." Mayhew divided the sizable "non-working" class into three groups: those

25

with a "physical defect"; those with an "intellectual defect, as in the case of lunatics and idiots"; and those with "some moral defect, as in the case of the indolent, the vagrant, the professional mendicant, and the criminal." In the first half of the nineteenth century, after his journey across America and his visits to its busy cities, Alexis de Tocqueville wrote of how the "lower ranks which inhabit these cities constitute a rabble" that menaced the young American nation. Over the years some, particularly those on the political left, have viewed this group as the potential vanguard of a revolutionary movement. But Marx himself savaged the "lumpenproletariat," as he called it. In *The Communist Manifesto* he referred to them as "the social scum, that passively rotting mass thrown off by the lowest layers of old society, that may, here and there, be swept into the movement by a proletarian revolution; its conditions of life, however, prepare it far more for the part of a bribed tool of reactionary intrigue."

More recently, commentators have come to view those "at the margin of society" as a threat not to the revolution but to society. Senator Edward Kennedy, in a rousing May 1978 speech to Detroit's twenty-third annual NAACP Convention, declared this group "the great unmentioned problem of America today—the growth, rapid and insidious, of a group in our midst, perhaps more dangerous, more bereft of hope, more difficult to confront, than any for which our history has prepared us. It is a group that threatens to become what America has never known—a permanent underclass in our society."

What to call this group? The problem with Kennedy's use of the word "permanent" is that for some members of the underclass poverty or antisocial behavior is not permanent; additionally, this description could become a prescription for giving up on certain people. In my interviews with experts and activists, I encountered a variety of terms—the "dependent poor," the "acute poor," the "bottom of the barrel," the "unreachables," the "dangerous class," the "disadvantaged." The problem with these terms is their inelasticity: the street criminal or hustler may not be poor, the "bottom of the barrel" is a blanket insult, many of the poor are not unreachable, a mother dependent on welfare is rarely dangerous, and the "disadvantaged" does not distinguish between a cold killer and a frightened teenage mother. Admittedly, any term that segregates a group of people risks oversimplification. But I came to believe that "underclass" was the most flexible term. This is the term used by the National Urban League and other civil rights leaders to describe the segment of our population with which this book is concerned, and it is the one used by the MDRC to describe its target population. A search through their voluminous records by the editors of the Oxford dictionaries reveals that the term "underclass" was first used in 1918, but in a different context. In the 1960s the term was sporadically used to describe a black or intellectual revolutionary vanguard. Its current usage commenced in the seventies. One of the first to use this term in its current context was Gunnar Myrdal. In his 1970 book *The Challenge of World Poverty,* Myrdal wrote of a third world rural and urban "underclass" cut off from society, its members lacking "the education and the skills and other personality traits they need in order to become effectively in demand in the modern economy." They were, he feared, "superfluous."

Size of the Underclass

How big is America's underclass? The answer depends on one's definition of the term. If one includes all those officially classified as poor, according to the federal census, in 1980 there were 29.3 million Americans living in poverty: 19.7 million were white, 8.6 million black, and 3.5 million were Hispanic.* But most students of poverty distinguish those who are temporarily poor from those mired in long-term poverty. Dr. Robert Hill, director of research for the National Urban League, guesses that about 30 percent are "acutely poor." Analyzing data from the University of Michigan's Survey Research Center, which tracked nearly five thousand poor families between 1967 and 1973, Frank Levy of the Urban Institute in Washington argues that the poor are more economically mobile than is commonly assumed. The majority of the poor, he says, are not trapped in a "cycle of poverty"; they were poor no more than two years out of seven, and the children "did better than their parents." About 45 percent—perhaps 9 million people—do not escape and become the "long-term poor," those who are poor at least five years out of every seven. Some students of poverty think Levy's 45 percent guess is high, guessing that the percentage is closer to Dr. Hill's one-third. But there is general agreement that the underclass has less upward mobility than earlier generations of immigrants. (In this sense, it threatens to become a permanent underclass.) In a paper entitled "How Big Is the American Underclass?" Levy wrote: "The underclass is about 70 percent non-white. About half its members live in female-headed households. About 70 percent of its members are children under eighteen."

The underclass need not be poor—street criminals, for instance,

*Broken down this way, the poverty population appears to total 31.8 million, but this is misleading, since the census counts many Hispanics as whites. The true size of the official poverty population was 29.3 million in 1980. This represents a one-year jump, due to inflation and a recession, from a poverty population that has remained at around 25 million for several years.

usually are not. Which brings us to a second characteristic that usually distinguishes the underclass: *behavior*. Whatever the cause— whether it is the fault of the people themselves or of society, whether poverty is a cause or an effect—most students of poverty believe that the underclass suffers from *behavioral* as well as income deficiencies. The underclass usually operates outside the generally accepted boundaries of society. They are often set apart, they say, by their "deviant" or antisocial behavior, by their bad habits, not just by their poverty.

Using this behavioral definition—one that is widely accepted— most experts would count as part of the underclass many of the 1.2 million "discouraged workers" who, according to the Department of Labor's Bureau of Labor Statistics, although they wanted employment in 1981, thought they could not find a job and were no longer looking. These "discouraged" individuals—two-thirds of whom were women, two-thirds of whom were white, and almost 40 percent of whom had never worked or had not been employed in five years— are distinct from the 9.5 million Americans who were officially unemployed at the end of 1981. Because discouraged workers are not looking for work, they are not taken into account in computing the official unemployment rate. "They are not looking for a job, and it is unclear whether they would take a job if offered," explains Samuel M. Ehrenhalt, Middle Atlantic regional commissioner of the Bureau of Labor Statistics. If they were counted, the offical unemployment rate at the start of 1982 would have swelled from just under 9 percent to just under 11 percent.

Then there are the hard-core unemployed. According to the Bureau of Labor Statistics, 21.4 million Americans sixteen or older were unemployed at some point during 1980. But of this number, 18.8 million worked at least one job during that year. The remaining 2.6 million—the hard-core unemployed—worked not at all.

An indeterminate number of unemployed young people could also be included in the underclass. The official unemployment rate for sixteen-to-nineteen-year-olds stood at 19.7 percent in the second quarter of 1981, with 40.9 percent of blacks, 24.3 percent of Hispanics, and 17.4 percent of whites counted as unemployed. Obviously, many of these young people are only temporarily unemployed, and cannot be included in the underclass. But a growing number of youths drop out of school and are without work experience or skills. In March 1980, the MDRC reported that if its 17 Youth Incentive Entitlement Pilot Projects were extended in 1980 to all those eligible nationwide, about 725,000 unemployed youth would qualify. Lester

Thurow, an M.I.T. economist, says if we counted those who have "disappeared from the system" and are living on the streets, the true figure would climb to about 1.1 million. The true numbers are hard to pin down. One could, for instance, subtract some of those who actually earn a living in the underground cash economy. Do that and the poverty and unemployment numbers shrink. On the other hand, one could add illegal, or undocumented aliens. It is variously estimated that there are three to six million not counted in government statistics, though no one knows how many of these are poor or in the underclass.

If just those eligible for MDRC's supported work program are counted, in 1975 there were 474,000 women enrolled in the basic Aid to Families with Dependent Children (AFDC) program who had been on welfare three or more years and had no children under six. These represented just 14.8 percent of all adult AFDC beneficiaries.* The MDRC also found that in 1976 270,000 ex-addicts and 422,000 delinquent youths or dropouts were eligible for supported work. Thus about 1.2 million persons qualified for supported work in a typical recent year—a figure that does not include the eligible ex-offender population, whose size the MDRC was unable to estimate (although by no means all of them would be included in the underclass).

These numbers could be multiplied. Should those with serious mental illness be counted? In 1955, before it became government policy to encourage the release of patients from institutions, 550,000 Americans were in state psychiatric hospitals. Today fewer than 150,-000 are. Some of the shoeless, gaunt, forlorn and sometimes frightening-looking figures encountered on city streets and sprawled across benches and patches of public greenery are homeless mental patients who have been released from hospitals.

What, then, is the true size of America's underclass? In fact, the experts are often as confused as the rest of us. Their figures hinge on their definitions, which in turn usually hinge on their values, their own life experiences, and their politics. Employing a narrow definition of the underclass—"those who've fallen out of the support networks and are not related to an organized family"—Dr. Marcia Freedman, a manpower specialist at Columbia University who is writing a book on the underclass, guesses that they number about 2

*This total excludes the 1,982,952 families who in 1977—the last year these totals were itemized—were dependent on welfare at least three or more years and had children under six.

million, or less than 1 percent of the population. In 1966, the anthropologist Oscar Lewis, in his book *La Vida*, using a broader definition—those who were defeated by the "culture of poverty"—estimated that 20 percent of the American poor qualified. In 1970 the Harvard political scientist Edward Banfield, in his book *The Unheavenly City*, used another term—"the lower class"—and guessed that perhaps 10 to 20 percent of poor Americans could be so described. Using a still broader definition, to include those who are "traumatized" or "hostile" or reject commonly accepted values, Dr. Hugo M. Morales, medical director of the Bronx Mental Health Center, one of New York's largest outpatient psychiatric facilities, gloomily guesses, "I think the working poor is a minority [of the poor], especially in the city of New York. In my country, the Dominican Republic, it's different. People work, mostly. In the city of New York you have many more people on welfare who are trying to screw society. I'd say about thirty to thirty-five percent of the underprivileged are sick and another thirty to thirty-five percent are the criminal element." If Dr. Freedman is correct, the underclass consists of about 2 million people; if Dr. Morales is correct, it could total 15 million to about 18 million. MDRC officials generally assume a figure of perhaps 9 million is closer to the mark; how many of these individuals are "deviant" as opposed to the long-term poor is of course anybody's guess.

Whatever its size or its origins, those who studied the underclass do not dispute its impact. Recently retired Ford Foundation Vice-President Mitchell Sviridoff, the principal architect and benefactor of the MDRC back in 1973, told the Bay Area Urban League in San Francisco in 1979:

> There is a segment of the nation's poor, small and sometimes invisible, that does not seem to be touched by . . . any traditional sort of outreach. For all our best efforts, this sector of the population is just about where we found them twenty years ago. To some extent the very programs that gave many poor families the means to move out of the ghettos left behind the disorganized families and restless, unskilled individuals of this chronic underclass. Their isolation and concentration has only exacerbated the frustration and hopelessness of their life and made their condition the most dangerous and intractable problem facing the cities in which they live. Numerically this group is relatively small, but it is extraordinarily destructive, and its behavior reflects intense anger, with consequences on a scale that mocks its size.

Causes of the Underclass

To attempt to discuss the causes of the underclass is to run smack into a ferocious political and ideological debate. At its root is the age-old dispute between those who insist that economic poverty and the formation of an underclass are the fault of society, and those who insist that poverty is ultimately the fault of individuals. Sometimes this conflict is described, too simply, as the race-versus-class debate. That there is an underclass is generally not contested. That its behavior is often antisocial and violent is also generally agreed. But here the consensus breaks down, and a fierce battle ensues over whether this behavior is a *cause* or an *effect* of being poor.

Many of those who blame society for the underclass cite racism as its root source. "If you're talking about poor whites in Appalachia, it has nothing to do with race," says Vernon Jordan, who resigned as president of the National Urban League in late 1981. "If you're talking about blacks and Hispanics in our cities, it has *everything* to do with race." Like most of the participants in this debate, Jordan exaggerates. The existence of an underclass clearly does not have everything to do with race. If it did, shouldn't *all* blacks be in the underclass? Judging by the numbers, Jordan's argument contains truth. By most comparative economic and social measures, blacks and Hispanics, particularly Puerto Ricans, fare dismally. Only 9 percent of white Americans are classified as poor, compared with just over 30 percent of blacks and 20 percent of Hispanics. The unemployment rate for members of minority groups is about twice that of whites. Dr. Kenneth Clark, the noted psychologist whose research on the harmful effects of segregation helped determine the U.S. Supreme Court's landmark separate-is-not-equal 1954 decision, blames "institutional racism" for the poor schools that blacks attend, for their poor housing, and for the difficulties they encounter in finding jobs. It comes as no surprise to Clark that even as late as 1981, a Washington Post–ABC News national opinion survey reported that almost one-quarter of white adults still believed blacks are inferior. This number has shrunk, but just as many Jews are scarred by the Holocaust, so many blacks are affected by a two-hundred-year legacy that includes slavery, lynching, poll taxes, twenty-nine states that as recently as 1930 outlawed mixed marriages, and separate and unequal facilities. Inevitably, racism conditioned many blacks to turn their hatred inward, sometimes resulting in negative self-images and crippling inferiority complexes, in physical and sexual violence, or escape into alcohol and drugs. In his autobiography about growing up in the South, Richard Wright wrote:

I had seen many Negroes solve the problem of being black by transferring their hatred of themselves to others with a black skin and fighting them. I would have to be cold to do that, and I was not cold and I could never be. . . . I could, of course, forget what I had read, thrust the whites out of my mind, forget them, and find release from anxiety and longing in sex and alcohol. But the memory of how my father had conducted himself made that course repugnant.

Another version of the argument that society is to blame assumes that the underclass is the inevitable by-product of an exploitative capitalist system. Marxists tend to see the underclass as "the surplus labor" produced by a system that worries more about profits than about people. Others, usually on the political left, also say that the underclass is a product of the mass migration from the rural South to northern cities, of sometimes stupid government policies, of generations of economic deprivation. Dr. Clark evokes the image of a flood when speaking of the poverty-stricken individual "overwhelmed by environmental neglect." One of the first to write of the ghetto's "tangle of pathology"—hostility, crime, dependence, drugs, alcohol, suicide, family dissolution—Clark believes these are effects of a society that projects its failures onto individuals.

University of Chicago sociologist William Julius Wilson, a black political moderate, takes a less conspiratorial view than Clark does. But he, too, claims that the evolution of the American economy has left many blacks (and others) behind. In his book *The Declining Significance of Race,* Wilson writes:

As a result of the decentralization of American businesses, the movement from goods-producing to service-producing industries, and the clear manifestation of these changes in the expansion of the corporate sector and the government sector, a segmented labor market has developed resulting in vastly different mobility opportunities for different groups in the black population. . . . The relatively poorly trained blacks of the inner city, including the growing number of younger blacks emerging from inferior ghetto schools, find themselves locked in the low-wage sector. . . .

This economic interpretation seems to contradict the view that racism alone is to blame for creating an underclass, for the vagaries of the American economy have punished rural whites as well as urban blacks. Homer Kincaid, director of West Virginia's supported-work project, says of the Appalachian whites with whom he works, "These people are victims of society. Let me give you an illustration. Technology hit the coal mines. Before that, you had families that saw no reason to get an education. They just went into the coal mines. Yet what happened in the fifties? These people were put out of work. No training programs, no jobs. It's not their fault. They lost their self-image. They went on welfare. Pretty soon the father was an alcoholic because government didn't do something about it. If we had had training programs we would have done something before their spirit was broken."

Kincaid's argument is also only a partial truth. Were it entirely true, then when the mines closed all able-bodied workers in and around the mine should have lost self-respect or gone on welfare. None of the sons should have escaped to Duke or Harvard, or become successes, as many of them did. Nevertheless, it is true that the American economy generates too few jobs, particularly blue-collar jobs. This is known as structural unemployment, and it worsens as a blue-collar population vainly chases white-collar jobs. Statistics help tell this story: white-collar jobs now comprise 59 percent of all U.S. employment, while blue-collar positions make up only 22 percent; service occupations make up 19 percent of all jobs. And the number of blue-collar openings continues to dwindle. In New York City, where the proportion of low-income people exceeds the national average, scarcely 8 percent of all jobs are blue collar.

Simultaneously, American public schools are failing to produce graduates whose skills match the available jobs. Nationally, an estimated 45 percent of Hispanics and 35 percent of blacks drop out of high school. In New York City, the number is well over 50 percent for both groups; 40,000 New York City kids abandon high school each year. Unavoidably, many will lack the job skills required in a service economy. Of the estimated 105,000 annual job openings in New York City, for instance, only 9,000 or so will be for the standard dropout —jobs as messengers, janitors, busboys, maids. There is a strong correlation between schooling and income. A head of family with less than three years of high school earns roughly two-thirds the median annual income of a high school graduate and less than half the income of a college graduate. A survey of welfare mothers, ex-convicts and drug addicts enrolled in supported work reveals that only 29 percent had earned a high school diploma, in contrast to 63 percent of the adult U.S. population.

That these dropouts often become part of the underclass is not disputed; what is disputed is who's to blame for creating this underclass. On one side are those like Vernon Jordan, Kenneth Clark and others on the left who assert that society is primarily responsible; they are sometimes called determinists because they believe society determines the individual's behavior. On the other side are those, usually on the right, like Edward Banfield of Harvard and Thomas Sowell, Senior Fellow of the Hoover Institution at Stanford University, who emphasize individual factors, including cultural history and personal attitudes. These behaviorists,* as they are sometimes called, ask some hard questions. If society is to blame for the increase in crime and welfare, James Q. Wilson of Harvard has asked, then why did both soar in the sixties, when the national economy was expanding and while unemployment declined? If crime is a form of protest against racism, asks Thomas Sowell, an economist who is black, then why don't Japanese Americans, who were herded into concentration camps during World War II, commit more crimes? Sowell has argued that racism does not explain why West Indian blacks are "disproportionately represented among black professionals" and their "education, income, home ownership" outpaces that of American blacks. If racism or economic injustice were solely responsible for human behavior, many ask, then why don't *most* blacks or Hispanics or poor whites turn to a life of crime or welfare? The true cause of the underclass, Sowell, Banfield, and others argue, is to be found in the interplay between cultural traditions, family history, and individual character; for example, someone born into a family with a long history of welfare dependency may, in the absence of strong personal qualities, fail to develop ambition, a rigorous work ethic, or a sense of self-reliance.

In his provocative book *The Unheavenly City,* Banfield distinguishes between those who are poor in income and those who are poor in culture. He argues that a "lower-class culture" is "pathological" and difficult, if not impossible, to escape:

> The lower-class individual lives from moment to moment. If he has any awareness of a future, it is of something fixed, fated, beyond his control: things happen to him, he does not make them happen. Impulse governs his behavior, either because he

*These so-called behaviorists differ, of course, from Harvard psychologist B. F. Skinner, whose behavioral theory of human psychology contends that individuals are exclusively the products of their environment and that free will is illusory. The distinction between the two groups can be tricky; it could be argued, for instance, that Sowell's view that cultural history determines individual behavior places him squarely in the so-called determinist camp. In a sense it does. But, in general, there are two clearly opposed sides in this debate, and the terms behaviorist and determinist are a useful if not precise shorthand.

cannot discipline himself to sacrifice a present for a future satisfaction or because he has no sense of the future. He is therefore
radically improvident: whatever he cannot consume immediately he considers valueless. His taste for "action" takes prece-
dence over everything else—and certainly over any work routine. . . . He is unable to maintain a stable relationship with a
mate; commonly he does not marry. He feels no attachment to
community, neighbors, or friends (he has companions, not
friends), resents all authority . . . and is apt to think that he has
been "railroaded" and to want to "get even."

The idea of a "culture of poverty" was popularized by anthropologist
Oscar Lewis some years before Banfield wrote this passage (and
almost a hundred years after Henry Mayhew's study of England's
non-working class). Both Lewis and Banfield guessed that perhaps 80
percent of those who were poor in the United States suffered only
from insufficient income, and with assistance or the passage of time,
they would triumph over poverty. But 10 to 20 percent of those who
were poor, they believed, were crippled by behavioral disorders.
Lewis, like Banfield, wrote that those belonging to this group lived
disorganized lives, were "present-time oriented," and rarely married. More sympathetically than Banfield, Lewis explored how their
behavior resulted from forces beyond their control. But he added:

The culture of poverty, however, is not only an adaptation to
a set of objective conditions of the larger society. Once it comes
into existence it tends to perpetuate itself from generation to
generation because of its effect on the children. By the time
slum children are age six or seven they have usually absorbed
the basic values and attitudes of their subculture and are not
psychologically geared to take full advantage of changing conditions or increased opportunities which may occur in their
lifetime.

Lewis showed how these traits were not innate to any race of people.
He wrote: "The more corporate nature of many of the African tribal
societies, in contrast to Latin American rural communities, and the
persistence of village ties tend to inhibit or delay the formation of a
full-blown culture of poverty in many of the African towns and
cities."
  Though Lewis wrote mostly about Latin American poverty, students of American poverty have built on Lewis' thesis, arguing that
each racial and ethnic group has ingrained cultural characteristics

that go back to their specific histories—the country, land, climate, experience and traditions of their ancestors. Thus Thomas Sowell argues in *Race and Economics,* one of eleven books he has authored, that a black child born today can be influenced not just by his parents but also by slavery and a history of welfare dependency which sapped self-reliance; by the rapid shift of rural blacks to Northern cities; by a "peasant" tradition that generally deemphasizes thrift and education. Generalizing liberally, Sowell extends his thesis to other groups: due to a hellish history, the Irish are said to be more prone to drink; due to their peasant background, Southern Italians are inclined to deemphasize education; and due to their nomadic history, Jews tend to fail at agriculture.

Of course there are many holes in this argument. If families were infected by a "culture of poverty," as Sowell and many conservatives claim, why does one member of an underclass family develop a work ethic while others surrender to welfare? If a bad home environment or "culture" can be a cause, as behaviorists say, then why not a bad school or a racist environment, as determinists say? To show, as Sowell does, that black West Indians fare relatively well because of their stronger traditions of self-reliance, is not to show that racism has not hindered far too many black Americans.

A more subtle version of Sowell's argument that underclass behavior is an inherited cultural trait is advanced by some black liberals. For instance, Eleanor Holmes Norton, who until early 1981 chaired the federal Equal Opportunity Commission, observes that "ghetto conditions attended all immigrants. The Irish, the Italians, the Swedes, were in their hovels. Their ghettos did not last long enough to equal a pathological status. Their ghettos disappeared . . . Forty percent of black households are headed by women. Most of these women are poor. It would be fine if these females enjoyed some advantage themselves. But they come to motherhood so early and so disadvantaged that they have nothing to pass on. So their children are raised by the streets. They get their values from the streets." Something fundamental happened to the ghetto in the sixties, she says. The ghetto "became a derivative environment. People were exposed to wholly different values. The churches and the family declined. The ghetto took on an influence of its own. . . . The causes are not simply economic or racial."

Former Health and Human Services Secretary Patricia Harris worries that this pathology and antisocial behavior is becoming the norm in many ghettos. Interviewed in her ballroom-sized Washington office soon after thousands of D.C. ghetto residents flocked to the funeral of Bruce Wazon Griffith—"Reds," as he was called—a convicted heroin dealer and suspected cop killer, Harris complained of the loss of "shared values, the shared expectations we took for granted twenty-five years ago. Now it is probably true that we have a culture where the drug dealer is a hero. In my childhood I grew up on the South Side of Chicago. I was not aware of the kind of culture that elevated a drug dealer to hero status. Even the Jones brothers, who were numbers bankers, were not heroes to young kids. They were grudgingly admired because we knew they could run the Chase Manhattan Bank. But we still knew they were outside the law. Today a group that is not pulled into our value system doesn't look up to doctors or lawyers."

But for many observers, especially those on the left, the notion of a culture of poverty, of a distinct lower class of "deviants," is offensive. They fear that implicit in this notion is the assumption that the underclass are somehow inherently—perhaps incurably—inferior. They fear that it will provide opponents of aid to the poor with an excuse to do nothing. It becomes, in psychologist William Ryan's terms, another justification to "blame the victim." Poverty, he writes in his book, *Blaming the Victim,* "is primarily an absence of money," and to shift blame to a culture or class is to remove the spotlight from the true causes, which he and others see as inequality caused by past and present racism and "our corporation-dominated economy." Robert Coles, whose sensitive interviews with the poor could offer instruction on the perils of generalizing, writes in the third volume of his study of the poor, *Children of Crisis,* that individuals are largely shaped by outside forces:

> We are not born to be what we are. We become what we are. We are raised to expect a lot or to expect virtually nothing. We are given hope or taught fear. We live in a time of progress, or we live amid a century's moment of chaos. And finally, we send our children to a school system full of experiments and inquiries or to one that is set in its ways and unwilling to budge much for anyone.

This debate is as old as civilization. When Cain slew Abel, was he personally responsible for murdering his brother or was he the victim of his sinful heritage? Because this debate is inexorably linked to personal theology and politics, it cannot be resolved here. In truth, there are probably as many varied causes of the underclass as there are combinations of notes on a piano keyboard. Unfortunately, those on the left tend to use one hand to strike a single set of keys, while those on the right also use only one hand. Yet in situations where real people and results matter more than abstract ideology, teachers like Howard Smith find it possible to strike all the keys. Smith is neither a determinist or a behaviorist. He believes members of the underclass are victims of racism as well as their own culture of poverty, of a society that produces too few entry-level jobs and of individual behavior traits that make it difficult for them to hold a job, of poor schools as well as poor attitudes. In fact, many community organizations now operate on the assumption that while government must contribute, the primary effort must be made by the members of the underclass themselves. Preoccupied as these organizations are by real individuals rather than global issues, they employ the tools they have at hand. Not surprisingly, they emphasize self-help and individual responsibility.

William Raspberry, the syndicated *Washington Post* columnist, who is black, believes that society should shoulder its share of blame for the underclass. But like Howard Smith, he worries that an enfeebling sense of "victimism" is created by those who stress society's culpability:

> There is no surer expression of superiority than to treat people primarily as victims. There is no more crippling an attitude than to think of yourself primarily as a victim. Victimism is a disease that blights our best-intended social programs, from school desegregation to affirmative action to public welfare, because it attacks the ability and the inclination of people to look after themselves. . . . If we aren't very careful, we teach drug addicts that they are essentially victims of society. And since the society isn't going to change, at least not very quickly, we also teach the addict that he is esentially hopeless. That's victimism . . . to attack victimism is not to deny that people get dumped on, horribly, illogically, repeatedly. Nor is it to suggest that victims of discrimination and disadvantage should be left to their own devices, with no proffer of assistance from the rest of society. The distinction is between being concerned about people and feeling pity for them. . . . Victimism is impotent. Its focus is on the hole you're in—how you got there, how long you've been there, who is responsible for your being there, whether there are more of you than of them in the hole. . . . The effective focus, which victimism obscures, is, "How do I get out?"

A major reason the underclass got into the hole, Raspberry and many who work with the underclass now say, is the ever-increasing numbers of female-headed families among blacks and Hispanics. Any number of causes have been offered to explain this phenomenon, but the handful of "experts" who have ventured into this thicket usually concede that no single, simple explanation will suffice. The facts, too often neglected, merit attention. In 1979, 55 percent of all black children in the United States were born out of wedlock and into female-headed homes, compared to an estimated 15 percent in 1940. In Washington, D.C., the current figure is 65 percent; in Chicago, the figure is almost 70 percent; in central Harlem it's 77 percent; and in too many ghettos the percentage hovers about 70 percent. Forty-one percent of black families are maintained by a single woman—up from 18 percent in 1940 and 30 percent in 1970—compared to just 12 percent of white families. In cities, where most black Americans now reside, a minority of black families—38.2 percent—are maintained by two parents. A recent study by the National Puerto Rican Forum found that 41 percent of all Puerto Rican families are headed by a woman, about twice the rate for Mexican-Americans and other Hispanics, and four times the rate for white families. The Census Bureau reports that 50 percent of all Puerto Rican children under eighteen live in female-headed homes.

Behind these statistics lie real economic hardships. A female-headed family is three times as likely to reside in poverty as a two-parent family—four times as likely for the majority of such families that now live in cities. Since women generally earn less than men, and since it takes an average of 1.7 wage earners to achieve the federally defined middle-income level, it follows that female-headed households, especially one in which the mother must stay home to care for young children, suffer most. The median income of a female-headed black family was just $5,888 in 1978, almost three times less than the $15,913 earned by two-parent black families. The median income of a female-headed Hispanic family was only 40 percent that of a two-parent Hispanic family.

American poverty has changed in the past several decades. For one thing, it has shifted to the cities. For another, the number of poor people has declined, although by how much is debated. Welfare and other income transfer programs have undoubtedly provided a safety net for most of the poor. But perhaps the biggest change is what has been called the "feminization" of poverty. Nearly half of the 25 million Americans classified as poor in 1979—12.8 million people—lived in female-headed homes; about 60 percent of all women on welfare are heads of households.

Between 1970 and 1977, those below the federally defined poverty standard declined by 2.2 million, or 8.2 percent of the poor. Poor black families headed by males declined by 25 percent. At the same time, however, the number of female heads of poverty families jumped by 710,000, or 38.7 percent.

This social earthquake leaves in its wake profound consequences. As long ago as 1940, E. Franklin Frazier, a sociologist who was black, described children growing up in fatherless homes:

> The disorganized families have failed to provide for their emotional needs and have not provided the discipline and habits which are necessary for personality development. Because the disorganized family has failed in its function as a socializing agency, it has handicapped the children in their relations to the institutions in the community. Moreover, family disorganization has been partially responsible for a large amount of juvenile delinquency and adult crime among Negroes.

Those without marriage ties seem more likely to become dependent on government support or to run afoul of the law. In its survey of supported-work enrollees, MDRC found that only 11 percent were married, compared to 70 percent of adult Americans. School enrollment is also linked to family status. The Children's Defense Fund in Washington reports that half of all single-parent families are headed by persons who have never completed high school. Unavoidably, in many of these homes education takes a backseat to economic survival. The son or daughter, emulating the parent, too often leaves school. A May 1979 MDRC survey of 7,553 youths enrolled in their Youth Entitlement Project revealed that most were raised in female-headed households, and concluded:

> The evidence also shows that family structure is a significant determinant in school enrollment. Approximately 74 percent of children living with both natural parents are enrolled in school, a rate which drops to 47 percent for children living with neither natural parent.

For too many, a cycle forms. Stuck at home with young children, lacking the skills to win most jobs, unable to afford or even to find day-care services, the mother frequently begins to rely on welfare. The children grow up in a home where welfare is normal. And it becomes normal, in part, because of an American migratory upheaval. Following World War II, 4 million blacks migrated from the South to the cities of the North, leaving behind their social institutions and familiar patterns of living. Yet in the North they found few manufacturing and blue-collar jobs. What they did find instead were social workers, doctors, counselors, psychiatrists, child-development advisers, family-planning experts, family courts—the "helping professions." This "organized altruism," as Christopher Lasch has called it, permitted the state to supplant the family, inadvertently making parents believe they were not responsible—perhaps incapable—of caring for their progeny.

Lacking role models at home, youngsters often look for them on the street. They begin to play what George Gilder in his book, *Visible Man,* once called the "virility game." Lacking the succor and confidence-building one can get from a family, many youths abandon school and, eventually, organized society. In society, they are failures; on the street corner, they are men. Hustling, holding up stores, and fathering babies become ways to assert one's masculinity.

Many minority leaders have come to believe that the subject of broken families begs attention. "Kids need to know what adults think," says Marion Wright Edelman, executive director of the Children's Defense Fund in Washington. "They need someone to supervise them, to provide role models." Dr. Terry Williams, who grew up in a ghetto and who now teaches at New York's City University and is Dr. William Kornblum's partner in the preparation of an ethnographic study of underclass life, says that the absence of fathers harmed the kids he grew up with and harms those he observes today: "It affects kids in that they do see role models. They do find it in street models. Boy, saying this is gonna get me in trouble. It's painful because people don't want to recognize that the father is important."

The argument that broken homes are the primary cause of the underclass can be oversimplified. For instance, a major criticism of then Assistant Secretary of Labor Daniel Patrick Moynihan's otherwise prophetic 1965 White House report on the Negro family is that it did not take into account the emergence, partly as an adaptive response to slavery, of the black extended family—the aunts, uncles, grandparents, and friends who don't always show up in statistics but nevertheless often provide role models and parental guidance. The Census Bureau says that about 11 percent of black children are raised in extended families. Similarly, it is foolish to brand a child "pathological," says Dr. Robert Hill, research director of the National Urban League, just because he or she was born out of wedlock or into an extended family. Leonardo da Vinci was an "illegitimate" child, as was Pope Clement VII, Erasmus, Alexander Hamilton and Frederick Douglass. Nor are broken families peculiar to American blacks or Hispanics. Although only 12 percent of white families are headed by a single parent, this represents a 75 percent jump since 1970. The

U.S. divorce rate has tripled since 1959. And the poor have always been plagued by broken families: for example, before World War II half the Irish immigrants living on the West Side of Manhattan were fatherless.

Almost no one familiar with the figures questions the devastating *economic* consequences of being reared in impoverished female-headed homes. The debate is over whether such households are psychologically harmful to the child? Not surprisingly, the answer people give to this question is related to their politics. Dr. Hill of the Urban League says, "I believe Moynihan was sincere. You know what his prescription was? Get her a husband. I say, get her a job. Getting her a husband is a prescription for the individual. Only the individual can solve the problem. Getting her a job is a solution that can only be determined by society." The chief concern of many on the left is that the focus on family dissolution as a *cause* of the underclass rather than as an *effect* of unemployment, racism, and economic inequality shifts blame to the victim and relieves American society of its responsibility for the downtrodden. Those on the right, on the other hand, don't want government to accept that responsibility, believing that government efforts undermine individual initiative.

Those who blame society for the growth of an underclass usually downplay the importance of another possible cause of the underclass: welfare dependency. The bulk of those receiving public assistance do so under the Aid to Families with Dependent Children (AFDC) program. In 1960, there were 3 million AFDC caseloads. By 1979, there were 10.4 million. Thus poverty has been altered in still another way. As poverty came to be associated more and more with female-headed households, many of the poor were not simply unemployed but were dependent on the state. And in combination with the earlier dependency that slavery inflicted on American blacks, many claim that welfare dependency has undermined self-reliance and self-respect.

Franklin Thomas is one who so argues. The president of the Ford Foundation, whose family is from the West Indies, says that welfare is one reason newer immigrants from Korea, Cuba, Vietnam, the West Indies, and elsewhere often seem to be eclipsing many blacks and Puerto Ricans. These newer immigrants, he says, know "that nothing worthwhile comes free. As a philosophy, that has consequences on how you approach your own personal life and kids. In Singapore, nothing is free. You pay the same amount for any social service. Welfare creates a dependency that is debilitating to the individual. I'm not saying we don't need welfare. But there ought to be some way to build in incentives so people can get off the system."

Frances Fox Piven and Richard A. Cloward, whose advice to the welfare-rights movement helped boost welfare rolls and make welfare more respectable, nevertheless concede in their extensive writing that it undermines the work ethic, inducing many of the working poor to ask:

> "Why work?" The danger thus arises that swelling numbers of the working poor will choose to go on relief . . . For all practical purposes, the relief check becomes a surrogate for the male breadwinner. The resulting family breakdown and loss of control over the young is usually signified by the spread of certain forms of disorder—for example, school failure, crime, and addiction.

Another consequence of welfare dependency, say others, is that feelings of helplessness, defeat, and victimization often lead to a fury that spills over into random violence or escape into alcohol, drugs, or mental institutions.

Effects of the Underclass

If one can circumvent the quarrel over whether the behavior of the underclass is adaptive or cultural, society's fault or the individual's, there is surprising agreement concerning the effects of underclass life. Prolonged poverty, William Ryan concedes in *Blaming the Victim,* can produce "stress," temper outbursts and vulnerability to "emotional disorder." "Culture of poverty" critic Charles Valentine concedes that "it is not my thesis that cultural distinctions confined to the poor are either impossible in principle or necessarily nonexistent in fact." Although he basically believes people are shaped by society, Kenneth Clark was one of the first to write of a "tangle of pathology" that attached itself to some Harlem families.

Although individuals often defy categories, in general members of the underclass seem to fall into four distinct groups. First are the hostile street and career criminals who openly reject society's dominant values, a surprisingly small number of whom are responsible for the majority of crimes in most cities. The second group consists of the hustlers, those who out of choice or necessity operate in the underground economy, peddling hot goods, reefers, or hard drugs, gambling, and pimping. Although their activities are illegal, unlike the hostile individual they are usually not violent; frequently they are skilled entrepreneurs. Third are the passive, those who have become dependent over the years on welfare and government support. The

43

fourth group is made up of the traumatized—those whose minds have snapped and who have turned to drink or drugs or roam city streets as helpless shopping-bag ladies, derelicts—or sadistic slashers.

For the average person, the most worrisome group are the violent criminals. Crime in America is now both more violent and more random. Crime statistics tell part of the story. In 1970, there were about 1,500 murders in the entire state of California. Nine years later, there were 1,975 murders in Los Angeles County alone. St. Louis, Missouri, which ranked as the murder capital of the nation, had 230 reported murders in 1978. In 1979, its murder rate jumped 24 percent. Eighty-four percent of the victims were black. Killings in Atlanta rose from 141 in 1978 to 231 in 1979; in Houston, from 462 to 632. Nationally, according to the FBI, violent crimes have risen in eleven of the past twelve years.*

In 1979 and 1980, violent crime jumped 11 percent. In 1980, New York City averaged five homicides a day (1,814)—more than triple the murder rate in all of Canada and ten times the declining murder rate in Tokyo, which has 40 percent more people. That same year New York had 3,711 rapes, 43,476 assaults, 210,703 burglaries and 249,421 cases of theft. There were an estimated 23,044 murders in the United States in 1980; in all of England and Wales in 1979, there were but 629.

Whereas most homicides used to be crimes of passion, usually among friends or family members, today violence has become more random. In New York City, for instance, a third of the homicides are classified as "murder by stranger"; in the city of Los Angeles in 1980, more than half the 1,028 murders were said by police to be the work of strangers. In the words of a St. Louis cabdriver, "A stickup in St. Louis used to be 'your money or your life.' Now it's 'your money *and* your life.' " City residents are terrified by the thought of sudden, unplanned, and unprovoked violence. In a 1980 Gallup Poll, more than a third of urban dwellers cited crime as the major reason they wished to move from their cities. A recent national survey of public fear of crime concluded:

> Fear of crime is slowly paralyzing American society. . . . Crime
> and the fear of crime have, like a dark dye, permeated the

*Some dispute this calculation, claiming that the FBI statistics are based only on reported crimes. These victim complaints, rather than climbing, have remained fairly stable. Others point out that if we placed crime in a historical context, then over the centuries crime has surely declined. However, few challenge the figures showing a rise in crimes of a violent, random nature. Or the growing public fear of crime.

fabric of American life. Yet the change has occurred so gradually, so insidiously, that society has accepted it.

Surprisingly, while crime has multiplied, officials say a very few antisocial and/or traumatized street criminals are responsible for most violent crimes. The New York City Police Department, for instance, inaugurated a Felony Augmentation Section in 1979 to track what they called career criminals in the borough of Manhattan. Police believe these people, who are between the ages of sixteen and twenty-five and who have a record of repeated arrests and convictions, are defiantly hostile and have chosen crime as their vocation. Deputy Inspector William P. Rose, who then administered the program, told me that about five hundred of these individuals "commit seventy percent of the street robberies in Manhattan. These are street people with no known livelihood, who are generally high on marijuana or alcohol. They are opportunistic—out in the streets with their antennae up, looking for pocketbooks to snatch or any way to make a dollar." Manhattan District Attorney Robert M. Morgenthau reports that career criminals comprise just 6 percent of those arrested for violent crimes in Manhattan—and are responsible for nearly a third of these crimes. These career criminals, a study by his office shows, average thirteen prior arrests, and each commits about thirty-four felonies annually. In the five boroughs of New York, Deputy Inspector Rose guesses that only about 2,150 individuals are responsible for 70 percent of the robberies. His boss, Police Commissioner Robert McGuire, thinks the number is closer to 6,000. These crimes include muggings, armed robbery, chain and pocketbook snatchings, rapes, burglaries, and larceny—the crimes citizens fear most. In violent crime, New York City ranks number one. Counting all crimes of violence, Bronx District Attorney Mario Merola estimates that perhaps as few as 5,000 young men are responsible for the majority.

A trailblazing 1973 study of crime in Philadelphia by Marvin Wolfgang and a team of scholars from the University of Pennsylvania zeroed in on 1,862 multiple offenders. They found that this group constituted 54 percent of those considered delinquent and committed 84 percent of Philadelphia crimes, including 95 percent of all robberies and 90 percent of all serious crimes. The chronic offenders, a subgroup of the multiple offenders consisting of those arrested five or more times, comprised just 18 percent of the larger group but were responsible for 52 percent of all offenses and 83 percent of the serious crimes listed on the FBI index.

Crime is the most visible product of the underclass, but not the only one. The National Advisory Council on Economic Opportunity observed that "unemployment has a demonstrated effect on the incidence of depression, and studies show that unemployment is linked to more drastic psychological impairments as well." The literature is filled with studies showing that poverty and unemployment and welfare dependency create stress and more serious disorders, including suicides, mental breakdowns, and heart and kidney failures. The National Association of Elementary School Principals released a study showing that a disproportionate number of low-achievement children come from one-parent families; a disproportionate number of reported cases of child abuse—711,142 in 1979, according to the National Center on Child Abuse and Neglect—occur in such families. Many ghetto residents feel cut off, isolated. Some lose hope. And, as witnessed in Miami's 1980 riots, some lose fear. Angry at police brutality or Cubans or unemployment or the system or whitey, or just bored with hanging out, these enraged individuals turn to senseless and wanton destruction. Herbert Denton, a reporter for the *Washington Post,* described Miami this way in 1980:

> They are small boys, eleven, twelve, and thirteen years old, still blushing when asked about their girlfriends, still chasing ice cream trucks when they have the money. But when guns and homemade bombs explode on the streets here, they stand on the sidewalks with the older boys, hurling rocks and bottles at every passing white motorist. They cheer when they hit a windshield and glass shatters. . . . Alex Moore, 13, takes small bites out of a hot sausage he has cajoled a reporter into buying from the ice cream truck. He talks about being on the streets of Liberty City, the site of two bloody riots in two months, about throwing rocks at whites—"crackers"—as they drove by.
>
> "I hit a cracker cab, then a cracker came down in a van. I hit him, too."
>
> Why? He smiles, sighs, gives the visitor a look of mock exasperation.
>
> Was he afraid out there with the fires and the police and the older boys exchanging volleys of gunfire?
>
> His smooth brown face hardens.
>
> "When they shoot me," he says, "they better had kill me."

The 1980 Miami riots were different from the racial disturbances of the 1960s primarily because of the "general air of approval that pervaded the scenes of violence," wrote Marvin Dunn and Bruce

Porter in their comparative analysis of the Miami riots and 1,893 racial disturbances that took place between 1964 and 1969. Many of those participating in the Miami riot, they wrote, "were not poor or unemployed or members of the criminal class." All were united by their rage. According to Dunn and Porter, they were protesting. But others would emphasize, as Eleanor Norton and Patricia Harris did in another context, that the value system of the underclass may have become the pervasive one in the Miami ghetto.

What is indisputable is that violence is more common among the underclass. Some see crime as a profitable or exciting career and would engage in it even if offered a good job. For others, hustling and behavior society considers aberrant becomes the chief means of achieving success. Observing sixties' street life in a Washington, D.C., ghetto, Elliott Liebow wrote in *Tally's Corner:*

> The street is, among other things, a sanctuary for those who can no longer endure the experience or prospect of failure. There . . . failures are rationalized into phantom successes and weaknesses magically transformed into strengths. . . . He explains the failure of his marriage by the "theory of manly flaws." Conceding that to be head of a family and to support it is a principal measure of a man, he claims he was too much of a man to be a man. He says his marriage did not fail because he failed as a breadwinner and head of a family but because his wife refused to put up with his manly appetite for whiskey and other women, appetites which rank high in the scale of shadow values on the street corner.

If one thinks in terms of the neutral word "habit" instead of the word "deviance" or pathology, it becomes easier to comprehend the often vexatious difficulties encountered by the underclass. Take the habit of work. "A love of industry is not a gift, but a habit," wrote Henry Mayhew in his study of nineteenth-century English poverty; "it is an accomplishment rather than an endowment; and our purposes and principles do not arise spontaneously from the promptings of our instincts and affections, but are the mature result of education, example, and deliberation." An MDRC survey of those enrolled in supported work as of 1978 found that only 39 percent were employed during the previous twelve months, and this figure included part-time positions. Imagine what a job would be like for Henry Rivera of BT-27. At the age of thirty-six, Rivera had never held a full-time job; he had never become accustomed to using an alarm clock, following a dress code, saying "please" and "thank you," taking orders or working in

47

concert with others. Habits most of us acquire early and later take for granted are foreign to Rivera and most members of the underclass. Some are scared and insecure, and prefer to fall back on familiar patterns. Many angrily rebel. Too many of Appalachia's white poor, says Homer Kincaid, director of MDRC's West Virginia supported-work project, can't cope with frustration: "I've had people who when they get their first check and it's in error or they think it is, the only way they know how to deal with it is to say, 'I quit.'"

Such habits or more severe behavior disorders among the poor sometimes defy conventional wisdom. For instance, MDRC's final report on the five-year national supported-work experiment showed that offering a job to a drug addict did not reduce his or her addiction. Contrasting a large experimental group of addicts enrolled in supported work with an outside control group of addicts, MDRC reported:

> The use of marijuana was widespread among both experimentals and controls and persisted at high levels throughout the study. . . . An examination of the use of drugs by employed and unemployed experimentals and controls provided no clear indication that employment and drug use are incompatible. The unemployed members of the sample show only a slightly higher use of drugs than those employed, and in the final nine months of the study this is actually reversed.

In reference to school dropouts, the MDRC found that supported work "appears to have little impact on the employment, drug use, or criminal activities of the youth target group . . ." Central to the work of the MDRC is the belief that the underclass suffer behavioral as well as income difficulties.

Of course, behavior difficulties are not unique to the underclass. Students of democracy are concerned with the "passivity" exhibited by the 46 percent of eligible Americans who did not go to the polls in the 1980 presidential election (compared to the more than 90 percent turnout of the West German electorate). "Deviance" can be observed among the well-to-do who snort cocaine and drink excessively. Broken homes are common in America, with 1.18 million divorces recorded in 1979. Teenage vandalism is rampant in the affluent suburbs. Cynicism is not peculiar to the underclass, as Watergate, Abscam, and Al Capone suggest. As a heroin dealer was lionized in the nation's capital, so Jesse James was—is—romanticized in song and legend. "Well-bred people steal far larger sums than those lost through street crime," Charles E. Silberman writes in *Criminal Violence, Criminal Justice*. "In the extraordinary Equity Funding fraud, the losses to creditors and stockholders have been estimated at $500 million—roughly 70 percent as much as was lost through all the robberies and burglaries reported to the FBI in 1973, the year in which the fraud was uncovered." The IRS has estimated that Americans cheat the government of about $18 billion in taxes.

Pathological behavior, street crime, and random violence are not unique to modern America. Charles Dickens described the "wicked cities" of his time, where poverty and disease created "infancy that knows no innocence, youth without modesty or shame." In *How the Other Half Lives,* Jacob A. Riis described nineteenth-century street gangs who by day "loaf in the corner groggeries on their beat; at night they plunder the stores along the avenues, or lie in wait at the river for unsteady feet straying their way." A decade before New York's draft riots of 1863, which were much more brutal than any since, the first annual report of the Children's Aid Society warned of a "dangerous class" of homeless, parentless, ignorant Irish immigrants "swarming now in every foul alley and low street." There were complaints at about this time of immigrant Jews who smelled and were dirty and, according to the *New York Times,* "cannot be lifted up to a higher plane because they do not want to be." When Jewish and Italian immigrants moved into a neighborhood, respectable Negro families often moved out. In the summer of 1981 England, with over 3 million unemployed, was rocked by riots very similar to those America experienced in the sixties.

Nor are those who live in Communist countries free of stress. Currently, it is estimated that the average Soviet citizen consumes twice as much hard liquor as the average American. The Soviet Union has endured "street arabs" who "succumbed to the temptations of the street." These young men, A. S. Makarenko reported in *The Road to Life,* his post–World War I study of the Gorky Colony, were often violent: "Teachers lived in perpetual terror, trembling in their beds lest at any moment a gang of robbers should burst into the colony, and a massacre begin." The youngsters were described as "illiterate" and "inured to filth and vermin"; "their attitude to their fellow man had hardened into the pseudo-heroic pose of aggressive self-defense." They required, Makarenko said, "moral re-education."

Finally, pathological behavior occurs in people of all groups. For example, Americans in general can be "pathological" in their narcissism, a point made (if overstated) by Christopher Lasch in *The Culture of Narcissism.* Too many of us are consumed by a desire for immediate gratification, for self-analysis, self-promotion.

Describing the hostility toward the outside world of working-class Italian Americans in Boston's West End section, Herbert J. Gans writes in *The Urban Villagers:*

[This] hostility . . . also allows the West Ender to condone illegal work activities. Consequently, little disapproval is expressed toward gamblers, and even racketeers, as long as their activities do not hurt the peer group society. . . . Parents are suspicious that education will estrange the children from them, and from the peer group society as well. . . . Although lower-class culture has innumerable problems, perhaps the basic one is occupational. It seems to produce people who can work only in unskilled jobs. . . . The female-based family seems to raise men who find it difficult to develop the skills and the motivations that are necessary for obtaining and holding the jobs that will be available.

But the subject of this book is not working-class or suburban or middle- and upper-class vices and pathology. This book is about the underclass. If we strip away the rhetoric of the right and the left, a surprising consensus emerges. There is broad agreement that America has developed an underclass, although some would prefer another term. There is sharp disagreement about the causes of this underclass, but rarely about its effects. Those on the right tend to use words like "pathology," "passivity," and "hostility"; those on the left tend to speak of "despair," "hopelessness," and "alienation"—different words that often mean the same thing. As Jacob Riis warned more than a century ago, a "few generations" of slum life might produce monsters. For the first time in America's relatively young history, the ghetto has become a permanent home for too many broken families. For some, upward mobility is a lie, and organized society is the enemy; for others, the temporary crutch of welfare has turned into a straitjacket of permanent dependency. Whether you are compassionate or scared, the underclass should command your attention.

The answers to this new American dilemma are not to be found in academia, or, I came to believe, in the partial truths of the "experts." To understand the underclass, one must consider real people, not abstractions like Edward Banfield's "lower class," President Reagan's "truly needy," or William Ryan's "victims." It's important to talk not just to the "knowns," as Herbert Gans, a professor of sociology at Columbia, called the people journalists tend to interview, but also to the "unknowns." To do this, let's follow Howard Smith's BT-27 class and the other "unknowns" who are participating in supported work or other MDRC experiments, and who are trying to enter the mainstream of society and the world of work.

3

The Class
Versus the Experts

The members of BT-27 are scheduled to meet at nine in the morning on a Friday at the Mid-Manhattan Library, at 8 East 40th Street. Few of them have ever been to a library. Howard Smith wants them to learn to do research for a paper they will write defining what he calls "the welfare mentality," but he doesn't show up. After huddling for forty-five minutes in the frigid lobby, the students who appeared—just five of them—decide to return to class. The five of them walk abreast down Fifth Avenue on the way back to the Wildcat Skills Training Center, on West 37th Street, seemingly unaware that they are monopolizing the sidewalk. Timothy Wilson evokes alarmed glances from pedestrians as he strides by in a black leather jacket, a black turtleneck, and an untamed Afro. Pedestrians step aside to let them pass, fixing me with a curious and sometimes startled look. As we walk west, into the garment district, the bustle of shoppers gives way to street life and black and Hispanic laborers unloading trucks and pushing racks of clothing. Here the five members of BT-27 pass unnoticed. The different reactions call to mind an observation in *Criminal Violence, Criminal Justice,* by Charles E. Silberman: "After 350 years of fearing whites, black Americans have discovered that the fear runs the other way, that whites are intimidated by their very presence."

Several minutes later they enter the familiar elevator, which creaks its way to the tenth floor of the training center. In the classroom, Howard Smith apologizes for not coming to the library, saying that his train was late. The other eleven members of BT-27 are already in the classroom; they say they forgot about the library assignment. All keep their winter coats on and complain that the room is too cold. But Smith ignores their complaints and plunges into his planned subject, "the welfare mentality," by reading aloud common assertions and stereotypes. "Most welfare clients stay on the dole most of their lives," he reads, and invites his students to respond.

"Yeah, I agree with it from what I saw in my environment," says William Penn. "I believe that the majority of people on welfare are trying to make a dollar right now."

"I feel it's up to them whether they're still on welfare the rest of their lives," says William Mason.

Leon Harris comments, "A lot of those on welfare stay on welfare 'cause they say, 'Why work? Someone is going to take care of me. As long as Uncle Sam will do it, why not?' Then they instill it in their children: 'Why should I have to go out there and bust my behind and have them take it out of my taxes?' "

Howard Smith, satisfied that he has sparked interest, reads another assertion: "Welfare drains most of the five-hundred-billion-dollar federal budget."

"Welfare is ripped off by welfare bureaucrats," says Pearl Dawson.

Concerning the federal budget, Smith asks, "Where does it go?"

"Support for the arms," William Penn says.

Leon Harris agrees. "Why'd they give Chrysler that kind of money to produce cars nobody buys? Then they use welfare as a scapegoat, you dig?"

In a flat, neutral voice, Smith reads another statement: "Most welfare males are loafers who don't want to work."

"True," Leon Harris responds. "It's the same as the welfare mentality, you dig? The average male—white, black, whatever—if he's got free dollars coming in, why not? He's going to be lazy."

"Most males coming from the penitentiary to the street don't know how to involve themselves with society," William Mason says.

"Some people don't want to go out there and work for it," says Timothy Wilson. "I know a lot of people on welfare who make more than those working, because they got their side hustle."

"No," interrupts John Hicks, who in turn is interrupted by William Penn: "Me, myself, when I first got out of prison I got on welfare. As soon as I got a job, I got out."

John Hicks continues: "I was trying to get on welfare but I didn't get anything. Not because I was a loafer. I didn't get on welfare. I got into Wildcat. Welfare got a law now where you can't get welfare unless you work—the PWP [the state Public Work Program] Program. You ain't gettin' nothin' for nothin'."

"What do you think of the idea that welfare encourages a welfare mentality?" Smith asks.

"I've known one lady who told me she would have a baby every year to stay on welfare," Pearl Dawson says. "That's the welfare mentality!"

"A lot of people get the idea of getting something for nothing," says Denise Brown. "I know people who live comfortably on welfare. They're satisfied with the food stamps they get. They know the rent is going to get paid. They have that something-for-nothing attitude."

Smith, pacing about the classroom, says, "I remember my days as a welfare recipient. The welfare center was like carnival time. We were drinking or shooting up there. I remember one time my girl-friend and I got drunk and went out and bought drugs. We shot up. The next day, we were sick. She said, 'Don't worry.' She went down to the welfare center with rags and barged in there yelling, 'God damn it, look what my baby has to play in! I didn't get my check!' She was crying. She could have put Bette Davis to shame. All recipients in the center played their part. They knew her game. But they all yelled out, 'Goddamn shame!' Half an hour later we were sitting at home shooting up with money from the extra check. From that point on, I played the welfare game."

The discussion continues in the hallway during a break, as the members of BT-27 smoke and sip coffee from a luncheonette down-stairs. Leon Harris complains about meager welfare allowances, which in New York State were frozen from 1974 to mid-1981 at $200 a month (tax free) for a family of three. It's not enough, he says. He now receives $105 a week (before taxes) from Wildcat, and it's not enough, he says. Of Bedford-Stuyvesant, he says, "It's a bad neighbor-hood. I really can't move out of that environment making the little money we do. Yet without proper training I can't make the kind of money to move. It's a depressing state. Some of us are now living in a fantasy. When we leave this thing, it probably won't be easy to get a job. Either we struggle. Or go to the penitentiary. Or get on wel-fare. As long as welfare's there and we can't get a job, we'll get on it. It leads you right back to the same cycle—from poor to worse. You haven't accomplished nothing till you find people who give you that chance." In addition to his weekly check from Wildcat, Harris says, he and the woman he lives with and their child receive nothing but $58 a month in food stamps. "That's for three people. This can't buy Pampers. Remember, it's only for food. I buy everything out of my $105-a-week check, which I don't see, because of taxes. I get $88 a week. But only if I'm here five days. Out of that, I got rent, which is $240 a month, baby clothes, toilet articles, transportation, et cetera. They only leave you two alternatives: hustle or accept it." Although Harris says welfare does not provide him a separate rent supplement, most welfare recipients in New York City get a rent supplement of up to $218 a month (for a family of four) in addition to food stamps, Medicaid, and their basic welfare grant. After he pays the rent, Harris says, they are left with about a hundred dollars a month to live on. "I hustle on the side," Harris says. "I d.j. I play music. That's not against the law. It's not against the welfare code. To make it, it's mandatory."

Gladys Miller says her after-tax Wildcat check is $83, and she gets $60 a month in food stamps. Her monthly rent is $150. "They clip me, I clip them," Gladys says of the welfare bureaucracy. "I go in and tell them I didn't receive my food stamps, even though I did." As a former heroin addict, Gladys is also enrolled in a methadone-maintenance program. Since she no longer needs either drug, she says, she sells her methadone doses for $120 a week.

Willy Joe says, "I got a hustle—like I went to a disco for a weekend, or during the week, that's extra change." Usually he works for his brother, who organizes dances.

"I even shoot dice," Gladys Miller says.

"I usually handle a little smoke," says John Hicks.

"I don't think there's too many black people don't have a sideline," Gladys Miller says.

"I can make a hundred dollars an hour selling loose joints and bags in front of Madison Square Garden," Hicks says. "But I'm only doin' it because I need the money right now. Times gettin' hard out there, boy. They got all them guards."

"All kinds of people, too—not just blacks," Willy Joe says of hustling outside the Garden. *"Everybody.* They're professional people. They wear three-piece suits."

Gladys Miller blames government programs for inviting cheating. "Take some of that money and open up something, something of interest to alcoholics or dope fiends or methadonians, you see, so they could create jobs," she says. "But, see, the programs—I been on welfare for about seven years—are not interested in the individual, understand? They only interested in you comin' in gettin' that methadone every day. They're handing methadone out. They are supposed to make sure you swallow if they give it to you. When they take your urine, they supposed to find methadone in your urine. Now, if they come and take my urine and see that I ain't got no methadone in it—that's their fault. It's their place to tell me, 'You don't need it, get off.' But they ain't. They only interested in their jobs. Counselor has to have a certain number of patients. So that's all they interested in—the patients. Just like the food stamps. I'm what you call a person who takes advantage of every opportunity. Don't give me no leeway."

I ask, "What if someone said, 'Gladys, you're stealing from taxpayers by ripping off the methadone and food-stamp programs?'"

"You look at the taxpayers that work for the system," she responds. "The government's ripping off them. They got to know I'm crooked, too. Whoever's overseeing them is also crooked."

"I got to make some money the best way I know how," John Hicks says.

"Hit 'em over the head?" Gladys Miller asks.

"No, not no harm," John Hicks responds. "Plenty of ways to make money—jostling, shoplifting."

"That's the worst way," says Willy Joe.

"I tell you, that's not hurting nobody," says John, who explains that stores or wealthy individuals won't miss the money. "Not Tiffany's or nobody like that who got it like that, or people who got the money. Macy's. Mr. Macy's, for instance. Take a little—five, ten dollars—that ain't gonna hurt him too much."

John Painter, the good-looking twenty-year-old who wants to be a basketball player and consider himself a dashing dude, says his hustle —serving as an escort for women and betting about $15 a day on the numbers—doesn't harm anyone. "On a bad week, I make $75 to $100 on the numbers," he says, pulling out white receipt slips with numbers written on them.

"I deal some marijuana. Coke, when I get a chance to get it," says Henry Rivera, the pale, goateed 36-year old ex-addict who refused to sketch his life in class and speaks halting English, although he does sometimes carry *The New York Times*.

"I used to hustle in the mid-sixties and early seventies," says Ramon Lopez, the handsome former convict and ex-addict with the pencil-thin mustache who always sits beside and is attached to Henry and once told BT-27 that school taught him "I was dumb." "But I don't hurt nobody, you know. I was in the street. That's where the hustling game is at for most of us drug users—hustling in the street. But at the present time I don't hustle."

I ask if hustling is necessary.

"Put yourself in our place, okay?" says Mohammed, the serene Muslim who dresses in black and who once hated whites and expressed his rage as a warlord of a Harlem youth gang. "Let's forget about middle class. You just come out of the penitentiary, or something. No job, so they place you in this program. They tell you when you first start, you'll make $110 a week. Okay, cool. You know you

55

gotta do something to stay in the street. You know you don't wanna go back." The take-home pay, he complains, is not $110: "Now you're making $87 a week. You're not accustomed to it. You're accustomed to hustling. Wipe out your middle-class background. The $87 a lot of money, still. Okay. You got a place of your own, you're paying rent, light and gas, food, clothing, transportation. Now they're paying you $87, $89 a week. What do you do? How do you survive? It's a strong person that can make it off $87 a week. It's a strong person that will stretch the money that far, because there's nothing to stretch. I don't hustle personally, that's against my religious code. Because of my lifestyle, I don't spend all that $87."

Their break over, the members of BT-27 return to class. Howard Smith asks, "Does welfare encourage alcoholism?"

"When you're bored and don't know how to use your idle time, people want to escape from reality," Timothy Wilson says.

"It hurts," Gladys Miller says.

"Why is reality so painful?" Smith asks.

Denise Brown replies, "The reality is that the person on welfare no have what they want. No have a job. Can't get one. Might live in a slum."

"It used to hurt my father that we didn't have the things we could have," Gladys Miller says.

"They just can't deal with the everyday hassles," Harris says. "Man, doors close in their face. They think, I tried. So they get on welfare and say, 'This is not as bad as I thought.'"

"That's where the loafin' comes in," William Mason says.

"He's got no one to push him," Harris continues. "His friends say, 'Hey, man, you're right. You tried. Let's go and get high.'"

"Listen, I can't live off welfare," Pearl Dawson says. "I cannot live off this money that I am getting—that's where your family and your friends come in. That's where my idea's different from going out picking somebody's pocket."

She is asked by Smith whether it is true that some of those on welfare prefer welfare, and have more children to qualify for more benefits.

"Yes. Have baby behind baby behind baby," she answers.

"If the money is so bad and welfare is so demeaning, why should this be so?" Smith asks.

"Some people don't want to do no better," Pearl says. "They can live, month to month or week to week, on just rice and beans. First thing I do when I cash my check at the bank? I get my tokens so I make sure I can get here. But when you get out and start spending it, hey, it's gone. That's how much I want to get here. I buy my tokens before I buy anything else."

Smith pauses to look over the class. Except for John Painter, who is reading the sports section of the *Daily News,* and Mohammed, who is asleep, all the members of BT-27 appear to be engrossed. Smith asks, "Is there any connection between the welfare system and what happened to the South Bronx?"

Denise Brown says, "I never was able to understand why certain welfare people live under certain conditions. I was on welfare and never lived that way. It seems to me that they don't take care of their houses well, the way they would if the money was coming out of their own pocket. People come to accept the garbage and dirt in the building. I never understood that. That's the welfare mentality."

"So what you're saying is that if these people were working hard to live in this building and paying their own money, they'd take better care of the building," Smith suggests.

"I believe so," she says.

"I've seen people waiting for the mailman," William Mason says. "And then it comes time to take a leak and they don't want to go all the way upstairs. So they go right there. That leads to deterioration. That's the welfare mentality."

"They keep us in a bunch!" Gladys Miller exclaims. "They keep us together."

"We can't live on East 96th Street, because we can't afford the rent," Leon Harris says.

"You find that most Afro-Americans and blacks are contained," Timothy Wilson says. "You can find a nice five-room apartment in Bedford-Stuyvesant cheap. The streets are filthy; there are no sewers. Yet you walk around Manhattan and see all these people dressed nice."

"They don't want no niggers. It's the same with the PLO," Leon Harris explains, referring to a recent newspaper report that the residents of an affluent Manhattan cooperative rejected a PLO representative as a neighbor.

"Suppose I'm black and I don't want you 'cause you're dirty," Smith says. "Is that a fact or a myth?"

"A fact," Gladys Miller says.

"As soon as blacks and Puerto Ricans moved in, the whites moved out of Bedford-Stuyvesant," Harris says. "They moved in with their attitudes. If you think bad, it will look bad."

Smith, who is obviously building toward something, asks why this should be the case. "Are you saying we're inferior?"

"I wouldn't say we're inferior," Timothy Wilson responds, somewhat hesitantly. "But we do have vandalism and graffiti."

"Why?" Smith asks.

"It could be anger," Wilson says.

"Sometimes it's just their way of fighting back," Pearl Dawson says.

"If you tear down enough buildings, they have to move you out of the neighborhood," Harris says.

"In order to get decent housing, you must be burned out, because there's a waiting list for the public projects," says William Block. "Most people say 'Fine.' So you get a lot of fires, because they know the only way to get into these projects is by fire."

"The landlords don't provide for many buildings," Smith says. "What does a landlord need to keep a building up? Is there a difference between a tenant who works and one on welfare?"

"He gives less care to welfare recipients," John Hicks says.

"A landlord feels that if you're working you'll take better care of the building, you dig," Harris says. "Whereas welfare people cause complaints."

"From working people, he can get the dollars," Denise Brown says. "From welfare recipients, he can't."

"The cost of buildings is going up and up," Smith says, switching gears. "But what's happening to the welfare check? Is it keeping pace?"

"This building is a good example," William Mason says, ignoring the question and rubbing his hands to keep warm. "Everyone else in this building has no complaints about the heat. Those on the tenth floor do."

"Look, we got to have heaters," Harris says, cutting in.

Most of the class members, their coats still on, chime in, wondering whether they haven't been singled out and given less heat because they're poor and black or Hispanic. Smith allows them to complain for a few minutes. Finally, he asks, "Is welfare responsible for the fires?"

"A lot are landlords who get the insurance money because they don't get their rent," Leon Harris responds. William Block agrees that many landlords burn their buildings to collect the insurance.

"A lot of the landlords disappear," says Carlos Rodriguez, the effeminate youngster who sits beside Pearl and always wears dark sunglasses. "So people have no heat or electricity or gas. I've seen it."

"Landlords always get theirs, one way or another," says William Mason.

"Is there a connection between welfare and crime?" Smith asks.

"I was talking about this earlier today," says Timothy Wilson. "Look at the statistics of the job market. The man on the lower level is black. He can't get jobs, and if he has kids he gets on welfare. I don't think that's living. The only food in the house is mashed potatoes or bread or spaghetti. People got to feed their kids. They're sick and tired of welfare. They may pick up habits like alcoholism and start committing crime. They're doing it to live. I've seen mothers on welfare who have their kids hustle."

William Penn disagrees: "As for me, my father worked twenty years and retired. He worked for private sanitation. Me, myself, I'm saying, the welfare mentality don't inflict crime or make you go on the street. I wasn't under that mentality. I worked. My whole family worked. First time I came in contact with welfare was March 1979. That's when I came home from prison and was forced to go on welfare."

"What about buying things hot?" Smith asks.

"You don't have to be on welfare to buy things hot," Pearl Dawson says, smiling.

"To go shopping nowadays, things are very expensive," Leon Harris complains. "And if you can buy it on the street for less, you going to get it."

"Where does the hot stuff come from?" asks Smith.

"Could be your next-door neighbor," Harris replies. "You don't ask where they got it from. You want to know the price."

"How has welfare affected the family?" Smith asks.

Willy Joe says, "I feel you lose your integrity and pride. You don't have the necessities of life—nice school, nice neighborhood. Most families are not together."

"It takes your manhood away," Harris says.

"It makes you feel less than a man. They'd take my heart away before I'd go on welfare," says Hicks, who earlier told of trying to get on welfare but being denied.

"The man's supposed to be head of the household," Gladys Miller says. "But when kids see there's not enough money they go out and hustle."

"Think of a child growing up in this environment," Smith says. "He knows nothing else—deteriorated buildings, urine in the hallways, father on alcohol who can't fulfill his role. What happens to him?"

"A lot of kids just have the attitude 'I don't care,' " William Block answers. "They sit down and think of ways how to beat the man out of welfare. For one person, welfare only allows I think $150 a month. A hundred and fifty dollars is really no money. Welfare will put you in these hotels that have all kinds of nuts in them—people from mental institutions, drug addicts. You can't keep anything of worth or value; to walk around with money in a place such as that is ridiculous. First thing you know, they got your wallet, if not worse." Block explains that he gets only $32 a month for food stamps and until he entered the supported-work program he received $122.85 a month from welfare. "That leaves you nothing," he says. "That brings about an idleness that brings about trouble. You always in the street, trying to get money. And if an opportunity presents itself where you can get some quick money, you just may jump into it. That will lead you to a life of crime or hurting someone."

"I've seen some children willing to pull away from welfare," William Mason says. "So many end up in the penitentiary because they want to do better. They don't have a born instinct for crime. They may be sitting home watching their mother crying because she can't afford milk. So they commit crimes to get away from it."

"I know one kid who lived in a building where he was constantly cold," Pearl Dawson says. "He set fires to keep warm."

"I know kids who did destructive things," Denise Brown says. "They broke up their rooms or didn't take care of their clothes. They did it to take out hostility."

"I think society tries to impose a welfare mentality on welfare recipients as far as the neighborhoods and the things that are presented to them," says John Painter, who has put his newspaper aside. "Something for some poor young child living in a predominantly welfare-recipient neighborhood, something that he can look up to and say he wanna be, is usually gonna be something he's seen and something he knows about. Might be something in the neighborhood, somebody driving a Cadillac. Whereas somebody else might wanna be a doctor or a lawyer or something. So if people do have a welfare mentality I think it's imposed on them by society, by the things that are presented to them. Most kids in ghettos and whatnot don't think about being a doctor. They be looking forward to being something closer to the reality as far as they can see. In a sense, welfare mentality is thinking you gonna get something for nothing."

To prevent that attitude, he is asked, should all welfare be terminated?

"No, no, no. That's essential in today's world, where you got this economical strife. That is an essential railing. But society plays a big part in the way the person is gonna accept it."

"You are what you eat," Timothy Wilson says, echoing the view, hinted by a few in the class, that the system, rather than the individual, is to blame. "If you eat garbage food, it affect you. If you have a kid and all he sees is pain and sorrow and garbage food, it's got to affect him. It hurts inside."

"Any hope for that child?" Smith asks. "Now he's seventeen, eighteen, nineteen, twenty-one—in his early twenties. He's gone the route—drugs, jail. He wants to straighten out. Is there any hope? Is there such a thing as the person who doesn't want anything else?"

"Some people on welfare don't see anything else," Wilson says. "They're happy with it."

At this point, Smith veers off in a new direction, reading a series of questions and asking for yes-or-no answers: Is it true that more blacks than whites are on welfare? Unanimously, BT-27 says more blacks are on welfare. Smith reports that just over 50 percent of those on welfare are white.

"Is it true that welfare drains most of the federal budget?" Smith asks. All but one member of BT-27 say it does. John Painter dissents, and Smith says he's correct: only 2 percent of the budget is earmarked for welfare. In fact, a glance at the budget shows that in 1981 the federal government shelled out $2.1 billion to farmers for surplus dairy products, paying 95¢ per pound for dry milk, almost 70¢ above the price on world markets. Close to $200 million went to subsidize the tobacco industry and about $1 billion was set aside to support grain and cotton growers. About $500 million in subsidies and special tax breaks was earmarked for the maritime industry. Private airplane owners pay for less than 25 percent of the government services they receive. The government offers a hand to veterans ($11 billion a year), small businesses, peanut farmers, homeowners, and college students through low-interest loans, not to mention loan guarantees to Chrysler or Lockheed, tax "loopholes," which David Stockman, President Reagan's budget director, said could be cut by $20 billion, and subsidies for the $3 billion Clinch River breeder reactor project in Tennessee, a program Stockman wanted to eliminate and Senator Gary Hart calls "a CETA program for nuclear engineers." According to a study by Gail Wilensky of the National Center for Health Services Research, when tax breaks for medical payments and insurance are added up, the government spends as much on health care for the rich as it does for the poor—between $21 and $27 billion in 1981, she estimates.

Howard Smith then recites a score of stereotypes:

"Blacks are shiftless."

"All Jews have money."

"Most of them," Painter jokes.

"Jews are stingy," Smith continues.

"Most of them," Painter says.

"Jews are tough," William Mason says.

BT-27's energy seems spent and the conversation begins to meander, but Howard Smith's long face looks satisfied. All of this, he says, was useful preparation for the paper he wants them to write describing what they mean by the "welfare mentality." Tuesday's session is again scheduled for the Mid-Manhattan Library, where they will learn to do the research for this project. At 12:40 P.M., Smith hands out their weekly checks and they break for lunch. Willy Joe lingers in the classroom and in his warm, open way shows me a deck of snapshots: his fifth-grade class from grade school in Brooklyn; a friend who is now "upstate"; a daughter who died of a birth defect; the woman he lives with and says he loves; their daughter; a son who is five and lives with his mother in Trenton, New Jersey. As Willy never knew his father, so he does not know his son in Trenton. Willy says the son was born when he was in prison. He lost a letter from the mother and doesn't know how to find the baby or the mother. "I think I would have married her," he says.

Willy wanders off to lunch; everyone is gone but Howard. "What were you trying to do today?" I ask.

"I was trying to get them thinking about the effect of welfare on a person's development, on the child, on buildings, on our values. The other thing—I don't know whether you picked up on it, but there wasn't much condemnation of burning buildings and throwing garbage out the window because they feel a lot of these things are justified . . . There's a lot of behavior in the class that is—for want of a better expression—'welfare mentality.' If you can get them thinking about welfare and its effects, then you can get them to change themselves."

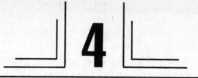

4

Howard Smith: Life-Skills Teacher

It is a wet, brisk Tuesday morning in January, and the students in BT-27 are to meet at the Mid-Manhattan Library at nine o'clock. By nine-thirty only five members appear. By ten, nine of the sixteen class members show up, and Howard Smith escorts them to the fifth floor. Absent instruction from Howard, at first they flounder about, leafing through the *Readers' Guide to Periodical Literature* and author indexes, unsure of what they're looking for. Finally, with belated assistance on how to look up "Welfare" and "Dependency," all nine disappear among the stacks of books and periodicals, returning after a period to sit at vast wooden tables and read, or pretend to read.

Howard Smith and I locate a quiet corner behind the stacks. He finds a chair, extends his long legs, wraps himself in a rumpled raincoat, and, sniffing from a bad cold, expresses the fear that many in BT-27 have a drinking or dope problem: "They find it difficult to function for any length of time without getting high. For most of them it's always been an integral part of their environment—in the home, at school, in the neighborhood. It's part of being in the ghetto a long time." The younger generation "are proud of the fact that they don't drink, but from the time their feet hit the floor in the morning they're high on marijuana."

Even though Smith decries the effects of marijuana, he concedes that without alcohol or drugs there would be "hell on our hands." He goes on, "I'd hate to be in the South Bronx if someone should suddenly stop the flow of cheap wine or drugs. The younger people, especially, wouldn't be able to tolerate the environment. Drugs have become the new religion. Drugs are the promised land. Drugs are salvation. It keeps them going."

Acknowledging that drugs are common throughout society, among the affluent as well as the poor, he says: "But the difference is that the suburban housewife can go to the doctor and get a prescription. In the ghetto the average person can't afford to get a prescription." The businessman who drinks too much or the rock performer who snorts cocaine don't suffer from a "welfare mentality" because "they're contributing to society. They live in a nice home. They have a job. 'It's not what you do, it's how you do it.' Hell, I can remember when I was on drugs. Carloads of middle-class whites came to the South Bronx to buy drugs. They dressed better, they smelled better, they spoke better, they drove nice cars. If they got caught or busted, they made phone calls. They had just as big a habit as I did. When things got over their heads, they were able to go away. They got money from their parents. This can't happen when you're visible, when you've got to depend on welfare, when you don't have a private doctor to go to. It makes a difference. It causes a lot of resentment, too. I can recall fellows in the penitentiary. Real bitterness. To a degree, society is responsible. Talk to any addict over thirty-five, like myself, about how drugs started in Harlem. There were never any drug programs. No rehabilitation. No help offered until drugs became not just a black and Hispanic problem but a white problem."

Everyone needs to escape, Smith says. "I did it as a youth through reading. One day I was Rhett Butler. The next I was Tarzan. Now you have ten- and eleven-year-olds on drugs." Smith admits that he is baffled by the cause: "I don't know what's happening to them. I really don't know. Is it because of a kid's need to escape? Or because he sees everyone else around him doing it?" On balance, Howard Smith thinks this dependency is part of what he calls the welfare mentality. Like the American Psychiatric Association, which labels substance dependence a mental disorder, he believes the mental addiction precedes the physical.

"Another aspect of the welfare mentality," Howard says, "is a lack of concern about one's environment because of the feeling that there is no real personal stake—in the apartment, the building." He pauses, and then says, "I know damn well that if I'm working hard every day and I'm paying rent to live in a nice place and I bought expensive furniture, I'm more interested in its upkeep than I would be if these things were given to me. How can you have respect—and I've thought a lot about this; I refuse to accept that we're an inferior species. How can a man have respect for himself who is a member of a family that has been on welfare for more than one generation when everything that's good and decent is supposed to be the opposite of welfare? Our entire system and society is based on the idea that a good man is one who works hard and provides for his family and is able to show some degree of success. If he was in Sweden and on welfare, it wouldn't have the same impact. In this country, it's definitely a stigma."

Members of BT-27 feel this stigma, but, according to Smith, their difficulties do not end there. If the Wildcat program adhered strictly to its stated policy of allowing no more than three unexcused absences and five unexcused latenesses during the first ten weeks of class, "we'd lose just about everyone in the class. It's my gut feeling that if we can extend ourselves a little there are a few it will pay dividends for." He's confident that Denise Brown, Timothy Wilson, William Mason, Carlos Rodriguez, and Hope Parker, a twenty-eight-year-old ex-addict who rarely speaks in life skills but stars in typing and other subjects, will win their certificates and go on to successful new careers. Pearl Dawson, John Painter, and William Block can make it, he feels, if they don't succumb to the lure of alcohol. He doesn't think that Henry Rivera will survive, and fears that the "peer pressure" of Henry's smoking joints and drinking will ensnare his friend, Ramon Lopez. Howard is similarly concerned that John Hick's surly attitude and William Penn's heavy drinking will influence Willy Joe, who moves in their orbit. He's not sure that Gladys Miller or Leon Harris will make it, but he suspects that if they fail it will be because of their low tolerance for frustration. Mohammed is another question mark. He has difficulty paying attention and seems constantly to be torn between his Muslim religion and organized society.

The life-skills class and supported work will succeed for any of them, Smith says, "only if they come to us with something. They have to already have something going for them. You reach a point where you get tired—tired of being scared when you see a patrol car, tired of hating your family, tired of going back and forth to jail, tired of hustling. Most of us get tired. Some can break away. With others, their rocket doesn't have enough rocket-boosting power. They just can't get away."

Howard talks about his seventy-nine-year-old grandfather, with whom he lived in the Bronx: "He remembers when things were worse for blacks than they are now. He tells me stories about South Carolina that sound like *The Rise and Fall of the Third Reich*. . . . In some respects we're so much worse off than when he was young. Here's where I feel most of my contradictions. A society cannot subject some of its people to the things blacks have been subjected to over long periods of time without certain abnormalities manifesting themself. Take what the Jews were put through with the Holocaust. That was a relatively short period of time. Yet I've read accounts of abnormal behavior when people got out of the concentration camps. It caused pathological behavior. So, yes, American society has a responsibility for the pathological behavior of some blacks. And yet, even though I believe society is responsible, as Dr. Kenneth Clark believes, individual responsibility also comes into play. That's where I get in trouble. Where do you draw the line? You can't get away from individual responsibility. I can no doubt trace some of my insecurities and problems to my mother. But I can't go through life wallowing in self-pity and saying, 'Look what my mother and father did to me.' At some point, Howard has to take responsibility for himself. That applies to David Berkowitz [the convicted murderer known as Son of Sam] as well as Howard Smith."

Howard Smith thinks the female-headed family is largely responsible for the "welfare mentality." "One basic common denominator is the matriarchal family. I deliberately didn't say, because the man split. That may be so. Even where the man is present, however, the mother definitely heads the family because the father can't get work or is dependent on alcohol. The mother is the one who faces the landlord, pays bills, encourages everyone to go to church or to school. Blacks are a matriarchal society, no ifs or buts about it. I see a lot of bad about it. The women, the mothers themselves, are not happy about it. Their sons grow up without any positive male role models to emulate. Usually by the time the son becomes a teenager he begins to resent that Mom is the one always giving orders. Especially now that he's beginning to feel his oats. Since he can't find a strong male role model at home, he turns to the streets for it. And what does he see? He sees Superfly, the reefer-smoking, coke-sniffing, numbers-running, drug-dealing, pimping, Cadillac-driving hustler, with expensive rings, expensive clothes, and lots of women."

Howard says that slavery ruthlessly uprooted the black family, that the black extended family often provides positive male role models, and that many mothers manage quite well against great odds. But he thinks that children—particularly minority children—are the victims of a seismic event that is shaking society: a crumbling family structure. "The difference between my generation and the majority of my class is that even though we may have had a female-oriented family, the average mother in the forties and fifties had different values," he says. "Welfare was wrong. Drugs were wrong. Every Sunday morning you had to put on a blue serge suit and a pair of shoes and go to church. You may not have been getting the best education in a segregated school, but you had to go to school. And they thought nothing of 'cutting your behind' with a strap. You respected your elders and didn't talk back. Those mothers were tough. Today it's a whole new ballgame. The kids aren't taught those same values. Now it's the parents whose behinds get cut with a strap. You have parents who are actually frightened of their kids. I'm frightened when I see a bunch of young kids on the street late at night. We have a generation of people coming up now with no family structures. The traditional institutions that taught them what was good and bad, church, schools, the family unit itself—there's an entire generation out there that has not had the benefits of family, church, or school."

5

Single Mothers: "The Feminization of Poverty"

The generation of which Smith speaks now forms the core of the underclass. The fact that poverty is increasingly linked to the matriarchal family is revealed by two startling facts. First, as noted earlier, the Department of Health and Human Services' National Center for Health Statistics estimated that in 1979 almost 55 percent of all black children in the United States were born out of wedlock, whereas in 1940 only about 15 percent were. In some urban ghettos, the percentage soars above 70. Also in 1979, 41 percent of black and 40 percent of mainland Puerto Rican families—compared with 12 percent of white families—were supported by a lone woman.

This leads to the second startling fact: One in three families headed by women is poor, compared with only one in ten headed by men and only one in nineteen headed by two parents. The issue is primarily one of economics, not sexism. Unavoidably, many of these single women become trapped at home, in poverty; in 1979, the median income of black and Hispanic families headed by women was only 40 percent of what it was for two-parent black and Hispanic families. Perhaps the single greatest change in American poverty is that it has been feminized. In 1979, 12.8 million people—just over half of those classified as poor—lived in families headed by women or were women living alone, or women living with nonrelatives. Between 1970 and 1977, the number of those below the federally defined poverty standard declined by 2.2 million, or 8.2 percent. The number of poor families headed by men declined by 25 percent. Meanwhile, the number of women who headed families below the poverty line jumped by 710,000, or 38.7 percent. And the thirteenth annual report of the President's National Advisory Council on Economic Opportunity, published in September 1981, carries an ominous warning: "All other things being equal, if the proportion of the poor in female-householder families were to continue to increase at the same rate as it did from 1967 to 1978, the poverty population would be composed solely of women and their children before the year 2000."

The poverty vise, government statistics show, clamps tightest on teenage mothers. About half of all out-of-wedlock births are to teenagers. In March 1981, the Urban Institute, in a study entitled "Teen Age Childbearing: Public Sector Costs," reported that more than half of all AFDC assistance in 1975 was paid to women who were or had been teenage mothers. In New York, an unpublished 1979 Department of City Planning document—"The Development and Growth of a Welfare-Dependent Underclass in New York City: How It Happened and What to Do About It"—found that "of all the children born out of wedlock in New York City in the last eighteen years, the equivalent of 75 percent—266,000—are on AFDC today." In 1979 in the United States as a whole, more than 560,000 babies—one in six—were born to teenage mothers; among blacks, the figure was one in four. Eighty-five percent of these black teenage mothers were unmarried.

Among the industrial nations, the phenomenon of teenage motherhood is most pronounced in the United States: in 1979, 16 percent of American births were to teenagers, compared with 9 percent in England, 5 percent in Sweden and France, and less than 1 percent in Japan. Such births are not restricted to minorities; in the decade from 1969 to 1979, the birth rate for unwed white women between the ages of fifteen and twenty-four rose by 25 percent; the increase for black women was only 3.2 percent. But teenage births are disproportionately concentrated in the minority community, as 1979 figures from the National Center for Health Statistics reveal: 13.8 percent of white babies were born to teenagers, compared with 18.9 percent of Hispanic babies and 27.5 percent of black babies.

"These teenage mothers are raising children," says Marian Wright Edelman, president of the Children's Defense Fund, in Washington. "Many are illiterate, unskilled, without health care. This is compounded by unemployment and by the language problem if they're Puerto Rican. I think about how hard it would be to raise a child if I were fifteen and I had an eighth-grade education and I didn't speak much English and I were in a big city. I can't imagine it. I can't imagine the isolation, the feeling of hopelessness and fear."

The Little Sisters of the Assumption, in East Harlem, is one group that toils to overcome such isolation, providing surrogate mothers for forty-five families headed by young women who, in many cases, became mothers while they were teenagers. The surrogates—older women—live in Harlem, and after getting permission from the young parent to enter her home they often instruct this child in how to mother her own child, and they also teach proper nutritional habits, demonstrate how to make appointments with the welfare agency or the local hospital, and free the young mother to leave the house and get away from adult responsibilities. These older women serve as both surrogate mothers and friends.

The surrogate-mother program of the Little Sisters of the Assumption, which the MDRC scrutinized in the course of designing its own program to help teenage mothers, in 1980, is now five years old, and has its headquarters in a battered three-story row house at 426 East 119th Street, across from a wall of gutted buildings. Fifteen of the sisters who work here, including some from other religious orders, live in East Harlem and receive only expenses—a major reason that the surrogate-mother program survives on an annual budget of just $40,000. The bulk of this money goes to seven grandmothers who work twenty hours per week as surrogate mothers.

Seated in their basement kitchen recently, several of the sisters described the fears, isolation, and dependency of the mothers they assist. Sister Ann Hayes, a short, white-haired sixty-one-year-old social worker who came to East Harlem in 1968, told of a twenty-year-old welfare mother who "left the baby here to go for food stamps and never came back." The mother, she said, had a drinking problem, had previously given up another child for adoption, had failed to appear for a welfare interview, and had not asked her landlord for a letter to give to the welfare department certifying the rent she paid. "She just didn't have the energy to get herself organized," Sister Ann said sadly. "She had all the help she needed."

Sister Maureen O'Keefe, who came to East Harlem from Philadelphia, where she was a social worker, in 1973, and still speaks in the accent of her native Massachusetts, said, "Many of the people we're dealing with do not live in the organized world. Our society is work-ethic-related. Our people are so linked into the bureaucratic system. They just don't fit." They know no other life, she said, because most of their mothers were dependent, just as they are.

The welfare bureaucracy becomes intimidating, Sister Ann said. "To deal with organized life requires a sense of consequences," she pointed out. "Many of our people don't think of consequences. They're responding to crisis, to the immediate. They don't have just a welfare appointment to keep but several children and apartments that have no heat or hot water, and they have to fight that. You are formed into that lifestyle. You can't think ahead."

Sister Maureen agreed. "Our families are dependent on the outside world," she said. "There is nothing in their existence that is not dependent on the outside world—their food, shelter, and clothing, and their medical expenses."

Sister Hertha Longo of the Congregation of St. Agnes, who at thirty-three has been the program coordinator for the past year, and came to East Harlem in 1977 from Fond du Lac, Wisconsin, said, "If a family comes here from Puerto Rico, they learn not to mention that the husband is in the home because they get more money. When I go into a house for the first interview they answer questions in a certain way because they feel I'll turn them in to welfare, which I never do. Even if there are ten people in an apartment, they tell you only the number allowed."

Abiding by the rules of the society at large, Sister Maureen implied, has become a secondary concern, and for understandable reasons: "When I grew up you never thought of what to eat or where to sleep. So in a sense you had the leisure to think about religion and love. Those become almost like a luxury."

Why do teenagers with little visible means of support have children?

"What else is life about?" Sister Maureen replied. "When they look into life, what do they see? It's not as if they were planning their life. Their life is planned, in a sense." They become victims of dependency. "Maybe in one day the mother has to keep three appointments—food stamps, welfare, a clinic. Depending on these systems for survival creates a way of life whereby your life becomes more and more organized by the systems. And remember, these *are* systems of dependency. You can sense a taking-away of family by the system." Strangers poke into your fate and begin to take it over, she said. Some people consider this normal, because that's what happened to their mother. "Twenty percent of the residential units here in East Harlem are vacant," she continued. "An additional ten percent of the units are near abandonment. So what do people look at when they wake up? They have no hope. What is within your ability? Becoming a mother."

Sister Ann said, "I've heard sometimes the statement 'I want something for myself. Something I can call my very own.' They don't think far enough ahead."

"To me, the problem is cultural," said Sister Hertha. "Lots of girls feel that if they get to be eighteen and they don't have a baby, they're not a woman. A baby is something everyone considers something of worth. You don't have anything valuable of your own. A baby is of value. People who are educated and work try to build something that lasts beyond them. It's the same for poor people." Returning to the subject of the twenty-year-old mother who had abandoned her child to their care, she said, "She was saying, indirectly, 'Help me. I don't want to hurt my baby.' "

Another reason for enormous increase in the number of out-of-wedlock births is the sexual revolution. In the late 1940s only 20 percent of all unmarried sixteen- to twenty-year-old girls admitted to having experienced sexual intercourse; by 1976, according to surveys, 55 percent had. There are biological reasons as well. While the birthrate overall has dropped, the age at which girls begin to menstruate has also gone down. In 1840, the average teenage girl in the United States and Europe first menstruated at seventeen; today she first menstruates at twelve. And, according to the Department of Health and Human Services' National Center for Health Statistics, during the decade of the sixties—the most recent decade for which statistics have been published—21 percent of black girls menstruated at age eleven, compared to half that percentage of whites.

Observers of teen parents tend, like the nuns at the Little Sisters of the Assumption, to emphasize social and psychological reasons for childbirth. In their ethnographic study of the black and white underclass of Louisville, Kentucky; Cleveland, Ohio; Lauderdale County, Mississippi; and Greenpoint and Harlem in New York, William Kornblum and Terry Williams of the City University concluded: "In the absence of educational and work experiences which can provide young women with positive identities, motherhood is viewed as a certain path to maturity and immediate income." Unwed births have lost their stigma. And a fear of contraceptives has spread. Their field report from New Rochelle, New York, reads as follows:

> Bernice said that boys just expected to have sex, first. And that some girls were afraid with taking the pill, because of all the news of cancer in the newspapers, the IUD caused infections, and the diaphragm took away from the fun. According to Sally, the student intern who had done an internship at Planned Parenthood, the girls were greatly misinformed. In some cases, a girl would take her girlfriend's birth control pill after having sex. According to Sally, the girls in New Rochelle considered the diaphragm middle class. . . . Linda, the nurse, said that it was difficult providing services because the girls did not come regularly. So often they had the welfare program, or had to pick up

their WIN coupons and at this stage—they are overwhelmed.
. . . Corale said that in fact the girls' mothers were tolerant of
their daughters' pregnancies in most cases. Many of the girls'
mothers' friends had pregnant daughters, so that it was almost
expected for their daughters to get pregnant. There seemed to
exist a peer group of not only young mothers but also a group
of grandmothers who were in their early thirties in the neighborhood. It seemed that the daughters continued having the
children that their mothers couldn't have.

Too few teenagers have a realistic sense of the consequences. "The
young adolescent (aged eleven to fourteen) is often not developmen-
tally prepared to understand the concept of pregnancy," Dr. Elizabeth R. McAnarney and Dr. Donald E. Greydanus, pediatricians
specializing in adolescent medicine at the University of Rochester's
Medical Center, have written.

Typically she may use pregnancy as a means of forging closer
ties with her mother, or possibly as a way of discovering if her
young body is physiologically mature enough to conceive without her thinking further about the consequences of her sexual
activity. The middle adolescent (fourteen to seventeen years of
age) may use this process as an attempt to compete with her
mother, as a means to acquire new autonomy or power, or as
a weapon to change attitudes or events about her. The older
adolescent (seventeen to twenty years) may have a specific motivation to solidify her own sexual identity or to improve a
perceived weakening sexual relationship.

The social and economic consequences of teenage motherhood are
all too clear. A young mother finds herself locked into a cycle of
poverty. Forced to drop out of school to have a baby, she becomes
dependent on welfare; lacking education and skills, she cannot find
a job. Frequently, the child's father is unemployed and unable—and
sometimes unwilling—to be the breadwinner. And marriage often
disqualifies a person for welfare because it lifts the family income
above the eligibility cut-off point. As time passes, welfare becomes
the only world that the mother knows, the only world that her baby
may know when he or she grows up. Many members of such families
become resigned to dependency. Not surprisingly, teenage mothers
often feel deprived of their youth and come to resent their children.
Some mothers, especially if they are unable to afford babysitters and
unable to find a day-care center, withdraw their love and neglect

their children; others physically abuse or abandon them. Too frequently, the child is left to be brought up by the streets.

One biological consequence of teen births is suggested by Wendy H. Baldwin, a demographer on the staff of the National Institute of Child Health and Human Development. In her report entitled *Adolescent Pregnancy and Childbearing—Growing Concern for Americans,* she wrote:

> Dr. Janet Hardy has reported data from the Johns Hopkins Child Development Study on the development of 525 children born to girls who were seventeen years or less at the time of delivery. At age four, 11 percent of the children scored seventy or below on IQ tests, compared to only 2.6 percent of the general population of four-year-olds. While in the general population approximately a quarter of four-year-olds will demonstrate an IQ of 110 and above, only 5 percent of the children born of very young mothers tested that high. Dr. Hardy noted that school failure and behavior problems are also more prevalent among the study population.

Finally, there are health risks to the young mother and child. The maternal mortality rate is most severe among teenagers, outpacing the rate for women forty to forty-nine years of age, who are usually thought to run the gravest risks. Babies born to mothers in their early and mid-teens also tend to weigh less and to die within the first year more often, and are more prone to cerebral palsy, epilepsy, and mental retardation than infants born to mothers in their twenties and thirties.

Life can be brutal for young unwed mothers, as two Harlem mothers, Brigette Skouloudes and Carmen Vives (the names of these women have been changed), can testify. Brigette, who is nineteen, is a thin blond with a mop of frizzy hair, chalk-white skin, a puffed upper lip, and a chipped front tooth. In 1980, she received $215 a month from welfare, $92 in food stamps, and $175 as a rent supplement. She lives with her children—boys three and a half and one and a half—in a four-room fourth-floor walkup on East 118th Street. Carmen, who is twenty-six, is short and chunky and has straight black hair brushing against a round, pretty face. She received $394 a month from welfare, which included a rent supplement, and $97 in food stamps. With her children, two girls, seven and nine, and a boy, six, she lives in a $200-a-month three-room walkup on East 114th Street.

Three times a week, Sister Dolorita Donachie of the Sisters of

Charity of New York, who is sixty-nine years old, conducts G.E.D. classes, so that young women like Brigette and Carmen can receive high-school-equivalency diplomas. Not long ago, Brigette and Carmen, seated together at a card table in a nearly bare second-floor conference room that serves as their classroom, discussed their lives. Living alone as a single mother was "hard at first," Brigette said. "My older son said he wanted to go back to his father. 'When are we going back on the train to see Daddy?' It's hard for him."

"Once they understand, they get used to you playing a double role," Carmen said.

"It's hard for me, too, being without a husband," said Brigette, but she added that living alone was better than being beaten by a husband, as she had been. Both are still terrified of their husbands, and don't let the men know where they are living. Brigette hardly knows her parents. Her father lives "I don't know where" in Florida, she said, and "I met my mother only seven years ago." Brigette fled her husband and their house, near New York City, after he stabbed her. She moved to Bedford-Stuyvesant, but he tracked her down, and then she moved to Harlem. Carmen became a fugitive after her husband, who is forty-four years old, cracked her skull with a bottle. She has not seen him in seven years, and he provides her with no support. Both men drank heavily, and both were extremely jealous.

"I never cheated on him," Brigette said of her husband, who was also white. "He would come home and beat me up. He cheated on me a lot. This is the father of my two children! He cheated and came back to me, and it wasn't easy. He expected you to cheer. He'd say, 'A man is a man.'" In the middle of the night, after collapsing in bed from drink, he would wake up and start to hit her. She was thirteen and newly married when the beatings began. "My husband told me he'd shoot me if I ever left," she said. "I just took off one day. I started a fire in the kitchen, so the firemen would come."

"Calling the cops doesn't do anything," Carmen said.

"Right," Brigette said. "He stabbed me in the leg, and I was lying there in a pool of blood when five cops came in, and he said, 'Don't touch her. She's my wife.' All they did was take his knife away."

"He used to beat me in front of the children," Carmen said of her husband.

"And it got to the point where my older son would hit me," Brigette said. "He broke my tooth by throwing a bottle at me. He thought it was a joke, because he'd seen his father do it. My son might grow up thinking that's how you treat a woman."

Carmen's current boyfriend, who is in his forties, strikes her in front of her children. "This is a funny thing about my kids," she said.

"They've seen me get hit by this man. I say to my daughters, 'What do you want to do when you grow up—have kids?' My daughters say they want to stay with me the rest of their life. They don't want anything to do with men. They think all men are the same."

Brigette feels the pressure of the conflict between her youth and her adult responsibilities. "I don't have my own life," she said. "Sometimes I feel like I have too many responsibilities. I just want to get away from them. But I can't. If I want to go downstairs to the store, I got to get them dressed and take them. It was like that when I lived with my husband. It was like they were just *my* kids."

After a pause, she said, "He's still looking for me." She said that he had surprised her when she returned to her former home to have her welfare case transferred to Manhattan. "He had a gun on him. He said he wanted the kids back. He said, 'If you want to stay with me, okay.' He wanted that because he didn't want to go back to work— I was supporting him." Brigette refused to stay but agreed to leave the two boys with him for two weeks. After two days, however, he gave them back. Her children are better off without their father, she says. "I'm giving them the best I can. They eat three meals a day. They're not suffering. They get what they need—but no extras, like rich kids have." Welfare provides the money for food and rent, but Brigette and Carmen, like most members of the BT-27 class, find welfare degrading and generalize about social workers. "You have to be running back and forth for your face-to-face interview," Carmen said. "You have to tell them what kind of shoes you wear. You have to tell them whether you sleep with a man. They invade your privacy. The women who can't find a decent guy and be supported, we are the ones who are stuck . . . I have found that dealing with social workers is bad. A lot of the time you find nice people. But there are those who talk nasty." Brigette chimed in, "They treat you like a number, not a person."

Down in the basement kitchen, the sisters talk about how dependency on the social welfare institutions robs many mothers of their self-confidence. "The key thing is lack of confidence—'I can't do it, man,'" said Sister Helen Kieran, a forty-year-old Dominican sister and schoolteacher, "I'm a Spanish teacher and I see it all the time. They feel they can't succeed. If they don't succeed once, their confidence is gone." Yolanda, an eighteen-year-old black girl who studied with Brigette and Carmen for her G.E.D., said she dropped out of public school because "I felt embarrassed to ask for help. I am not educated. Here no one tries to be smarter than the other."

Sister Caryl Hartjes, a forty-six-year-old nurse and member of the

Congregation of St. Agnes, talked about Rosa Deligne, a black grand-mother and former welfare recipient who now serves as a surrogate mother to four welfare-dependent mothers. Of Rosa's "over-whelmed" families, Sister Caryl said, "Over a protracted period of time, Rosa was able to establish a schedule for the family, so now she doesn't have to spend as much time with one family." A new problem arose, however. One form of dependency threatened to replace an-other. Now, Sister Caryl said, "we're going to wean the mother away from Rosa so she doesn't become dependent on her."

Jean Madison (her name has been changed) is one of Rosa Deligne's unwed mothers. At thirty-nine, she is older than the other dependent mothers. And she produces babies at a phenomenal pace—twenty-seven or twenty-nine by her various counts. "Our objective," Sister Maureen said of Jean Madison, "was to give her a sense of herself as a person beyond being a childbearer. She tended to define herself by giving birth." Rosa Deligne said she freed Jean to get out of the house, to visit a community center where she is learning to sew, to take day-long summer excursions. "Jean is a different woman," Sister Maureen said. "Three years ago she was rigid. Mattresses were all over the floor. Not a bed in the place. She was excessive in her discipline of the children. She didn't nurture the children. We've helped her to share more." As a child, Jean was on welfare, watched her mother produce babies, and helped her take care of the house. As an adult, Sister Maureen observed, Jean "repeated what she knew. She had her kids cook and clean, like she did at six. These patterns will be continued unless there is new learning."

Jean Madison lives with seven of her children behind an unmarked door on the second floor of a walkup on East 116th Street. To get to her apartment one must walk past mailboxes that have been ripped open by the addicts who congregate in the hallway and have ran-sacked Jean's apartment five times in five years, up squeaky wooden steps past a broken window opening onto an alley piled almost one story high with household garbage. The stench of urine wafts through the building.

Jean Madison lives in a railroad flat, with a long hall bisecting the apartment. To the left as you enter is a laundry room with clothes-lines crisscrossing the ceiling; next door is a bathroom with a bare light bulb protruding from the ceiling and a linoleum floor with gaping holes through which the floorboards are visible. Beyond this is a bedroom with two single beds jammed together for five of her sons, the oldest fourteen. In this room, exposed electrical wires crawl from the wooden floor to the ceiling. Finally, one comes to a guest bedroom, which appears unlived in and is kept like a hotel room: bed freshly made; dresser polished; trunk, area rug, and radio kept spotless. This room is reserved for her private moments, and is in stark contrast to her bedroom across the hall. Here a faded, stained carpet lies at the foot of two mattresses jammed together on the floor, which two young daughters share with her. Half-drawn black shades shield the windows in the living room across from the boys' bedroom. Box springs serve as a sofa and are covered with fabric and several pillows, as are two armchairs facing the sofa; a low coffee table sits between the sofa and chairs. At one end of the room is a varnished bar and wooden phonograph; at the other, a closet with a drape for a door. Through an archway, which also serves as a pantry, is a small kitchen in which electrical wires dangle from the walls and cockroaches race across the bare wood floor. The family eats at a small round formica table, cooks on a miniature white stove with three burners, stores several weeks' food supply in an ancient refrigerator Jean Madison purchased when the landlord refused to provide her with one, and relies on a washing machine that spins all day long. Electricity costs $61 a month, mostly for the washing machine and the four television sets that labor overtime. She also pays for four telephones and sends $214 a month to the landlord, who lives in Englewood, New Jersey.

Jean Madison, who is five feet, two inches tall, puttered about the house in a loose-fitting crew-necked flowered housecoat, her hair up in pink curlers. Relaxing in a living-room chair, her hands resting on a stomach swollen by another pregnancy, she talked about her life. Since March 1966 she has been on welfare, receiving tax-free payments of $456.35 every two weeks in 1981 from welfare and $247 per month in food stamps. "It's not a hassle any more," she said. "You get used to it.

"I didn't have any parents to help me," she said of her childhood. "My mother just left us. Just walked out." Her father, a merchant seaman, drank himself to death when she was a baby. "I had to cook for my sisters and brothers when I was six years old. My mother was an alcoholic. My parents weren't together. We lived right here on 98th Street, between Central Park West and Columbus Avenue. I went to school at night and stayed home taking care of my younger brothers and sisters during the day." At the age of eleven, Jean Madison became pregnant and gave birth to triplets; at twelve, she had another set of triplets, and at thirteen, twins. By thirteen, she boasted, she was the mother of eight. By twenty-six: "I had over twenty kids." At thirty-nine, she is the mother of twenty-seven children (in a subsequent interview the figure she gives is twenty-nine), eight grandchildren, and another baby was on the way.

She had babies so young, she said, "because I had no one to tell me what to do or not to. It was a way to escape my aunts and uncles. They made me do a lot of household chores. I knew if I got pregnant they'd throw me out." Her first eight children had the same father. He and she never got married, but he helped support her, as did an Italian-American woman from East Harlem who watched over her and the kids. "I could have been a dope addict," she said. "But at the time I wanted to become something. In high school I took nursing. I became first a practical nurse, then a resident nurse." More children and other boyfriends forced her to abandon nursing school.

Why so many children? "I don't know," Jean Madison said, a pleasant smile spreading across her attractive face. "One fella that I met, his mother used to call me a cat. If I had a husband I wouldn't have so many kids." Pointing to her stomach, she continued: "This time, it's like a mistake. I used the thing they gave me and it didn't work. If I was married I'd have had my tubes taken out. My children's fathers are all nationalities. One was West Indian. One was Puerto Rican. When I love, I love. I'm down to earth." The father of several of her sons was shot and killed in 1969; others she's lost touch with.

Jean Madison considers herself a good mother, although Sister Maureen said Jean has placed several daughters in foster homes and rarely visits them. "I think I'm a beautiful mother," Jean said. "Because a lot of women my age want to stay at a bar or on the corner. I want to stay home." Other mothers "go out and have a good time. I don't. I think of my children first. Some people lose their drive. A lady across the hall, every time she's broke she throws a fit. I'm in her age category. I feel I should be the one to shop, not her. A lot of parents look for it to come on a silver platter. It doesn't come that way. They stay in bed all day."

Jean Madison's goal? "I'd like to have a house on Long Island, have my feet up in the air, and have me a strawberry shortcake or ice cream. That's what I'd like to be doing five years from now. Maybe one day I'll get it—if the right man comes along and I get married. If not, I'll be right here, waiting."

6

BT-27 on Broken Families, Unemployment, Racism, Crime...

Welfare-dependent mothers are one of several subjects that members of BT-27 discuss with me over sandwiches and sodas in a grim, cell-like conference room at the Wildcat Skills Training Center in February. For seven hours, members of BT-27, divided into groups of five or six, sit around rectangular tables and talk about growing up in broken homes, racism, unemployment, Wildcat, the cause of soaring crime rates, why people kill and whether they have remorse, and other topics.

At one point in the discussion, Pearl Dawson says that single mothers and their children, especially in the city, face different kinds of problems from the ones she faced, because of different backgrounds. She explains, "Well, I was living down South, and it seems to me that most of the people from down South have different values from the people that left the South and came up here. Because in my childhood you don't see no child smacking its mother or cursing her out. In the South, we have more unity—family unity. It's like rooted. Your grandparents done it this way, your momma done it this way, and you in turn take it that way. But once you come to New York City it's a whole different aspect of life. When my family came up here, they came for opportunity."

Gladys Miller cuts in to say, "When you're reared up in New York, there's so many hustles and schemes and things people got to learn, you know, to get along with each other and stuff. Whereas in the South it was family. You say good morning to somebody up here, they look at you like you was crazy!"

Pearl resumes, "If you had, say, no food, no clothing, there was the church, the neighbors. You could always go there. Everybody had a house. It might not have been the biggest, but they had land to grow the vegetables, they had chickens, birds, and all of that, and a mother doing sewing, making clothes for them children. I think it's more a matter of pride. And schooling. If you went to school, and you don't know what you was studying, you gonna stay in that same place until you learn what you supposed to learn. In the first place, *respect*—you learn that in the home."

I ask if she is saying that many city residents aren't learning respect from the home.

"That's true," Pearl says. "I'm talking mainly what I know. They don't have to be worthless. They got some very rich kids. The parents don't have time for them. Especially the ones that out hustling. They don't have no particular values, really. The kids don't because the parents do not take the time."

I remark to Willy Joe that statistics show that in 1979 almost 55 percent of the black children in the United States were born to single mothers and 40 percent of Puerto Rican families living in this country were headed by women, and ask if he thinks those are the children who get into trouble.

"Those kids are under the influence of what they see," Willy says. "They looking at their parents. Now, the parents, they telling the kids one thing and they doing the other. They gonna look at this, put two and two together, and say, 'Why should I?' That's why you get a lot of disrespect between the child and the mother. Because the mother's poor, right, and don't have enough money to give the child food a lot of times, and clothing, and things of that nature. Plus the environment. The child's being around people who just cursing all day, getting high and drinking. That kid don't get a chance to see nothing else. So it's like what the child learns."

Why do some parents seem to communicate the wrong standards to their children?

"Mostly, it's that way because the fathers do not contribute to that family," Pearl Dawson says. "No matter if they can get along, it's still your child. It's there for you to clothe and feed. My husband and I, we separated. No problem. Best kids in the world. My kids are grown. One is in Germany, and the other one is still living here. But their father was always their father. And I was always their mother."

Gladys asks, "He was always there?"

"Right," Pearl says. "Might not be in the same house, or even in the same state. But his presence was always felt."

I ask Pearl if she thought that mattered to the kids.

"Oh, it matters a lot, honey. A lot of women that have kids teach their child when they split up to hate their father. 'Don't you mention that man's name, hear? That no good so-and-so.' And then the child sees what's so and how they fool around and how that mother struggles, he begins to hate the father."

Why does the father leave?

"I would think he would get upset if he cannot do for his family like he would like to," Pearl said. "That's where the drugs and liquor come in."

I ask Ramon Lopez if he feels that kids who grow up in a home without a father suffer more than kids who grow up in a home with two parents.

"The problem in our community is that we let a woman have maybe seven kids, you know?" Ramon says. "That seven kids take maybe fourteen years. Maybe seven kids and the mother just stay home, maybe let the kids go out, do what they want to do. Nobody tells them right or wrong because today nobody tells nothing. And the kid grows up doing wrong. Nobody to guide him."

Why doesn't the mother guide him?

"Mother might guide him in the house, you know," says Ramon. "But out of twenty-four hours, he might be in the house two, three hours. Might just come to eat and go right back out. So he grows up to whatever he sees other kids doing. That's what he might do. He might see a kid hitchhiking the bus; he might want to hitchhike. He grows up listening about people mugging other people; that's what he might do because he has no guide. Nobody, you know, to take him to the park, take him to the baseball, take him to the swimming pool. He's all by himself, you know. Got nobody to teach him anything. He got no school. He just do nothing; just stays around and does whatever he wants to. That kid might grow up doing things that are bad. Mother have too many kids, maybe. More than she can handle." I ask Ramon why the woman would have so many kids.

"You know, they just don't stop to think about it," says Ramon. "That it will create problems in the future. That's what happens. Not only one lady or one partner. Maybe a lot of partners. And there are a lot of kids. I, myself, in my family we have seven."

Was your father around?

"Yeah, my father always stays with us. He stays with my mom and he goes to work. He took my mother's beefing and all of that. He's a nice guy. He was in the streets a long time, didn't do too bad."

Leon Harris says that young males rarely fear their mothers. "It's hard for a lady to ever fill a man's shoes. I have friends who were brought up by their mother—and when we was younger, my father used to beat me. They used to get accidentally beat also, because they was with me. But not by my mother. It's that thing that a man's supposed to do. Certain things a woman just can't do. When I be bad, my mom only scolds. When she beats them, she's too aggressive. She tried too hard to be like my father. I used to say to my friend, 'Man, what's wrong with you? You got it made. You want a father to whup you?' And he'd say, 'Yeah, 'cause I miss it. I never had a man to hit me, to make me know that I'm doing wrong.' My mother told me right from wrong, but I feel that she's good at talking to daughters, you dig?"

Even with a strict father, though, Leon got into trouble. I ask him why.

"See, I left home when I was fifteen," he says. "I thought I was grown. And when I left home, see, I was hustling. Money was easy to me. I wasn't even worried about it. I got into trouble because I was hanging out with the wrong people. That society was wrong, and at the time I thought it was right. At the age of fifteen, I was one of the youngest guys on my block—in fact, the first young guy on the block —to buy a house for my family. My brothers, now, they got to compete against me—the youngest kid in the family, out of eleven, doing more than the other ten. You dig? So that started hostility. And when you get hostility with your peers—brothers, sisters—you have a tendency to take it out on strangers. And that was me. I couldn't beat none of my brothers. I would be a fool. Like a five-year-old kid to run up on me now. Can he win? No. I'm no fool. It doesn't take much strength to pull a trigger. But, like I say, I couldn't beat them. So I figured, I know who I can beat. Them suckers out there. White, black, Puerto Rican—I didn't care. He could have been Jesus Christ at that particular time. When the frustration came on me, I said, "Somebody gonna pay for this.' And I went out and did wrong."

Harris said that he made a lot of money being a stickup man and a drug pusher, and I ask how much.

"At age fifteen, I was getting something like fifteen hundred dollars a day, I was getting something like three grand a day. It was good money. I'm young. I'm not even thirty, and I'm getting this kind of money. And my father? He's still living, and isn't making that!"

I ask Harris where his father works.

"In Queens," he says. "He's capping tires and stuff. I didn't like supervision, dig? Somebody other than my family telling me, 'You got to do this to get this.' I'm gonna work forty hours a week and bring home maybe a hundred, a hundred and fifty dollars when I can work fifteen minutes and come back with a thousand dollars tax free?"

In an earlier class, Howard Smith mentioned the notion of defeatism, of people giving up. I ask the class members why they think people give up.

"It may have a little bit to do with values," Mohammed says. "In the sense of religious values, maybe moral values. Many poor people, some of them just give up, just accept their conditions, our conditions. It's like welfare, for example. I know many people been on welfare a long time. My mother was on welfare for a long time. And I'd hear her say such things as 'I can't get nothing else,' 'I can't do no better,' 'I'm too old to go back to school.' She's not too old to go to school. I mean, it don't give one ambition to a better life. We become satisfied with that condition."

I ask if they think there are many people who are passive and defeated.

"Yes," Leon Harris answers. "My community, a lot of them out there, you know. They are dissatisfied, but they won't admit it to themselves. They'll admit it to us: 'Hey, man, I got to do something about this little retirement check every two weeks.' But when that check comes today, count fourteen days later. They don't go out to look for no job."

Could he explain why?

"Because they're afraid to go out there and try, to compete," Leon said. "It's like trying to compete with Mohammed. He's a specialist in radio technology. I know a little bit because I work on my personal radio. Who's going to get the job?"

He is, I respond.

"I'm afraid so. Why should I compete against him? When he gets that job some of his money is going to come to me anyway on welfare. And then I ain't got enough heart to compete. But I got enough heart to steal. I might meet him when he gets paid, dig?"

Then the passive person is not the one who will steal.

"No, he'll just sit back and say, 'Well, brother Mohammed got the job. We on welfare. What the heck, some of his paychecks coming to me anyway,'" said Leon.

In view of the notion that some people on welfare are passive, and so don't go out to look for work, I ask Leon if he thinks that they should be taken off welfare and forced to work.

"You would take that passive person and change him into an animal," he says. "Because now he's got to survive. This is mandatory. He's still scared to compete against somebody that got more learning or more experience. So he says, 'Hey, a pistol ends all of that. If I go to jail, they gonna take care of me anyway. And if I die, all my worries are over.'"

Thirteen members of BT-27 are black. I ask if they think that racism has held them back?

Willy Joe says that whites "look at blacks as unskilled and lazy," and goes on, "Because they see black people robbing, doing this, that. So, generally, they look at us as if we all like that, which we are not. Some of us about 'good,' some of us about 'bad.' "

"But we always get the lowdown, the dirty part, of everything," Gladys Miller says.

"If you see a crime in the paper and you read about it and it doesn't say 'black,' you know a white person done it," Pearl Dawson says. "They never say 'white.' You got more arrests at the police station that never get published. A lot of your own kids in the higher white middle class, they get busted with speed, they get busted with everything."

"I'm from the South and I've seen poor white people as well as poor black people," Gladys says. "The poor white people still look at the poor black person like they nothing, you know? And you on the same level."

Do they feel that whites are racist?

"Most of them," said Gladys. I point out that they have complained in class about the stereotyping of people on welfare and ask if they aren't guilty of stereotyping themselves.

"Yeah, but in my line of work some of my best clients are white folks on methadone," Gladys Miller says. "Some of my best friends are white people. I don't know if it's because I got what they want. I think most prejudice is out there on Long Island, where there generally is a bunch of them together. I got on the train about three weeks ago and it was crowded. I was this close to this white dude, and I said to him, 'You know, I never been this close to whitey in my life.' He said, 'I never been this close either.' And I said, 'You smell the same.' "

"It never bothered me about black and white at all," Pearl Dawson says. "I like a person. It never really bothered me, and I was raised in the South. I like a person for himself."

Willy Joe says "From day one—slavery time—you know, when Abraham Lincoln passed that Emancipation Proclamation and everybody was free, right? Free from physical chains, but not mental chains. Most everybody's got some prejudice in him. Everybody has that thing in him, not just blacks and whites, Italians and Jews, and everybody else."

In the 1980 presidential campaign, Ronald Reagan said, "The *Los Angeles Times* carried sixty-five full pages of help-wanted ads, and you wonder how we call someone unemployed if there are employers taking out ads begging someone to come to work." I ask the class what it means when unemployment is high and yet newspapers advertise hundreds of jobs.

"That means those jobs are for people who usually have experience, education, or somebody who knows somebody," John Painter says. "I'd say half the new jobs, if not more, I could go any time of the day and they would be filled. You know how today is, you got Ph.D.s working on hundred-and-fifty-dollar-a-week jobs. So them things on paper look good. You go through the paper and see this and that, but once you go for them, you know it's not for you."

The members of BT-27 say that at one time or another they have all tried, usually unsuccessfully, to follow up help-wanted advertisements in the papers. "I have followed ads that speak on specifics of what they want," William Mason says. "I'll apply for the job. When I go for the job, the specifics are whitewashed—they might not want me for that position, but there's a place over in the corner that's open. They looking for somebody for this corner over here. So you ask, 'Why wasn't that corner in the ad?' And I wouldn't take the corner job, because I knew that I wasn't moving my best in that corner."

"Most of those jobs are agency jobs," Willy Joe says. "A lot of times, I'll go check out some of these jobs at lunchtime or something. And I'll get there and they say, 'Fifty dollars for the job.' Or fifteen dollars, or twenty. You got to pay the fee. Or you got to have a skill to get the job—three years' experience, or five years' experience. Always something you got to have before you can get the job."

"And if you go to the same job on your own, you can't get it," Pearl Dawson says. "But if you go through that agency and give them that fee, you can go back to that same job and get it."

"But with them agencies, though, the job is not guaranteed. You might work two or three days, or a week or a couple of months," Gladys Miller says.

"They got so many people coming to do this type of thing, and they need money to keep the agency going on, so they'll let the guy go," Willy Joe says.

Gladys adds, "I was on a job and in about two more days I'd have been in the union. I'd have been there a month. And they fired me so that I couldn't get into the union, and they hired about a hundred and twenty some-odd more people."

Henry Rivera has been silent throughout the discussion, so now I ask him about the apparent contradiction between the high unemployment rate and the large number of job advertisements in the newspapers.

86

"But me, I never work in my life before," answers this thirty-six-year-old ex-addict. "I got no experience working. You need experience to work."

I ask why some class members lack interest in the Wildcat program.

"The reality is that the money we receive is not a hundred and ten dollars. It's about ninety after taxes," Mohammed says. "Personally, I haven't received over eighty-seven. Could also be a lack of interest."

Lack of interest?

Mohammed explained, "You got typing, life skills, math, and so forth. Our English teacher, he talks a lot. Many people just don't want that. Typing's a good skill. Life skills you learn in the street. Many people, including myself, think that when their twelve months is up, what's it going to be? They say they'll give us a job if we pass this and go to an advanced class. We might get a job. Suppose we don't get this job?"

"Wildcat doesn't show us anything that's going to set us for life," John Painter says. "Like, people are coming here mainly for the jobs. What Wildcat mainly spells to everybody is money, first of all. Now, this training, although it's nice and everything, they don't show us any promise that, you know, after you leave here you're definitely going to be able to go do this. And they have an old saying at some penitentiaries when you get ready to go up for parole—they say, 'You look for the worst, and you hope for the best.' And that's the same attitude a lot of people have to take about Wildcat and what kind of job they're gonna have after this, if they're gonna get one at all. Their absenteeism and lateness is probably a habit, something that they've had for years and years. If necessary, if they got a good job or something, that's probably a habit that everybody in the class could break. If they had something like a reward. 'If I do this, I'll be rewarded in this way.' But Wildcat doesn't seem to be very rewarding. When I sit down and look at Wildcat, I see them not as slave drivers, but we're like—how could I say it?—somebody who's making money for them. Because somebody has to be in the school for Wildcat in order for the program to get funded. They take us and place us next to city workers making $300 and $250 a week, and we not making a hundred. Yet Wildcat is making money off of us—off of us going out there doing a job for the city. If they could promise us, 'You definitely will be able to get a job here if you meet these requirements.' Well, they just tell us, 'You have to meet these requirements and then, maybe, you can go to an advanced class. And then, hopefully, you'll get a job.' "

"Now a lot of people come here with the intention of, well, it's just the money," says Timothy Wilson. "They don't look at the education. Recipients of Wildcat are being utilized as far as I'm concerned. I didn't have problems as far as habits—getting up in the morning, dressing properly, learning how to hold on to my emotions toward supervision and authority in general. A lot of people come here and the money they make, some of it is deducted from their welfare. So I see Wildcat utilizing that to pay us. It enables some people to go back to where they came from, back to crime. I knew that this was the type of environment I was coming to, so I came here with the attitude, 'Well, okay, I'm looking at what they have to offer. I'm not looking at the politics of it.' "

Carlos Rodriguez mentions the fact that he was offered the job of foreman at his supported-work site. "I said to myself that if I took the foreman position, that would be only temporary for twelve months. And I wouldn't have the experience I would gain here. So I preferred coming over here, which I don't feel sorry about, because I picked up speed in typing and brushed up my math. And I am looking forward to staying here for the thirty weeks."

I ask them if they agree with John Painter's argument that Wildcat's a dead end because there's no guaranteed job.

"For me it's not a dead-end program because if they don't promise you a job, you know, you could go by yourself and look in the newspaper and so on," Carlos Rodriguez says. "Before I came into this program I was looking for a job, you know, and for clerical positions the minimum requirement was fifty words per minute."

"I can't say I knew exactly what I was getting into when I came, because I didn't investigate the place," William Mason says. "I didn't send no one to inspect it. But the way things were running with my life and my family, any one thing beat a blank, you know? So I came into Wildcat hoping that it would be better than what I was into."

On being asked to explain the many absences and latenesses of the class members, Gladys Miller says, "Myself, that's a good one. Like yesterday. When I called in, she"—the deputy director—"said, 'What's the matter?' I said, 'I lost my—my will, the drive, you know?' I got up out of bed and called and told her I wasn't coming in. I don't want to come to some place that I know they going to get on my ass after I come in. First of all, it's a hassle getting on the train. Where I live, it's a job in itself trying to get to work. Then, once you get here, it's cold. Please. I live in whitey's house. I freeze to death there. Then I come here and freeze."

Twenty-two people were enrolled in BT-27 the first day, I observe. This morning, only fourteen attended class. Some days, only half a dozen attend. Why?

"As far as I see, it's a lot of talking, you know, about work," Willy Joe says. "Sometimes I feel like I just don't care, man."

"I'm not too much up on Communism, but I think I know a little bit about it," Gladys Miller says. "I think it should be like that. Because over there everybody's equal. Nobody has more than anybody else."

"Well, I don't want to do that," Pearl Dawson says. "Honey, that's the only thing you got—equals. You can't go where you want to go. You can't come in when you want. Here you can go right up and cuss the President if you want. That's your right. You go over there and cuss that man over there? You going to Siberia! If everybody was equal, there wouldn't be nothing to strive for."

Crime

How do they explain the heavy drinking, the drug abuse, and the high crime rates in poor communities?

Leon says, "It's basically jobs. Most of the drinking and crime stuff is welfare victims. That's the people that society say is outcasts. And, see, by labeling people like that—and people you're supposed to be looking up to are talking about you—society gives you the feeling that you're not worth anything. And a lot of times when you spend a little money you ain't got, and you sit down and it's 'I got to get some clothes for the children, or clothes for me,' and you can't get no job, or welfare doesn't give you enough money, you got two alternatives: to borrow—but you can't pay back because you're not working—or to steal it. That causes a lot of crime. And drinking? That's in every neighborhood, but it's mainly the poor because it's their spare time. Mostly all the crimes and alcoholism, vandalism, all that's due to the lack of jobs, lack of money."

"I think they have to try to provide some more work for the community," Henry Rivera says. "Maybe better schools for the kids coming up now."

The night before, William Mason's kid brother had been robbed and stabbed. He was in the hospital, in pretty bad shape. The robbery occurred early in the evening in his own Crown Heights community. He had no money on him. I ask why the muggers did a crazy thing like that.

Henry answers, "The community got no jobs. The people have no money. They will rob other people."

But why stab him five times? I ask.

"Because they made a mistake, too. Maybe they mistake him for somebody else, no?" says Henry.

I mention a conversation I had had with two pretty big high school dropouts from Bedford-Stuyvesant who said they were afraid of certain "dudes on the street," as they called them, who look at you real mean and would "cut you" for no reason.

"That's what you call a bully," Pearl Dawson says. "You have people that do crimes to live. And then you have people who just do crimes because they can do them. Before they passed that law for young kids [the New York State juvenile-offender law stiffening penalties for youths under sixteen who commit serious felonies], you had kids that would do crime because they knew they couldn't be punished. Then we have people with just sick minds. One thing to me about the black people, when it come to crime they don't think. A lot of crime is done without thinking."

Gladys Miller says, "Most of all they robbing the people that's in the same state they are, and of course they're not getting anything! If people have anything, they wouldn't be in that neighborhood themself. Go up Park Avenue, Fifth Avenue. Go rip those folks off if you got to rip somebody off."

I ask Willy Joe, who lives in the East New York section of Brooklyn, one of the city's worst slums, if he sometimes feels afraid on the street.

"Yeah, I could say that," Willy says.

"It just happened to you," Pearl reminds him.

"Christmas Eve, right," Willy says. "A fella I know took money from me. There was three people. It was dark. I just happened to walk by, coming back from the store. And we talked and everything, and then somebody put their hand around my throat and choked me. Tried to make me not see who was doing it, but I'm looking back to see who's doing it."

I ask if these men had weapons.

"They say they did," Willy replies. "I couldn't see none. One kept banging me in the eye so I couldn't see. They was trying to make me not see who it was. But it was too late already, I knew who it was."

Has he seen them since?

"I see them now and then. I'm not gonna walk up to nobody, because I'm not like that. I'm not gonna say what I'm gonna do or whatever. Be cool about it."

I ask if it's easier for those men to be street criminals than it would be for them to take a job.

"It's easier," Willy says. "They figure like you make $125 or $135 a week with a job. You got to be on time. You got to go through a lot of changes. They don't want to have no responsibility. They just want to hang out all day, make some money, get high, dress a little.

They in a fantasy world. They looking up the flicks—*Superfly, The Mack.* They think about having prostitutes, big cars, telephone and bar inside."

"Poor people don't get too many opportunities to, you know, to be good, to want to do things the right way," Ramon Lopez says. "What they see on television is a lot of violence all the time. All the time is violence on television."

"You know, we are human beings like everyone else," Leon says. "And we have these needs—for shelter, clothing, food, for good jobs, good-paying jobs. Violence is committed for these necessary things. And unfortunately we commit unnecessary crimes on our own. It don't matter. Because in a sense this is a cold, cruel world, you know? People are real cold. New York breeds this into a person. You go to the West or the South, people are more hospitable."

I recall for them what happened to Herbert Finn and his wife, Ruth—an elderly couple from Phoenix, Arizona. The Finns were visiting New York in October 1979. As they were parked outside a relative's house with other members of the family, in the Riverdale section of the Bronx, three young men armed with guns robbed them. One of the robbers took Herbert Finn's money and demanded his wallet. Without becoming belligerent, Finn tried to hold on to his wallet, hoping to save his credit cards. Finn's assailant shot him, and he died instantly. The story was on TV and on the front page of the papers. If the three robbers picked up the newspapers the next day, I ask, do you think they felt sorry?

"I would feel sorry," Ramon Lopez says. "I say there's no need for that."

"That happens," Harris says. "That stuff's always happening, 'cause that kind of people have no respect for authority. They were afraid. The man might not have had nothing in his hand, but they didn't care. They got what they wanted. And by him making that sudden move to reach, dig, they didn't think to look in his hand. They just shot him. And this is how I used to be, you know, because I used to be a stickup kid. Before I was that, I was a potential stickup kid. I was always scared. I always pulled a pistol. And, you know, they say, 'If you pull it, use it.' "

I ask whether that means he would use a gun right away if the victim made any move.

"He asked for their credit cards and then he reached, which was wrong," Harris says. "He should never have reached. We were taught, 'You don't reach for nothing.' When you reach for things, especially if they have a pistol on you, you don't know if they gonna shoot, if they're nervous, if they're bluffing, or what. Now, you can

91

find some that'll pull a pistol and you can say, 'Get that out of my face or I'm gonna hurt you,' and the guy will figure you're crazy, you dig, because he's got a gun in his hand. Or you don't care about life. And if you don't care about life, one bullet won't stop you."

Harris has admitted to having shot people in the past, and I ask if he has ever felt any remorse about this.

"That's a hard question," he says. "At that time, I was young, you know, and stupid. I use the word 'stupid' not in the sense of education-wise but street-wise. A young guy with a big pistol. Man, I could whip the whole block, you know. Anybody mess with me and I'll show them how bad I am. But as far as feeling sorry, hmm—maybe a little touch of remorse. A little. Because I really didn't understand it. How could I be sorry? 'Hey, brother, he asked for it. Should have never made *me* scared.' I'm standing there with a pistol, and he ain't got nothing to be scared of. He scared *me.* Because he showed me he didn't care. That authority, that pistol, is just like a badge of a cop. When it says *stop,* you stop. Or it stops you. He made me scared, so I pulled the trigger. So feel sorry? I doubt it. I didn't want him to go down like that, but better him than me. That's an old cliché—better the next one than you. That's how most of them think. I sent him something with no return address. A sorry letter. No money. Now, don't get me wrong. I've sent cards. You know, they say 'Sorry for what happened.' "

"Listen, when you go out with a gun and you do not intend to hurt anybody with it, you leave the bullets home—right?" Pearl Dawson says. "Because you cannot shoot no gun without bullets. When you go out with a loaded gun to rob somebody, I call that premeditated from the word go."

John Painter cuts in to say, "The dude was supposed to be in control of the situation. And by his saying, 'Give me back my credit cards,' as far as I understand it he snatched it back, his wallet back. That's like him rebelling. The average black guy who's robbing don't like a white person. They can't look at you and say, 'I don't like white people.' But if they know one person who's white, and he's all right, they don't hold it against him. But they might still say, 'I don't like white people, but he's all right.' So when they're robbing somebody, especially whites, they say, 'Well, I don't like them anyway.' When you robbing somebody, you supposed to be in control of everything at all times. That gun makes you the boss."

Do you think he felt remorse? I ask.

John Painter says, "Only if he's got a religious background. The only regrets I think some of these guys that rob might have about killing somebody is if the cops caught the guys that were with them and those guys just might go home free if they start singing a tune.

When you set down and there's three people and you say, 'We're gonna go rob this place,' you're not gonna go in there with two people that's down and one that's gonna fold. You're going in there with three people that you know, where you say, 'You got the front, you got the back, and I got the middle.' When I was young I did that one time with this older guy in Brooklyn. He was like a pro at it. He said, 'We're going in there and we're gonna tell them to freeze. And if somebody's got an idea and moves, I'm gonna shoot them, and then I'm gonna shoot you.' "

I ask if he would have shot them if they moved.

"I can't say," Painter answers. "That was like four years ago. It all depends. If I thought they was strutting it big, maybe. At that time I felt I was invincible. I thought, you know, at that time guys were killing people and doing three months. I was fifteen, sixteen, man, and people were doing like three months for things like that."

I ask them whether the threat of punishment serves to deter street crime.

Painter answers, "No, why should it? I seen people when I was incarcerated. They just run around like it's an everyday thing. What they worry about, first thing in the morning, is that they got the latest tape, or the latest sex magazine, herb, wine, whatever. It's just a brag: 'Oh, yes, well, I did this to such-and-such a person.' He brags because this person may have three years for the same thing. 'Oh, I got off lucky—I only got three months.' "

I mention the rise in senseless violence, especially by teenagers, white and black, and ask them why they think it's occurring.

Timothy Wilson says, "If you kill somebody, you might do it because of hostility; or you might have flashbacks of your childhood when you were beaten. Then there are people who enjoy killing other people. It's been proven before—people like Charles Manson. It didn't mean anything to him to kill anybody. It didn't mean anything to the .44-caliber killer to kill anybody. There's a few people who kill people that really feel it. And then some people really don't have no conscience at all."

I ask Leon Harris how he'd respond if someone said, "You behaved like an animal."

Leon answers, "I'd say, 'How does an animal act? Survival.' Dig? That would bring on a potential barrier. You call me an animal. I'm trying to survive. I tried it legit. It didn't work. Couldn't get the right jobs. I had a family to take care of. Most people that got kids are kids themselves who got kids, you dig? Who's gonna hire a kid to work? He has no responsibility. He's not to be trusted. He's young. He's got all these strikes against him. He's black! You dig? He's coming from Bedford-Stuyvesant or Harlem. He's got a reputation. His block's got a reputation. So he goes out and gets a Saturday night special. Am I an animal for trying to live? A lion will kill a weak prey to survive, not just to kill. And the same with people. When he put that pistol in his hand and do stickups, he's saying, 'Hey, somebody's gonna get it. But before they do, I'm gonna enjoy myself. That's part of my life now. I don't know anything else. I can't get a job where I can get a thousand dollars a day.' Well, what job's gonna be like that? What job pays you that? Once you get used to that kind of money, it's hard to let that go."

So even if there were no discrimination and racism and there were sufficient job opportunities and the schools worked, we'd still have a lot of violent crime.

"You always gonna have that," Leon says. "You will always have crime. You know, the United States is based on crime. Couldn't exist without it. Without crime, there would be no need for a police department. There'd be less jobs because now they got to find jobs for the cops. The United States got a big interest in crime."

I ask Leon what his last statement means.

He replies, "A penitentiary itself makes more money than any garment district. While we were there we had to work. We had to make for factories, cabinets, chairs, soap, perfume, license plates. They pay you seventy-five cents a day. But one of these chairs? They might go out there and sell them for fifty, a hundred bucks. And we made something like thirty to forty apiece."

Ramon Lopez interjects, "Most likely a man has a gun, he's not thinking right. He's thinking of doing something with it. Whatever it is, I don't know. But if he has a gun, he's not thinking of doing anything right—unless he's a police. Police, too, don't do things right sometimes. There are cases of police doing things with a gun nobody would have thought they would do with a gun. I remember one time they shot a guy in Brooklyn over fifty times. That's not right. That just show to prove what a weapon comes to. Maybe the racial problem, too, has something to do with it."

About the growing number of killings of cops, John Painter says, "One reason is the image police give people. The way they treat somebody who doesn't break the laws and hasn't broken the laws—like a dog. They stop you and say, 'Come here, nigger.' That's one reason. The other reason is that a lot of people weigh the odds. Another reason is because a lot of people don't value death—especially a cop's death. A lot of people despise cops. A lot of cops, they're punks. They're overplaying their role. They're not just taking their role as cops. They're playing Superhero. Trying to instill fear in the younger generation."

7

Crime: The Law-Enforcement View

The mural on Bronx District Attorney Mario Merola's office wall assaults a visitor. Painted in vivid shades of yellow and orange and black by Fred Taylor, a black artist, it is a mosaic of the conflicting images from the New York City blackout of 1977: helmeted police officers, haunted black faces, raised billy clubs, clenched black-power salutes, looted stores, buildings swallowed by bright flames. "I test everybody who walks in here on that painting," says Merola, a chunky cherubic-looking man with bushy eyebrows and a warmth that one wouldn't expect to find in a man who has been district attorney since 1973. "I can tell what they are by how they react to it. Liberals see deprivation and police brutality. The right-wingers hate it. They see animal behavior and say it doesn't belong in the D.A.'s office."

Merola's mural is a metaphor for the ideological debate surrounding crime and its causes—a debate in which liberals tend to see victims and conservatives see villains. Members of BT-27, for instance, think crime is an understandable, if not justifiable, response to the pressures society inflicts on the poor. This view of crime as a form of social protest has many advocates, including Dr. Kenneth Clark. According to Clark and others, injustice and unemployment underlie the soaring crime rate.

Others on the left, including psychologist William Ryan, believe that headlines and talk about street crime are a form of ideological warfare against the poor. He writes in *Blaming the Victim*:

Large numbers, perhaps a majority, of all races and classes commit serious crimes, most of which they get away with. . . .

To blather on and on about the slum as a "breeding place of crime," about "lower class culture as a generating milieu of delinquency"—presumably liberal explanations of the prevalence of crime among the poor—is to engage (surely, almost consciously) in ideological warfare against the poor in the interest of maintaining the *status quo.* It is one of the most detestable forms of blaming the victim.

On the other hand, many conservatives, including Banfield, Thomas Sowell, and James Q. Wilson, tend to blame individuals, class, cultural factors, or human nature. "Lower-class youth in every generation and in every ethnic and racial group are extremely violent as compared to middle- and upper-middle-class adults," writes Banfield in *The Unheavenly City.* Sowell focuses on broken families and the distinct cultural traits of different ethnic and racial groups. Thus he writes in *Race and Economics* that historically

> groups characterized by a high incidence of broken homes have also been characterized by high incidences of exaggerated "masculinity" in the form of violence, liquor, obstreperousness, and sexual exploitation. The Irish were commonly associated with violence in the nineteenth century; they continue to have a very high rate of alcoholism (fifty times that of Jews), and long ago acquired the title "playboy of the Western world." These same characteristics have also been observed by many in the American Negro, with drugs to some extent replacing alcohol in recent years.

D.A. Merola, like an increasing number of students of crime, manages to blend these discordant views. He sees the criminal as both victim and villain. Asserting that there is no simple explanation for the root causes of crime, he says, "Kids view it as the haves versus the have-nots. They can't cope educationally. Don't ask me why. They can't hack it. The education system doesn't want 'em. You got to be an idiot not to recognize what the sociologists and philosophers say—that society is to blame. But on the other hand, that shouldn't excuse people. Let's be honest. It's too late when the problem comes to me." Merola says many of the criminals he prosecutes are monstrous: "They'll kill you for nothing. They'll stare through you. They're cold and callous. They have no remorse." To see street crime as a form of protest, he and others believe, is to disdain one uncomfortable fact: most street crimes are committed by ghetto residents against their fellow ghetto residents. On a national per capita basis, in 1978 black citizens were murdered at six times the rate of whites, and were raped and robbed more than twice as often.

There are, experts say, other causes of violence, including the glamorizing of crime by television and the movies, the premium America places on success, racial and ethnic and class tensions, and the general decline in respect for authority. But whatever the responsibility of society, the view that there are bad, perhaps irredeemable, people out there is now widespread. "Some of these kids are just some mean human beings," says former Urban League President Vernon Jordan. "Not unlike the Klansmen or some vigilante group. I think somehow you've got to separate that criminal mind from the guy who steals from the fruit stand because he's hungry. Those kids who enter the subway and terrorize, they're mean kids. What you don't do is parole them."

What produces street criminals and what to do about them are hotly debated. Their effect is not. Though violent crime is not unique to this time or this country, the extent of random violence is new. As a result, many urban residents feel under a state of siege; they alter their living habits, change their locks, bolt their doors, and nervously glance over their shoulders.

Citing FBI reports, Charles E. Silberman writes in *Criminal Violence, Criminal Justice*:

> The chance of being the victim of a violent crime such as murder, rape, robbery, or aggravated assault nearly tripled between 1960 and 1976; so did the probability of being the victim of a serious property crime, such as burglary, purse-snatching, or auto theft. . . . In some ways, the crime statistics understate the magnitude of the change that has occurred, for they say nothing about the nature of the crimes themselves. Murder, for example, used to be thought of mainly as a crime of passion— an outgrowth of quarrels between husbands and wives, lovers, neighbors, or other relatives and friends. In fact, most murders still involve victims and offenders who know one another, but since the early 1960s murder at the hand of a stranger has increased nearly twice as fast as murder by relatives, friends, and acquaintances.

What is also new, says Silberman in his authoritative study of crime, is that today people "kill, maim, and injure without reason or remorse." Gruesome, senseless crimes are chronicled daily in the press, so routinely that citizens have become inured to them except when the victim is prominent—for example, John Lennon, Michael Halberstam, or Allard Lowenstein, each senselessly gunned down in 1980, or President Reagan and Pope John, who were shot by crackpots in 1981. Those who senselessly murder ordinary citizens are all too alike. Eighteen-year-old Eric Thomas, for instance, is one of many street criminals who made headlines in 1980. Thomas, who is five feet three inches tall and 125 pounds, is suspected by police of having committed nine murders in just seven months. In at least two cases, Thomas shot his victims after they made offhand remarks about his "manhood." Silberman tells of three youngsters who set fire to three derelicts as a prank; "they simply wanted to see the men's reactions when they woke up and found themselves on fire." Silberman explores their lack of remorse: "This absence of 'affect,' as psychiatrists call it, is the most frightening aspect of all. In the past, juveniles who exploded in violence tended to feel considerable guilt or remorse afterwards; the new criminals have been so brutalized in their upbringing that they seem incapable of viewing their victims as fellow human beings, or of realizing that they have killed another person."

Sometimes these juveniles are, or feel, brutalized by society or its institutions. Sometimes they are, or feel, brutalized at home. Juan Williams of the *Washington Post* recorded this account in 1980 of a brutalized child. At the age of twelve, Mickey grabbed eighty-seven-year-old Gladys Merlich's purse and, when she resisted, cracked her skull with a Coca-Cola bottle, killing her.

> His mother is a heroin addict. His father comes by the house "sometimes," according to his mother. Mick-Mick [as he's called] is one of seven children his mother had with three different men. "The children drove me to use drugs," she says. Her children and her two sisters' children—in all about 20, including Mickey—live with their grandmother on Willard Street. . . . Grandmother says she couldn't always keep track of Mickey. "He'd be gone for days," she said. "He liked to go downtown and be around the hustlers and the pimps. . . ." Mickey's lawyer, Dennis O'Keefe, agrees: "His problem is that he finds himself involved with older kids. He is easily led by his peers. . . . He has no inner drive of his own. He goes along with the crowd. . . . This kid was without any acceptable role model of what he should become. With all the kids in the house, his grandmother couldn't control them. He was cut adrift to mingle among kids, roam the street. His male model was older kids. For them, street robberies or anything else is acceptable."
>
> O'Keefe and the boy's mother say the child does have a conscience. O'Keefe says that, according to a social worker's report,

Mick-Mick cried one day while talking about the Merlich murder. But both the lawyer and Mick-Mick's mother say the fifteen-year-old has no sense of what will or can happen if he goes along on a robbery or is involved in a killing. The boy does not live in a world where actions have consequences. He does not see himself as a member of society or an adult world.

Because many white citizens are fearful of blacks and Hispanics they encounter on the streets, they often assume that there are Mickeys swarming all over city streets. That is not the case. Throughout America, violent crimes are committed by a disproportionately small number of individuals, the vast majority of whom—although by no means all—are members of the underclass. It is this small number of criminals that police are increasingly turning their attention to.

The police tend to view criminals—particularly the ones they identify as "career criminals"—as opportunists taking advantage of a "permissive society." Approximately 70 percent of all the robberies in New York City, according to Deputy Police Inspector William P. Rose, are committed by only approximately 2,150 individuals. These crimes—muggings, chain- and purse-snatchings, rapes, burglaries, and armed robberies—are the ones that most terrorize citizens. In Manhattan, the Felony Augmentation Program was established as a pilot project by the Police Department in January 1980 to keep a watch on 500 of those 2,150 or so individuals, most of whom had long criminal records and committed at least two Manhattan robberies subsequent to October of 1976. Under the program—which the department expanded outside Manhattan in September 1981—each person merits a separate folder, containing mug shots, known aliases, and computerized arrest sheets, often running to several pages. "We have fellows with thirty-six, thirty-seven arrests," said Sergeant Daniel Hannon, who is white and was formerly one of fifty policemen assigned to this special unit, which is based on Randall's Island, in the East River. "It's a pattern of life. I'm not talking about the organized-crime sort of criminals. I'm talking about street criminals. People who turn streets into nightmares." The fifty policemen in this special unit study the faces, the folders, the aliases, and the hangouts of these criminals. They drive in unmarked cars and dress casually as they try to track down these fugitives, place them under surveillance, and apprehend them in the commission of a crime.

After an arrest, the unit calls in a special investigative squad, which seeks to build a solid court case by getting witnesses to appear in court and alerting the district attorneys to these cases, in the hope that the suspect will not slip through the cracks of the criminal-justice system. The cracks are pretty wide. According to a

January 1981 investigative report by E. R. Shipp and Joseph P. Fried of the *New York Times,* "Ninety-nine of every hundred people arrested on felony charges in New York City never serve a state prison term, and more than eighty are not even prosecuted as felons." All but the most serious felonies were usually plea-bargained down to misdemeanor charges. Of 104,413 felony arrests in 1979, 88,095 were dismissed or plea-bargained down to a nonfelony offense. People in every segment of that system protest that their job is made impossible by a lack of funds. The district attorneys say they lack the resources to bring all those cases to trial, the courts say there are too few judges, the corrections system says there are too few prison cells, the police say there are too few policemen. By beginning to narrow their focus to career criminals, law-enforcement officials hope to seal the cracks.

Leafing through a stack of folders that contain mug shots mostly of black and Hispanic males, Sergeant Hannon displays the folder of a white male with three aliases, six arrests, and one conviction. Another folder features a six-page arrest sheet listing four aliases, ten arrests, six convictions, and only seventy-two days spent in jail. Another shows twelve convictions and seven months spent in jail. Portraits of the kind of people that this police unit tracks can be glimpsed by an inspection of the records of several street criminals recently prosecuted by District Attorney Merola's office.

In June 1979, Robert, Ernest, Henry, and Curtis Bolden ranged in age from seventeen to twenty-one. They lived in the Bronx, and, among them, had been arrested approximately 125 times. According to Neal Hirschfeld of the *New York Daily News,* who first brought them to public attention, the police say that the Bolden brothers were responsible for "anywhere from twelve hundred to six thousand crimes." All were street criminals, and Henry, then nineteen years old, was serving eight to twenty-five years in jail for a 1977 robbery conviction. It was no ordinary robbery. While an accomplice held a knife to the throat of a seventy-four-year-old woman, Henry Bolden was said to have ripped the teeth from the mouth of her eighty-four-year-old husband. On the day Henry was sentenced, Hirschfeld reports, he "entered the Bronx courtroom laughing." Robert Bolden, then seventeen, had been arrested eighteen times before his sixteenth birthday, according to Hirschfeld, and the charges included robbery, grand larceny, jostling (picking pockets), possession of stolen property, and burglary. He was then in jail. Ernest Bolden, then eighteen, was back on the streets after completing a ninety-day sentence for drug possession and criminal mischief. In the eighteen months before his incarceration, Ernest had been arrested sixteen times. Before his sixteenth birthday, he had been arrested twenty-three times. The oldest brother, Curtis—then twenty-one—had been indicted for the rape of three Bronx women. He had previously been arrested at least twenty times and served two years in prison for robbery. In March 1980, after having been convicted the previous month for two of the rapes, Curtis Bolden was sentenced to thirty years in prison. The Boldens' parents were divorced, and their mother could not control them. Their father, the Reverend Henry Bolden, who is the pastor of a Bronx Baptist church, told Hirschfeld that he did not know for certain whether his sons were in jail or out.

An account of one of Curtis Bolden's crimes bears repeating because it suggests the ease and brutality with which he earned his living. According to the official police report, on a Saturday afternoon in April 1979, Curtis and an accomplice spotted an eighty-two-year-old widow walking her dog and followed her home. She slowly climbed the two flights of stairs to her apartment and placed the key in the lock. Suddenly Bolden grabbed her by the mouth and barked, "Shut up! Give me money!" Pushing her inside, Curtis locked the dog in the bathroom, grabbed a knife from the kitchen, and demanded her money. When she said she had none, Curtis dragged her into the bedroom, beat her, and ordered her to lie down on the floor. He closed the blinds and the living-room drapes and came at the trembling woman, ripping off her shirt, bloomers, and girdle. "Before raping her," Detective Judith Fehily's report said, "perp. [perpetrator] asked compl. [complainant] 'if she had anything inside her.' Investigation discloses compl. has a dropped womb and has a device requiring the use of a jock strap. Perp. removed the jock strap when he removed the other articles of clothing. While compl. still on bedroom floor perp. exposed himself and lubricated his penis with Vaseline taken from a jar that compl. had on the bedroom sewing table. He raped compl. after she told him she had nothing 'inside her.' After the rape perp. asked compl. for money and when she told him she had none he kicked her in the face, threw knife on the floor and fled." The right side of the widow's face was partially caved in, and when detectives interviewed her a second time one week later the print of Bolden's sneaker was still stamped on her cheek.

A detective who has reflected on the attitudes that prevail in the slums in which the Boldens grew up said not long ago that to people like Curtis Bolden "education is not important," and added, "Impressing your girlfriend is important. Wearing fine threads is important. Getting revenge against whitey is important."

The Bolden boys' father saw something else. "This whole thing is a frameup," he said. "It's ruining our name."

Curtis's victims remember him as an animal, but Anne M. Andersson, one of his elementary school teachers at P.S. 55, in the Bronx, has a different recollection. In a letter she writes:

I was Curtis and Henry Bolden's second-grade teacher, and of all the children whom I have taught, I was the closest to Curtis Bolden. Curtis and Henry were not hardened in the second grade. I know because I loved them. I was very close to Curtis' desperate need for love and acceptance. In reaching beyond his troubled exterior, I found a frightened little boy who wanted to be good, who diligently struggled and successfully overcame his delinquent behavior, if not his retarded academic performance. This was a boy who craved his mother's love, but who still cared about other living creatures.

Curtis needed daily doses of praise for behaving well and also for his nice clothes, which stood as proof of his mother's love.

We had a close relationship, Curtis and I.

In return, on Valentine's Day in 1966, while the class wrote cards to their parents, sadly but poignantly, Curtis wrote his card to me.

On the last day of school, he wanted one of the classroom plants to care for during the summer. I gave him the plant along with an award for good behavior and then the class went out to the park for the final time.

My lasting image of Curtis, at age nine, is in that Claremont project park—an image of a superb basketball player in midair, sinking the basket as always. At that time I had silently prayed, "Maybe his athletic ability will save him—just maybe, he'll make it."

The psychiatrist retained by the prosecution saw still another Curtis Bolden. In a report dated January 17, 1980, Dr. Daniel W. Schwartz, an associate professor of psychiatry at the Downstate Medical Center, in Brooklyn, wrote:

On examination the patient shows no indication of psychosis. He is alert and passively cooperative, responding to all questions in a relevant and coherent manner. . . . There is no indication of delusions, hallucinations or otherwise disordered thinking. His mood is neutral and his display of feelings quite subdued.

The patient is well aware of his present legal situation, correctly identifying the other two men as "my lawyers" and myself as "a psychiatrist." He knows that he has been arrested for "robbery and rape" and that in regard to his defense, "one possibility is a plea of insanity."

The patient shows no indication of mental deficiency. He reads such words as "for Municipal Credit Union information" correctly, subtracts 56 from 80 with pencil and paper and correctly adds 16 and 17 in his head. He correctly names the President, says that he watches the news on television every night, and correctly gives the current big news as the fact that Russia has been "coming in on other countries and stuff like that."

Dr. Schwartz, who is also director of forensic psychiatry at Kings County Hospital Center, made this diagnosis: "Antisocial personality disorder." His conclusion: "It is my professional opinion, with a reasonable degree of medical certainty, that at the time of the present offense the defendant did not, as a result of mental disease or defect, lack substantial capacity to know or appreciate the nature and consequence of his conduct or that his conduct was wrong."

The psychiatrist retained by the defense, Dr. Augustus F. Kinzel, who is a clinical instructor in psychiatry at Harvard and was formerly an associate in clinical psychiatry at Columbia, looked at the same defendant and saw someone else. His report, dated December 28, 1979, stated:

There may have been a considerable discrepancy between the way the [two] girls were raised in this family and the way the boys were raised. . . . On direct examination he appears mentally dull. His responses are quite slowed. His affect is very flat. He attempts to answer questions relevantly, but appears unable to bring any judgment or insight to his situation. His responses are impoverished. He is unable to elaborate on anything. . . . He draws the hands for three o'clock imprecisely. Asked to subtract 7 from 100 and keep taking 7 from his answer, he shows marked confusion, actually subtracting 6, 8, 5, 12, 11, 7, 10, 2, 7, 4, 7, 7, 0, 7, when all of these should be 7's. Asked to interpret the proverb don't cry over spilt milk, he states, "Never cry over something that you lose," indicating poor comprehension. He believes the day is Wednesday (it is Tuesday). . . . He is able to write the sentence: My name is Curtis Bolden, but omits the period.

103

Dr. Kinzel offered this diagnosis: Curtis Bolden was "so psychotic at the time of the alleged incident that he lacked substantial capacity to understand the nature and consequences of his acts and know they were wrong due to acute mental illness." His recommendation: "Attorneys on both sides should consult to consider dropping criminal charges in view of lack of criminal intent (mens rea) and arranging for civil commitment to a psychiatric hospital for treatment." Dr. Kinzel's report is so different from Dr. Schwartz's that one wonders whether they interviewed the same person.

These disparate views did not perplex Acting State Supreme Court Judge Howard Goldfluss. He told a crowded courtroom on March 12, 1980, "The attacks inflicted upon aged and defenseless women defy description. They are almost too horrible to relate. So vicious. So cruel. So lacking in sensitivity and compassion. I am totally bewildered as to how one human being can treat another human being in this manner." He sentenced Curtis Bolden to thirty years in prison.

Unlike the Boldens, Clifford Bright is a pro who planned his crimes carefully. He is, like the young Leon Harris, a hostile professional stickup man, and, like Harris, he got caught. On April 5, 1979, he gave a videotaped confession to Bronx Assistant District Attorney Ross Weaver at the 47th Precinct station house. Bright, a wiry six-footer, sat behind a desk, his legs casually crossed, and, faced by Weaver and several police officers, was openly defiant. "Man, shoot the shot if you going to shoot it, man," he challenged, sitting up and pounding the desk. "All these questions are not relevant, man. I don't even want to hear it. I want to hear what's going to happen."

Weaver said, "I need to know the answers to these questions."

"You don't need to know no more than I tell you," Bright replied.

It was established that Bright and an accomplice robbed a supermarket, Bright brandishing a nickel-plated five-shot .38 pistol. When police surrounded the store, Bright took a hostage rather than surrender. The police ordered him to drop his gun; Bright did. "That's when they came in and started kicking me," he said, displaying large welts on his face and a nasty cut under one eye. As the camera continued to record the session, Bright loosened up, referring to his rather lengthy arrest record, and boasting, "I'm the best stickup man in the business. I do things on my own." Previous charges were dropped, he said, and he continued:

Nobody didn't want to complain, 'cause I didn't hurt nobody. It's not about hurting nobody. It's survival and out there in the world you have to survive, my man. You sit here; you got on a tie, sports jacket, whatever. Me, I'm casual. . . . Whatever you going to do, do it, baby. Could I get a cigarette please, sir.

"You ever rob a grocery store before?" Bright was asked, and he replied:

Yes, I did. . . . I did a lot of them. That's my business. That's all I been doing all my life. . . . I never rob anybody on the street 'cause there's no money on the street. Really, if you go in somebody's pocket the most money you going to get is four hundred dollars. I carry—the less amount of money I ever had in my pocket was nine thousand dollars. . . . I have big knots in my pocket 'cause when I went to the movie and seen that picture *The Mack,* I said to be black and rich means something and in another part of the movie they say, the nigger told Goldie, she said, "I'm going to have you walking around like your pockets have the mumps."

The Mack is a movie about a black pimp who owns sleek cars and is trailed by gorgeous women. "I use no drugs," Bright said during the interrogation, "only thing in my head to do like they said in that movie *The Mack,* 'to be black and rich means something.' " Bright admitted that by choice he never sought a steady job. "I had little jobs," he said. The last was as a deliveryman for a Manhattan delicatessen. "I work, but see like this here, my man, that money I was working for them six days a week. I had two days off, to be exact. I had Sunday, I had Saturday and Sunday off. Them five days I was working. Money that I go in the store and stick up for, I make four times that much money. I was making eighty dollars a week, my man."

Others who often frighten citizens and even police officers are those so "traumatized," in Dr. Hugo Morales' phrase, that their minds snap. Why or when this happens to an individual remains something of a mystery to psychologists. What is clear is that some of these traumatized people are capable of violence at the slightest provocation. According to police and psychiatrists like Morales, "traumatized" individuals incubate in the underclass. They may be harmless shopping-bag ladies wandering aimlessly through subway arcades, the released mental patients who populate single-room-occupancy hotels, the kids rejected at home and left to roam city streets, the zombielike men who loiter on West 42nd Street or brood behind a cabin door in Appalachia. Some are black, and some—like the "Son of Sam" killer David Berkowitz—are white. These are people who, for whatever reason, cannot cope with the pressures of their environment and lives. The phenomenon is not restricted to America or urban slums. Anthropologist Nancy Scheper-Hughes, in her book *Saints, Scholars and Schizophrenics: Mental Illness in Rural Ireland,* has written of a white "residual population" in rural western Ireland, where the land and the society can't support the population, which partly accounts for the fact that Ireland has "the highest hospitalization treatment rate for mental illness in the world."

> The combined effect of the steady erosion of the community through childlessness and emigration, the disintegration of traditional values and familism, the constriction of village social life and institutions, and the national policy to retire even young and able-bodied farmers can be observed in the contagious spread of a spirit of despair and anomie. . . . This anomie is expressed in drinking patterns and alcoholism, in a sexual devitalization, and most profoundly, perhaps, in the high incidence of mental illness, especially schizophrenia. . . . The concept of anomie focuses attention on the primary importance of men's and women's work to their sense of self-esteem. . . . For the more psychologically vulnerable . . . a gradual withdrawal from peer activities, such as sports events, Sunday dances, and cooperative turf-cutting and haymaking, signals the onset of an engulfing spirit of depression and despair—sometimes climaxing in fits of rage or violence directed against neighbor or self.

Until his most recent arrest, twenty-one-year-old Michael Machuca of the Bronx had committed an assortment of street crimes. He spent his youth in foster homes. Then one day in January 1980, Machuca's mind snapped. Without apparent provocation he murdered his mother. With his powerful arms folded before his naked chest to "ward off the devil," Machuca, an American Indian with bushy hair, a square jaw, and blank, expressionless eyes, impassively told Bronx Assistant District Attorney Nina Speigler: "I saw the devil in her eyes, and I, I, was trying to keep—I was trying to keep it out of her, but it took her over. So I put some crosses—I put her hands on the cross, and she was, you know, yelling all this stuff, you know, I'm your 'hose-child' and stuff. So I told her well, you know, it's time." He threw Blanca Machuca to the kitchen floor and wrapped a blue scarf around her neck. She struggled and managed to remove it. "I put it back on, and she kept on taking it off. So I tied the scarf up—this is later. I had her on the ground, I was trying to put crosses on her face. You know, to get the devil out. . . . I dragged her in the living room, and I crossed the scarf, one of the scarfs, and I stuffed it in her throat, and she kept on biting me and stuff. And I kept on stuffing it in there. She had just got teeth removed a little while ago, so I stuffed it in that side, and I kept on stuffing it in there." She continued to fight. He stuffed another scarf in her mouth, then two drill bits. She kept squirming, frantically trying to escape. He punched her, and then ripped the leg off a table and pounded her repeatedly. He continued: "She stopped moving. And then—oh, then I took her eyes out, plucked them out, 'cause I was trying to put crosses on her. . . . Then the crosses just wouldn't fall out."

Clifford Bright, the Boldens, and, to a lesser extent, deranged individuals like Michael Machuca are the kind of people the fifty cops in Manhattan's Felony Augmentation unit spend their time tracking. Roy Miller, Tom Fennell and Vinnie Pepitone were assigned as a team to that unit. Roy Miller, the eldest of the three, has been a policeman for sixteen years. He is in his mid-forties, and on one winter day his undercover outfit consists of thick blue corduroy pants, a shirt, a heavy sweater, a windbreaker, and loafers. Tom Fennell, a short, bearded man, has been a cop for nine years. He wears a green-and-blue ski jacket zipped to the neck, with jeans and casual shoes. Vinnie Pepitone lives in Brooklyn, where his older brother, Joe, became something of a sandlot baseball legend—"the next DiMaggio"—before rising to become a New York Yankee. Vinnie has been a policeman for twelve years. He sports a cap atop long black hair, a brown-and-white checked lumber jacket, wool sweater, jeans, and Hush Puppies. The three partners are white.

A typical day on patrol consists of trying to find and trail three of the five hundred "career criminals" identified by the Felony Augmentation Program. From the folders they've selected, Miller, Fennell, and Pepitone study mug shots, aliases, last known addresses, and hangouts before setting out in an unmarked four-door 1977 white Plymouth to hunt their prey. Experience has proved that the best spots to search for career criminals are near Macy's and Gimbels, in the West 34th Street area; outside the department stores and shops on West 14th and East 86th Streets; in Minetta and Washington Square Parks, in Greenwich Village; in Bryant Park, at Sixth Avenue and 42nd Street; in the diamond district, on West 47th Street; on Third Avenue in the low fifties; around the Port Authority Bus Terminal, on Eighth Avenue; and on the north side of West 42nd Street between Times Square and Eighth Avenue. These are places where they can blend into the urban landscape and where wealthy commuters, shoppers, and tourists with unguarded habits often make inviting targets.

Most policemen don't blame society for criminal behavior. "There's got to be poor people no matter where you go," Miller says as their Plymouth crosses the bridge into Manhattan. "But because you're poor you don't have to steal, right?"

"I come from a neighborhood of poor people," Fennell says. "Yet most made it. You know what it is? It's becoming so easy. Here's a guy arrested ten times." He flips open a folder. "And he's done less than two months. If you can make a killing and not do any time, it more or less pays."

Miller calls criminals of the type they're seeking "businessmen, not animals," and adds, "I'd be quicker to call the members of a parole board that let a guy go animals. Manhattan juries let anyone go."

"I think that the juries must not believe us," Fennell says. "They think we have something to gain."

"You can kill a cop and maybe get seven years," Pepitone says.

"Jail is the furthest thing from their minds," Miller says. "They know they can get away with it. You lock up the same people all the time."

Miller says, "I don't blame the kids. I blame the parents. If my kid came home with a watch or a bicycle that I didn't buy him, I'd want to know where he got it. But those parents are delighted. I'd lock the parents up."

Many of the career criminals use and sell drugs or drink heavily, and these addictions, because they diminish earning capacity, often qualify them for welfare. Many are professional burglars or stickup men. The younger street criminals, in particular, make their living by mugging and jostling, on occasion armed with a gun or a knife. Their weekly haul can range from about $500 to $2,000.

Today, the three undercover policemen are searching for someone named Hally and two other career criminals. First, they will check a list of last known addresses, showing neighbors or doormen mug shots for leads. Hally has vanished, but if they can find where he lives and place him under surveillance, perhaps they can catch him in the commission of a crime. Their list of last known addresses usually comes from parole or arresting officers, whom Hally, obviously, has conned. After leaving the second address, a stately brownstone just off Fifth Avenue, Pepitone angrily says, "How can a guy accept that address?" They check a methadone center that Hally once attended, then a fourth address. No luck. They turn to the folder of Willie and his last listed address, in the West Nineties. It is a seedy five-story residential hotel—the kind of place that houses released mental patients, addicts, and single welfare recipients. The man at the desk is locked in a small, glass-encased office that has no openings for a

potential robber. The main foyer is pervaded by the smell of marijuana and the stench of urine; faint moans rise from behind closed
doors. After considerable prodding, Fennell and Miller get the clerk
to acknowledge that Willie, a known drug pusher and professional
mugger, lives there. But Willie is not in. After waiting fifteen or
twenty minutes, the policemen decide to go to Eighth Avenue and
42nd Street in the hope of spotting Hally, Willie, or another familiar
face.

"I don't think these people"—blacks and Puerto Ricans—"are
ready for society," Miller blurts as they leave the West Nineties.
"Civil rights came too fast, too soon. Most blacks don't have a family.
There's no father image. I see the way these wise guys dress. They
dress like broads. They wear flowered hats and weird colors. They
relate to their mothers. I see more black fags than white fags. There's
no father that runs the family. Kids rely on their mother. Whereas
in the white family the father runs the family. So you don't have
discipline. You know yourself that you can always con your mother
out of something."

Unlike John Painter, of BT-27, who views policemen as an occupy-
ing army of "punks," a policeman like Miller sees himself as a victim
of punks and public attitudes, locked in an unending and unyielding
war against crime. Members of BT-27 would consider Miller a racist,
particularly when he speaks of "these people"; Miller considers himself a realist. Yet despite the differences, it is not uncommon in
talking with policemen to find that they harbor the same feelings of
helplessness as members of BT-27. "I feel that the public doesn't
realize what's out there, the garbage on the street," Pepitone says as
the Plymouth moves down Broadway. "My wife is very liberal. She
don't believe what I come home and tell her."

"See, we're the good guys, they're the bad guys," Miller says. "But
we live by their rules, they don't live by ours."

"By the same token, not every kid in Harlem is a thief," Fennell
says. "Many kids go to college, become cops and firemen. Many
middle-class kids have parents who are alcoholics. Many kids from
places like Harlem don't succeed. But to have someone say 'I didn't
make it because of my neighborhood' is crap. Where I grew up, you
either played basketball or played with drugs. People make choices.
I seen a lawyer say to a black judge, 'My client was forced into this
way of life.' The judge said, 'I grew up on Eighth Avenue. That's
crap!'"

One great obstacle to winning convictions, says Pepitone, is getting witnesses to cooperate. "They're afraid that if this duck gets out
he'll come after them. They always ask, 'If he goes in, will he go in

for a long time?' What do we do? We can't say yes. They want to be helpful, but they're afraid. They want to tell you. They want to be good."

Miller parks the Plymouth on West 43rd Street, just off Eighth Avenue. He remains there while Pepitone and Fennell get out, take their pistols from their holsters, and slip them into their jacket pockets. "With these people, there may not be time to reach for your holster," Fennell explains. As a further precaution, Pepitone walks about fifteen steps behind Fennell as they enter the subway arcade on the west side of Eighth Avenue—"the subculture station," Fennell calls it. Here they pass a gallery of derelicts, prostitutes, winos, shopping-bag ladies, sneakered young toughs, gaudy transvestites, mink-coated pimps, heavy-lidded addicts, and drug peddlers. Fennell, whose right hand remains glued to his gun, emerges from the arcade and stations himself to one side of a fast-food store just east of Eighth Avenue—a place he calls the single worst hangout in New York. The store's front window is broken—the result of a fight and shootout earlier that day. Within inches of Fennell's shoe is a pool of dried blood, either from a mugger who was killed or from a policeman who was wounded just hours before. Young boys saunter by, many of them wrapped in expensive-looking furs. A few feet away, a teen-ager leans against the broken store window, beckoning passers-by—"Smoke, smoke, smoke"—to buy marijuana. The faces are familiar to Fennell and Pepitone, and the two policemen are familiar to the inhabitants of this gallery. The regulars long since recognized them as "deeks"—street slang for cops—but not because they had seen the policemen's snapshots or because they were white. (Other whites congregate here.) Perhaps it was because they were strangers, and were not quite scruffy or cool enough.

West 42nd Street is a subterranean world. "The urban, middle-class idea of the street is that it is fraught with potential trouble," Terry Williams and Vernon Boggs wrote in the chapter they contributed to *The Bright Light Zone,* a study of Times Square street life prepared for the Ford Foundation in 1978. "There is violence, danger, and harm to be found on the street. After a certain hour, the streets are to be abandoned for the safety of the home. But for others, the street is a home—a place to stand, sit, drink, eat, sleep, converse, defecate, urinate, fight, and work." After observing West 42nd Street for two months, the authors estimated that "more than 12,000 drug transactions alone took place between Seventh and Eighth Avenues." In this "supermarket," as they call it, the hustlers know one another: "Members of the street network who at first appeared individualistic and competitive were part of a clique often seen conversing, sharing drugs, loaning each other money, calling each other names. They often arrived promptly each morning as if they were going to a regular job, which, in fact, they were by conducting their business as usual and then returning home." In the supermarket one can find drugs and a variety of stolen goods, including typewriters, radios, televisions, jewelry, coats, and food. Other common activities include male or female prostitution, with a choice of young boys or rotund women; con games; dice games (cilo and crap); three-card monte; pickpocketing (called dipping); and shoplifting. In their sympathetic account, Williams and Boggs say the only alternative to the street life these people lead is "often ennui, unemployment, welfare, and physical violence."

To Fennell, Pepitone, and Miller—and to much of the public as well—that street is populated by parasites, shrewd and sometimes skilled at what they do. But the cops do not think of these street people and dealers as nonviolent. Standing nonchalantly beside a pay phone on the corner of Eighth Avenue, Pepitone, who is six feet four inches tall, is bumped by a beefy black man wearing a gold earring. "Push me, man, and I'll beat the shit out of you," the man suddenly erupts. Pepitone looks away, ignoring the taunt. Why? Because, he says later, to arrest the man would tie up an entire day in the precinct house and in court, diverting him from more important duties. Besides, such behavior is customary on the streets he visits. For these policemen, the outrageous has become normal, just as crime has become a normal burden of urban life. At the end of their shift, the three-man police detail will file a report stating that all of Hally's listed addresses are phonies, and supplying Willie's address so that another shift can place him under surveillance. In the war on crime, progress is measured in inches.

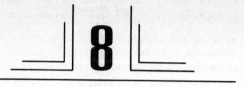

8

The "Welfare Mentality"

The students in BT-27 are on average about six to seven years older than the street criminals the cops chase. But just a few years ago many—Mohammed, Leon Harris, John Painter, John Hicks, William Mason, Willy Joe—might well have been on the list of career criminals kept by Vinnie Pepitone and his colleagues. Getting off that list is in part a function of age. As they get older, street criminals often get tired of being chased by the police, of shuffling back and forth to prison, of hanging out on street corners, of not knowing where money for the next meal will come from. Many of them mature, settle down, get married, have families, and learn to accept responsibility for more than themselves. Many are murdered. "When they get to be about thirty-five, we rarely see them any more," says New York City Criminal Court judge Irving Lang.

Most members of BT-27 are struggling to stay out of the criminal courts. Today, after a three-day weekend, BT-27 is scheduled to present their "welfare mentality" papers. But because Howard Smith is late with the keys, the training center is locked and the class congregates in the lobby at 240 West 37th Street. The members of BT-27 are angry. The previous Friday the classroom was so uncomfortably cold—despite the presence of three portable heaters—that BT-27 staged a walkout in midafternoon. "Sally told us we wouldn't get paid for it," grouses Gladys Miller about Sally Grueskin, the young native Iowan who directs the center. "We're going to go and fight it. Nothing physical, nothing violent. Just words. They want to know about a welfare mentality? We come in every morning and they are taking advantage of us. It's cold. You don't talk to grown-ups like children." The wait, the cold, and the threat of lost pay fuel their paranoia, the sense of exploitation they had in prison or on welfare or at employment offices—or now have at Wildcat. "They want us to sit in the cold!" exclaims William Mason, usually the most easygoing of men. "They're not placing enough people," Carlos Rodriguez complains. "I have a friend who told me they may lose their contract because they're not finding jobs for people."

Their anger is shared by several instructors who also huddle in the lobby. John Barnes, who teaches reading, vocabulary, and math at Wildcat, snaps that he will go home if there is no heat today: "They dock me, I quit." Delores Licorice, the short, stout typing teacher, says her thermostat read 52 degrees on Friday. "This program is partially funded by welfare," she says, "so the students are working off part of their welfare checks. Other programs are funded independently. So in a sense it is a slap in the face because they are saying that as welfare recipients the students are not entitled to the same consideration and educational opportunities as other folks. That's why they keep saying, 'They're treating us like cattle.'"

Sally Grueskin arrives at 9:55 A.M., explaining that Howard Smith was supposed to open up but his train broke down and she came right over after he called her out of a previously scheduled meeting. The director of the center is a thirty-year-old woman with shoulder-length blond hair and a friendly manner. She smiles at the trainees but is greeted with icy stares. Sally stiffens, puts the key in the door, turns on the lights, directs the students to sign in and not to complain, and goes off to search for the superintendent to turn up the heat. Members of BT-27 huddle in the hall outside their classroom, and John Barnes, one of four of the seven staff members who are black, says, "If we are to convince them that we have the solution to their personal problems, we should be models in every way. Yet we don't have our act together."

Howard Smith, obviously suffering from a cold, arrives to open his classroom and turn on the portable heaters. "That's why he's sick all the time," says Denise Brown sympathetically, pressing her fur coat closer as she and her classmates confer outside the classroom. Sally Grueskin returns to report that a representative of the landlord has explained that the oil gauge was broken. The students express disbelief. Standing beside a trash container overflowing with several days' worth of garbage, Sally lays out two options: keep their coats on and stay, or report to Wildcat's parent offices at 660 First Avenue. "We will definitely not cancel classes," she announces. William Mason reminds her that there was also no heat on Friday. Seeking to channel their anger into a lesson, Sally Grueskin asks, "Does anybody have a positive attitude?"

"My feet are cold," Mason responds.

"The owner of this building just refuses to give us heat," gripes Leon Harris. "It's his fault. Maybe they're trying to get us out of here to sell the building. Who knows?"

"All right," Sally interjects. "This is what we're going to do."

"Says who?" interrupts usually mild-mannered Willy Joe.

Promising to assign them to a warmer room, Sally orders, "Go to class."

"Break time—it's ten-twenty," Gladys Miller announces defiantly. Sally repeats her command, more softly this time. The class agrees with Gladys. Howard Smith sticks his head out of the classroom to agree with Sally. "Why sit out there and be cold? There's heat in here."

After a stony silence, only Timothy Wilson takes Smith's bait. "Just 'cause they weren't here, they can't take our break away," Gladys says. "We're together," says Mason, turning to his friend Leon Harris to ask if he wants to follow Timothy.

"We don't break no rules," says Leon. "I'll go to class. But they don't break no rules on us by canceling our break."

Both sides see a larger issue here. Members of BT-27 believe that they are once again being victimized. "They have a point," concedes Sally Grueskin privately. But, she believes, "it's an attitude thing. They were given an alternative on Friday—to go to 660 or to come back after lunch and see if the heat was up. It was. But the attitude feeds on itself. No longer were they saying, 'How do we do it beside the lack of heat?' Instead, it became 'How do we go home?' " Sally admits she plans to dock them part of Friday's pay. "The theory I have to uphold is that this is a work site. An employer would come up with an alternative. He wouldn't send his employees home." Wildcat attempts to prepare people for the real world of work, a world where special counseling and other supports are absent. Perform or be fired. But Delores Licorice says private employers are not always so absolute. "In every training program I've worked in, if there was no heat the students were dismissed. I've never worked in a program where they were docked." At RCA, if there was no heat, they would close the plant, she said.

Sally and Howard's primary concern is that if the students are permitted to give in to frustration they will not break a lifetime pattern of surrendering to impulse. It is a familiar pattern, one observed by Richard A. Cloward and Robert Ontell in the study they did for New York City's Mobilization for Youth of Lower East Side youths:

> We are plagued, in work with these youth, by what appears to be a low tolerance for frustration. They are not able to absorb setbacks. Minor irritants and rebuffs are magnified out of all proportion to reality. Perhaps they react as they do because they are not equal to the world that confronts them, and they know it. And it is the knowing that is devastating.

But the choice is not always between uncontrolled rage and docility. Sally Grueskin and Howard Smith could have chosen to teach their lesson in some other way. They could have gotten the members of BT-27 to organize a delegation to visit the superintendent or the landlord of the building. Most working people would not be expected to sit in a room and freeze. They would doubtless turn to their union or instigate some sort of job action. For the members of BT-27, a group with little experience in the organized world of work, the lesson could have been: don't quit and don't surrender to Sally Grueskin, Howard Smith, or a cold classroom.

By 10:45, eleven students are in the classroom, nine of whom keep their winter coats on. Howard says today each will be called to stand before the class and read his "welfare mentality" paper. Timothy Wilson, the nineteen-year-old former foster child and drug addict who now lives at home with his mother, is first. This, in part, is exactly how Timothy's paper reads:

> First I would like to elaborate on the affects of the welfare mentality, in the home. Most welfare recipience are deppressed finantialy becuase of the amount of money that they get. To be a little more practical there are some welfare recipience recieving 27$ a month for food. . . . Most of the Welfare recipience eat potatoes, rice, bread, grits and cheese; they hardly ever eat good meats cause they cant afford it. On a personal note I think that who ever gives out this food stampt at the rate of 27$ a month is insane. . . . I believe that a percentage of crime and arson are committed by frustrated welfare recipience.
>
> Now I would like to focus in on the socail aspects of the avarage welfare recipient. I witness every 1st and 16th of the month what I call the grattified welfare ricipient. They tend to get a few beers or so and just let it hang loose. They no these good vibes will come to an end so they just stagnate in gradifica- tion. . . . It seems to me as a fact once your on welfare your

doomed. I feel that your subjected to "placement unvolintaraly" and also you are being contained like sardines in a can.

After he finishes reading his three-page paper, Timothy fields a few questions from his classmates. Several chime in to protest skimpy food and welfare allowances. Howard Smith, playing devil's advocate, prods: "How come there is so much of the numbers game, alcohol, and drugs in areas where there is a high percentage of welfare recipients, especially on days when they get their checks? Where's all this money coming from?"

"They play the numbers to make more money," Gladys Miller responds.

"I know people who bet their last dollar," Leon Harris says.

The numbers are cheap, says Mason. People only bet nickels, dimes, quarters, maybe a dollar. "It gives them a day off from crime if they win."

"Why not use the money for groceries?" Howard Smith asks.

"They can't take the pressure of knowing that five kids need shoes," Gladys replies.

"It depends on the mother," says Mason. "Some hustle. Some do drugs." But then many stay home despite the pressure, and care for their children.

"Why do many of those who complain there is no money, when they get it it's not food or clothes that are on their mind," Smith asks. "Getting high is on their mind. Why?"

"Check day is a day off from crime," says William Block.

Smith asks Gladys Miller to present her paper. It reads, in part:

The word "welfare" comes from a system that started centuries ago, but then it was called aid. Its purpose then was to help the poor and disable. Those that were able to work but didn't, were wipped or put in jail for three days with nothing but bread and water to eat.

Today we have a system that has changed in form but not thinking. Its terrible that a system that started out helping, now takes more than it gives, like a person pride, self-respect and family unity.

In the 60's instead of helping those on welfare, the employes helped themselves to very large amount of money. Then we have the recipient who decides to get more than just their bi-weekly rashing. Because we receive so little, most have a side hustle, which are all elegal. This means jail when caught and causes the breakup of familys.

But who should get the blame for such a bad system? The

system by a landslide. . . . Times have changed, prices are sky high, and the system still dates back to beging, trying the poor, given just enough to stay alive. . . .

A mine is a terrible thing to waste. Welfare spelled backward means fare-wel to caring, respect, self being.

In a question period that follows, Gladys Miller continues to blame the system, not the individual, for welfare cheating. She asks, "How can we continue to go down there and get two or three food checks a month without them knowing?"

"Let me stop you there," Smith says. "Aren't we taking money out of taxpayers' pockets? Where does the money come from?"

"The government's going to take it anyway," says Ramon Lopez.

"I'm hearing two different things," Smith says, pointing up the contradiction between the system they complain is so loose it encourages fraud and yet so tight it provides inadequate support. "Which way do you want it?"

"It's a little of both," Gladys Miller says. "Can't I have both?"

"You say welfare treats you bad," Smith says. "Or is it because people feel bad?"

"I feel bad," Gladys Miller says. "But they still treat you bad."

"You can feel like you're one hundred percent self-sufficient," says William Mason. "But when you come out of there you feel like two cents."

"You lose self-respect," Gladys Miller says.

"It rips a man's integrity," says Timothy Wilson. "They have to know everything. They're always coming over to the house. Looking at this, looking at that."

"When was the last time a welfare inspector looked under the bed for a man's shoes?" Howard Smith asks. An inspector can't come into your home unannounced, can't deny you a TV, he says.

"The reason they don't get away with that is that they walked social workers off the roof and into trains," Mason explains, obviously exaggerating. "They was getting rid of social workers. That's why it changed."

Howard invites William Block, who has on his customary dark pants, black shades, and rust-colored leather jacket, to present his paper. This normally reticent man has obviously poured himself into this project, producing thirteen neatly printed pages that at times sound as if they were transcribed:

Why are the recipients of charity vomiting in rage and laughing in scorn at their benefactors? So much charity—why no gratitude? In fact, why so few improvements? We argue that the people in power have served only in "safe" ways that will not threaten their power. . . . Before the advent of Universal Compulsory education in the United States, the rulers of society did not believe that education was a necessary welfare service for all citizens. . . . The general public still thinks of welfare as public assistance. . . . Most people do not, however, think of Social Security (old age, survivors, dependants, and hospital insurance) as "welfare." Nor are they likely to view unemployment compensation or workmen's compensation as "welfare," because they are told that they are entitled to those benefits because they worked for them. Still less, are people likely to view farm subsidies, oil depletion allowances, or tax write-offs for big corporations as "welfare" even though they involve more government spending than public assistance. . . . No legislation has ever been passed in the United States to guarantee a job to everyone who wants it. Business men consider some unemployment desirable, because a fully employed work force would drive wages and reduce profits. . . . People cannot be forced back to work if there is no work for them; and the lack of employment opportunity is the reason many are welfare recipients in the first place. . . . What is needed in my judgment is a very careful examination . . . to set a livable standard of help in the form of money, better medical service, better housing, programs geared to provide jobs for those who complete its [training] course. . . . And parents should get back into a religious atmosphere with their family to promote a sound well being of oneself and to society as a productive participant in the working classes.

Howard observes that Block's paper is somber, and inquires about why he is so pessimistic. "You either be in the grave or you be in jail," Block responds. "'Cause you not going to get the money you need to live on. So you go out and steal and get caught. Getting caught, you either get caught in jail or you get caught and put in the ground."

"Why do you think the death penalty is so popular?" Howard asks.

"I see it as a getting-even mentality," answers William Block. "You know, burn a few."

"You tell me that for twenty-five years I got to take care of that 'nigger' who bumped off my neighbor?" Smith asks.

"I don't feel that's good, the death chair," volunteers William Penn. "If they do pass that bill, understand, all it will mean is more killings. These people on the street when the cop comes are going to hold court right there. It's then a do-or-die situation."

118

"Personally, I'm for the death penalty," Smith says. His point of view is shared by 29 percent of American blacks and 42 percent of black college graduates, according to an August 1980 poll conducted by Data Black. A November 1978 *New York Times*/CBS News poll showed 46 percent of American blacks favored the death penalty.

Turning to other forms of subsidy in which the federal government is involved, Smith says, "You don't hear too many people screaming and hollering about farmers' subsidies or workmen's compensation. How come?"

"Working-class people have pride," says William Block. "They work and provide for their family. They are productive people. They look at people on welfare who can't read or write. Society is not screaming about those that need help. What they're screaming about is when they come out for lunch and see a man walking up and down with a three-hundred-dollar radio. Some on welfare are making more than those working. You come home at night after working a whole day and you be worrying about getting pushed on the subway—you're mad."

Smith asks if anyone can offer a solution.

"A stricter screening of welfare recipients, for one thing," Block says. "Second, screen only those people you can give jobs. And, third, I think families in general should get back into religion. Put kids back into Sunday school."

Coming around to a theme he often brings up in class, Smith asks if Block is blaming the individual or the system.

"It's mostly the system, because if the system allows this, it will become a reality," Block says. He goes on to say that if ex-convicts are to lead stable lives they must have jobs, yet because they are ex-convicts many cannot find jobs, and he recounts his experience in applying for a job when he got out of prison in 1979: "They offered me a security-guard role. I said, 'I'm on parole.' They said, 'Next.' "

Block and many of his fellow supported workers realize that although they have been abused by the system, they have also exploited the system. And many of them have conflicting attitudes toward the system. Block says, "If you walk in a house and see a color TV, you know someone's stealing. If you walk down the street with a big radio blasting, you telling people you don't care." In the next breath, he says, "When you have a system that tells people it's all right to loaf . . ." Similarly, although black Americans vote overwhelmingly for liberal candidates, according to a March 1981 *Washington Post*/ABC News national opinion survey, nearly half of all black adults—47 percent—take the more "conservative" position that "most blacks don't have the motivation or willpower to pull themselves out of poverty." This response could be viewed in one of two ways: as a disturbing but understandable sign of self-hate or as a frank assessment of the damage done by welfare dependency.

Smith agrees that the welfare system often encourages cheating, and that welfare promotes idleness and "an unreal world" where work can become aberrant and bad habits are shaped.

"Yes," Block says. "Prisons promote more idleness than anything else." Most of the people he served time with in jail did not have a high school diploma or any skills. Block then tells of the five months he spent at a supported-work job before coming to the Wildcat Training Center. "I worked in the park," he says. "They put you in the park all by yourself. *He* says, 'You clean up,' and then he leaves. You pick up a few things, and then you lie in the grass. If I see a hundred people on welfare, I doubt whether five are trying to use that welfare ladder to escape."

The class breaks for lunch, and during the break Smith and I discuss the conflicting opinions held by a student like Block. "For the most part, the way I interpret it is that they recognize the negative aspects of welfare on an individual basis," he says. "But they feel that ultimately it's the result of the system. They're saying, 'Hey, look, I know it's wrong. I know it's negative. I know what the middle class says. I understand that. But what you don't see is that it's not all the fault of the poor.'" The thrust of life skills is to concentrate on individual responsibility, to make people believe they can leap barriers, that they need not be victims of the system.

As for whether the class should have been docked pay for leaving school on Friday, Smith admits, "I have ambivalent feelings. You can't just walk off a job and expect to keep it. In life skills, when you come you have an employment agreement. They have obligations. So do we: heat, clean bathrooms, pay. That's where I'm caught at. I understand what the administration is saying. They don't. And what they're doing is coming back to me and saying, 'Howard, you told me the company has certain obligations. They're not keeping theirs. Why should we keep ours?' And most of them don't have positive work experience. Most are just out of prison. They are not traditional nine-to-five people. It doesn't take much to throw them off, to make them fall back into negative patterns. They resent the system, and in this case the system is Sally Grueskin and Howard Smith."

Four days later, eleven members of BT-27 are in the classroom at 9:00 A.M. to read their papers on the welfare mentality. Smith calls on Pearl Dawson, the forty-five-year-old woman who has had her troubles with two husbands, alcohol, a manslaughter conviction, and welfare. Somewhat nervously, Pearl reads from her paper:

> Speaking as a member of the black race and not from books, newspapers, radio, TV, or any other sources, these are my thoughts and feelings on the welfare system.
>
> 1. Welfare mentality. To me welfare mentality is the state of mind of a person having to depend on welfare to survive.
>
> 2. What does welfare do to a person? . . . I do know that it takes something away from your pride. Not everyone wishes to be on welfare, but there comes a time (or a point in time) in one's life where there is no other choice.
>
> To the male, or I would like to think to most of them, it's a lowering of self-esteem. They seem to feel or fear a lack of respect from family and loved ones.
>
> To the female, it means a way of survival for their children when there's no father, and jobs are a rarity for untrained persons. . . .
>
> 3. How does Welfare help financially? To be sure the amount of monies that is doled out is not sufficient for one person (not speaking of two or three) in a household. . . .
>
> 4. Education. Another sore spot because the family on welfare usually cannot afford decent clothing, lunches, books, and other material things that a child should have in order not to feel ashamed or embarrassed to be seen in school. Therefore, many young children decides to heck with school, take to the streets and start them a hustle. . . . Does welfare have any good points? Welfare does have some self-defending points in that there are scores of people who are physically as well as mentally unable to work, and without the little dole could not make it at all. But the bad part of it is that people have to go through so much hell to even get that meager handout.

At 9:45, two more members of the class arrive—Mohammed and John Painter. As they take their seats, Carlos Rodriguez, who is nineteen, and who always sits beside Pearl, approaches the lectern. He has been reading *Blaming the Victim* by William Ryan, the psychologist who wrote: "To suggest that anyone—or at least more than a tiny handful of erratic or disturbed persons—would choose the bitter existence of AFDC as a way of life except as a last resort, is to demonstrate ignorance either of the basic nature of humanity, or of what life is like on AFDC." Ryan would no doubt be appalled by many of the statements made in class. Rodriguez's paper echoes Ryan's book:

> The so-called welfare mentality is a belief or mental picture held in common which is based not necessarily on the truth or facts. Unfortunately, welfare is generally used in a very narrow sense to refer to the unfortunates at the bottom of the economic ladder. (THE POOR) Those who are sometimes called the Welfare Bums. So when we use a term like welfare mentality we are using a stereotype, in the same way we use a stereotype if we refer to a Female Mentality, a Puertoriquen Mentality, a Negro Mentality, or even a Homosexual Mentality. So we cannot refer to such ideas as a Welfare Mentality because in fact it is a stereotype. . . . This is a good example of Blaming the Victim.

"You hit a few buttons there," Timothy Wilson says, offering congratulations. Smith then asks if Rodriguez agrees with a statement Pearl Dawson made in an earlier class, to the effect that many women have more children to qualify for more welfare.

"There are women who have more children in order to stay on welfare," Rodriguez says.

"Do you think the child is affected as he grows up?" Smith asks.

"Yes."

"Why?" Smith asks.

" 'Cause she doesn't take care of the child," Rodriguez responds.

Smith asks if that characterization is a stereotype.

"A stereotype is to say, like, all Puerto Ricans eat rice and beans," Rodriguez says. "Or all teachers are dumb." The class breaks into laughter.

Smith asks, "So what stereotype is not true?"

"That they're lazy and irresponsible and like to hang around," Rodriguez says. "That's not true. Many people on welfare need that aid."

William Penn enters the room at 9:55. Taking no notice, Smith calls on Mohammed, who lifts his head from the desk to say he does not have his paper.

Denise Brown volunteers to read hers. With the exception of Pearl Dawson, Denise is the only other member of BT-27 whose dress and manner would blend easily into a Wall Street brokerage house. She reads:

> When I meet someone with a welfare mentality, I know how it came about. It causes people who always wanted the best for themselves to learn to settle for less. They no longer have a

standard of living, just merely surviving. They later raise their children to enjoy welfare mentality and learn to think little. They are forced into unhealthy conditions and humiliations. Also, after a while they begin to relax into this nothingness, enjoying this crutch welfare has provided for them. This is welfare mentality. It can make us irresponsible, lazy and depending on the system we claim treats us so unfairly. . . . I am not opposed to the purpose of welfare, as long as it does not become a permanent condition . . . even though I am a part of the system, I will use my mentality to keep welfare mentality away.

Smith once again brings up the question of various kinds of government subsidies. Seeking to broaden the class's frame of reference and to reduce their sense of victimization, he asks, "Who receives welfare in America?"

"Farmers," William Penn says.

"Unemployment insurance," Denise Brown says.

"Workmen's compensation is another form of welfare," Smith says. He asks where the programs under the Comprehensive Employment and Training Act (CETA) fit in.

"Same soup, different bowl," says John Hicks, a sometimes defiant ex-convict who is the only married member of BT-27.

Smith asks if the decline of small farms and the movement of people from rural areas to cities might have anything to do with welfare.

"We are more dependent on the system than people like that," Denise Brown says of rural people. "They had food. They didn't worry about housing, because they'd chop down their trees and build it."

"We all moved here to the city looking for this manufacturing," Ramon Lopez says. "I don't know. I think too many of us came at the same time. Can't find job. I don't know—maybe some of us are dumb. Now we're stuck here."

Next, Smith asks how American communities have changed over the years.

"In my neighborhood, when I was young there was always the Boy Scouts and an older person to take you to play ball," says Penn, sounding much older than his twenty-three years. "It's not a community no more. I hear babies four and five talking words even I don't use. That's what they're looking up to."

"When I was growing up, the church member helped you if you were sick," Block says. "This way, you kept your dignity. Now, with the playacting and lying for the welfare system, you lose your dignity. Kids see it as 'Get what you can.' "

Hope Parker, a former addict who rarely says a word in life skills, enters at 11:00 A.M., taking her seat as William Mason says, "When I was incarcerated, the church took care of my family."

"Kids now at a disadvantage," says John Painter, who is twenty. "You have thirty-five to forty in a class. When I was a kid, we had some teachers who were friends. Now teachers wouldn't think of visiting your apartment and talking to your mother in Bedford-Stuyvesant."

Again, Smith asks how neighborhoods have changed.

"No trust," says Penn. "My mother's still in the same place where I was born. The door was always open. If you leave the door open now, you better be ready."

"Used to be you could have a fight—didn't mean you hated the guy," John Painter says. "Now it's a one-punch fight before someone shoots you. It didn't use to be where the guy would try to kill you."

"Little kids, twelve, thirteen years old, say, 'I slice your throat, turkey,' " Timothy Wilson says. "Another thing that changed is traditional pride. I grew up all around the whole racial thing. You know, 'Black is beautiful'—I forget the dude's name who said it. There was pride. Nowadays they're never satisfied. Always looking for more. When I was a kid, I was proud to have a pair of shoes."

Willy Joe enters at 11:25 A.M. As Willy makes his way to a chair, John Barnes, who sometimes sits in on the life-skills class, asks, "What effect do the media have on this change?"

"When you were younger, you didn't think of TV," says Leon Harris. "It was no influence. You may have heard of drugs or killing, but you didn't see it. It was cops and robbers. But as you grew up and watched this on TV, people started to act it out."

"When I was a kid our role models were teachers or doctors," says John Barnes. "How are we presented by the media? *Superfly!* That was a stereotype. And that's what we related to—'make it hustling.' They call it subliminal suggestion. It blew our minds."

"They go and see *Superfly* and he's got a Rolls-Royce," John Painter says. "The majority want to be Superfly."

"Why is *Superfly* more popular than *Sounder?*" Smith asks.

"The majority of our community is about hustling, and people can relate to Superfly," William Penn says.

"How have whites affected your community?" asks Smith.

"They moved out," says Denise Brown. "When they left, the community died. No longer any stores where you can shop. No more services."

"Use your imagination," Smith coaxes. "Make up a story—a musical comedy—of the saga of the South Bronx. Think of just one thing that caused it. Start in 1945 and go in sequence."

"Don't use the South Bronx," interrupts John Painter. "Most of us are from Brooklyn."

"We all know bad neighborhoods," Smith says. "I'll start. Franklin Delano Roosevelt died in 1945. Lots of Irish and Jews were living there. GIs came home from the war. They got benefits. What happened?"

"They buy a house out of the South Bronx," Gladys Miller says.

After a long silence, Smith contributes, "The federal government built highways." He goes about the room, putting everyone on the spot. Mohammed volunteers, "Blacks came from the South looking for better opportunity."

"The Jews and the Irish move out," says John Hicks.

"The Dodgers win the pennant!" says William Penn, and his classmates crack up.

"A large group of immigrants come over from other countries," says William Block.

"A war broke out, 'cause, like, the Russians took over Afghanistan," Willy Joe says.

Neighborhoods deteriorated, says Denise Brown. Poor housing, Smith adds.

"Increased racial violence," says William Mason.

"Crime," says Leon Harris.

"Why?" asks Howard.

" 'Cause there were no jobs and they had to get something to eat," Leon replies.

"There was no money for taxes, so there were less services," Howard says, completing the circle.

By the time the class period ends, at one o'clock, eleven of the sixteen people enrolled have read their "welfare mentality" papers, and Smith asks Pearl Dawson to collect the papers. He also announces that, beginning the following week, the life-skills class will concentrate on practical questions concerning jobs, discuss the various occupational choices that may be open to them, and learn how to write letters and act on job interviews.

9

BT-27:
Goals and Obstacles

If Howard Smith was asked to gift a single word of advice to BT-27 it would probably be *confidence.* As part of the process of building self-confidence, Howard has asked the members of the class to draft a brief statement about their career goals. Each member of BT-27 is to stand before the class and talk about him or herself, about something he or she has done before. This time, however, is different. Each student will be asked to engage in self-analysis. And the talks will be videotaped, with the tape played back so the entire class can join in the evaluation. To ease the pain, Howard has distributed a two-page form—"Who I Am and Where I Want to Go"—listing the questions he wants answered. To prepare them for the world of work, Howard must ready the members of BT-27 for businesslike encounters with job interviewers and personnel managers.

Few job interviewers would accept the excuse offered by one supported worker attending a special two-week life-skills course in December 1979: "One day I was late because the alarm clock didn't work, and the next day I was late because the clock was wrong." His classmates roared, but Howard Smith followed up on that topic by asking such elemental questions as "Besides laying out your clothes, what else is involved in getting ready for work?" Most adults don't think about such questions because they are in the habit of working. Those in supported work are not. Nor are they used to being interviewed by personnel officers.

To break the ice Howard asks John Barnes to stand up and answer the assigned questions: "Who am I and where do I want to go?"

Barnes talks about his parents, his youth, and his vices, particularly his inability to distinguish "the ideal from the real." Barnes concludes, "I was born to teach. And I'm a good teacher, believe it or not." The twelve students in class applaud.

At 9:40 A.M. William Penn arrives, followed five minutes later by John Painter. Howard calls on Hope Parker, who is the best typist in class and does well in English and math. For unexplained reasons she has refused to submit a "welfare mentality" paper or speak in class, and today is no exception. John Painter is less shy. When he wants to be, John is a garish dresser, and today he wears a wide-lapeled gray suit jacket, a black shirt, and a thin black tie—more Nathan Detroit than Shaft. After touching on his orphaned youth, Painter hams it up for the camera: "My main interest is being one of the most prominent and successful black men who ever lived on this planet earth." First he wants to go to St. John's University and be a basketball star, a dream he often talks about but has so far done nothing to advance. "The only thing I like about my present job," he says, "is the skills that it offers and the determination the teachers have. The thing I don't like is that I spend too much time traveling to it, and it's cold." His career goal? Instead of being "my own boss," as he vowed earlier in life skills, John says he wants to be an executive in a big firm and have "my own desk."

Henry Rivera and Ramon Lopez, who sit beside each other in class and have become close friends, are in a foul mood and refuse to speak. Timothy Wilson pushes aside a copy of Alex Haley's *Roots* and moves to the lectern wearing a blue-and-white T-shirt pulled over a beige turtleneck. Timothy does not mention how his parents split, the homosexual attacks he fended off while living in four foster homes, the heroin use, the time he spent in prison. He talks about his reading habits and his enjoyment of poetry. Today he says, "I believe that my best abilities are communicating and socializing." He hates the cold in the classroom. But most of all he hates people prying into his personal life: "In my next job I would like a very simple boss who is just concerned about my work, not my personal affairs."

Sleepy-eyed Willy Joe is next. Willy is burdened by problems at home, but rarely is he without a kind word for someone in class. But his performance at Wildcat has been marginal, particularly in the areas of typing and attendance. Willy Joe no longer wants to be a chef, an earlier ambition, but now has decided he would like to use his math skills to land a job in a credit department. "Some of the things I have to do to better myself is to be on time and to be persistent."

Pearl Dawson, who is consumed by a desire to get off welfare, says one thing she likes about Wildcat is that John Barnes teaches "proper English." She does not like the cold classrooms here or the scarcity of school materials. Her goal is simple: to "get to a point where I can look back and say, 'I made it.'" Pearl says she knows that because she is older she is more set in her ways and must learn to get "in tune with a hundred people. I been through what they going through, and I don't want to go through it again." She claims to be confident of success as an office worker but says, "I got four strikes against me—my age, my race, my sex, and my lack of experience."

While the class takes its break, Howard Smith whispers to me that with the ten-week cutoff point just two weeks away, Sally Grueskin and the six other members of the Wildcat staff have begun to discuss who will receive a ten-week certificate and go on for the final twenty weeks of training, and who will be sent back to the job sites. One decision they have made unanimously: John Hicks, the handsome twenty-two-year-old with the bushy sideburns, will be terminated this afternoon. This means he will return to his supported-work job site, finish out the year there, and come back to the center for a two-week life-skills orientation before he begins the search for a job. The reason for his sudden dismissal, Smith says, is that he is a "bad influence" on some, particularly John Painter and Willy Joe. Hicks drinks too much, smokes dope, is usually late, carries a chip on his shoulder, and recently almost came to blows with John Barnes. At the end of supported work, says Howard, "If he doesn't find a job, it's back to the welfare rolls." The evaluators also expressed concern about William Penn's drinking; about John Painter's dislike of regulations and the danger that he will decide he can make more money hustling than he can at Wildcat; about Willy Joe's poor attendance, poor typing, and passivity; about Mohammed's preoccupation with Islam. Hope Parker's erratic attendance record was excused because she is in poor health, lives with an ailing grandfather whom she looks after, and recently had a flood in her home. The remaining problem student is Henry Rivera, thirty-six, who like Hope Parker says little in life skills. Henry has never held a regular job, hustles drugs on the side, and says he does not live with a daughter and mother who are supported by welfare. "Unless he shows a great turnabout in the next two weeks, he will not go on," Smith says, and then elaborates: "He's in another space and time. What really frustrates you with Henry is that every once in a while he'll come into class sober, and he really is an extremely intelligent, bright guy." His math is good, his English is not. But the big problem is marijuana: "He's fine in the morning. But after the break, when he's had an opportunity to have a couple of joints, he's another Henry."

The class resumes and Leon Harris, drawing his words out slowly, says, "I know I have a lot of faults and misunderstandings with people. But I want to get a job. I work good, but I work at my pace, which is bad." What he does best is "talk and get along with people." In the future he'd like to be a counselor: 'You know, sit around and talk. A person come and bring me their problems, you know, because I can help them. The things I have to do to better myself? I have a bad temper. I blow off. Can't do that if I want to be my own boss." Wildcat "gives you good training—if you want to learn. Typing is really beautiful. Life skills, to tell you the truth, was boring to me. But I learned." How was Smith as a teacher? "We had our run-ins, but he's cool—a good teacher." At this Smith and Harris flash the V-for-victory sign at each other.

Gladys Miller approaches the lectern hesitantly, shaking noticeably. She begins to read her notes, stops, lowers her head, apologizes, and returns to her seat. Denise Brown follows, explaining that she is skilled at the martial arts, to the point of owning a brown belt. "I just like to talk," she says. "I don't do it very well, but I just like to talk. This here's really helping me because I don't like to stand up and talk. I don't mind being told what to do. I enjoy working under supervision." Denise would like a job in communications, perhaps as a receptionist in the Air Force. She is currently taking Spanish lessons at night and "I speak French fluently. As far as the writing, I just got to learn to join the verbs and adverbs together." She describes other realms that need work: "I find at times in talking to someone that I lack confidence. I don't know how to express myself, so I don't say anything. You're about the first group of people that I expressed myself to. . . . I felt I didn't have to change myself to deal with other people. I found I had to."

After considerable coaxing, Ramon Lopez agrees to speak, and while staring down at his shoes, he quickly recounts his childhood, noting that the longest he ever held a job was for seven months. He looks up and smiles, displaying a dazzling set of white teeth. "I like you all," he concludes. "You're all my friends. I like being here."

William Block tells the class of his dislike for city life: "I like mostly countryside. The thing I don't like was that in the city there is a lot of backbiting. People telling on other people. I can't say what kind of job I'd like to be on because I'm gonna relocate. I'm getting out of New York. This is my home, but I can't stand the crime. It's paranoia trying to step out here." Block worries that if he is mugged and resists and is hauled before a judge, the law will pay attention to nothing but his criminal record, and he'll be sent back to prison. "But I know also that to go somewhere else without experience, to a home where you have no relatives or anything like that, it's gonna be hard." He'd like a job "close to social work. Either placing myself in a church or some sort of community organization."

Mohammed, wearing dark clothes and his customary black hat, begins by saying, "I'm not good at this." He describes his youth, a period of "racism" toward whites he felt as a teenager, and his hope to one day use his drawing skills to become a draftsman. But his most fervent hope is "to serve humanity in the way the Koran tells us to."

Gladys Miller then tries once more to speak. She tells the class she is a good cook, a talent confirmed by her waistline, and mentions that she is also good at sports and likes to read. Her supported-work job as a messenger paid too little "even though it made me lose weight." She would like to improve in the areas of persistence and follow-through. Her immediate goal is to get her G.E.D. In the long-term, she says, "You know when they say first class, I'd like to find out what that's about."

And finally Smith calls on Hope Parker, who surprises everyone by getting up to speak. Her hair is braided and rolled into buns that rest over each ear. She has on a gray turtleneck, tall boots, corduroys, and thick, brown-framed eyeglasses. When Hope begins to speak, her hand instinctively reaches for her mouth, covering her two missing front teeth. Hope is twenty-eight and lives in Coney Island. She was brought up as one of six children in the Fort Greene projects in Brooklyn, and she tells the class that she remembers those years as full of "love and self-development," which she received from her grandparents—"who I was raised by from day one." She never finished high school because "I started going in all directions." For unspecified reasons, she got hooked on drugs. She finally explains her reticence in the life-skills class: she doesn't like "life skills because it reminds me of group-therapy sessions, which I don't like because I don't like talking about my personal life." She also doesn't like group therapy because she endured too many sessions in overcoming her heroin habit. Her goal is to become a secretary. She lists her weaknesses as a hot temper and the need "to get confidence within myself."

Only Henry Rivera and John Hicks refused to speak. Smith seems quite pleased. "I think you know why you were asked to do this—to get confidence," he says. Looking straight at Hope Parker, he continues, "Unlike in group therapy, in life skills *you* determine what you talk about." Smith tinkers with the large TV set. Suddenly William Mason's face comes into focus. A loud cheer is followed by groans, giggles, and taunts as Howard plays back their presentations. The class members watch themselves with a mixture of awe and embarrassment. They are the stars of this show, and as the performance continues their bashfulness gives way to pride and confidence.

The class breaks for lunch and John Hicks, who has not yet been told he will be terminated as of this afternoon, agrees to talk to me privately. "I haven't been coming in here on time," he says. "I got an insufficient alarm clock to wake me up in the morning," he explains. "I sleep through nine o'clock because I have a newborn baby and I'm up at midnight every night. It won't be that way any more because now we have an efficient alarm clock. I don't know what was wrong with the old one." Proudly John mentions that recently he registered for college, that he loves his fourteen-month-old daughter, and that his wife attends York College. "I worked during the day while she went to college during the day."

"My attendance is very well," he says. "Only been absent three or four times." (He has been absent three and a half days this week alone.) He would like to get the certificate for the first ten weeks. "I would like to make the advance class," he says, "but I have to type twenty-five words a minute to make the advance class. If not, I'll go to the job site." I ask what he would like to improve. "When I take care of that punctuality problem, everything should be all right," he says. "I came here typing no words a minute. Now I'm past the halfway mark—fifteen to twenty words." He returns to the topic of punctuality: "In this new house there is no sun shining in my face like in the old apartment. So there's no sense of time. I had an alarm clock that wasn't effective. Something always went wrong with it. The other one my wife didn't set right."

Later that afternoon John Hicks received the news that he was being sent back to his job site with a city agency. Pearl Dawson, Denise Brown, Timothy Wilson, and Hope Parker are notified that they have been selected to participate in a special secretarial training program sponsored by McGraw-Hill. Two mornings a week they will attend advanced typing classes at McGraw-Hill's corporate headquarters on Sixth Avenue. Honored, each eagerly accepts.

During another life-skills class, Smith pursues the question of social conformity and racial assimilation by singling out Jerome Patterson, who began to call himself Mohammed when, in prison, he became a convert to the Nation of Islam. Smith says, "I hope I'm not being too personal, but do you think Mohammed's religion will be a problem as he pursues his vocational goals? Knowing what you know about our system, do you think we as Americans, as a society, have really matured and grown up so we're tolerant of life styles? Will a family from Middle America have trouble accepting Mohammed?"

"It depends on the individual," says William Penn, the only other member of BT-27 who has embraced the Muslim faith, and who sometimes goes by the name Akim. "If Mohammed is good, he will be accepted beyond a shadow of a doubt."

"You will have a problem, because you have two forces," Mohammed says. "More you stand up for truth, more you have the forces of falsehood."

"If you be dealing with truth, you keep going," Penn responds.

"Playing devil's advocate, I'm a little confused," Smith breaks in. "From my own experiences in the penitentiary, I'm aware of prejudice against those following the Islamic faith. Everything's fine, no hassles, as long as you went along in prison. But when they got out, Muslims encountered problems. My question is: In terms of the economic structure and the working world, what's happening with the Muslim there?"

"He'll always have problems," Leon Harris says.

"And let's be fair," Smith interjects. "Those prejudices are not just of whites. I know lots of black men prejudiced against Muslims."

John Painter agrees, saying, "Average Muslim, his co-workers will have animosity because of his religion."

Harris concurs. "A lot of people on the job no like Muslim because he speaks out," he says. "In the penitentiary, Sunni Muslims never liked because they were militant." He goes on to say that they argued with other prisoners about what they ate.

Smith says, "That same Muslim who gave me hell in the penitentiary for eating pork—guess who I saw eating pork on the street when I got out. That same Muslim."

Muslims used to call the white man "a blue-eyed devil," Penn says, but they no longer peddle that message, and yet whites are still afraid of them. "So once you say you a Muslim, they get scared," he adds. "They shouldn't, but what I'm saying is that people don't accept them as having changed. When you say Muslim on your application, first thing guy thinks is you no like whitey. You a militant."

"I heard Mohammed say he doesn't like to wear a tie," says John Barnes, who is again sitting in on the class. "But at some point we have to talk assimilation. The only way you will not have a problem is if you play the game and convince white folks you don't hate them. I play the game. I wear a tie. I come to work on time. I let the quality of my work speak for me. A tie is just something around my neck." He continues, "We tend to do the opposite—to let them know we're here!" Barnes says that's wrong, because "a person can be accepted in his lifestyle if he puts forth a conscious effort to be assimilated," and adds, "After five o'clock, I become something else. Between nine and five, what's on the inside can't be altered."

But such an effort can "take its toll on you," John Painter says, half insinuating that Barnes is an Uncle Tom, half questioning whether Barnes is not right.

Smith asks Painter, "How do you feel playing the game?"

"If the man says requirement is shirt and tie and no drinking, he's telling you the requirement before you take the job," Painter responds. "The only way I feel it's right is if you are told ahead of time."

Mohammed has another concern. "What I mean about wearing a tie, see, I come from Bed-Stuy, and in my community if you wear a tie it causes a lot of jealousy."

"Who is it you're obligated to—yourself or Bed-Stuy?" John Barnes asks.

"I'm hearing contradictory things here," Smith says. "Isn't that a form of assimilation and 'playing the game' when you wear the dress code of a community?"

"Clothes don't make it, you do," Mohammed says. "I don't like ties, 'cause I feel like I'm choking." But Mohammed has another practical problem. He is in the process of legally abandoning the name Jerome Patterson. "I can walk around calling myself Popeye," he says. "Name isn't what counts. It insults me to call myself Jerome Patterson. My mother called me Jerry. But Patterson, I don't know where it comes from." He does not know who his father was. When he was released from prison in 1979, his Muslim name and the cap that many Black Muslims wear were proud badges of honor. Nevertheless, he is convinced that they have hindered his efforts to find work. He says that prospective employers have taken just one look at his cap and his name and decided against hiring him. "They said, 'We'll call you,' " he tells the class. "I thought I had the job. They never called. My friends said, 'You should have waited until you got in there.' The name makes no difference to me, 'cause once in there I am what I am." But he knows that it makes a difference to some employers, and is torn between his convictions and his common sense.

Practical compromises are required, John Barnes says, because progress is being made by black Americans. "Harlem is no more dangerous than Madison Avenue," he asserts. "You can walk through streets and it's like an oasis. Harlem is going through a renaissance."

"It didn't look like that to me last weekend," Painter says disdainfully.

Barnes repeats the claim, and says that several friends of his have taken out loans to buy Harlem brownstones.

"You gonna put some $30,000 house on Lenox Avenue and 135th Street and some niggers gonna knock it down," Painter says.

Smith sides with Barnes, saying, "It seems to be a trend. I know that most of my friends would love to get a brownstone."

133

"People are just not gonna be intimidated any longer," Barnes adds.

"We can't move out to Long Island," Painter counters. "You let them move up to Harlem. You think that won't be a hustler's paradise?"

"Thing you got to know is economics," Barnes says. "Bankers won't pour money into a bag with a hole in it."

"They're gonna give to middle-class blacks like you, John," Painter says.

"That's right!" Barnes answers.

The thrust of Smith's argument is that there has been economic and racial progress, and that striving is worthwhile because blacks can succeed. South Philadelphia, near where he's from, is experiencing a renaissance. "Some of the blacks who lived there held two jobs in order to get out," he says. "Others, who worked equally hard, stayed behind and restored their homes. Now the area is fashionable, and they no longer want to leave."

The thrust of Painter's argument is that blacks are victimized by racism. "The difference between Harlem and South Philly is that you said people in South Philly worked hard," he says. "People in Harlem are not working. They're on welfare. They're not looking to go nowhere. The Jews came to Harlem. They left. The Italians came to Harlem. They left. The Irish came to it. They left. The blacks came to Harlem. They're still there. I'd like to see a white man move to Eighth Avenue and 116th Street. They'd look at that white man and say, 'Let's get him.' Just like it was in Queens. Black man move to Rosedale, Queens, and he gets his house bombed. Not 'cause of money. 'Cause he's black. Ain't supposed to be out here, he don't know nobody here, if he yells no one will hear him. So they rob him." Painter curses, and is quickly upbraided by William Penn, who says, "Watch your mouth. Mohammed is here."

Painter looks over at Mohammed and apologizes.

The discussion shifts to how blacks feel about whites.

"In Comstock prison, I got close to a white dude," Penn says. "Very close. He was in for a murder charge." But the friendship collided with prison custom: in the courtyard and the cafeteria, blacks were expected to gather with blacks, whites with whites, Hispanics with Hispanics. "I couldn't go over there and he couldn't come over here."

"You can only be so tight with a white boy," Painter says, explaining that if he took me to a playground in Harlem "they wouldn't hurt you," because "you was with me." He continues, "But they'd tell me and you to get out of here. They can know somebody white and like him. But as a whole they say, 'I hate white people.' "

"John, it took me a long time not to resent Jews—I learned they got it up here," says John Barnes, pointing to his head. "What we got to learn is that when a brother gets up a business on 125th Street we got to look out for him. I just love the way they run the garment district and the diamond district and the financial district."

The conversation stretches on, with opinions, resentments, random experiences, and stereotypes exchanged in a good-natured way —the way, no doubt, many whites exchange stereotypes about blacks. A white person who did not know these people might feel threatened, but their resentments and bigotries seem impersonal. (The black poet Amiri Baraka recently wrote in the *Village Voice* newspaper, "Even as I spouted ideas that could be called anti-Semitic, I did not think I hated specific Jews.") These jumbled feelings are perhaps best expressed by Willy Joe, who says, "Most black people don't like whites 'cause of past experience with slavery. We still have slavery in Pittsburgh, I heard. They have auctions for slaves. I heard this from a girl. I don't have no prejudice against no race. Whatever problems I have with somebody, I don't generalize. If I have a fight with a Chinese person, I'm just mad at that person."

BT-27
After Ten Weeks

Those who successfully complete the ten-week BT-27 course will receive a certificate and go on to a twenty-week course called advanced office practices. During the two weeks before the ten-week cutoff, a number of changes take place in BT-27. Mohammed announces that he will be married. The class is invited to the ceremony, at a Bronx church. (Only William Mason attended the wedding, which was scheduled to begin at four in the afternoon, but did not get under way until eight.) For the first time, Hope Parker volunteers to read something in the life-skills class. William Mason's brother, who has been robbed and stabbed, is taken off the critical list. His nineteen-year-old sister is arrested for fighting with a cop. Because of poor attendance and drinking problems, John Hicks and William Penn are dismissed from the training school and return to their jobs to complete their year of supported work.

On this Friday, the day the members of the class are to either receive a certificate stating that they have successfully completed ten weeks of training or be dismissed from school, only ten of them arrive on time. Smith starts by informing them that on Monday four new students will join their class, and urges them to be helpful and serve as role models.

The members of BT-27 listen, but obviously their minds are elsewhere—on their fear of failure.

"What happens to those who fail?" William Mason asks Smith.

They report back to the Wildcat operations division, Smith says, and if their Wildcat job is still open they get it back. If not, Wildcat will try to find another job for the remainder of their year of supported work.

Everyone is nervous. The class members know that after lunch today they may be rejected—may be back on the street, may go back to welfare or crime. Smith encourages their insecurity in order to enhance the worth of the ten-week certificate. Acting as if this might be the final day for all of them, he solemnly begins the morning session by asking everyone to write an essay evaluating the life-skills class. He hands out blank paper and departs. Groans and whines fill the air. Everybody is bored with these written exercises. "I just hate this class! I hate it!" Hope Parker explodes.

Many class members spend the next hour or so ignoring Smith's assignment. John Painter ponders a book of crossword puzzles. Ramon Lopez reads the sports section of the paper. Leon Harris borrows Willy Joe's backgammon set. Willy Joe sleeps. Hope Parker stares straight ahead.

When Smith returns, he asks Painter, whose pen has not touched the paper, to present his composition, and Painter ad-libs, in the voice of Howard Cosell, "Life is a big life-skills class, and when you are writing about life skills you are writing about yourself."

Smith calls on Hope Parker, who says, "Life skills to me in the last ten weeks was really hell. It reminds me of group therapy."

Gladys Miller dissents, saying, "It taught me to speak out in group discussions."

Carlos Rodriguez chimes in, saying, "I feel much better about myself."

Pearl Dawson praises the class, but says that "the class time is too long" and that the class "has a tendency to get boring." Something else is on Pearl Dawson's mind. She is disturbed by journalists and others who refer to supported workers as "ex-convicts" and "ex-welfare mothers."

But isn't she an ex-welfare mother?

"That's what the program is, but the way the words come out—it comes out cold," she says.

How should they be described?

She says they should be described as "ex-welfare mothers and ex-convicts who are trying to help themselves."

Pearl Dawson's comments trigger a discussion about a shared feeling that supported workers are victims of stereotypes.

"As far as I'm concerned, Wildcat has a bad name," Timothy Wilson says. "It's a dead end. All people who are ex-cons, when they go look for a job they're looked down upon."

Smith asks why Wildcat has a bad name.

"A lot of people on the job site are high on drugs," Wilson says, adding that Wildcat sounds like a place for wildcats.

"We don't want to be labeled," Gladys Miller says.

"For me, I like it, 'cause it takes my mind off negative things," Ramon Lopez says.

Glaring at Wilson, William Mason says that those who don't like the name Wildcat should leave.

"It doesn't have a bad name to me," says Wilson, reversing himself.

"If it's got a bad name, what are you doing here?" Leon Harris asks, echoing his friend Mason. Timothy Wilson now praises Wildcat. And Ramon Lopez, seeking to dispel bitterness, says, "I started something, and I usually don't finish things I start. So I'm proud." He looks at Howard Smith and says, "You, you're a good teacher." Looking at Wilson, he smiles and understandingly says, "Tim here is a young guy," so he should be excused if he said something foolish.

Getting back to life skills, Denise Brown says, "I became more relaxed in this atmosphere."

"I still don't dig it," Leon Harris says, and he turns to Smith and asks him to evaluate the class members.

"When I think of BT-27 in terms of evaluation, I think of the first week," Smith says. "I remember there were sometimes not enough seats to go around. Now look around." The class has shrunk from twenty-two members to fourteen now, and there are only ten people here this morning. "I remember how positive everyone sounded during the first discussion in life skills," Smith continues. "How determined they were. I think about some of the most positive statements coming from people who are no longer here." Those, he says, were people who couldn't cope with the stress of organized life: the regulations, coming to work on time, the orders from supervisors. Turning Harris' question around, Smith mentions that eight members of the class—more than a third of those enrolled in the Wildcat program to date—have already been dismissed, and asks, "Why do you think a large percentage of the class dropped by the wayside?"

"They really didn't want to come to school," Harris says. "They felt more comfortable at the job site."

Why? Because it was a habit?

"It was comfortable," Harris says. "Maybe some were able to get away with things there they can't do here."

"I feel that a good percentage come here who are not serious," Timothy Wilson says. "They don't want to change. They couldn't deal with coming to school, and a lot of people had a defeatist attitude. Maybe they could do it, but they copped out. I said, 'Me, I'm going to make it.' A lot of people wanted to hang out at lunch break and smoke dope."

Smith asks why the eight people who left the training center did not resign but waited to be dismissed.

"A lot of people like to feed themselves rationales," Wilson says.

"I feel if you can't make it here, you can't make it outside," Mason says.

"Bill expressed our philosophy," Smith says. "If you can't make it here, you can't make it outside. We know that, no matter how good the class, if you can't get punctuality and attendance together you won't make it outside. Outside, you're always going to have to deal with something. It may be personality problems or personal problems. Do you always stay home every time you feel a cold coming on? Out there in the real world, that doesn't work."

Maybe the individual lacks skills, Ramon Lopez says, and is "used to so many years of laying up and doing nothing." He goes on, "Maybe coming here and sitting here, he can't cope with it. He's not used to doing something. He doesn't have a routine of doing things as other natural people do who have done it all the time."

Smith is intent on driving home a point. If you don't like the situation here, he asks, how do you get out?

"Go to Sally," Harris says, referring to Sally Grueskin.

"But I got a problem with that," Smith says. "It's like I can't deal with it. It's almost like saying, 'I can't make it.' What's my way out?"

Talk to a social worker, Rodriguez suggests.

"Okay, he wants to know what I want out of life," Smith says. "I tell him, 'Man, I need a little time to get my thing together.' He takes twenty minutes. He tells me how important confidence is, to talk to myself."

"You need a psychiatrist!" suggests Ramon Lopez.

"He really doesn't want it," Leon Harris observes.

"Why does he have a problem saying, 'I really don't want it?' " Smith asks.

"There's nothing left," says Gladys Miller. "He has trouble admitting he doesn't want something."

Harris says, "It's like saying you acted lies."

"It's their image," says Henry Rivera, making a rare observation.

"I know a lot of people say they want to get off welfare and get a job," Harris says. "But you never hear of them going for a job."

"I have a brother like that," Hope Parker says. "He says he wants a job. But he refuses to go out there and skimp and scrub to get it. I say, 'What you expect to get?' He says, 'I ain't working for no $105 a week.' I say, 'You ain't getting nothing for nothing.' "

"People give up," Mason says.

Smith asks Willy Joe for an opinion.

"I'm tired," Joe says, lifting his head slowly from the table. "I didn't get much rest last night. I haven't been here. My head's somewhere else."

Smith persists, again asking Joe why people give up.

"It could be because personal problems keep holding them back," Joe says.

Smith asks if alcohol has been a problem in BT-27.

"Yes," Wilson says.

"Marijuana, too," Lopez adds.

"I wouldn't say alcohol or marijuana," Mason says. "I would say it is the individual himself."

"The individual can make excuses, but his problems are really his own fault," Lopez agrees.

"We often lose fifty percent of our classes, but we've never discontinued a class," Smith says. "Once we had a class where a hundred percent went on. Once a class got together for one person who was shaky and applied peer pressure."

"It happened here," Harris says, glancing toward Mason. "It happened to me right here." Harris and Mason slap each other's palms, classmates smile, and Smith picks up a stack of graded evaluations from their teachers to distribute. He asks them to study the grades and return from lunch promptly at two o'clock.

Willy Joe stays behind, eyes fixed on the grade he received in typing—a failing grade.

I ask if the grade is a fair one.

"She's right," he says of the typing teacher. He admits that his typing speed dropped from twenty-one words a minute to fourteen because he wasn't concentrating.

Why? And where were his thoughts when Smith called on him in class?

"Last night I had an argument with my old lady," he says. "I was deciding whether we should split up, 'cause for the nine months we're together it doesn't seem like she really learn anything or want to do anything. I told her I can't deal with it any more. I'm putting too much energy into it, and nothing succeeds." He's convinced that he won't receive a diploma this afternoon.

Now twenty-four, Willy Joe has been on drugs, in jail, on welfare; he has bounced from job to job; he has a son he'd like to see who lives somewhere in Trenton, and a woman at home he no longer wants to see. Outwardly, Joe is a warm, considerate person. He always offers classmates the thin black briefcase containing his backgammon set. He borrows a cheap ballpoint pen one day and goes out of his way to return it the next. He is unfailingly polite. It is hard to imagine that he once prowled city streets mugging people, sticking a gun in their

140

face. "I used to be very wild, a cold person," he says. "If something occurred I didn't like, I'd react."

Did he commit violence?

"Yes. I didn't care."

At the time, did he feel remorse?

"No, I didn't care. I didn't have feelings about nothing." But deep down, he says, he and the people he was hanging around with had a conscience. They acted cold, he says, to cover up. "They feel like they're a man already, 'cause they going out and getting it. They feel like a man isn't supposed to cry. If they feel something, they hide it. They live in a—what do you call it?—a fantasy world. These pictures that come out, like *Superfly*. They go out and check it out. Every young kid looking for his role model." Welfare, which he was forced to go on after he was released from prison, helped rob Joe of self-confidence. "I didn't want to get on welfare," he says. "'Cause you lose your integrity on welfare. You can't move if you want to."

Now, looking down at the floor, Joe says simply, "I just feel crushed." He has been through several training programs. "I didn't keep practicing the knowledge I learned in the programs, so now I see myself as a failure," he says. "It seems like all the things I learned is wasted. I think about it constantly. In a way, it has to do with lack of confidence." Most of all, he thinks about the pressure at home. "It affects my ability to do better," he says. "I'm constantly thinking about the pressure of my old lady. She don't want to leave, and she knows she's making me unhappy." He says that, at nineteen, she doesn't have a job, doesn't comb her hair, often doesn't wash, and wants only to be with Willy. "I would like to have something motivate me rather than pull me down," he says. "She not doing anything for me to keep me motivated. When I bring my friends over, my old lady gives them the wrong impression. She makes me look bad. We argue. She doesn't want me to have friends. Her whole world is surrounded by me. She don't want to do nothing. I'm like her god. I don't want to be no dictator. You don't need nobody with you that you got to help when you got to help yourself, too. I feel bad all the time because of that. I still has a daughter by her and a son by another woman. I haven't seen my son yet." The son's mother, who gave birth while Joe was in prison, sent him her address, but he lost it. His daughter stays mostly with her mother's mother. "I haven't seen her in a while—two or three weeks," he says. He thinks his daughter wants to be with Daddy. "She miss me," he says. "She was telling her mother she wants to come and see Daddy. I don't want her to see me and my lady arguing and think that's what it's about." Still, he's burdened with the thought that staying with her grandmother may be worse for his daughter. The grandmother drinks—"three pints a day," he says. "She doesn't want to do anything for herself. She has a man coming to stay with her from time to time. She's on welfare, and she's comfortable with it."

Willy Joe wants to succeed at Wildcat, but he can't shake the pressure from his indolent "old lady," or the concern about a daughter who is in the care of an alcoholic, or the guilt about a son somewhere in New Jersey who does not know him, just as Willy did not know his own father, or the anxiety that he will be mugged, again, on his way home at night, or the agony that once more he may fail.

As for Wildcat, he says, "This thing here really has nothing to do with what I want to do," explaining that he would like a job in the Postal Service or as a cook. "I didn't really know what this was about when I came here"—on the recommendation of a parole officer. Still, the program does matter some to him. "I want to pass just for the satisfaction of completing something," he says.

After lunch, the members of BT-27 file back into the classroom, engaging in nervous chatter while Smith, Sally Grueskin, and Ann Marie DiNapoli, the academic-affairs manager, who like Sally Grueskin is white, hold court in a tiny conference room down the hall.

The first to be summoned to the conference room is William Mason, who is greeted with warm words from Sally Grueskin: "You are promoted to the advanced class."

This should have been no surprise to Mason. He is easily the best male student in class, a stabilizing, mature influence on others in life skills. Mason emits a loud sigh of relief.

Harris follows, and returns to the classroom moments later sporting a big smile. He announces proudly, "I made it!" and bows to a round of applause.

Hope Parker is shaking as she enters the conference room. Sally Grueskin immediately puts her at her ease by proclaiming her "the best typist in the class," and adding, "Don't rest until you've typed sixty words a minute." After praising her abilities, Sally Grueskin says that her attendance "is a problem," as is her lack of patience.

"I know I have a temper," Hope Parker admits, covering her two missing front teeth as she half smiles. She gets her certificate.

Pearl Dawson is next, and Sally Grueskin tells her, "You're promoted. Did you have any doubt?"

"Nope," Pearl Dawson says matter-of-factly. But her wet eyes suggest otherwise, and so do her next words. "I need this," she says, trembling. "I really need this."

To outward appearances, John Painter is the least affected. He struts into the room and asks, "Gas chamber or electric chair?"

"I'm going to put you at ease and say you're going on to the next class," Sally Grueskin says. Painter grins. She sternly continues, "There were a lot of reservations." "*Are* a lot of reservations," corrects John.

"English is not one of them," Ann Marie jokes.

"The problem is not academic," Sally Grueskin continues. "It can't be what it's been like. The business of wearing jeans or coming late from lunch or coming in high. Now's the time to change patterns if you want a good job. So we're making this acceptance conditional." For the next four weeks, Painter will be on probation. Every Friday the Wildcat supervisors will review his performance.

As Painter is told this, his eyes narrow into slits; he seems to be listening intently. Sally Grueskin then hands him a certificate and he rolls it up and says, "This ain't nothing compared to the one I'm gonna get after the twenty-week course. Let me go collect money. I laid twenty to one I was gonna make it!"

Grueskin, Smith, and DiNapoli are still smiling when Denise Brown enters the room. She had the best attendance of BT-27, Miss Grueskin tells her, and is an outstanding student.

Wearing a chador, Mohammed's wife-to-be sits nearby as he enters the conference room. "It was not a cut-and-dried, clear decision," Sally Grueskin tells him, "but we're promoting you to the advanced class." Their reservations had to do with attendance, punctuality, and Mohammed's preoccupation with Islam. "There were times you didn't call in," Grueskin says. "You have to understand that I can't accept the excuse that you slept through. Because you were getting married, we took that into consideration. But I'm not sure an employer would."

Ann Marie DiNapoli warns Mohammed that he must work to improve his math. Smith compliments him for participating more in life skills lately and polishing his typing skills. Mohammed is told that he will be on four weeks' probation.

Carlos Rodriguez and William Block, who was absent this morning, are promoted. Henry Rivera, perhaps sensing that he was one of two students who would be sent back to their jobs, told his friend Ramon Lopez that he was dropping out. And Lopez, so nervous that he drank his way through lunch, wobbles into the conference room. "Have a seat," Sally Grueskin says solicitously.

"No, that's all right," Lopez says, eyes cast downward, pulling on his fingers.

"You're promoted," Miss Grueskin announces.

Lopez gulps audibly.

"You've been extremely dependable and made real progress," she says.

"That's nice to hear," Lopez says. "I'm like a kid all the time. Ever since I was a kid, I told my mom I didn't want to go to school. I didn't want to go through torture. I never tell no one about my good points. I tell them about my misfortune. But I like this. My friend Henry didn't come in. I'll miss him. But I'm used to being by myself."

Gladys Miller arrives, fanning herself with one hand. Sally Grueskin tells her that she is promoted, and says, "It matters a lot that you showed you cared in the last two weeks." Gladys Miller began removing her ever-present stocking cap in class in compliance with regulations, and brought her typing speed up to twenty-five words a minute. She says "Wow!" as she receives the certificate.

Timothy Wilson kisses his, moving in and out of the room quickly.

A pall falls over the room as they come to Willy Joe's name. Joe is to be sent back to his job site. The door still closed, Sally Grueskin asks if Smith would prefer to do the talking. His hands shaking, Smith says, "This is difficult."

I asked him earlier that day why Joe would fail and others with equally bad attendance and punctuality would pass, and Smith replied, "That's the problem I always have. When I go to Sally to argue —and we started two weeks ago—and she asks 'Why should he stay?' the only thing I could come up with was that Joe is a nice guy. Nothing more. He's apathetic. With Mohammed or Painter or other students, if they come in at ten o'clock they make an effort to come up with an excuse. I say to him, 'Late again, Joe.' And he says, 'Yeah, I was up late again.' Then he smiles. You can't keep people here just because they're nice guys." Smith admitted that the Wildcat administrators bend the attendance and other rules. "We're talking about people who just got released from the penitentiary," he said. "The type of behavior changes you're talking about are unrealistic to expect in ten weeks. Our people need time." But time was not Willy Joe's problem, he said. Motivation was. "Joe? He won't respond. It's like ho-hum, like he really doesn't care. Now, what bothers me is, is that a true evaluation? Is that the real Joe?"

The staff reluctantly concluded that it was the real Joe. A belief that their task is not to support people permanently but to prepare individuals to make it on their own led them to make their decision. "He didn't do well in any areas," Sally Grueskin says, convinced that they had no choice.

The door opens, and Willy Joe enters in a long, tattered black overcoat with a narrow fur collar, his hands jammed into the pockets. His mood appears glum as he takes a seat.

"Considering your evaluation in all three areas of training, I'm really sorry to tell you we can't pass you on to the advanced class," Smith begins. He says that Joe's math is weak, and Joe nods agreement. "Your life-skills work is good, but not your attendance." Joe nods again. "Finally, your typing is weak." Joe makes it easier by nodding again. "And yet, despite all that, all three of us really agonized over Willy Joe. A really nice guy. But that's not enough. We feel bad about it."

"I do, too," Joe says. "I just have to work on it."

"There's a way of pushing a little more if you want something," Sally Grueskin says, handing Joe a certificate proving that he attended the class at the training center for ten weeks. He stands up, offers his sad smile as he shakes hands with each of them, and is told by Sally Grueskin that he should report Monday morning to Wildcat's main headquarters, at 660 First Avenue, to see if his old supported-work job is still available.

"Well, better luck next time," Joe says, passively but sincerely. "Everybody have a good weekend."

Joe shuts the door and does not return to the classroom, heading instead for the elevator. "I told everybody it was going to happen," he says to me. Failure is no longer a surprise to Willy. Still, as the elevator arrives, he says, "I wanted the satisfaction of knowing that I would be able to continue, even if this was not the thing I wanted to do. It would be good for me to be asked to go on."

Who Is to Blame, the System or the Individual?

The four new students are to join the class today, but only two are present. (The other two arrive after the morning break.) As an initiation rite, Smith asks them to sketch on a piece of paper the highlights of their lives. By way of demonstration, he shows them a sketch of a Liberty Bell with the date "1942" written inside and, just below that, a large hypodermic needle. He asks Herbert Washington, one of the two, to interpret the drawing. Washington, a thin black man with a neatly trimmed, graying beard and mustache, guesses that the person was born in Philadelphia in 1942 and at some point became addicted to heroin. Smith stuns Washington by announcing that the drawing depicts his own life.

The tactic is a great seducer, and moments later Washington accepts Smith's offer to stand before the class and explain his own drawing. He is about six feet two, wears an emerald-green sweater with matching green corduroy pants and a pale-green knit cap, and has a giant gray scarf flung once around his neck and stretching down to his waist. Washington speaks flawless English. The drawing begins with the year 1933, when he was born. He grew up in Harlem, with his parents and a sister; they moved to Brooklyn when he was seven. When he was nine, his father died. Washington finished the eleventh grade at Boys High, but "I dropped out in the last year and took up in the streets," he says. "I was making money in the streets." Determined to straighten out, he married in 1961 and later migrated to Canada, where he worked as an office file clerk. Obviously talented, he rose to become the manager of the entire office. The next six years, he says, were the best of his life. But in 1970—the year is prominently printed on the page—his marriage dissolved. Depressed, Washington returned to New York. He started running numbers, and eventually became a numbers banker. "I could count well, so I was making $200 to $300 a day as a numbers banker," he says. He was arrested and sent to prison for four months. He hated prison, and when he was released he became "street-wise," he says. "I promised myself I wouldn't be back in prison. I gave police respect. I gave them the whole block." He also became addicted to heroin. The streets became his home, and his nemesis: he says that he was accidentally shot (but does not explain how) four times in the right leg—an injury that still prevents him from standing for prolonged periods. His last steady job was the one in Canada that ended ten years ago. Over the past three years, he has held no job longer than four months. Washington's autobiographical sketch includes a large question mark, which he explains this way: "I'm still on the streets. The question mark is still there. If I can find the answer in Wildcat, I'll be appreciative."

Aubrey Powers rises and displays his sketch. He is a light-skinned black man with short hair and a neat beard; he wears a gray crewneck sweater slipped over a button-down white shirt, and blue slacks. His good looks are marred only by a two-inch scar under one eye. With a suit, a tie, and a briefcase, Powers could pass for a successful executive. Wildcat records show that he has a B.A. from Queens College, has completed eighteen credits toward a master's degree, and in the early seventies worked for the city government as an assistant borough coordinator of the Urban Corps. When he speaks, another Powers unfolds. Blankly staring straight ahead, he begins by saying that he was born in Brooklyn in 1943. "I've lived inwardly, always running from people," he continues. "I've tried hard at some things. When I didn't want to do no more, I didn't. I'm a sick individual. Before 1974, I was a nice guy. After 1974, I was a fugitive." Powers' sketch resembles a Jackson Pollock painting: a mass of tangled lines—in his case, names, schools, projects, dollar signs, the word "dignity." His life story is confusing, and the somnolent, sometimes incoherent manner in which Powers explains it baffles the class. "I have a style built from punishment," he says. "I can identify with punishment. I have a lot of creativity, but it's suppressed right now. I'm prideful, but I'm full of shame." The class members begin to glance about at one another, not quite sure whether he is serious or joking. When they realize that this is no joke, several cover their mouths to smother their laughter.

"I left out a lot, because I don't like laughter," Powers says.

"We're all adults, and any time you want to express yourself we're not about to laugh," William Mason says.

Powers does not respond. He continues, "I always had trouble in school." Teachers would strike him with rulers, wash his mouth out with soap, order him to a corner with a dunce cap, he says. "I've been in lots of programs. I don't like New York. I deal in metaphysical things."

Smith asks what Powers meant when he said punishment influenced him.

"I used to love the five-cent paper," Powers says. "Now everybody is talking about rebuilding New York. To me, I had to develop an understanding of who I was. I wondered how to encourage myself, and I realized I'd have to eat someone's heart. To deal with pain is a pleasure. This last war proved it."

Timothy Wilson asks why Powers feels he has nothing to offer.

"I enjoy people," Powers says. "But right now—see, I went to college, right? And I graduated. For me, the only thing to do was go on to graduate school. I cut my own throat. I have amnesia, is how I said it. Like you, I sound conservative. But I don't believe that too much. The world is somebody else."

"I think what Powers is trying to say is that we all have different ways of dealing with life," Smith says. "All he's saying is that he sees these problems in terms of pain."

Powers concurs. "You can get some growth out of pain," he says.

As the class takes its break it takes a moment to shake off the memory of Powers' bizarre behavior. Aubrey is clearly a traumatized individual. At some point his mind snapped. Psychologists do not generalize about why this happens or at what point in life someone becomes traumatized. They say it varies from individual to individual. Some are born poor, some rich. Some members of the underclass are born with psychological problems; some become traumatized while very young. For Aubrey it seems to have happened in adulthood. Why a mind snaps is often not clear: the pressures of poverty, perhaps, or family background, a lack of love, a single crushing experience, inherited or physical deficiencies. According to Aubrey's original Wildcat psychological profile, "sexual conflict" was "at the root of his problems." He was judged to be paranoid.

Another person members of BT-27 sometimes laughed at is Andrei Williams, the Wildcat maintenance man, who is often drunk or high when he barges into class sessions to remove trash. During the break Andrei talks eagerly about his life. Twenty-six, he has long wisps of black hair protruding unevenly from his chin and upper lip, and for the past three and a half years has been employed by Wildcat. His work uniform consists of a faded University of Hartford T-shirt, jeans, thick-soled work shoes, and a black knit cap. "I come from the Fort Greene projects," Williams says. "But the friends I had, if you weren't with it then you was a target to be robbed. To protect yourself and family you had to become part of everything—part of the drug scene, part of stealing. You had to become *one of*. If you weren't *one of*, you'd get taken off. That was like the scene in charge of everything. You wouldn't go to the police and blame me—I have fifty-five friends ready to blame you. And then at fourteen, fifteen, you wasn't going nowhere."

Williams has been to prison several times for assault, robbery, and drug possession. Today, with a wife and four kids, he says he's straightened out. Like Willy Joe, he lives in the East New York section of Brooklyn. Of the street criminals who mugged Willy, he says, "They don't bother me. I know a lot of them from jail. I just want me a steady job where I can support my family." His goal in life is a simple one: "I just want a maintenance job. I'm not asking to be president of the United States or senator. I've been doing it so long that I enjoy maintenance work. I enjoy painting a wall and seeing it nice without fingerprints, and knowing you did it. You strip a floor and put wax down and buff it and shine it so you can see your face in it and people say, 'Oh, Andrei, looks good!' And I feel good. I know I did my best."

After the morning break, Smith asks the new students what Wildcat job they held before they came to the training center. Michael Mathews, who arrived after the break, says he was employed in the reproduction-and-collating department of the city's Human Resources Administration. The job was all right he says, but he resented the fact that CETA and civil-service workers who did the same work were paid more. Most of all, he resented the lack of job security.

"None of us felt secure," Washington agrees.

That's not unusual, Smith says, trying to provide a larger context. "I don't have job security for the future. It's a very subjective thing. If the federal government stops funding Wildcat, I'm out of a job, too."

"Ever a time ten years ago where you felt, if I had a job like that I'd be secure?" John Painter asks.

"I was thrilled when I got a job as a messenger," says Smith, and he goes on to argue that insecurity and frustration are normal, and not insurmountable obstacles in the path to success. Like the people in his class, he was on the streets, unemployed, on drugs, on welfare, and in prison. And today he confronts new frustrations. He says that he's underpaid and that the training center is understaffed. There are personal frustrations, too. He says he procrastinates too much and does not budget money properly. Then he adds, "I have to overcome my fear of being responsible to a female. Twice I've been engaged, and twice I've reneged."

"Attaboy, champ!" John Painter calls out.

"Marriage is a rewarding experience," Smith says. "But it can be hell. I'm going to have to change the attitude I have. I'm just afraid." Fear is normal, he repeats. "You'd never believe it if you'd seen me a few years ago that I'd be up here now. The key thing—more than money and a raise—is job satisfaction. And I have job satisfaction. And that's who I am."

Michael Mathews is invited up front. He is a square-jawed, goateed, ebony-skinned man with a smooth manner, dressed in well-tailored dark slacks and a beige turtleneck. He was born in the Bronx in 1949, he says, and he and a sister were raised in part by their mother, a domestic worker, and in part by relatives in twelve different states. His last full-time job was in 1970–71, as a payroll clerk for the New York Telephone Company. He spent much of the past ten years at the upstate Auburn Correctional Facility, for armed robbery and peddling drugs, and he earned a high-school-equivalency diploma there. He was an addict for several years. Now he hopes to learn hotel-and-motel management, in order to use his "ability to remember names and make people feel at home."

The fourth new recruit, Ivy Ford, explains that she was late because of a death in the family. She is just under five feet tall, a plump, cocoa-skinned woman of twenty-nine who parts her Afro in the middle. She has on large, circular earrings, jeans, and a bulky dark sweater. She says she was one of eight children born in White Plains, and her family moved to Bedford-Stuyvesant when she was a teenager. There she slipped into the wrong circles, dropped out of school in the eleventh grade, messed around with drugs, was arrested for a felony (she does not say what), and at the age of seventeen was sent to prison for a year. When she got out of prison, she got hooked on heroin. Once she was shot in the leg. "I was so high that I didn't notice," she says. She moved from job to job, entered a variety of training programs, and in 1976 met Howard Smith when she worked briefly as a messenger in a Wildcat job. She kept moving, kept hustling, kept shooting heroin. Finally she entered a methadone treatment program. She says she has now reduced her daily intake from a hundred milligrams of methadone to five. "In October of 1979," she says, "I went back to Wildcat and started all over again." Her hope is to become a computer operator or analyst.

Smith compliments Ivy Ford and the others on their presentations.

The class members begin to chatter and laugh among themselves as he inspects some papers. Suddenly, Aubrey Powers barks, "I'm for humor, but there's too much talk, too much laughing in class."

"Laughing is healthy," Herbert Washington says.

"I'm not looking for no contradiction, either!" Powers says. The other members of the class shrug and exchange glances. After a moment of incredulous silence, the class breaks for lunch.

Although members of BT-27 have at times taken advantage of society, many are baffled by and fearful of organized society. To ease this fear and acquaint them with the world of work, Howard Smith employs such tools as *Ten Occupational Fields,* a student manual explaining various types of jobs and the qualifications needed for them. He also uses other booklets prepared by Winthrop R. Adkins, director of the Life Skills Education Project at Teachers College, Columbia University, including *Keeping My Job: Habits That Help* and *The Job Interview: How to Be Effective.*

Howard also uses tape-recorded playlets performed by actors. In one of these, the main character, whose name is Cliff, is out of work and out of sorts. Like many members of BT-27, Cliff has few skills, little work experience, and even less self-confidence. His wife nags him to look for a job, so Cliff finally makes an appointment to interview for a good-paying blue-collar position. That morning the wife inspects Cliff and coaches him on the way out the door. Cliff is a nervous wreck. The interviewer asks Cliff what he wants to do. Cliff doesn't know. Yet for some reason the interviewer offers Cliff the job. Cliff impulsively says no.

Hurrying from the interview, Cliff realizes what he has done. He was afraid to take that job; now he is afraid of his wife. Cliff walks aimlessly about for the next several hours, hoping to come up with a good excuse, but when he gets home, he tells his wife the truth. Angrily she asks how he could turn down such a job. How can they pay bills? What the hell *does* he want to do, anyway? Cliff doesn't know.

Howard Smith flicks off the tape recorder, turns to the class, and asks, "What do you think was on his mind?"

"I think he was getting ready to throw a brick," says Michael Mathews. "The pressure was building up."

"Have you ever been offered a job and turned it down?" Smith asks.

"I feel like any given time if I can handle the job offered I'll take it," William Mason says.

"He didn't know what was available out there," Smith points out.

"Didn't know what his skills were or what he wanted to do. In other words, Cliff did not know the occupational fields, which is what we're doing now." Howard asks why Cliff turned down a good-paying job when he needed one.

"He wanted something better," says Denise Brown.

"But did he know what he wanted?" Smith asks.

"He wanted a change of scenery," Ramon Lopez suggests.

When Cliff comes home, Smith says, "What important questions does his wife ask him? She said, 'What about bills?' He said, 'What about me?' She said, 'What do you want to do?' He said, 'I don't know.' Any of you ever feel that way? I know I did."

"I used to feel that way before I became a Muslim," says Mohammed.

What adjectives would you use to describe that feeling?

"Blue," Gladys Miller volunteers.

"Frustrating," Denise Brown offers.

"Perplexing. Disillusioned," Pearl Dawson puts in.

"Broke," says Ramon Lopez.

What do those words mean? Smith asks.

"You want it," says Pearl, "but you don't know what to do."

Any other adjectives?

"Mad. Angry," says Ramon Lopez.

"How about this one—empty, lost?" counters Howard. "I think we've all felt this at one time or another. Now if this condition lasts too long, how do people go about dealing with it?"

"Sometimes in the morning when I have to get up and it's cold," Gladys Miller says, "I have to stroke myself. I take a joint."

"Take it out on the family," Pearl Dawson offers.

"They let it out on someone else," says Mohammed. "Take, for example, myself. I didn't have to steal nothing. But my mother would do something to me and I'd go out there and do crazy things just to let out frustration in myself. To feel better, I'd do badder and badder things."

"I became withdrawn, myself," says Denise Brown. "I just gave up for a while. I withdrew. I just didn't want to do anything."

"You say, 'It's not my fault,'" Gladys Miller says. "Blame someone else."

Who?

"The system," Ramon Lopez says.

This is just the kind of response Howard Smith's life-skills class seeks to deter. Smith thinks that as long as members of the underclass feel victimized by society, they have an excuse to do nothing. What Smith and Wildcat and, indeed, the national supported-work experiment, seek to do is to induce trainees to accept the responsibility for their own fate.

I thought about this later in the week while listening to New York Civil Court Judge Bruce M. Wright address an assembly at Manhattan's Martin Luther King, Jr., High School. At a time when many civil-rights leaders seem to have lowered their voices, Bruce Wright is one black leader who still asserts loudly that white society is racist. Judge Wright, whose policies on bail and sentencing have led critics to call him "Turn-'em-loose Bruce," firmly maintains that racism predetermines where most American blacks wind up.

A striking man of about sixty, Wright has the taut body of a wrestler and the closely cropped hair, tailored blue suit, polka-dot tie, pinched collar, and horn-rimmed glasses of a staid jurist. On this particular day his thundering voice and grave mien command the attention of several hundred students, most of them black and Hispanic, who gather in the school auditorium. "My assumption is that you know the difference between law and injustice," he opens, skipping the usual pleasantries. "I come not to discuss law but injustice. . . . Any black person in America who is not paranoid is sick. You are my fellow inmates of black skin. You are on a permanent blacklist. If you want to make it you have to be like Avis—try harder." Wright mentions two incidents in his own life that confirmed his belief in the intractability of white racism. The first came in the 1950s when he visited McGeorge Bundy, then the dean of the faculty at Yale, and "was referred to the freight elevator." The second occurred while he was attending a cocktail party on the East Side of Manhattan. A partner in the prestigious law firm of Lord Day & Lord "came over and put his hand on my arm and said, 'You know, if we ever have slavery again in this country, I'd like to own you.' " Wright draws the moral: "So we are always an endangered species. No matter what kind of jobs we have." He catalogues instances of police brutality. "People ask me why I'm angry," he says. "I have four black sons. That's reason enough to be angry."

Paraphrasing Alexis de Tocqueville, who believed the nobility of America was rooted in its laws, Wright tells the students that he believes we have too many laws today. He is particularly concerned with New York State's new juvenile justice law. "Now we can bring thirteen-, fourteen-, and fifteen-year-old children and send them to adult jails"—the same jails, he points out, that fail to reform adults. "People say I have allowed murderers, pimps, prostitutes, and muggers to go free. Not true. I now have been burglarized eight times and subjected to threatening notes, some from cops. Every year at

153

Christmas time I get a box from Tiffany's filled with dog shit. They don't know I can't smell. I know there are depraved, wicked people out there on the street, and we're in danger of them as well."

But those relatively few "wicked" people do not shake Judge Wright's deep conviction that racism is responsible for the lives full of pain led by many blacks and Hispanics. Rapidly he offers the following evidence:

· Eighty-five to 90 percent of all defendants are black or Hispanic, and they receive harsher sentences than whites committing the same crimes.

· An unnamed white judge upbraided a defendant in open court by shouting, "How's he going to be rehabilitated when he lives with a colored woman?"

· "This Christian country, if you will, owned blacks as property," Wright says. "George Bernard Shaw said, 'America is the only country in the world to suffer a decline and fall of civilization without having a civilization'—and it's true." When Mohandas K. Gandhi was asked why he did not become a Christian, he said, "I would, except for those who are."

· At the age of fifteen Wright won a scholarship to Princeton. The president of the university, surprised to find that Wright was black, exclaimed, "'Professor Goldstein didn't tell us you were *colored* when he arranged your scholarship.'"

· Federal Judge Constance Baker Motley, a black woman, once said that in twenty years on the bench she never suffered discrimination. Wright comments wryly, "And I wondered what she had to drink that day."

The thrust of Wright's message is that the students should be angry, should focus on white society as the enemy. He believes that pride and achievement will emerge from anger and defiance. Wright would agree with Frances Fox Piven and Richard A. Cloward when they write in *Poor People's Movements* that the rising crime rate and disorder of the sixties show "that old patterns of servile conformity were shattered; the trauma and anger of an oppressed people not only had been released, but had been turned against the social structure." Wright tells the story of Hannibal, a black slave in ancient Rome who was buried neck deep in the Coliseum. Only the slave's head could be seen by the spectators. A ferocious lion was then released from its cage. The animal circled Hannibal, finally leaping at him. By quickly moving his head, Hannibal escaped the lion's jaws; as the lion turned to resume the attack, Hannibal reached up and bit off the animal's testicles. Wright delivers the punch line: "Fifty thousand Romans rose in the arena and yelled, 'Fight fair, nigger!' So much for fairness. So as you go through life keep in mind that there is no fairness."

Judge Wright concludes by urging the students to study hard, to become professionals—pilots and doctors and lawyers—and above all, to register to vote. "I leave you with this piece of graffiti, and I hope it's burned into your mind: the graffiti on the wall of my courthouse says, 'Kill the niggers, the spicks and the Jews first.'"

Applause fills the auditorium. During the question-and-answer period that follows, Wright more fully explains his views. One student asks what deterrent against crime would exist without jails. "Unless the country is prepared to redistribute wealth," Wright says, "there will be redistribution through larceny." He insists that the resources are there: "A country that says it has no money and yet has the nerve to offer $400 million to Pakistan" is not broke.

A student asks about the job market. "If you read the classified section of the *Times* every Sunday," he answers, "there are thousands of jobs. People lack the skills." He suggests that this is not the fault of individuals but of the system. Many qualified blacks and Hispanics don't get those jobs because they are not trusted, he says. And: "It is the lack of trust that brings on recidivism."

He is asked if he is a revolutionary, an opponent of capitalism? "It's the only system of government I know," he says. "I'm not a revolutionary. I'm an arch Tory. I didn't blow up the Jefferson Memorial because he kept slaves. I just call it to your attention—in case *you* want to be a revolutionary."

Outside, a white man emerged from the auditorium and passed a cluster of black students, who glared hard at him. The man continued to walk briskly along the snow-covered sidewalk. Soon snowballs crashed all about him, none thrown very hard but all aimed at him. The man turned and saw the students snickering. Were they just kids being kids? Or were they acting out the hostility it could be said Judge Wright condoned?

Today, Judge Wright's pessimistic views are challenged by an array of minority leaders. The Black Muslims, who used to preach that the "white devil" was to blame for the condition of people of color around the world, now urge people to accept responsibility for their own lives, to become self-reliant. Before he was assassinated, Malcolm X, who first popularized the "white devil" phrase, wrote: "I have learned that not all white people are racists." Before he was murdered in 1968, Dr. Martin Luther King, Jr., was shifting the focus of his efforts from civil rights to economics. "What good is it to be allowed to eat in a restaurant," he asked, "if you can't afford a hamburger?" King believed that society had an obligation to provide jobs as a matter of right. Today many minority leaders, particularly those who work at the community level, focus not just on economics and government assistance but on self-help as well. The Reverend Jesse Jackson, head of the Chicago-based Operation PUSH, says that "self-mastery is a revolutionary concept" and that "nobody can save us from us for us but us." Self-help is embraced not just by Howard Smith, Jesse Jackson, and the Muslims but also by drug-free therapeutic centers, Alcoholics Anonymous, Jehovah's Witnesses, est, and the sponsors and supervisors of supported work, among others.

This emphasis on self-help is more cyclical than new. At the turn of the century, for instance, go-slow integrationist Booker T. Washington and black nationalist Marcus Garvey beseeched their followers to become more self-reliant and economically independent. They did not agree on means and goals—Washington spoke of "privileges" and dreamed of an integrated society, while Garvey spoke of "rights" and dreamed of a back-to-Africa movement—but they both tried to promote self-help. Both Garvey and Washington believed that a sense of "victimization" can retard a person's ability to help himself, can become an excuse to surrender to frustration and adversity, can become another form of dependency. To succeed, individuals need to have *faith*—in themselves, in their future, in society. If they believe they will be put down due to the color of their skin or to the social class they belong to, they will have less incentive to strive, to struggle, to believe.

Howard Smith does not believe that people like Bruce Wright desire to see blacks wallowing in self-pity; he does believe that self-pity can be one unintended by-product of speeches like Wright's. "I used to say, 'The devil made me do it,'" says Howard Smith, "and the Black Panthers and the Muslims used to say the white man was the devil." But Howard says he has come to believe "man is responsible for his actions. And I am not apologizing for the white man or the inequities of our system. We are still victimized." He admits a "conflict" between "how much of it is due to a lack of individual responsibility and how much is attributed to the system and prejudice."

Of course, Howard Smith's audience is small. His obligation is to a handful of individuals attending the life-skills class. He wants to influence his students, not the federal government or the larger society. And of the individuals he teaches, Smith says: "You can actually get comfortable blaming whitey or the system for the discrimination and racism that has gone on for four hundred years. If you're not careful it can become a convenience. . . . I'm not saying the reason is not valid. What I'm saying is that I don't see any redemption in going through life blaming whitey. And yet I see so many of the brothers and sisters doing just that." Ford Foundation President Frank Thomas, who worked with ghetto kids when he was head of the Bedford-Stuyvesant Redevelopment Corporation, says, "As soon as you help a youngster orient his head to believe the problem is external and therefore that there is no obligation to reorient their behavior, you've done them a disservice. The better message is to tell them they don't know their own limits."

Civil-rights leaders, in contrast, speak to a broad audience and urge governmental action. They argue that racism and, to a lesser extent, economic policy are the root causes of the underclass. Consequently, only a massive governmental effort can correct what society has caused. Those on the political left generally believe that economic inequality and structural unemployment can only be cured if society accepts responsibility and redistributes its wealth.

There are dangers inherent in the emphasis of either approach. Those who stress self-help may inadvertently relieve pressure on government and society to correct injustice, while civil-rights leaders risk having their message justify hostile acts or a sense of "victimism."

Who's to blame, the system or the individual? Perhaps both. People like Howard Smith or Frank Thomas have learned from experience to harmonize the two schools of thought. People may be victims of racism or failed institutions, they say. But they may also be victims of broken homes, of too many years of dependency, of the lure of the streets and the quick buck, of bad habits, of a pathology that runs deep. "For the majority of poor people," observes William Grinker, President of the MDRC, "it is a resource problem." They are poor because they lack income. But for the majority of those enrolled in BT-27 and supported work—for the estimated one-third of the poor who are in the underclass—Grinker and Howard Smith believe it is more than just a "resource problem."

12

Appalachia:
The White Underclass

It was with the Bruce Wright/Howard Smith debate in mind that I sat in class one day pondering my impending trip to rural Appalachia and Mississippi. A visit to the poor whites of Appalachia and the rural blacks of the Mississippi Delta would test Wright's thesis that racism and urban poverty largely explain the growth of an underclass.

These thoughts were interrupted by John Painter, who asked, "Howard, anyone else you hung out with doing good?" The question was as revealing as the answer. The life-skills course that Howard Smith teaches attempts to enlarge a student's understanding of society and the organized world of work—to give him an idea of how to get up on time, how to dress, how to talk, how to get a job, how to temper frustration. But Painter was searching for people to model himself after, for confirmation that Howard's success was not an aberration, that the effort the members of the class were making was worthwhile.

Similarly, when Smith told the class that I would soon be traveling to Appalachia, Mississippi, and elsewhere to study similar training programs among rural whites and blacks, I was bombarded with questions: Were there white people who lived like them? Were they on welfare, too? Did they hustle? Did they have the same disappointments? The same family woes? Was it less hard for whites? For rural blacks? In sum, was anyone else, like them, doing poorly or feeling bad?

After sitting in on Smith's class for four months, I flew to Morgantown, West Virginia, the headquarters of the MDRC's Appalachian supported-work experiment—the most rural of the twenty-one supported-work sites that the MDRC has supervised. From the air the rolling hills that rim Morgantown resemble the back of a porcupine: bare pine, maple, and birch trees rise like quills from the black earth. The monotonous sameness of the terrain is occasionally relieved by scabs of white snow, by nuclear power plants belching plumes of steam, by the twisting Monongahela River, which snakes north to Pittsburgh. The West Virginia A.F.L.-C.I.O. manages supported-work and other training programs through the Human Resource Development Foundation, or HRDF, a local nonprofit corporation whose supported-work program is supervised by the MDRC. Seven counties in the north-central part of the state, with a population of just under a quarter of a million, are included in the experiment. Fifteen percent of the people live in hollows up to six miles from the nearest paved road. From 1975 through 1980, 1,054 supported workers entered the program, of whom about 90 percent were white.

Density is but one of many differences between New York City and West Virginia. The biggest city in the seven counties is Morgantown, in Monongalia County; its population is 27,500, and is shrinking. In Preston County, the most rural of the seven, the population density is just thirty-nine people per square mile. Unlike the cities of the North, where ghetto residents constantly shift addresses, almost 70 percent of Preston County's 25,000 residents have lived in the same house all their lives; another 20 percent of the people there have moved, but within the county. Upward mobility is relatively rare: male adults have, on the average, less than a ninth-grade education; only 31 percent of them have completed high school; and the 1977 per-capita income of the county was $3,986, which was 69 percent of the national average ($5,751). In the same year, 31 percent of the population was classified as poor, as opposed to 11 percent of all Americans. And those who hold regular jobs usually work in coal mines, at lumber mills, on hog farms, or for a government agency. The houses tucked amid the rolling hills of Preston County are often trailer homes or wooden shacks resting on cinder blocks. Television antennas sprout from most houses; for many of the people, TV serves as the sole contact with the outside world. In the seven counties, the average mother receiving Aid to Families with Dependent Children (AFDC) has been on welfare more than six years—one of the longest average periods of any supported-work site in the nation. As was true of the rural Appalachian mountain community brought to life in John Fetterman's powerful book about rural poverty, *Stinking Creek,* much of "the rural populace in the countless hollows have adopted the welfare rolls as a way of life."

Welfare as a way of life is no easier to change among whites here than it is among blacks and Hispanics in the North. Jackquelyn Bishop, who was the chief recruiter for HRDF in West Virginia, recalls how she collected the monthly printouts of those on welfare and then walked from house to house banging on front doors and pleading with people to let her tell them about supported work. Most were friendly, she says, but she still couldn't reach them. Many didn't want to "move where the work is," she says. "They're happy where they live. But, unfortunately, there are no jobs." Others feared any disruption of their daily routine. They lived by habit, including the habit of welfare. "In many counties, there's no social stigma if you're poor," Mrs. Bishop says. "A lot of these people don't know they're poor. They're happy. I taught school in Webster County"—one of the seven—"and I had some welfare children. They thought I was strange. They didn't know what nail polish was. One day a group of girls stood around the desk and stared at my fingers." Mrs. Bishop says that many of these poor whites, like Wildcat recruits, have never worked before. "They have poor work habits," she said. "Don't know how to get up in the morning. Don't know how to regulate their life to go to work." Like most urban training programs, the HRDF program also competes with alcohol. Family troubles haunt people here, too, with incest common. According to David Walker, a thirty-seven-year-old former Neighborhood Youth Corps instructor, who is the programs manager at the HRDF, many residents of Preston County have the same surname, and "they all look alike." As in the North, alcohol, unemployment, family problems, frustration, and boredom generate violence in the home.

Police Captain John T. Fahey, Fetterman recounts in his book, once subdued a wife-beater:

I tried to talk to the man, and told him: "Look, you've got four kids. What if they found out you beat up their mother? Why did you do it?"

The hillbilly said, "She got out of line and I stomped her."

I said, "What would you have done if your father had done it to your mother?"

The hillbilly said, "He did it all the time."

With few private jobs available, what supported-work jobs there are in Preston County are often with local government. The Preston County Community Action Agency, in a frame house in the hamlet of Kingwood, supplies two such jobs. Cheryl Hall (the names of all the trainees have been changed) travels twenty miles each way to her clerical job. A heavy-set woman with a moon-shaped face and straight brown hair, she is twenty-eight and has two children. Her husband, Fred, who is in his forties, also works at the CAA. Cheryl Hall qualified for the program as a long-term welfare recipient; she has now been at her job—the first one she has ever held—for seven months. "When I got out of high school, I got married," she says. "No time to do much of anything." Two children quickly followed, tying her to the house. Though she went on welfare to support her family, she has contempt for many whites on welfare. "Trashy," she calls those who "walk in and stink and you can't see their faces." She goes on, "Welfare gives them everything. Welfare rebuilds the house." Unlike Jackquelyn Bishop, Cheryl Hall believes that welfare recipients are stigmatized. "Around here, when you're on welfare people consider you trash," she says. "Most of these people don't have education. Not willing to get it. I'm not saying all. I'm saying most of them." Later she says, "Most people on welfare have two, three cars per family." Cheryl Hall is happy at the center, and happy to be working. "It's got me away from home, training me," she says. Like Pearl Dawson in the Wildcat program, her motivation is high—and for the same reason: she hates welfare, and hates what it did to her. Her attendance is outstanding and, according to a written evaluation, "she is very willing and would make some employer a great worker."

Sam Clendenin's future seems less promising. Clendenin is a carpenter at the Community Action Agency in Kingwood. Four of his front teeth are missing, and the rest are decayed and blackened to the gums. He has shoulder-length dark hair, and he often wears a red bandanna around his head. Clendenin, who is now twenty-two, has a sixth-grade education and an I.Q. of 65; he spells his own name with difficulty, and admits to having a drinking problem. He has been in jail seven or eight times, he says. "I was in there three times for drinking," he says. "Once for stealing. Once for breaking down a window. Once for being cruel to animals. And I just got out for being drunk again." Sam lives in a trailer home in Indian Rocks, close to his mother; he keeps a respectful distance from her, though. Recently, she went after him with a shotgun, and after a short chase she fired, nicking him. Clendenin's father abandoned his family—eighteen children in all—leaving his wife on welfare. Clendenin's parents, one local evaluator wrote, were "not really interested in his personal problems." Of his mother, Clendenin says, "She had to have eighteen kids"—to get more welfare. Although he has been supported by welfare, he shares Cheryl Hall's harsh attitude. "Some of them just don't want to work," he says of welfare recipients. "They

161

can just live good on welfare." If Clendenin could quit drinking, his supervisors say, he might be a modest success as an employee when he leaves supported work. But the drudgery of his life is an invitation to drink. After work, he goes home and "sits around and watches television." Cheryl Hall, who looks out for him, says, "The only thing around here is a bowling alley and a lot of beer joints."

There are more distractions for Mary Paul, nineteen, who is a supported clerical worker at the HRDF's state headquarters in Morgantown. A skinny, freckle-faced girl with straight dirty-blond hair, she lives in a downtown trailer court with her son, Michael, who is two years old. Unlike 80 percent of West Virginia's poor, she was not born in the state but moved here several years ago after an altercation with two police officers in Massachusetts, her native state. She qualified for the supported-work program as a mother on welfare. Unlike the members of the Wildcat program, Mary Paul earns about twice as much from the program as she received from welfare—she earns $320 a month, and also gets $60 a month in food stamps—but is still $30 a month short of what she needs to live. She says her monthly expenses are $100 for rent, $25 for home heating gas, $18 for electricity, $40 for gasoline for a 1969 Volkswagen, $100 for groceries, $120 for a babysitter to watch her son while she works, and $7 for her cable TV. She covers the difference by borrowing from her parents, who now live in the same trailer court, or from $10 a week she earns cleaning the house of an elderly man.

Mary Paul does not consider herself poor. "I'm happy," she says. "My son has nice clothes. As long as Michael looks normal and doesn't look shabby, I don't consider myself poor." Her husband used to drink and became so violent that she had him arrested. "Now he comes over to see the baby," she says. "At times I forbid him to come over. He's dried up now and looks like a normal twenty-three-year-old." Her husband provides no child support, and depends on unemployment insurance and the largesse of his mother. Despite the absence of a father in the home, Mary Paul does not believe that Michael suffers. Of the boy's father, she says, "He's around enough. The kid knows who he is. I don't think it affects him at all. One of the reasons we separated was because of the fights. I can give him all the love like his father could give him. There's not as much confusion now." She has a firm hand. "If he needs a whipping, I give it to him," she says. "I don't beat him. But he gets cracked when he needs it."

Mary Paul likes supported work but does worry that her job is drawing her away from Michael. "I'd love to stay home," she says. "Pretty soon, my son's going to think I'm the babysitter." But that danger is outweighed by her distaste for welfare. "I don't want to be on welfare," she goes on. "They're too pushy, too nosy. They act like they should rule your life, know everything you do. For the little bit of money you get—no way that half the people in town who are on welfare are not doing something on the side." Welfare paid her $164 a month and $74 in food stamps. "I lived in a four-room apartment, no running water, no bathroom, no heat except for a gas stove," she says. "That's where I lived. Now if you had welfare come in to look and show them where you were living they'd tell you you'd have to find something else, because there was no running water. They don't approve of places you're living in, but they don't give you enough to live anyplace else but the dregs. If I had me a thing for the president to change on my say-so, it would be to straighten out the welfare system. Get people in there who know what they're doing. People who don't treat you like you're lower than them. I told a woman one time not to get excited, because if not for people like me she wouldn't have work. I said, 'You don't talk down to me. I don't have the same nice clothes, but everybody is equal. Even the potheads walking the street.' "

The bureaucracy bothers Mary Paul, but so does welfare cheating. "I know a few who just have a ball on it," she says. "I have a girlfriend who likes to stay on welfare. She enjoys it. In fact she was supposed to come here with me. She wouldn't." Mary Paul's attitude toward husbands is similar to her attitude toward welfare. "Before I started working, I was one hundred percent dependent on him," she says. "Even for a cigarette. Now I feel that if I can't earn it I don't need it. I don't want to be dependent."

Because she is young and because she fears she will be superseded in her son's affections by a babysitter, Mary has a poor attendance record that endangers her success with supported work. Other things—"little things," as Mary calls them—complicate the life of a single mother, as this account drawn from Mary's official records suggests:

11/14:   absent "because my babysitter's son was sick" and "I couldn't find my mother to sit in for a sitter."
11/16:   left early because son was ill.
12/1:   "I had to leave for 1½ hours to have my utilities hooked up."
12/5:   left at 2:30 P.M. to "rent a trailer" to move.
12/6:   left at noon "to go to Legal Aid office and family service."
12/14:   out all morning to visit clinic.
12/17:   "Left at 3:30 Monday afternoon. I was sickie at stomach."

12/19:	out from 9:30 to 2:00 to visit doctor and clinic.
1/4:	a half-hour late; no call in.
1/7:	out sick. Called in at noon.
1/21:	called in sick at 12:12.
1/25:	late due to icy roads.
1/28:	ill, leaves at 11:00 A.M.
1/29:	Mother calls in sick for Mary.
1/30:	"I need time to go to the welfare department to have my case reviewed."
2/1:	requests time off to visit clinic.
2/6:	three hours off for sick leave.
2/7:	called supervisor to request vacation day to be with son on his birthday (approved).
2/14:	Mary did not phone in or come to work at all this day.

Mary Paul admits, "I have to improve my attitude. I joke around a lot. It breaks up the boredom. The secretary asked me to do something and I said no. It wasn't taken as a joke. So my attitude needs improving. Also my attendance." David Walker asserts that Mary has the brains and talents to succeed in the world of work, but that she, like many of the people he deals with, doesn't know "how to deal with the supervisor. She feels people are picking on her."

Mary's attitude problem is not uncommon at HRDF's largest supported-work site in downtown Fairmont, a city of 23,000 residents twenty-one miles southwest of Morgantown. Since 1978, the program has owned and operated the Fairmont Hotel, a seven-story red brick building, which employs fifteen to twenty supported workers as waitresses, maintenance men, maids, and kitchen helpers. The hotel has fallen on hard times since a suburban shopping mall was built about ten years ago, draining downtown Fairmont of its commerce. With many boarded-up stores and only desultory street traffic, downtown is more or less a ghost town. Today, the hotel relies on about seventy elderly tenants and a handful of out-of-town salesmen who reserve rooms there for their one-day-a-week pilgrimages to Fairmont. Tensions between tenants and workers have been common. The guests, according to the hotel's manager, Claude Arnett, "do not appreciate supported workers." He adds, "A portion of the tenants don't appreciate having ex-convicts here. And because the supported workers are underskilled they make a lot of mistakes." Theft has dogged the program. "At a conservative estimate, in the three years we've run the hotel we've lost about ten thousand dollars' worth of hand tools," says David Walker, who, like all the staff except three supervisors, is white.

Like the people enrolled in Wildcat, supported workers here are drawn from the ranks of ex-convicts, long-term welfare recipients, and delinquent high school dropouts. (Ex-addicts, the fourth group represented in the Wildcat program, are not enrolled, since heroin addiction is rare in West Virginia.) The names, dress, and mannerisms may differ, but the attitudes and the behavior of these supported workers and the ones taught by Howard Smith are noticeably similar.

Mary Sue Boggs, who is forty, found her opportunity in the Fairmont Hotel. After completing the supported-work program there, in November 1979, Mary became a cook in the hotel's dining room, where she works today. On her right biceps is a tattoo—a snake curling around a knife, with "TRUE TO DEATH" printed below. She has jet-black hair and a heavily made-up, bony face, which make her appear to be Indian. She grew up as one of two children in a poor family. In high school she got pregnant and dropped out to get married. She had five children before she and her husband, a truck driver, separated. He was disabled on the job, and provided no family support, so Mary Sue Boggs searched for work, but, lacking any basic skills and having young children to take care of at home, she found none, and applied for welfare. She was on welfare for four years. "When you're on welfare, they just think they own you," she says. "Act like it's coming out of their pocket. I even hated to go over there. When you're on welfare, you're like a prisoner. I'd rather be in jail. They look at you—I don't know how to explain it. They make you feel guilty." When she heard of the supported-work job at the hotel, she applied at once.

Although welfare kept Mary Sue Boggs alive, she believes that too many white welfare recipients are loafers. "A lot of them don't want to get off of it," she says. "I guess because they don't want to work. The young kids today would rather get pregnant and go on welfare. They do it just to keep from working. But I'll tell you, when they start raising kids they'll find out how hard it is."

Even now it is hard for Mary Sue Boggs, whose monthly take-home pay of $446 does not cover expenses: $90 for rent, $25 for electricity, $110 for home heating oil (in the winter), and $250 for food. To help make ends meet, her mother-in-law, who lives with her, contributes part of her Social Security check; her twenty-one-year-old son also contributes. Some months the family skimps on food to pay bills. "I signed up for food stamps," Mary Sue Boggs says. "I want to see if I can get them. I won't go into that if my older boy gets in the mines."

Like Mary Sue Boggs, Lora Paranski, who is now twenty years old, dropped out of school and got married when she became pregnant. When she lost the support of her husband, who is now serving time in prison for armed robbery, she turned to welfare. Lora Paranski joined the hotel program as a kitchen helper five months ago. "I just needed a job and came down," she says. "My husband used to work for the program before we were married." She knows how difficult it is for mothers on welfare who have younger children. "People won't watch children till they're at least three or four years old, and it's hard to find babysitters," she says. She pays her sister to babysit for her two children. Her monthly salary is $440 before taxes. She pays $70 a month to rent a four-room house in downtown Fairmont (she hopes to buy the house someday); $80 for her sister's babysitting; $7.50 for electricity; $48 for heating gas (down from $106, the figure before she insulated the windows with plastic); and the rest for food. To supplement her income, Lora Paranski does domestic work. "I do a little washing and cleaning house on the side," she says. This brings in about $30 a week.

She was placed on probation for six months after a brush with the law, and spent one year on welfare. "I really felt bad," she recalls. "Like they owned me. They send you a check once a month and then food stamps once a month. You can't live off of that. And they send you food stamps about a week or so after you get your welfare check. So you can't save. You're borrowing money. So when you get your check you're paying back. I felt like I was trapped." Others on welfare don't feel that way, she says, echoing a view expressed by several members of the Wildcat program. "There's people I know in Fairmont just having babies to get more money. I wouldn't want a baby for that. They just say, 'I'll get more money if I have a baby.' They just want to lay around. I couldn't stand it." She spots the same indolence in her brother-in-law, Cecil Breeden, who also works at the hotel. "He's hard to get out of bed in the morning," she says. "He's lazy."

I ask Lora why her husband got in trouble. "He was doing real good," she says. "Had a good job, making $130 a week. He just got in with a bad group. Drinking a lot. I didn't know till they took him to jail. He said he couldn't stand not making enough money to pay rent and have enough money on the side. So he drank and gambled." Something else gnawed at him: "His father died when he was about fourteen. That bothers him a lot. He said he never had time to really know his dad or something. Every time I go see him he says he wishes his dad were alive. I guess he felt left out or something. And his mother? She can't stick with one man. And the reason she does what she does is because her children are in trouble all the time."

When she is asked about her goals, Lora Paranski says, "I like to do carpenter work—to work on things like cement." Eventually she would like to own a construction company. "I'm tired of being poor," she says. "I'd like to climb up that ladder and make it where rich people are. And if I have to climb up the ladder myself with my kids, I'm gonna do it. I've come a long way in a year. I plan to go further." Indeed, supervisors say that Lora Paranski's attendance and attitude have improved. David Walker says that she has the potential to climb the ladder, but he worries that she will slip off. She drinks, and she smokes too much marijuana, he explains, and sometimes she works as a prostitute. "She runs around with a wild crowd," he says.

Walter Roberts, who is twenty-two, has also run with a wild crowd. The only black supported-work employee at the hotel, Roberts was referred to the program by a probation officer. ("I was caught with a pistol in my car," he explains.) A muscular five feet eight inches, Roberts is light-skinned, and has a thin mustache that droops just below his mouth, long sideburns, and two front teeth blackened to the gums. Roberts, who is one of five children, was born in Fairmont, and now lives down the street from his parents. After finishing high school, he worked at odd jobs, collected unemployment compensation, and hustled. Officially, Roberts did not work in the two years before he entered the program. "They wouldn't give me any welfare," he says. "I had two cars at the time, and my own house." Unofficially, money came in because he owned a truck and hauled materials and garbage for people. "Also," he says, "I had a couple of girls staying with me. They helped me out a lot." He will not say whether their contributions came from work, welfare, or prostitution. He bought a house for $3,000, as well as four used Cadillacs. "I have a girl who stays with me now," he says. "We got two kids. We're not married, 'cause she's on welfare. That's not the only reason. I'm not ready for it yet."

Roberts, though his household is partly supported by welfare, says he is unlike people on welfare, because he has ambition. "I know a lot of people, if they can get that welfare they're not worried about anything," he says. "Me, I want my money. A lot of people asking me how I can afford four cars. I tell them it all depends on what you do with your money. I feel a lot of them like being on welfare. They get a check. They get food stamps. They don't have to do anything."

Roberts says that being black is not a particular handicap. "I don't think it's a problem," he says. "Maybe with certain people. But you have that everywhere." He says better pay would change things a bit at the hotel. "A lot of them get the supported-work job because their parole officer makes them. I feel if they paid more they'd have better attendance." If a better-paying job comes along, Roberts says, he will probably leave. He now makes $3.35 an hour, having recently been promoted to maintenance-crew chief. His goal is to "open up some type of business—maybe a customizing shop for cars."

Claude Arnett says of Roberts, "He's hard to understand. He's got some leadership ability. But he'll take issue with me." One day at work Roberts suddenly flared up, and he was suspended for three days. But over the past few months he has been steady and reliable. "He's got a good chance to succeed," Arnett says, "if he can resist the lure of the quick buck."

Cecil Breeden, twenty, is a member of Roberts' maintenance team and is Lora Paranski's brother-in-law. But unlike them, he seems to lack the spark of ambition. He speaks in a slow drawl, pausing often between words, his eyes usually fixed on the floor. He has dark-brown hair parted in the middle and cascading to his shoulders. With two children and another on the way, the Breeden family survived on welfare before Cecil found work at the hotel. Welfare wasn't particularly healthy for him, he recalls. "It helps out, but it didn't give you a sense of responsibility," he says. Breeden is disdainful of friends who are satisfied with welfare. "Some people like that," he says. "This one guy I know, his wife's working. She quit her job after he was working. Then she got a job and he quit."

One of eight children, born in Fairmont, Cecil Breeden was two when his father died. His mother remarried and had three more children. Cecil wasn't happy at home, and dropped out of school in the tenth grade, after falling more than three grades behind in reading. He was laid off from his last two jobs, his marriage is shaky, and he feels uncomfortable with his current job and salary. He complains a lot. There are too few supervisors at the hotel, he says—only one in maintenance, rather than two or three—and the supervisors he does have are arbitrary. "In handbooks they gave us, they had holidays and stuff we get paid for," he says. "After a while, around Veterans Day, they decided we wouldn't get paid for them, though the handbook said we would." Breeden concedes that his attendance is bad—he has been absent or late thirty days out of just over a hundred workdays—but blames the supervisors, in part. "We sit down—me, Claude, and the counselor—and we was having a little discussion about that," he says. "He said he'd meet me halfway if I tried. I told him I would. Next day I saw him and he asked me *again* about it." Breeden felt pressured.

He is asked why, if he loses pay, he is absent and late so frequently.

He stares at the floor for a few moments and then, without lifting his head, says, "I was here almost every day. Some days I'd call in sick. Some days, when I was sick, I'd tell my sister and she wouldn't write it down. One time I took two sick days off because I was looking at another job. In September, there were some personal problems. I just didn't feel like coming in here. I came down and talked to the previous manager and he said he could get me time off if I needed it. If Claude keeps pressing, I'll tell him what to do."

Claude Arnett offers a different perspective on Cecil's troubles. "He didn't mind coming in five, ten minutes late every day," he says. "He wants to be excused. He didn't show up yesterday. Last week, he was late four days and absent one day. Whenever I sit down and try to help him and straighten him out, he listens, he talks good. But that's as far as it goes. He's really got something on his mind. Something's eating him bad, and I think it's his wife. He's downright jealous of his wife. He wanted me to change my electric time clock to the time on his alarm clock. He's way out."

Tolbert Pickens, who is forty-seven, is not hostile, like Breeden, or a hustler, like Roberts. He is simply passive, like Willy Joe. He has bad skin and rotting teeth. A short man, Pickens has blanketed his body over the years with tattoos. "Everybody else was getting them," he explains. On one hand, the word "LOVE" is spelled out on four fingers; on the other hand, the word "HATE." The names of his son, his daughter, his former wife, and countless cousins are tattooed over both arms. From 1951 to 1964, Pickens commuted some two hundred miles between his job as a shipper's helper for a steel company in Lorain, Ohio, and his home in Fairmont, where he spent weekends. When business slackened, in 1964, he was laid off. He got a job as a truck driver with a small Fairmont company, but eventually the company went bankrupt. His difficulties, however, result from more than bad luck. He has been in and out of prison—most recently, for grand larceny. "I got all drunked up and took some junk laying over on the river," he says. He is an alcoholic, and has been for as long as he can remember. "Nothing to do, I guess," he says by way of explanation. "Sit around and watch TV. Some of your buddies come in and say, 'Drink with me.' You do."

Pickens' wife divorced him twenty years ago, taking their two children to Florida. "I heard she was remarried," he says. "The boy was twenty-two on January seventh. The girl'll be twenty-one the twenty-fourth of April." He neither sees nor supports them. "My wife, she wanted me to leave them alone," he says. "I still miss them. I used to send them money when they were young." He pauses, and then says, "I didn't think she was going to get a divorce. My mom showed me it in the paper. All a surprise to me." He doesn't write to his children. "They wouldn't write back," he says. "I figure that if they want to see me they can. They're old enough. I shouldn't have to go to them."

Before Tolbert Pickens went to work at the hotel, he washed dishes for $2.90 an hour at the Poky Dot Restaurant, in Fairmont. He is much happier today, painting and doing plumbing and electrical work around the hotel, where he also lives. "At night, I'll be here and a lady asks me to do something," he says. "I'm not supposed to, but I went to her room and fixed her TV. After working hours, you're not supposed to do it. But I like to help people out." One of his deep regrets is that he dropped out of school. "A big mistake," he says. "In A.A. meetings, they tell you to go to school, but I didn't go. I thought I was too old to go and sit in class. But there was older men than me going. I found that out later. A big mistake. Most jobs you can't get without high school training."

Claude Arnett says that he likes Pickens, but offers a harsh judgment on his potential. "He'll never make it with another employer unless we straighten him up," he says. "And he's not very bright."

One former employee of whom Arnett is particularly proud is Joyce Haun, who is known as Susie. Susie is a high school dropout who, after an unsuccessful marriage, supported herself and a daughter by working as a nurse's aide. She was able to make a decent living until her right knee collapsed in an accident. Seven depressing years on welfare followed. She learned of supported work through a doctor, and became one of the HRDF program's first recruits. When she graduated from the program, she was offered a position as assistant manager of the Forest Glen development—a mixed low-income and middle-income housing project in Fairmont. Since 1976, the development has been owned and managed by the HRDF. One of Susie Haun's duties was to supervise ten supported workers employed there. Within seven months, she was promoted to manager. Today, at thirty-seven, she has lost forty pounds, is remarried, and earns a weekly salary of $286. She also receives free housing and utilities as the live-in manager of another HRDF-owned project. She says it's "a far cry" from the $124 a month she got in welfare payments.

Success has taught Susie Haun to be a tough taskmaster, like Claude Arnett. Seated in the Fairmont Hotel's dining room with Arnett and David Walker, she says that pride is often the missing ingredient that determines whether the ten supported workers she supervises will succeed or fail. "Most people are on welfare by choice, in my opinion," she says. "They're lazy. The problem with people on welfare is that they would rather sit at home. I think we should make them go to work if they're eligible—maybe because I know what HRDF can do for you, and they don't." Of her seven years on welfare, she says, "One of the fears you have when you're on welfare and you go through training is 'What if I lose the job?' "

"It's dependency," says Walker, who agrees with Susie Haun that there should be a work requirement for able-bodied persons on welfare.

"They get into security and hate to lose it," she continues, and she turns to Arnett. "When you sent me a letter that it was time to go out and search for a job, I was scared to death. You're afraid to let go, for fear of not being able to support your child."

Walker refers to the program's target population as "the disadvantaged," but, like Howard Smith, he believes that most people in the underclass are more than just poor—that they have behavioral difficulties requiring special help. "I think the people we're dealing with for the most part are at the bottom," he says. "In our AFDC group, we're dealing with people who've been on welfare at least twenty of the last twenty-four months. And many a hell of a lot more. I sincerely believe a lot of people are unemployed simply because they don't know how to get a job. No one ever took the time to tell them. They don't know how to present themselves. They don't have the self-confidence to look a guy in the eye and say, 'I'm a good man. Can you help me?' And many people from the rural counties don't have much contact with working or with the public. To come to Morgantown is a big trip, a big deal. I can't believe it. People from Preston County, for instance, never had to deal with blacks before. It's difficult for them to do it." Many lack education or skills, he says, and others have a surly attitude. "How to deal with a supervisor is often a problem," Walker says.

Walker believes that self-confidence is often the key. One mother on welfare stayed with the program eighteen months and was frightened at the thought of leaving, he says. "She didn't believe anyone else would want her. I thought that after eighteen months we had built up her confidence. But there are a lot of other things. You've got to consider that we as an employer have been more tolerant than most employers would be." In his opinion, Consolidated Coal, which pays close to $85 a day for work in the mines, wouldn't be so tolerant. "That's one of our problems," he says. "We're hesitant to write people off. Maybe we're wrong." Walker is as troubled by this dilemma as Howard Smith was over whether to flunk Willy Joe. Demand too much of people unaccustomed to regulations and discipline and you risk chasing them away, he says; demand too little and you risk not preparing them for the more rigorous world of work. A guaranteed job does not turn out to be the answer for everyone. Nor is preaching about the rewards of the work ethic and about punctuality. After years of poverty or hustling or dependency, people become inured to the demands of society. "Usually they come from a family with no work experience," Susie Haun says. "And when they haven't been taught about work from an early age, not working comes to be a bad habit. A family habit."

Claude Arnett says that some supported workers have "real tough lives," and this view is shared by Homer Kincaid, a local labor leader and community organizer, who now serves as the director of the HRDF. Kincaid, who is forty-seven years old, has long, thin, graying sideburns and a full mustache, and he speaks in a soft voice. "If you been a welfare recipient in West Virginia, it's sometimes because it's been passed down to you," he says. "The children of long-term welfare recipients have an attitude. In 1967 we recruited two brothers from a mining community for the Neighborhood Youth Corps. They didn't show up for two days. We sent out a counselor to find out why. The counselor asked them. They said, 'We signed up. We're waitin' for the check.' That's the kind of attitude we've had to face." Others fear straying from their homes or communities. "We've had AFDC mothers, really good workers, who when they got out of supported work went right back into the shelter of their homes," he says. To someone lacking self-confidence, the home is safe; a job is threatening.

A violent home life imposes another obstacle. Kincaid says of some of his recruits, "They've grown up in violence. What they expect in life is that who's the toughest survives. In some communities, the family name is passed down as a no-gooder. They're branded. Even if a guy's done nothing, he's branded."

"And because of the brand, no matter how much skill they have they don't get the job," Walker adds.

All the programs that the MDRC has supervised in recent years struggle with dilemmas, none of them easy to solve. In West Virginia, for example, there are too few job opportunities, so there is sometimes difficulty finding jobs for supported workers, particularly in Preston and Taylor Counties. With the exception of the HRDF's hotel and housing projects, the work sites are so small and so scattered that supervision and such supported-work techniques as peer-group pressure, graduated stress, and close supervision become next to impossible. Without mass-transit facilities, travel to and from work is a hardship; to go from Morgantown to Wheeling, for instance, takes an hour and a half by car. "The price of gas really hurt us," Jacquelyn Bishop says. "A lot of people couldn't get in to interviews with us because of gas. It's bad enough for me to pay a dollar-thirty for gas. Imagine how it is for them!" The program reimburses workers at the rate of seventeen cents a mile, but only for the first ninety days of employment.

172

"But of all the barriers to employment," Homer Kincaid says, "lack of education is the greatest handicap." Referring to America's renewed reliance on coal production, he explains, "We're about to face an economic boom here in West Virginia. The coal companies are not going to accept people without skills when they can get a high school grad. We have to give them something more tangible. To get people into meaningful jobs will take more education and skills training."

Contributing to this problem, Walker says, is the design of the MDRC's national supported-work program, which he feels is too rigid. Twelve months of supported work is simply too short a period for those lacking a high school education. "You can't learn basic skills and education skills at the same time," he says. "And what of the illiterates? No program touches them. All programs screen them out."

Kincaid offers no magic cure. He concedes that there is no readily apparent way of helping illiterates. "The cost is prohibitive," he says, because illiterates need individual instruction. Nor is there any quick and inexpensive way to reclaim the 64 percent of the people who have enrolled and dropped out of this supported-work project in its first five years. Many illiterates and dropouts, Homer says, become "a class on welfare the rest of their lives—they are wards of the welfare system."

Over all, the results of the West Virginia program matched those of other supported-work programs throughout the nation. Of the 1,054 workers enrolled between April 1975 and December 1980, 40 percent were ex-offenders, 37 percent delinquent youths, and 23 percent AFDC mothers. Almost 400 completed the training program and graduated to regular, unsubsidized jobs. To understand why a majority left the program, the MDRC conducted interviews in 1978 and 1979 and issued reports, one of which said, "A sample of eighty-two participants who preferred to be unemployed rather than stay in the program had numerous reasons for their departure. The most often cited reasons, in order of frequency, were low wages, personal health problems, transportation difficulty caused by lack of vehicle or distance to the work sites, disappointment with what the program offered, and friction at work sites with HRDF supervisors." The most common cause of both suspensions and dismissals was absenteeism—49 and 27 percent, respectively, compared with a national average of 52 and 28 percent. (The West Virginia numbers would have been higher if the program supervisors had suspended or dismissed workers in 1975, their first year of operation.) The MDRC's analysis of the West Virginia program shows that through

December 1980 the greatest success was achieved with ex-offenders (38 percent went on to unsubsidized employment); next came AFDC mothers (32 percent); and the least success was with young people (31 percent).

But "success" is a subjective word. One can choose to focus on the 64 percent of those enrolled who failed to finish supported work or the 36 percent who did finish and went on to full-time, unsubsidized jobs. It is the MDRC's contention that normal definitions of success or failure should not be applied to the underclass—people so battered by years of neglect, habit, and hostility that they are difficult to reach. A 1979 MDRC evaluation of some of those who succeeded in West Virginia observed that, "while this post-program activity . . . may be absolutely low, it far surpasses any expectations based on previous trends or prior knowledge of the target area, its population, and its economy."

13

The Rural
Black Underclass

In rural Mississippi the MDRC supervises a program that has attracted scant notice but could have profound national implications. The Youth Incentive Entitlement Pilot Project here—one of seventeen MDRC supervised nationwide—is, in the words of MDRC President William Grinker, "the first legislatively mandated guaranteed jobs program in the nation's history." Which is to say, any poor youth between the ages of sixteen and nineteen who lives in one of seventeen designated cities or rural areas is guaranteed part-time employment during the school year and full-time summer employment if he or she agrees to return to or remain in school.

Of the seventeen designated areas, Mississippi's was the most rural, encompassing as it does nineteen southeastern counties where only five cities have populations in excess of 10,000. It is also the site of the nation's most severe poverty, at least in terms of income. Mississippi's per capita income ranks last among the fifty states: $5,736 in 1978 compared to a national average of $7,810. And this fact tells only part of the story. Although blacks comprised 36 percent of the state's population in 1976 (down from 49 percent in 1940), 63 percent of black Mississippians are poor compared to 16 percent of white Mississippians. The state's welfare benefits trail those of any other state in America. In 1979 the maximum monthly payment, including rent supplements, for a mother and three children was $120. This contrasted with comparable monthly payments of $487 in California, $476 in New York, $386 in Denver, $292 in Cleveland, $267 in Baltimore, $249 in West Virginia, and $235 in Louisville. In the nineteen rural counties covered by Mississippi's program, 36 percent of the population falls below the federally defined standard of poverty—triple the national average.

Any poor youth living here is entitled to a job, but few white youngsters apply. All eighteen youths holding down part-time jobs and attending special alternative education classes at the high school in Port Gibson, not far from Meridian, Mississippi, are black. The reason few whites enroll, says Benita Burt, who is black and serves as the assistant director of youth programs for the Governor's Office of Job Development and Training, is because it's "looked upon as a black program. We have been pushing for white enrollment. The white kids may want to participate, but their parents don't. They don't want to admit they're poor." More than pride is involved. Burt and others also say that whites don't want to associate with blacks.

Tales told by these youngsters are similar to those told by young people in West Virginia or New York. Michael Louis Brown (the names of all youths in this chapter have been changed) dropped out of a Chicago high school in the tenth grade and moved to Port Gibson three years ago to live with his grandmother. His childhood was not a happy one. He was born with one arm shorter than the other. Of his father, Michael says, "I haven't seen him since I was nine years old. Maybe younger than that. I don't even know if he's living or not. You could line up my father in front of me and I wouldn't know who he is." His mother, he says, "is kind of mentally ill," and is now institutionalized. At nineteen, Michael has been arrested several times, the last time for robbery. He says he was a hostile youth and blames "family problems." Michael explains: "I guess everybody's up on me 'cause I did this and did that. They didn't want to give me a second chance. So I thought they didn't care about me. Now I know they do care. They cared ever since I was born."

Unlike William Block of BT-27 or Mary Sue Boggs of Fairmont, West Virginia, Michael yearns to return to city life. "I don't like it down here 'cause of the people," he says. "They're too nosy. They know your business better than you do." He believes that Port Gibson offers no respite from drink and violence and family neglect: "They got a bunch of winos in this town, put it like that. They be drinking a lot. They be shooting down here. The place so little, but every time you look around somebody died." He complains about families here: "Twenty-five percent are all right to kids. Twenty-five percent are sometimes nice. And I believe that fifty percent of them just don't care. I seen this woman's—this ain't none of my business —kids walking the street. I asked her son, 'Where's your coat?' He said, 'I don't have one.' I blame the mother for that. She drinks, too.

I been seeing her up in town more than I see her with her kid."

Michael's goal is now a fairly simple one: "I gonna take care of me, myself, and my mother and buy her a house if it takes twenty years. I ain't hardly seen my mother since I was nine." Michael no longer blames his family or the system for his difficulties. "I'm blaming myself now," he says.

Mary Anne Thompson does not apportion blame. At nineteen she has three children, the first born when she was fourteen. Her children have two fathers, both of whom do not see or support her or their offspring. Why did she have the children? "I don't know," Mary Anne drawls slowly through chipped front teeth. Her father died when she was a baby, and Mary Anne and her seven sisters and five brothers were raised on welfare. Similarly, Mary Anne also supports her children on the $120 she receives each month from welfare and the $209 from food stamps. Mary Anne's expenses include $40 for rent (she shares a "two-sided house" with an uncle), $200 for food, $14.50 for electricity, $32.50 for home heating gas, and an unspecified amount for the cost of a TV purchased from a pawnshop. She gets her clothing from the Salvation Army.

Mary Anne never finished high school. "Mommy didn't let us finish 'cause she had a baby. She'd keep me and my sister out of school— she'd stay out a day and I'd stay out a day—to watch the baby. She had nobody to keep him." Today Mary Anne tries not to victimize her own children in the same way. While she works or attends school she relies on her mother and an older sister to babysit. This is the second time Mary Anne has tried to return to school. The first was after her earliest pregnancy when she found that she "couldn't get along with those dumb children in school. They'd talk about me 'cause I had a baby." But the opportunity offered by the Youth Entitlement Program is different: "I like it. I want to try to get my diploma. The people are nice in it. The teacher tries to make you understand. He'll break down a word until you understand what it means." Still, there are psychological barriers ahead. Mary Anne is frightened. She says she hopes to get a full-time job, but she is afraid to leave welfare: "I won't know how to take care 'cause I might not find a job."

Eldore Jones dropped out of school because, she says, "the teacher wasn't teaching nobody nothing. So I just stopped going." Like her mother, she became a teenage mother supported by welfare. Now seventeen, she and her two-year-old daughter live with her mother, stepfather, and eleven brothers and sisters (three others have moved away) in the town of Tilma. Eldore still sees her daughter's father and admits to contemplating marriage. "He wanted to" when the baby was born, she says. "I didn't want to. I said I was gonna wait till I was eighteen." She feels she "just wasn't ready" to be a mother at age fifteen, but now she believes she has matured. Her part-time job teaching Head Start children four hours a day has helped her mature, she says, and now she is ready to settle into marriage and eventually to become a kindergarten teacher.

Betty Lydon, nineteen, is learning to be a better mother to her four-month-old daughter, Aquarius, whom she at first resented. "I learned to love her," says Betty, a hefty girl with hair dyed a bright auburn, a nice smile, and a solid gold front tooth. "At the time I wasn't ready for one, but after she got here everything was all right." Although she didn't want the baby, she refused to have an abortion: "It didn't seem fit to do it." She dropped out of high school during her pregnancy because "I got sick a lot" and the "teachers were mean 'cause I was pregnant."

Betty lives in Port Gibson and receives child support from her daughter's father, who is married to someone else. Her sister babysits during the day. Like so many unwed teenage mothers, Betty grew up in a household consisting of a mother and eight children, all dependent on welfare. Today she receives $60 a month from welfare, the maximum permitted in Mississippi for one child (aid in Mississippi, like West Virginia and unlike most states, including New York, is earmarked for the child, not the family head, and is called Aid to Dependent Children). Food stamps add $112 a month. Her part-time entitlement job pays the minimum wage, or $254 a month. Her monthly expenses include $125 for rent, $80 for food, $25 for heating gas. She has a TV but no car. "I spent $250 this week for clothes," she says. "Week before last I spent $43." And like most participants in MDRC programs, she has no savings.

Betty also detests welfare. "They have to interview you every six months," she says. "It's the questions they be asking you: 'Who all living with you?' 'Are you living by yourself?' And then they be trying to find out everything about you, and then they try and trap you with difficult words and questions. If I can find a job I'd be willing to give up this ADC." Betty would like to be a secretary, and the advice she would offer her daughter is consistent with her own middle-class values: "My advice would be I wouldn't like for her to smoke or drink. I'd like her to go to church, like I do."

Peggy James, sixteen, is an unusual teenage mother in that she is married. She, her husband, and their five-month-old daughter Aneriana live in a trailer outside Hamanvelie. Her mother, she says, "wanted me to get married," warning her that "Sometimes boy leaves girl after they get pregnant." Abortion was out of the question:

"When baby comes here, you start loving your baby. It's nice to have somebody to look after." Peggy, a pretty girl with an irrepressible giggle and cornrowed hair, feels she received the kind of love as a child she now tries to offer. Fortunately, her mother, who lives nearby, babysits while she and her husband work. Many young girls she knows don't have that advantage, she says, and go on welfare "'cause they have nobody to take care of the baby."

James Goldsbarn is also secure, even though he has several strikes against him: he is black, his father died when he was seven, he was raised in a large family that depended on welfare, and he dropped out of school. Yet James believes he will pass his G.E.D. exam and eventually become an electrician. But first he wants "to get away from here. There ain't no jobs for the young ones, and when they come up there ain't gonna be nothing to do but sit around the house and wait." He adds, "When I grow old, it ain't gonna be the same." He can't explain why his friends lack self-confidence. "Some of them just don't have it in mind," he says. "They could be what they want to be, but they just don't have it in their mind that they could do it."

A short black man who speaks with a slight stutter, Arthur Jackson coaches the eighteen students for their G.E.D. exams. But all too frequently he runs into the same roadblock. "The students feel a lack of self-confidence," he says. "When we think they're ready to take the G.E.D., we give them a G.E.P.I. [General Information Performance Index]. If they score at least forty percent in each section we let them take the G.E.D. Some of them fear that if they pass the test they'll be out of a job." Like Howard Smith, Jackson blames welfare dependency for robbing his students of self-esteem. "About eighty percent of the students in my class are receiving welfare and food stamps. The student or parent learns to be dependent on that. They have no type of job skill. Most students I'm working with function between a fifth- and a seventh-grade level." Doesn't racial discrimination also lessen self-confidence? "I don't think so," he responds. "In Cleveland County we have a seventy-five to twenty-five percent ratio of blacks to whites, and in the city about sixty-five to thirty-five." But his students seemed unusually polite for dropouts, answering questions with "Yes, sir," or "No, sir." Was this because I was present? Did they fear a white person? Jackson politely smiles at my naïveté and explains that they are simply respectful of adults: "It goes back to first to sixth grade when the teacher could paddle and nobody said anything. Now things are changing since the Supreme Court changed that. Without discipline the classroom is not a suitable environment for learning."

The chief weakness of the Youth Incentive Entitlement program,

Jackson thinks, "is that my students are tired after working all morning and coming to school in the afternoon. Then they don't do the assignment." Herman "Chuck" Wells, the retired Air Force colonel who manages the program division of the Governor's Office of Job Development and Training, sees other flaws. "Our program is like an individual who sits down and plays the piano for the first time. There's an awful lot of discord in there," says the white native Mississippian. What Wells calls "turf fights" bedevil their efforts. His agency vies with the State Employment Service for jurisdiction over the youth program, and by early 1980 it was losing the battle. "They have potentially strong political backing," Wells says of the employment service. "They lease in every community. They have sixteen centers in the state, and an office in practically every town. And if you're sifting through ten to eleven million dollars of public employment funds and then you contract with the president of the county board of supervisors, I would say that gives you political clout." Political infighting is not uncommon in these programs; for instance, a bitter feud between the Detroit public school system and the Detroit Employment and Training Department over how to run its Youth Incentive Entitlement Program has retarded that program. But the politics in Mississippi are special. On the same day in March 1980 that I interviewed Wells in downtown Jackson, the Mississippi House of Representatives voted 109 to 7 to abolish Wells' state agency, a move endorsed by the incoming governor. The next day the state senate ratified the change.

Wells, who knew his own job was imperiled, said that if the rival State Employment Service gained control of youth entitlement they would push aside the community-based and largely black organizations responsible for outreach and would smother the program with bureaucracy. "Doggone it," he said, "there's got to be some restriction so that the local education associations"—with whom the employment service is allied—"don't put the funding into more staff and equipment. They got enough."

This civil war between state agencies not surprisingly works to the detriment of the youngsters. "An underlying fact that emerged" during one of his visits to Mississippi, Tony Santiago's February 28, 1980, MDRC field report observed, "is the anomalous situation" of a state agency responsible for running the program that cannot adequately control the agency it subcontracts to. Wells' parent agency was undermined, but so was the program. Youths who complete their training and schooling and await a job are classified as "on hold," and Mississippi has an unusually large number of those. Compared to the other sixteen sites around the nation, in early 1980 the

Mississippi program had 16.8 percent of its enrollees on hold, the second worst record in the nation (due to severe management turnover and conflict with the public school system, the Denver program had 39.6 percent on hold). MDRC tried to correct this flaw, to no avail. Its second annual report on the Youth Incentive Entitlement Project said of Mississippi: "By October 1978 there were nine hundred participants in holding status, about three hundred of whom had never been assigned to a work site. Various efforts, programmatic and contractual, have been attempted to remedy this problem. However, it continues, and the percentage of unassigned youths has not decreased. ES [the State Employment Service] claims that given their rural economy, acceptable jobs simply do not exist, although in some areas, like Hattiesburg, there are available work sites. As of August 1979, there were over 1,000 enrolled youths 'on hold,' and 21 percent of them had been classified in this status over ninety days."

Why are youths on hold if there are jobs available? "It was probably a lack of real effort to match the kids to available jobs," says MDRC President William Grinker. "The State Employment Service was not what you'd call a dynamic force. That's the nature of the bureaucracy." Since most of these youngsters were black, Grinker did not doubt that the predominantly white bureaucracy may have dragged its feet.

One community-based effort in Mississippi that is generally considered a success is MACE (The Mississippi Action for Community Education). Spawned by the civil-rights movement and founded in 1967, MACE is a nonprofit development corporation covering fourteen northwestern counties, an area commonly called the Delta. There are 23,000 dues-paying members. Although the MDRC has no formal connection with MACE, Gary Walker, MDRC's bearded vice-president for operations, has journeyed south to inspect an organization that he and other MDRC executives consider one of the two or three most effective community self-help organizations in the country. Walker plans to discuss with MACE a possible joint venture as part of a proposed national test to aid teenage mothers in five communities.

Walker hopes that MACE will bid to join this experiment as one of the five sites. "It takes a sophisticated organization to meet MDRC's demands for research," says Walker. "They, like the other two or three or four really competent community development organizations, really pride themselves on being able to deliver services themselves. They don't send kids to G.E.D. program schools. They do it themselves. But in developing that service delivery capacity and pride it means that when an organization like us comes in they will say, 'You have money for teenage parents? We know what to do.' But the whole idea behind MDRC is that you're researching a particular design or structure. You can't just research teenage mothers. In order to do research in six or seven cities, you've got to have assurance that you're researching the same thing in all cities so we can aggregate data. What we also have to do—and this is hard for the local operators—is to test an idea. But if you're into a program six months the operator may say, 'No, we're doing long-term research.' " Tensions are constant. In the Youth Incentive Entitlement Project, for instance, MDRC set a maximum of twenty hours a week for youngsters to work. Yet most local operators want more. To conduct its research, MDRC demands uniformity. To best serve individual needs, local operators demand flexibility.

In order to view the work of MACE we drive from the state capital of Jackson to the town of Belzoni, where MACE conducted an early organizational effort. The drive takes about an hour and a half. While there are indications everywhere in Mississippi of the progress blacks have made there, a ride across the Delta, once the site of all the great plantations, serves as a reminder of how wide the gap between white and black remains. East Broadway in Yazoo City, the site of many a stormy civil-rights protest, is a street of colonnaded white homes, expansive porches and lawns, freshly painted picket fences, and a modern downtown business district. This is the white area of town, as Park Avenue south of 96th Street in Manhattan is white. At the railroad tracks on Water Street, same as the railroad tracks that burst forth from beneath the flowered island north of 96th Street, another world begins: boarded-up stores with long-neglected FOR SALE signs, junkyards, fetid creeks, sagging wooden shacks enveloped by laundry lines rather than lawns, and wrinkled, stooped black men resting on shaky milk crates. Just outside of town a stone bridge crosses the Yazoo River, and one enters a vast plain, the land so flat it seems ironed, the moist earth yielding cotton, rice and soybeans.

Belzoni is a sleepy little town whose sole industry is an aging soybean processing plant. The town is part of Humphrey's County, in which MACE operates a farmer's cooperative, a clothing cooperative, and a restaurant. Profits from these enterprises are recycled into lowered prices, new black-run businesses, and the location and training of community leaders. "The whole effort is to make money in the black community spin around at least five times," says Malcolm Watts, a tall, ebullient black man in his early thirties who recently moved back to Mississippi from New York to become MACE's director of public affairs.

We are going to visit Aaron Hazelwood, who is something of a local legend. At eighty-one he is old enough to have known former slaves, to have personally fought against plantation owners and for desegregated public facilities. He has been physically beaten by whites, has been branded a radical by blacks, and has lived a few miles from Belzoni in the same tar-paper-roofed wooden shack perched on wooden stilts for as long as he can remember. In this shack Hazelwood has sired ten children and entertained forty-nine grandchildren and twenty-six great-grandchildren. He still drives a battered 1946 Plymouth, which sits outside on a rare patch of dry land. The years are revealed in Mr. Hazelwood's gaunt face. His smile is toothless, his eyes are bloodshot, and his denim shirt, trousers, and loafers are caked with mud; unruly hair rises in dark-gray puffs from his head. But he holds his shoulders as straight as any drill sergeant's. Patti and Aaron Hazelwood are poor, but they'd be insulted to be called that. They live on $183.20 a month from Social Security, plus $149.10 a month from federal Supplemental Security Income (SSI) checks. They say they are eligible but have been refused food stamps by the state. Their meager income barely covers their expenses: $120 a month for their home mortgage, $74 for hot water and electricity, $122 for gas for the car and tractor, and an uncalculated amount for food. They make ends meet by selling vegetables, eggs, and chickens.

Mrs. Hazelwood is in the kitchen watching a religious revival program on television and cooking marinated chicken necks while ironing the shirts of a grandson who lives with them and goes to college. Mr. Hazelwood locates a hard chair in his living room, fidgets with a straw hat, and talks about a lifetime of fighting: "The struggle I went through to get voter registration here! The first time we went to register they had a twenty-one-question test. She was the first one to register"—pointing toward the kitchen. "The man who was giving the test was a 'third-grade scholar.' So we subpoenaed him to Jackson and *he* wasn't able to analyze it. I had three children go to jail in Jackson. They put it down to a six-question test. We had people go to register there. They turned thirty-four of them down. We went to Washington, and they sent federal registrars here. We registered everyone."

In the autumn of their lives, Patti and Aaron Hazelwood have lost none of their spunk, although they believe many of their black neighbors are resigned, passive, defeated. "The underprivileged people stopped pushin'," says Patti Hazelwood, joining the conversation. "They went to sleep and didn't push no more. Stopped pushin' for jobs."

"Some of us got satisfied with the little handout they was giving us," Aaron Hazelwood says. "Like in Head Start school, the little handout they was giving to hush your mouth."

"They scared," Mrs. Hazelwood adds.

"I had one tell me when I was working that they wouldn't buy my cotton, my bean," he says. "I had one teacher tell me he'd lose his job. He's supposed to be a leader!"

Mrs. Hazelwood suggests this passivity has its roots in slavery: "A lot of people live on these plantations here, and they're afraid. We outnumber whites in the county, but most are scared to join forces." Scared to change life's habits and customs.

"When we started work here," he says, "we had black people tell us, 'Why don't you quit?' We had white boys and girls in here with us and they said, 'Why don't you go home?' " Gesturing toward the land just beyond his dirt road, Mr. Hazelwood continues: "My neighbor over there, they won't come out and do nothing for themselves. They get welfare." Spitting tobacco juice into a coffee can, he adds, "Welfare crushes a man." Like slavery, he implies.

Hopes for black advancement, he believes, rest with the children: "When Isaiah was the doorkeeper for Uzziah, he forgot everything else but being a good doorkeeper. But after Uzziah died, he saw the Lord. Some of our people got to die out for children to see results of being independent." Suddenly Aaron Hazelwood's face brightens and he adds, "Of course I ain't gonna die for a while."

Driving the few miles back to town, Malcolm Watts discussed Aaron Hazelwood's views on welfare. The attitude of welfare workers is that they are doing their clients a favor, Watts says. "I don't know who's responsible for the attitude, recipients or the government. But it really has an effect on people's ability to organize a network." Poor whites have more choice, he says. "But black people who are poor are rooted in the mentality that this is the way black people are supposed to live."

That serves as Malcolm Watts' definition of the welfare mentality. Joyce Leroy, a defeated welfare mother, serves as his chief exhibit. Joyce lives on Cain Street in a block-long row of connected flat-roofed shacks. She dropped out of school in the ninth grade after becoming a mother, and now at twenty-one has five children by two fathers, both of whom have vanished. Joyce relies on $144 per month from welfare and $248 from food stamps.

Her thick hair straightened and tinted red, Joyce is a heavy-set woman who keeps her eyes fixed on the floor when she speaks. She has never looked for a job, never thought of going back to school, never sought help. She does not know what type of job she would prefer, but "I would not like to clean nobody's house." Her own house, which rents for $40 a month, is immaculate. The living room is in front, and the furniture consists of a red leather couch, a double bed where three of the children sleep, a television set, and bare light bulbs suspended from the low ceiling. Behind the living room is Joyce's bedroom, where an infant sleeps on top of a carefully made bed. The last room of this flat is a miniature kitchen with a two-burner stove. A bathroom was not included, but Joyce's brother built one when the landlord, who owns the row of connected plywood houses on Cain Street, said he was not responsible for plumbing. A large tin tub hangs from a hook by the back door and serves as the Leroy family's bath.

Like her own children, Joyce Leroy says she never met her father. Her ten brothers and sisters were brought up in similarly cramped quarters and made do on "commodities"—now called welfare. "It's a lot better now," she says. "It was hard then." Her five kids sometimes make it difficult for her: "I keep telling them to do something. But they don't pay attention. Probably if I was a man they would." Yet Joyce is not dissatisfied. She says her days are spent "just sitting at home." What else do you do? "Lay down and take a nap," she answers. The television is on all day. For herself, Joyce has given up. Her hopes rest with her children. "I still believe," she says. "I depend on my children."

Barbara Harrison, like Joyce Leroy, is twenty-one, a dropout, a mother on welfare who lives in Belzoni. There any similarity between the two ends. Barbara's two-bedroom shack on Hayden Street is as messy as Joyce's is neat. She and her two children, plus a sister and her two children, and their grandfather live here amid clothes and cans strewn all over the floor. Grease cakes the kitchen pans; the bathtub is ringed with grime; the smell of urine suffuses the four rooms. But while Joyce takes pride in her house, Barbara clearly takes pride in herself. She has studied for and received a G.E.D. Last year she married the father of her children, a soldier on duty in Germany, who sends part of his paycheck home. Barbara's determined to leave Belzoni, and in a few days plans to move to Jackson, where she has been accepted in a program to train electricians. The pay, when she graduates, will be $9 an hour.

"There ain't nothing around here to do," Barbara Harrison says, looking directly at her visitors with big, dark eyes. Aaron Hazelwood is "my godfather," she boasts, and like him she rejects a sedentary life on welfare: "A lot of people feel welfare will take care of them. Not for me. I want a lot more out of life than welfare." Welfare is wrong, she says, because: "You don't get enough. Then they want to know too many personal things for what you do get. To rent a trailer around here is $100 a month. And then welfare only give you $60 a month for one child and $96 for two children. And they expect you to pay rent and gas and everything else. Not possible. Many people don't want to get off welfare. They just want to sit down. Not me. I want to own my own farm. I want a house and my kids to look up to something and to say, 'That's mine.' Welfare just keeps you from starving. That ain't enough."

Barbara Harrison would agree with Unita Blackwell, mayor of the tiny Delta town of Mayersville, and one of nineteen black mayors in Mississippi in 1980. "One lady just left here a few minutes ago," Blackwell says. "She has five children. She is single. She's thirty-two. She's had a husband. He's now got somebody else. So she's trying to take care of those children, including a fourteen-year-old with a baby and a sixteen-year-old with a baby. So that's two more folks. She had to drink. She had to do something. Well, we talked, and for the last two years she got herself out of welfare. We talked it out. Now she reads books. Now I see a lot of women in this condition who need a push. She's got all kinds of problems. She feels defeated on the inside. She wants a man. Then she goes in to the welfare department and they ask a whole lot of degrading questions. She tried to get off but found herself on a merry-go-round. While she looked for a job, she tried to get her daughters on welfare."

"Welfare eats away at the self-image," says Malcolm Watts. "I've never met anyone who's been on it a long time that didn't have that problem. Take Joyce. No reason Joyce can't find someone for twenty dollars a week to take care of her baby. But something causes her to stay home every day and watch *The Edge of Night.* She's got five kids at twenty-one!"

"But isn't she trapped?" says Benita Burt of the Governor's Office of Job Development and Training. "The welfare system is not an incentive system. It gives her no motive to go out."

Malcolm agrees; but like Howard Smith or Homer Kincaid, he believes it is more productive to stress self-help. "What we try to do," he says of MACE, "is paint a picture of what is possible. First you got to give a feeling that things can change. They have it bred in that things have to be this way. For years and years they have it pounded into them that they can't succeed. There are fears that have to be overcome. A low self-image. No feelings of belonging, in many cases. Everybody feels isolated, even though others are in the same condition."

In cities, hostility and a low tolerance for frustration seem to be more prevalent. In Mississippi, passivity, apathy, and the "low self-image" that Malcolm mentioned and novelist Richard Wright wrote of appear to be more pervasive. Recalling his youth in the Deep South, Wright wrote in *Black Boy*:

> I began to marvel at how smoothly the black boys acted out the roles that the white race had mapped out for them. Most of them were not conscious of living a special, separate, stunted way of life. Yet I knew that in some period of their growing up —a period that they had no doubt forgotten—there had been developed in them a delicate, sensitive controlling mechanism that shut off their minds and emotions from all that the white race had said was taboo. Although they lived in an America where in theory there existed equality of opportunity, they knew unerringly what to aspire to and what not to aspire to. Had a black boy announced that he aspired to be a writer, he would have been unhesitatingly called crazy by his pals. Or had a black boy spoken of yearning to get a seat on the New York Stock Exchange, his friends—in the boy's own interest—would have reported his odd ambition to the white boss.

"In a lot of ways we're our own worst enemies," Malcolm Watts says while driving from Belzoni to MACE's headquarters in Greenville. "I can go out on a street corner and talk to the brothers and ask them to help me move a lady's furniture and they'll say, 'What you want me to do that for?' And yet a white person asks them and they'll do it. It's deep-rooted. Same reason a black man won't buy from a black store." The importance of the civil-rights movement and such organizations as MACE, he believes, is that they help instill pride and encourage assertiveness. Still, Malcolm distinguishes between the majority who are simply poor and those who are in what he calls the underclass: the underclass consists primarily of "people who see themselves as poor. The poverty is in their attitude."

MACE employs 329 people—80 in Greenville, a city of 55,000 near the Arkansas border. MACE operates a variety of enterprises: a training center; a foundation that provides venture capital and technical assistance to small black firms; the number one radio station in the Delta; a jean manufacturer that produces 2,000 dozen pairs of Fine Vines jeans a week; a reading program for one hundred illiterates; cattle cooperatives; a housing development for 76 families; a technical-assistance arm for some of the black-governed towns or cities in the state. MACE is supported by the money from these enterprises, by the dues collected from members, by gifts from foundations and private individuals, and by government program subsidies.

187

A building that once housed the Shriners and was off-limits to blacks is now MACE's training center. This three-story complex on Washington Street contains a 150-seat auditorium, classrooms, and an immense ballroom for instruction or dances. MACE's Rural Youth Housing Project is similar to MDRC's Youth Incentive Entitlement Project. MACE provides twenty rural black youths with part-time work as carpenters and maintenance men; in return they attend G.E.D. classes at the training center. Conversations with most of these teenagers illustrates the emphasis MACE places on the development of positive attitudes.

Ricky Wild is a victim of bad luck. At the high school in tiny Isola, he was a football and track star, the president of the student body, a good-looking, dynamic leader destined for later success. Then bad luck intervened. His mother, a Head Start teacher, got cancer and was forced to leave work. His father was old and enfeebled. Ricky, the oldest of eight kids, had to quit school and get a job. "I didn't have a choice," he says. "We had to survive." Ricky does not come from a typical underclass home. He does not lack drive or strong parental influence. He is just poor. The $440 he makes each month, along with $160 from welfare and $235 from food stamps which the family receives, helps support ten people. Repeatedly addressing a visitor as "sir," as do most of these teenagers, Ricky says of MACE, "Recognition is important to me 'cause it makes me feel important. It also gives you courage, makes you feel you can do something. That is what MACE is all about."

"I have a girlfriend," he says, pulling her picture from his wallet. "She has a kid. It's different than guys in the streets. I support them." They plan to marry. Supporting her and his family is taxing, but he accepts his responsibilities. With the faith of a missionary, Ricky says, "You just got to have the courage to keep going. You can't lose 'cause you have nothing as it is. In the end, it will pay off." He commutes 104 miles each day to come to work and classes in Greenville. A strong positive attitude keeps him going, an attitude he fears friends, including some colleagues in the MACE program, lack: "We often talk about where you be tomorrow or five years from now, and a lot of people say nothing. Ask why and they say, 'I just want to have fun and party all the time.' It hurts me, a person like myself having a negative attitude. We often think things gonna come down and give us something."

Like Wild, Carl Bailor dropped out of school to support his family. He married a sixteen-year-old girl, and they have a baby daughter. He realized that he no longer had the freedom to hang out with friends in Belzoni, that he was responsible for more than himself. "It was hard for me, but I made the adjustment," Carl says. "Some dudes don't care, but I want my kids to come up much more better than I did. Since my mother and father separated, it created a downfall. It's unhappy in some ways. It just don't feel right for your mother and father to be separated. You just feel more together if your mother and father are together. You don't see too many dudes marrying. They say, 'I'm young. Too young to settle down.' " Carl has settled down. His wife's mother teaches his wife "things she don't know about kids." He has a steady job, a career goal (to become a carpenter), an immediate goal (to get a G.E.D. diploma). Unlike some of his friends in Belzoni, Carl says he won't steal to put food on the table. And unlike some young men he's met in Greenville, he finds street hustles like pimping or hawking marijuana unattractive alternatives. "Some people just start off and when it don't work right, they just give up," he says.

Like members of BT-27, these young people often say surprising things, things that if said by a white youngster might be dismissed as insensitive or bigoted. Listen to Carl Green, eighteen, from Rolling Fork: "Where I come from it's just a whole lot of young people walking the street and their parents don't care. They don't give them nothing. They just have to quit school. You know how kids do when just turning teenagers. They like to go out and start having babies, and then they go down the drain. They could have trained their kids better. All of a sudden they're a mother. Have to quit school to take care of their kids. Go on welfare."

Roy Grayson, seventeen, whose father was shot and killed when he was six, is equally stern about friends who impregnate girls and disappear: "If I had a child and me and my lady can't get together, I'd take care of my child. Some want her to get on welfare and then come back and live with her. They're not taking from her. They're really taking from children." Henry Lane, nineteen, agrees: "A lot of the guys don't care. I have a friend who did that. He had two babies and moved to another state."

When asked if they had ever felt discriminated against, many of these black teenagers say no. "I don't feel disadvantaged," says Carl. "All men are created equal. That's the way I see it. If he really wants it he can go out and get it." Henry says flatly, "I have never been discriminated against." And Robin can recall but one time: "I had this teacher who had something against black folks. She put them down. Tried to put them lower than they are. We had a few words."

Marie McBride, their G.E.D. teacher, an affable woman in her early thirties, says that in working with these young people her foremost challenge "is motivating them, making them feel they can learn. A lot of them don't feel self-confidence." Economic pressures weaken family ties; this weakening of family ties in turn shakes self-esteem: "I grew up in a home without a father, and I remember the shame and burden my mother had to carry from people in the community who made her feel unworthy. All of my life I've been ashamed. I don't blame my mother for what happened. Still, there's a stigma attached to it, and people make you feel like less of a person." She says, "I'd never bring up a kid without two parents." Of the six children in her own family, five finished school and hold good jobs. The sixth, an older brother, refused to work and became an alcoholic. "He's just a real trapped person," she says. "He feels a lot of self-pity. A lot of 'I'm no good. Nobody loves me.'" McBride believes that broken homes and the economic pressures of poverty outweigh race as factors holding black youth back.

How did she square her students' statements about the absence of racial discrimination with MACE's dedication to end racism and unequal treatment? "I don't feel nearly as discriminated against in Greenville as I did in Boston," she responds. "Here a salesperson asks, 'Can I help you?' In Boston they ask, 'What are you trying to steal?'"

Marie McBride's boss, MACE's thirty-nine-year-old executive director Charles D. Bannerman, sees the racism question from a different angle. Over dinner at The Rib Hut, a restaurant in a remote part of town whose soul food has attracted white governors and senators as well as civil-rights activists, Bannerman says the teenagers were asked the wrong question. "If you had asked them 'Do you think you have been treated the same as white boys?' you'd get a different answer." Unlike McBride, Bannerman believes that institutional racism is at the root of the poverty afflicting black Mississippians. "Humphrey's County has the kind of poverty no program can cure," he says. "There's a whole class of people who control everything and are basically oblivious to surroundings." Not until 1979 did Mississippi raise welfare allowances. Nevertheless, they remain the lowest in the nation, as the schools remain basically segregated. "Whites still control the school board, even though there are only maybe fifty white students in Humphrey's County. There's no compulsory education in Mississippi. No truant officers. There are six hundred thousand illiterates in the state, and we have less than three million people. And I would say eighty-five percent are blacks. Those conditions create repetitive poverty."

And over the course of time, he says, "It becomes a cultural thing. In black communities unwed mothers are no big deal. Always been part of our culture. We come from a slave culture. Marriage and divorce is not a big thing. Poverty becomes a culture. It sustains you. It's a lifestyle. If you can have rich people adapt in a counterculture —and that's their big option—imagine what people who have no option do to sustain mental health. Around here, because of slavery and racism, you're talking about people who have had to suppress natural desires." They learned: "You don't take risks. You try not to be seen. To be seen is to have some problems. You learn to be devious. You learn how to avoid bill collectors and controversy. You want to see this culture? You go out there and stand on the street and you'll be ripped off. They'll say it was your fault. You shouldn't have been there. There are fast rewards. Ripping off is a value."

Richard Wright's autobiography makes the same point about this adaptive lifestyle:

> No Negroes in my environment had ever thought of organizing, no matter in how orderly a fashion, and petitioning their white employers for higher wages. The very thought would have been terrifying to them, and they knew that the whites would have retaliated with swift brutality. So, pretending to conform to the laws of the whites, grinning, bowing, they let their fingers stick to what they could touch. . . . He was white, and I could never do to him what he and his kind had done to me. Therefore, I reasoned, stealing was not a violation of my ethics, but of his: I felt that things were rigged in his favor and any action I took to circumvent his scheme of life was justified. . . . True, I had lied. I had stolen. I had struggled to contain my seething anger. I had fought and it was perhaps a mere accident that I had never killed. . . . But in what other ways had the South allowed me to be natural, to be real, to be myself, except in rejection, rebellion, and aggression?

But Bannerman, who was born in Harlem and could pass for an actor with his muscular good looks, barbered mustache, camel-colored sport jacket, dark trousers, and striped tie pinched at the collar by a thin gold pin, extends this argument to cover the behavior of some Northern as well as Southern blacks. He asks: Why are 80 percent [the actual figure is just under 50 percent] of the prisoners in America's jails black? He answers: "What happens is that our values are already different to start with. And when institutions become unresponsive, we revert to what we know." The heritage of slavery and Jim Crow has defeated some blacks, he says, leaving them to believe they can knock themselves out and not get anywhere. "I see that a lot." Although Bannerman believes this attitude is a practical response to institutionalized racism, he also worries, as does Thomas Sowell, that this passivity has hindered the progress of American blacks: "You'll find most black people in New York who are somebody are West Indian. A very different culture than black people in the South." Both have the same skin pigment; both suffered slavery. Yet the West Indian, he says, developed a more positive self-image. "They come from their own country. They have strong family ties, a strict British school system."

But this is an argument fraught with danger. It can be twisted into a polemic that goes like this: American blacks are poor because they are culturally "inferior." Since this is a long-term if not permanent handicap, it is not correctible by money or compassion or governmental effort. Bannerman says he's aware of the danger, confident that the many blacks who have climbed from poverty due to the efforts of MACE refutes this argument.

But Vanessa Green, MACE's program assistant and the director of the Delta Arts Program, is plainly nervous with the conversation. "I agree with the culture of poverty," interrupts this thirtyish woman who wears a stylish burgundy-and-orange wrap around her Afro, "but if you look at it from a complete pathological viewpoint you lose something. You're talking about people who are going through the culture of survival. Lots of positive things come out."

Bannerman readily agrees, but he continues to stress the pathological behavior of those he calls the "underclass," as opposed to those who are simply economically poor. "My brother has a master's degree—and a criminal record," he says. "He works now and then. He's a classic underclass mentality. He doesn't believe in working. It doesn't bother him to do nothing. I would never hire him because I know his value system is totally different."

But is that value system unreasonable?

"I judge it to be unreasonable. Especially since he's my brother. His problems started in the military." He was thrown out of the Air Force, lost his self-esteem, became a heroin addict and a thief. "He couldn't keep up. He lost prestige. He found prestige in prison."

But whites gain prestige in strange ways, too. "Look at me," he says, pausing to scan a table laden with hickory-smoked ribs, chicken, hot sausage, bowls of smoked beans, cole slaw and potato salad. "In this town I'm considered powerful. Yet I can't get in that country club. And I go to the White House more than them—going next week. So who am I 'to be seen of'? That's what motivates people. Money is only one way to keep score."

"This is a multicultural society," says Vanessa Green. "Not just in race and nationality, but economically. Look at what's considered crime. There are things the dominant society considers crimes that may not be. Stealing a loaf of bread to support a family is not necessarily considered a crime you should be sent to prison for. Looting is not necessarily a crime."

I ask if she is just making excuses for those poor people who commit crimes.

"No," she insists. But Bannerman is not sure. He relates a recent experience. MACE hired an ex-convict as a bookkeeper. Several months later they learned he was forging checks. Bannerman says he was outraged; the majority of his staff was not. Vanessa sided with the staff. "There are crimes against persons and crimes against property," she explains, suggesting the latter are more acceptable.

Was she not contradicting the belief in shared values promulgated by MACE?

"In terms of holding society together," she says, "middle-class values are false. I could not do things my middle-class white friends could do. They had access and mobility I did not have. Black folks exist with a kind of duality."

Bannerman echoes her: " 'If you're white, you're right. And if you're black, stand back.' " He points out that black Americans are treated differently yet are expected to act the same. Hustling and jostling and cutting corners results from this brainwashing by society. "We have no problem understanding brainwashing in the Korean War. But we do have trouble understanding the brainwashing of Americans and America."

What did Bannerman do about the bookkeeper?

Heeding staff pleas, Bannerman said he kept the bookkeeper in his employ and no one reprimanded him; two weeks after the event the bookkeeper still seems to be working diligently.

Is there a contradiction between preaching individual responsibility and then excusing a person who forges checks?

"Learning is by mistakes," says Bannerman, recalling his own childhood. Home was the Lincoln Projects in Harlem. He remembers resenting all authority figures: his parents, his teachers. At fourteen, he dropped out of school and ran away from home. He got into trouble, was arrested, and was threatened with a visit to jail. He was terrified. But his father, a subway conductor, while refusing to condone his behavior, let him know the family stood by him. The judge gave Bannerman a break; he returned to high school, went on to Ohio State, and came to work in Mississippi. He escaped the ghetto, but his brother did not. "You look back and wonder why you got out and other people didn't," he says. "I wonder. My father gave me values. He would ask me, 'You spell this?

You spell that?' He gave me values." Bannerman applies this lesson to the bookkeeper: "What if someone hadn't taken a risk with me?" Still, he's not sure they chose the wise course. "Maybe we were too paternalistic?" he asks.

The subject of his father brings Bannerman to the issue of unwed mothers. He knows many black and white civil-rights and political leaders downplay the issue, and that Daniel Patrick Moynihan was vilified for raising it in 1965, but like most poor or community-based people I encountered, Bannerman emphasized it. "In a moral sense, I don't care," he says. "But from a practical sense, I care."

Vanessa, who is a feminist, interjects: "It's incorrect to say there are negative social consequences. That's a dangerous generality."

Bannerman arches an eyebrow at her and insists that kids need a male role model: "Your parents have an effect on you. I'm not saying aware single parents can't have an effect on you. But in general it's harmful. I've seen it. I've seen kids identifying with all sorts of things. Boys in particular are gonna identify by the time they're six or seven years old. They lose Momma then and identify with some male role. When I grew up in the project in Harlem, I was one of the few people with a daddy." The cause of broken families, he believes, is economic pressure on men who cannot find work. He also blames welfare: "Maybe what we're reaping now is the man-in-the-house rule. If you had a man in the house, you didn't get welfare."

Does being raised in a female-headed family have negative social or psychological consequences for the children? "I see it as a social problem," Bannerman says. "You lose all your options. You lose your mobility. And when you lose that, you lose your will." It is this loss of will, this passivity, that is so hard for MACE to overcome. Bannerman blames slavery, continued racism, broken families, and welfare dependency for this apathy. But he is quick to add that it would be wrong to blame only the individual. "The majority of people don't vote in this country. And why don't they vote? Because it doesn't make a difference. So if you expect no different from the majority, why expect different from poor people who feel equally if not more helpless?

"Appalachia is a good example of how welfare makes people passive," he says. "White people living on a different plantation, the coal company plantation. You've got to give people the capacity to develop themselves rather than being dependent." That requires jobs, which are far too scarce in the Delta, Appalachia, or Harlem. But it also requires something else, says Bannerman, again reflecting the basic ambivalence of many community leaders who simultaneously stress society and individual responsibility. Bannerman goes back to talking about instilling a proper attitude, about self-esteem, initiative, values. Then he concludes, "There's real good evidence that if I have an investment in the stock exchange I'll watch the Dow-Jones averages. If I don't, I'll just read the sports page. If people don't have an investment in society, there will be no change."

Differences: The White, Black and Hispanic Underclass

When I return to New York, the members of the Wildcat program are eager to learn about Appalachia and Mississippi. What were the people like? they ask. Are there differences between the rural and urban poor? Between blacks and whites? Or Hispanics and whites? Interrupting their stream of questions, Howard Smith invites me to the lectern to give an impressionistic account to the class.

In appearance, I say, the Southern poor seem worse off than the poor in the North. In Appalachia, one of the first things a visitor notices is rotting teeth—"green tooth," as it's called there. While broken or missing teeth are common in the North, decent dental hygiene is more prevalent. In general, health care is worse in the South, with fewer Medicaid services and other social programs. This in part reflects the different traditions of the two regions. Government, for all its flaws, is often thought of as an ally in Northern cities, and as a meddler in the South. Because of these varied traditions, welfare benefits and government support are usually less generous in the South. Perhaps because of this, the infant mortality rate is steeper. According to the Atlanta-based Southern Regional Council, in eleven key states in 1980, 14.3 percent of the population lived in poverty, yet only 3.4 percent received AFDC support. And the maximum monthly support in 1980 for a family of three in Mississippi was $96, in Texas $116, and in Tennessee $122. In New York a similar family could receive almost $500 monthly.

There are also differences in behavior. The MDRC has generally found that passivity, as opposed to hostility, is more pervasive in the

South. Or as Anne Ward, the MDRC's representative for urban Baltimore and rural West Virginia said, "I think the rural underclass seem more content with their lives. Life doesn't change much for these people. When I talk with kids in Baltimore— Their parents come from the South. They're very mobile. The people in West Virginia are not very mobile. They don't know that they should ask for more. They don't complain, women in particular, that they're only getting the minimum wage." Because of their passivity and fear of venturing from the familiar confines of the home, she says, "West Virginia has a terrible attendance and lateness problem. The myth is that blacks have no respect for time. These people are no different."

Sometimes far from the nearest road, with few job opportunities or skills and very little self-esteem, a person is probably more likely to give up in the South than in the North. Passivity and dependency are the most frequently cited woe of MDRC and MACE recruiters. Those with ambition and energy often migrated to Northern cities in search of opportunity. Or as Robert Coles writes in *The South Goes North:*

> The streets, then, offer hope. The streets have received, continue to receive, men and women and children who have had to leave their homes elsewhere; they are people driven and forsooken, compelled by fate to seek not merely a new life, but the conditions under which survival is possible.

The lifestyle is different, I tell the class. As Charles Bannerman of Mississippi told me, "Rural kids don't stand on corners because there are no corners." The so-called clock life is different. With less to do at night, people generally rise when the sun comes up in the morning and go indoors when the sun goes down. With fewer strangers to contend with, shopkeepers more freely extend credit to their customers. Where ghettos exist, they rarely sprawl. In rural areas it's not uncommon—as it is in the North—to find the rural poor living next door to more affluent families. The hills of West Virginia contain expensive red-brick houses beside ramshackle trailers. In the suburb just beyond the city line of Greenville, Mississippi, wooden shacks lurk behind modern ranch houses with two-car garages. "My next-door neighbor is on welfare," Henry Myles, director of public affairs for MACE's Delta Enterprises, told me. "I don't mind as long as he trims his lawn."

One result of urban stress and steeper unemployment is more crime—particularly violent crime—in cities, where the majority of the underclass now live. Gary Walker, who is the MDRC's senior vice-president and spends part of his time visiting MDRC sites throughout the nation, says, "Violence is one area of human behavior that can be analogized to the behavior of rats. In rat experiments, they've found that if you put rats in a crowded space you get more violence." Resentments build. A resident of Preston County on his way to work, for instance, encounters neither the strangers nor the opulent wealth that a Miamian or Harlemite would on his way to work in midtown Manhattan.

What frightens citizens most about urban crime is its random nature. Homicide rates are soaring everywhere, but a truly startling statistic is the geometric rise in murders by strangers. Pocketbooks and gold chains are grabbed in broad daylight along crowded thoroughfares; rapes and homicides have become almost commonplace. But random crime does not plague West Virginia in the same way. "People are closer," explains Homer Kincaid. "They know their neighbors. I go driving in Preston County, and the people wave. You find the crime rate not that great in rural counties. People are not afraid to talk to strangers. There's violence here, but you don't find severe crime. People are not afraid to walk down the road. Most crimes are from people getting high on alcohol. No one's coming into a community from the outside." While in cities disputes are more and more frequently settled with guns, in rural areas, Kincaid says, people resort to "fisticuffs."

In cities, an underground economy tends to flourish. Most members of the Wildcat program have side hustles—selling drugs or "hot" goods, running or playing numbers, organizing dances, cheating on welfare programs or food-stamp programs or methadone programs. Fewer rural supported workers have such hustles, and those who earn outside income tend to do so in what are considered less antisocial ways. On the corner of Mill and Amite streets in Jackson, Mississippi, for instance, every morning thirty or so black men, ranging in age from about twenty to fifty, wait on a corner as if in a shape-up line. All morning long, people pull up alongside, roll down the window on the passenger side of the car, and barter over an odd job they'd like done—painting, carpentry, masonry, a garbage detail. On a good day, the men are off the street by early morning. On a bad day, by afternoon they are drunk.

MDRC officials report that 15 percent of all supported workers enjoy some illegal income—a figure that they think is low, because it is based on volunteered information. Indeed, there is some evidence that the underground economy is more extensive in smaller Southern cities than is commonly assumed. Terry Williams and William Kornblum of the City University of New York, who are engaged in an unusual research project on the underclass in New York City,

Louisville, Cleveland, and Meridian, Mississippi, were surprised to find that Meridian, a city of fewer than 50,000 inhabitants, ranked second among the four cities that they studied in illegal earnings among young people. (Cleveland ranked last.) The reason, they suggest in an unpublished study, is that poorer communities that have "accessibility to more affluent white and black patrons" have broader markets. They write: "The existence of a large naval base at the outskirts of Meridian has created a thriving market for drugs and sex in this small city. Thus we find that youth in Meridian do perceive opportunities for earnings in the illegal economy. We have a surprisingly large number of individual cases of youth who have been employed in drug dealing and prostitution."

While some of this illegal activity—particularly pimping, prostitution, drug peddling, street crime, and vandalism—debases the quality of city life, it must also be placed in a financial context. The underground economy is not monopolized by the underclass. The Internal Revenue Service, for instance, estimates that Americans, many of them affluent, cheat the government of $18 billion in annual tax revenues. Some economists have estimated that the total underground economy—including maids and workers paid off the books, inflated expense accounts, pilfering, tax avoidance—could be as high as $250 billion a year.

Rural or urban, broken families are often an indicator of poverty. When the number of families headed by single women goes up, income goes down. This is true among blacks and whites, within or outside of metropolitan areas. But the percentage of broken homes is greater among urban than among rural blacks, and greater among urban than among rural whites.

While children in the white underclass are more likely to grow up in a two-parent home, incest is more common in these families, according to people who work with the underclass in Preston County, West Virginia. The absence of stable family life remains a distinguishing trait of the underclass everywhere. In a national survey of all the teenagers participating in its Youth Incentive Entitlement Pilot Projects in 1979, the MDRC found that 39.7 percent of the whites lived with just their mothers; 48.3 percent of the Hispanics lived with just their mothers; and 61.4 percent of the blacks did. Nationally, only one quarter of all the teenage participants lived with both parents.

The similarities between the rural and the urban underclass are striking. There is the same general lack of exposure to the world of work, the excessive violence in the home, the absence of role models, the same dependency on and rage at a degrading welfare system, the same lack of self-confidence. Cecil Breeden in West Virginia resents authority, just as John Hicks of Wildcat does. Mary Paul rages against the indignities of the welfare system just as Pearl Dawson does. Teenage motherhood rises, in the North and in the South.

Also, the stereotypes are alike. The Wildcat trainees sat in rapt attention when I told them of whites in Appalachia who denounced "trashy" welfare loafers or those "who live good on welfare" and rode about in their "fancy cars." They were surprised, and not a little amused, to hear of Sam Clendenin, in Preston County, being chased by his mother with a shotgun. The description of Tolbert Pickens' rotting teeth raised a few eyebrows, as did Cecil Breeden's hostility and his inability to get to work on time, or Lora Paranski's working as a prostitute. They heard of Pickens' alcoholism and passivity, of Susie Haun's former dependency on welfare. Members of the class could identify with teenage mother Joyce Leroy's five children and dependency on welfare in Belzoni, Mississippi, with Barbara Harrison's messy Belzoni home and strong desire to escape the clutches of welfare, with Ricky Wild's being forced to resign as the student body president of Isola High School in Mississippi in order to support his family. Wild, like Pearl Dawson or Denise Brown of BT-27, was not born into the underclass. He was the victim of bad luck, not bad attitudes or a culture of poverty.

Silence followed my presentation. Finally, Howard Smith said, "The most important thing I heard is that all races behave the same. Many people feel inferior. What was said is that whites, when in poverty, behave the same. It is not anything intrinsic to a certain race of people."

On that note, the class broke for lunch. The members went off to McDonald's and the other fast-food emporiums where they usually ate. I walked up Eighth Avenue, past the addicts and alcoholics languishing in doorways, past the bars where the pimps hang out, past the Port Authority Bus Terminal where the surly prostitutes, truculent chain snatchers, and dope peddlers ply their trade, past the dazed shopping-bag ladies and drunks, past the crushed dreams and the dirt and decay and hopelessness and spiritual poverty of Eighth Avenue. Heading for the subway I thought of these people who hover around West 42nd Street, many of whom could be members of BT-27. And I thought of what Howard Smith had said. Howard is right, I think, that all races behave the same. But in the rural South, defiant anti-social behavior is less prevalent; the underclass is less visible, part of what Michael Harrington called "the other America." In urban America, the members of the underclass are as omnipresent as potholes, and can be considerably more dangerous.

15

BT-27
Graduates

All participants in MDRC programs—white, black, and Hispanic; rural and urban—are taught that the standards of success in the world of work differ from those on the street. They are repeatedly told of the importance of having the right attitude. "If they are to be placed in permanent slots, we try to work on attitude," says Wilhelmina Baert, an instructor in a Manhattan skills-training program run by McGraw-Hill which is attended by four members of the Wildcat program, who were chosen because of their success in typing class. Mrs. Baert teaches very basic social skills, she says. "Be pleasant. Try to show willingness when someone asks you to do a job. When we get to telephone training, we try to get the students to be pleasant, because the person on the other end doesn't see them. We try to get a good image across, because that's what counts."

As proof that attitude counts, Wilhelmina Baert and others point to the want ads in newspapers. Despite the bankruptcy of scores of manufacturing companies, the loss of jobs everywhere from the North to the Sun Belt, and statistics showing that 9.5 million people in this country were unemployed in late 1981, Wilhelmina Baert and others say that thousands of jobs go begging. And they often blame the lack of a proper attitude as much as the lack of skills. "If you want a job, we can place you," says Melvin Rosen, the associate vice-president of Wildcat and the supervisor of its job-development staff. "Anybody who wants to work—even if he's unqualified—he can get a job. Motivation is much more important than skills."

This does not alter the fact that there are fewer low-skilled manufacturing and blue-collar jobs, especially in America's aging cities, than there were for earlier generations of immigrants. Today's high school dropout is usually judged to lack the reading, writing, typing, math, or social skills required by the post-industrial service economy. Knowing this, many lack the self-confidence even to try. It is this lack of self-confidence that employers may confuse with the wrong attitude.

Nevertheless, few dispute the notion that there is a "skills gap," with a blue-collar population vainly chasing white-collar jobs—what is known as structural unemployment. After studying this problem in 1979, the Carnegie Council on Policy Studies in Higher Education concluded that nationally "one-third of our youth are ill-educated, ill-employed, and ill-equipped to make their way in American society." New York City's largest private employer—the New York Telephone Company—reports that six of ten applicants fail the competency test it gives prospective employees. The telephone company, which hires something over three thousand people annually, says that it sees twelve to fifteen applicants for every candidate who meets the skills and attitude requirements.

The Wildcat Skills Training Center tries to impart the proper skills; Howard Smith's life-skills class works on developing the proper attitude. Four months into the seven-month training program, poor attitudes claimed five more members of the class, in addition to John Hicks, William Penn, Henry Rivera, and Willy Joe. And in each case, lack of patience or drive or a sense of security played important roles. Gladys Miller, who had learned to remove her stocking cap in class and had improved her typing—and was so nervous the day she received her ten-week diploma that she couldn't eat lunch—unexpectedly told Howard Smith she was bored attending classes. "At school I was given courses, but I didn't want that kind of course," she said later. Gladys asked for and received permission to return to her supported-work job as a messenger for a city agency. Ramon Lopez, who spoke with such enthusiasm the day he received his ten-week diploma—"I started something and I don't usually finish things I start, so I'm proud"—suddenly declared he too was tired of the classroom. Ramon told Howard he had been "lonely" ever since his friend Henry Rivera left. He later told me, "I just got bored, tired of being there." Ramon returned to his supported-work job in the printing and reproduction department of a city agency, a job that may well be another dead end for this twenty-eight-year-old. John Painter did not mend his ways. After repeated admonitions about his attendance and lateness—Wildcat records show he was absent one out of five days and late 49 percent of the time—Painter was dismissed from the training center. A few weeks later John went to work as a typist with a personnel agency, a job unlikely to set him on the road toward his stated goal of becoming a major executive.

Two of the four students who joined the class in the eleventh week had also left. Herbert Washington, the forty-seven-year-old former office manager who had been unemployed and on the streets the past ten years, mysteriously stopped coming to class on March 28. Attempts by Wildcat to contact him proved fruitless. Aubrey Powers, the traumatized college graduate who did not like to be laughed at, was returned to Wildcat's main office for psychological help after he tried to strike typing teacher Delores Licorice. The evaluator wrote of Aubrey: "Has been verbally and physically disruptive and threatening on every assignment which he has been given. . . . he is possible [*sic*] very dangerous."

Seven months in a classroom proved enormously frustrating to many. With the exception of Aubrey Powers, they were all high school dropouts. Many had earned more money on the streets than they received at Wildcat; their Wildcat salary barely exceeded the money they could receive on welfare. And there was no job guarantee at the conclusion of their year of supported work. Not seeing immediate results, not knowing if all these classes would lead to a job, many began to feel that they were being exploited, taken advantage of. Their suspicion was compounded by impatience. "Many of our people were just getting out of the penitentiary or drug centers," Howard Smith said one day. "They weren't prepared for punctuality and attendance. They had just got half a foot into the work world. They're used to being in prison or at home with soap operas. Suddenly they're bombarded with work requirements. It's unfair to them—and to us."

Just two months shy of the final graduation day, the Wildcat class I sat in on, whose enrollment had been as high as twenty-six students, now had eleven. Nevertheless, Smith and the eleven students pushed on. For the remaining two months, Smith concentrated on practical lessons. He reviewed the six steps involved in writing a letter to apply for a job: "*Why* I am writing. *Where* I learned of the job or training program. *What* I can do. *Who* I am. *How* I can be reached. *When* I am available for an interview." He played a videotape recording of a black man identified as Mr. Jones on his way to meet a personnel officer. To steady his nerves, Jones went first to a bar, and he arrived for his appointment a few minutes late. The personnel officer immediately noticed that Jones' application was blank regarding his most recent employment and his criminal history. Asked about this, Jones responded evasively, "I had personal problems." During the interview, Jones rubbed his nose, shifted about in the chair, chewed bubble gum, and spoke in street slang. The people in Wildcat readily agreed that Jones failed to sell himself.

Smith hammered home the point that this was Jones' fault, not the system's, and launched a discussion of the do's and don'ts of going for an interview. Don't wear a sexy, low-cut dress, an enormous wig or hat, heavy perfume, cornrowed hair, a furious Afro, or a dashiki. Don't walk jitterbug style, take along a radio, lie about a criminal or narcotics record, or resort to street slang such as "my gig," "What's happening?," "cool," "You dig?," "I've got to pick up my juice" (methadone) or "I been upstate" (in prison). Among the do's: in responding to want ads, make sure to ask the address and time of the interview; during the interview, say "please" and "thank you," listen to the questions asked, be relaxed without acting too familiar, look at the interviewer, clasp your hands and cross your legs.

After watching actors being interviewed in job situations on videotape, the class members were invited to pretend that they were at actual interviews. These performances were videotaped and re-played for the class. At first a few of the students resisted, but during the last several weeks all participated, analyzing and re-analyzing their performances and assessing each other. Sometimes Smith was the interviewer, hitting the students with hard, antagonistic questions. Sometimes he asked me, the only white person there, to act as a personnel officer. Sometimes he asked one of the class members to be the personnel officer. They wrote sample letters, reviewed the qualifications needed for various jobs, and asked hundreds of practical questions.

During New York's one-week mass-transit strike in April 1980, BT-27 vigorously debated whether the training center should be open or closed and whether they should be docked a day's pay for failing to attend classes. Most of the students in BT-27 said that they could not walk six or more miles each way from their homes in Brooklyn, the Bronx, and Queens, and thought it unfair to be penalized a day's pay for an absence due to circumstances beyond their control. Although Howard Smith recognized the merit of their argument, he insisted that supported work was about self-reliance and positive thinking. As was true when they argued they should not lose pay for going home rather than sitting in a cold classroom, members of BT-27 felt picked on, much as youngsters do when punished. The staff arrived at a compromise: the trainees could take each missed day as a vacation day, but it would be subtracted from their vacation time.

By mid-May—one month short of graduation—Howard sat in his

cramped tenth-floor office munching on a hero sandwich and handicapped for me the prospects of the remaining eleven members of BT-27:

Smith worried that Leon Harris might drop out. Harris' wife was pregnant. He missed the kind of money he made on the streets. And last week he had been absent two days and didn't call in, Howard ominously noted.

He also worried about Hope Parker. Problems at home were getting her down. Her grandfather died after a long illness. A week later her Coney Island apartment was flooded and the floor collapsed. She stayed at home to repair her apartment. Then her teeth hurt, and she required oral surgery. She needed approval from the local Medicaid office, and they hassled her about the cost, requiring regular visits to their offices. "Sometimes she comes in and seems depressed," Howard observed.

Timothy Wilson, Howard said, "is up and down. He needs a lot of attention." Like most of the young people who enter supported work, Timothy had a low tolerance for frustration. One day he would be full of enthusiasm, and the next he would storm into Howard's office and threaten to quit and go on welfare. "He saw it as the easy way out," says Howard.

William Block was also a borderline case, Howard said. The poor health that has plagued William ever since two .38 slugs ripped open his chest sometimes dragged him down. "He's still very reticent," said Howard. "It's hard to get to him unless you have the time and patience."

Howard Smith was more confident of some of the other members of BT-27. He felt that William Mason, interviewed recently for a clerk's position with a private firm, would succeed whether he stayed through graduation or not. Pearl Dawson, Denise Brown, and Carlos Rodriguez were doing fine, as were Michael Mathews and, to a lesser extent, Ivy Ford, two of the students who joined BT-27 in the eleventh week.

The big question mark was Mohammed, who like John Painter had been put on probation because of poor attendance and punctuality. Mohammed's problems were special, and instructive of the individual attention each member of the underclass can require. After some improvement, Mohammed had fallen back into his old habit of poor attendance. Depressed, Howard Smith stared at his half-eaten sandwich and offered this explanation: "He hasn't been able to match his sect of Islam with what's going on out in the streets. Even among the staff here, who are supposed to be sympathetic and understanding, when he comes to the training center and his wife meets him there's a feeling of strangeness. She doesn't talk. All of her body is covered except her face. When spoken to she won't respond without looking in his direction, and he responds for her. You see the pride he has in religion, but the reaction the staff has is that it's strange. Once a day he'll ask me or one of the staff for an office for fifteen minutes of prayers. It can't be any office. It has to be facing east. You go by the room and people ask, 'What's that strange noise?' It creates strains. And also, don't forget, it's only one year since he's out of jail. He was a leader of the Muslims in the penitentiary. Muslims are treated with respect in jail. Now he comes out and, if anything, he's looked on as strange."

Graduation day is a damp and overcast June day. After seven months of classes, the Wildcat students assemble in a dingy, pale-yellow fifth-floor conference room at Wildcat's main office. The 660 First Avenue office is a seven-story former printing factory several blocks south of the United Nations. To get there the members of BT-27 took their usual subways to midtown, and then walked or rode a bus. All had been here before—to interview for the supported-work program, to collect a check, to see a guidance counselor, a staff psychologist, or any of the 126 staff members employed by Wildcat. A receptionist sitting behind a glass window buzzes visitors into a cavernous room dotted with hand-me-down metal and wooden desks, as well as supported workers or fresh applicants waiting to claim the attention of a staff member. In all, the Wildcat Corporation in 1980 had an annual budget of $7 million to supervise 450 to 700 supported workers, a maximum of only 120 of whom attend the training center and Howard Smith's life-skills class. The rest were assigned to a new training center in the South Bronx, or to one of ninety-eight government and private job sites.

The graduating class has shrunk to ten. Leon Harris dropped out three weeks ago to take a $150-a-week job with his brother in construction. "I wanted to start working as soon as possible," Harris later explained. Smith has another explanation. "He had applied for a grant from the government," he says. "He got it. He may be like so many people I know, traveling from one program to another. They hustle programs." Leon, Smith adds sympathetically, also had a personal tragedy. In May, his new baby died during delivery.

Joined by Wildcat officials, including the organization's president, Amalia Betanzos, the remaining members of the class convene around a set of metal card tables arranged in a horseshoe shape in a back room without adornment. Hope Parker sits at one end. Personal and medical pressures got to be too much for her, Hope says, so two weeks ago she asked to return to her supported-work job, with the city's Human Resources Administration, before completing the course. Nevertheless, because she mastered the required skills, Wildcat has invited her to receive a diploma, even if technically she did not finish the course. In her spare time, Hope says, she reads the want ads and goes out on job interviews. "I been looking," she says dejectedly. "But unemployment is rising. I went to one place, and a lady made me feel that being twenty-nine is a sin. I went to four job interviews, and I'm getting tired. I got the skills. I can type forty-five words a minute without mistakes. But I got to get me some more skills to compete. I'm going to take shorthand." Tears welling in her eyes, her head down, Hope says, "I'm in the same place I was when I got here."

Denise Brown, who sits beside Hope, is only slightly less depressed. "I had a tough morning," she says. Her sister, who is eighteen years old and the mother of eighteen-month-old twins, ran away this morning, and could not be found. "I'm the oldest of the kids, and they tell me I have to take the twins or they'll separate them," she says, no doubt feeling that her life is repeating itself. As a child in Montreal, Denise had to look after her younger brothers and sisters. The sister's disappearance only adds to Denise's depression about her own vain job search. She applied for a clerical position at CBS, but she has been waiting so long for a promised second interview that she is convinced that the job has been filled.

Moments before the ceremony commences, Howard Smith surveys the room and one by one summarizes for me his impression of each graduate: "If you had asked me about Denise Brown two months ago, I'd have put her in the same category [outstanding student] as William Mason and Pearl Dawson. I'm not sure why, but in the last few weeks I'm not so sure. I've seen this phenomenon before. Just before graduation students who were outstanding in performance and behavior suddenly begin to fall to pieces as graduation approaches. It is not unique to Wildcat or similar programs. The same thing happens in high school. It happened to me. I quit two months before graduating from high school. It's less controllable with our type of population. That's what I saw happen to Denise. She became afraid. She suddenly realized how comfortable the training center was. It wasn't so cold any more."

Next to Denise sits Michael Mathews, who enrolled in the eleventh week. Two weeks ago, Mel Rosen arranged an interview for him with a midtown-Manhattan branch of D'Agostino supermarkets. Michael was hired as a dispatcher, coordinating grocery deliveries. "He'll make it if he can give himself time to become acclimated and make positive friendships at D'Agostino," Smith says. If not, he'll return to drugs and the streets.

Next is Ivy Ford, who several years ago attended Wildcat alongside another ex-addict—Howard Smith. Ivy appears relaxed and self-confident. But Smith is not sure that she'll succeed. "She's playing so many games that she's ultimately the victim of her games," he says. "In many ways, she doesn't know the difference between the games she plays and reality. She'll come into class and if there's too much typing pressure suddenly she gets ill and has to go home. Her attendance was erratic during the week, but you always knew you'd see her on Friday." Friday was payday.

Smith is more hopeful about William Block, who sits beside Ivy. Block's attendance was sporadic. Yet he always phoned in, and supplied doctors' notes. "Despite being out a lot, he catches right up," Smith whispers. "He's a very reserved, very modest, very nice guy. I think he'll make it." Block seems to think so, too. Just this morning, he was interviewed for a clerical position, at $4.25 an hour, with a company that manufactures police badges, and he believes he has a good chance of getting the job.

Next is Timothy Wilson, who of late has alternated between bravado and depression. Today, he seems depressed, and keeps to himself. "Tim's main stumbling block is his youth," Smith says. "He's never had the type of guidance and direction most young people need." Looking at Wilson, Smith crosses his fingers, silently wishing him good luck.

Finally, at the far end of the horseshoe table are William Mason and Pearl Dawson. Mason is the valedictorian speaker. "He's the type of person who will succeed," Smith flatly declares. He feels the same about Pearl Dawson, who has been judged the outstanding academic student in the class and today will receive an award of twenty-five dollars. Tomorrow, she has an interview with Montgomery Ward for a receptionist position. "The awards are nice," she says, "but it won't mean anything if there's no job." She offers no sympathy to those who are downcast. "If anybody should be depressed, it should be me," she says. "I'm older than anyone in the class, and I feel that if I don't get down and don't feel like I'm beating my head against the wall, they shouldn't, either. I could stay on welfare if that's the way I felt."

The only graduates not taking part in the ceremony are Carlos Rodriguez and Mohammed, who both have already found employment; neither could leave his new job to attend the graduation ceremony.

Instead of their normal diet of hot dogs and hamburgers or ham sandwiches brought from home, the graduates peered at and finally wolfed down box lunches catered by a local French restaurant—pork pate with pistachio nuts, cold slices of stuffed chicken breasts, string beans vinaigrette, a slice of brie and an apple. The ceremony began with remarks from Amalia Betanzos, the personable woman who is the President of Wildcat. "Your training class was the most difficult we've ever had at Wildcat," she says, and she recites a catalogue of woes—inadequate heat in the classrooms, a leaky ceiling, an eleven-day transit strike, and the resignation of Sally Grueskin. Nevertheless, Amalia Betanzos says, Mel Rosen reported that "there is not a single person in this group who isn't qualified for a job."

One by one, the Wildcat teachers offer their congratulations. Then Howard Smith rises slowly and, with obvious emotion, says, "This will be the most memorable class for me." His eyes pass from face to face, and he continues, "Classes in the past had the best of conditions. Not this one. We first started out with twenty-two students. [Four more were added later.] Everyone was full of hope, said what we were going to do. And yet you were—you are the ones that endured. If you watch any race, some runners start out with a burst of speed. Somewhere around the track they get a cramp, give up, lose sight of the goal. You're the ones that endured and finished the race. And though some of you don't have the reward of a job, I'm confident you will. There's always the intangible reward called self-esteem."

Each member of the class receives a diploma, after which William Mason delivers the valedictory address, in a deep voice that commands attention. "The turn of events here has left us with less people graduating," he says. "And it doesn't make me mad. It makes me sad. We winded up as friends. I must admit there were times I resented the rules and regulations. I'm glad I stuck it out. I had a lot of pushing and a lot of pulling. I now have a lot of education." He heaps praise on Wildcat, on his teachers, on his colleagues, and concludes, "I'm leaving with more confidence in myself. I'm overcharged with confidence. Look out, world, here I come!"

16

What Became of the Members of BT-27

Early in 1981, Howard Smith and the Wildcat Skills Training Center moved from their sunless offices on West 37th Street to more comfortable quarters, at 241 Church Street, in lower Manhattan. By January 1981—seven months after graduation—the twenty-six people who left Wildcat's program had taken several divergent paths.

William Mason had wanted to become a beautician, but he soon abandoned that plan. Failing to find work immediately, he shifted from one temporary job to another, and earned extra income by singing in local clubs. "They say they're not supposed to show prejudice because of previous convictions, but they did," he complained to me. Yet Mason did not give up. With the aid of an introduction from a nephew, on August 21, 1980, he started work as a private security guard for a federal public-housing complex in Brooklyn, at a salary of $125 a week. A few months later, he had risen to sergeant in the security force. By the end of the year, he was Lieutenant Mason, earning $161.50 a week, and commanding a force of sixteen men on the four-to-midnight shift. And Wildcat's job developers now called him to find work for their trainees. Still, Mason's entrepreneurial sights were fixed on bigger things—on opening, with his brother, a barbecued-chicken-and-ribs restaurant with an adjoining pool hall. "I'm ready to go into my own business," he said at the end of the year. He credited Wildcat with liberating and channeling his ambition. "They did a lot for me," he said. "They gave me a step back into society."

Carlos Rodriguez had got a $150-a-week job as a cashier with

Daitch-Shopwell, through the Wildcat job-development office, but he left it after several months. "I had an argument with the manager," said Rodriguez, who is a homosexual. "He didn't respect me. He used to make remarks about my personality, and I just told him where to go." Rodriguez pondered the want ads. On September 10, 1980, he started a job as a clerical worker with a nonprofit medical society. He worked in a Park Avenue office with thirty-two other people, earning $150 a week. "I love it," he said at the time. "They treat me nice here. With respect. It's interesting. I plan to stay here a while and get promoted." Not long after that, Rodriguez was dismissed. He told his friend Denise Brown, "I had problems with people there and their attitude." One day, they told him not to come in any more, and paid him for the week. The next week Carlos went on unemployment.

Although Wildcat officials had predicted that Denise Brown would be sought after by employers, she did not get the job she had applied for at CBS, and spent months racing to job interviews. All led to dead ends. "I was discouraged at first," she said. She remembered her past. "Before Wildcat, I went into a terrible depression," she told me later. "It was loss of hope. I was so far gone the courts recommended me to see a psychiatrist. I felt like nothing. I felt dead. I felt like something was drained from my soul." She was beginning to feel the same way after Wildcat. But she struggled to retain her newly won self-confidence, and then her luck changed. A Wildcat job developer arranged an interview with an employment agency. On the basis of the interview and a typing test, Denise was offered a clerk-typist job with a national company; the salary was $131.35 a week. "I like what I'm doing a lot," Denise said in early 1981. She had received a $10-a-week raise and was expecting another. But her rewards were more than financial ones. "I'm getting a lot of experience here," she said. "I write my own letters. I answer letters. I'm kind of well known within the three insurance companies we deal with." Today Denise is optimistic. "I don't get depressed any more," she says. "I may get frustrated, but I've achieved a lot in the last two years."

Mohammed, heeding Howard Smith's warning that employers might reject a Muslim, gave his name as Jerome Patterson when he applied for a job with an architectural firm in Queens. He was hired as a draftsman-trainee at $140 a week. Once he felt comfortable with his co-workers, Mohammed dropped his guard, and ceased to hide his religion. "They know me as Mohammed and as Jerome Patterson," he said at the end of the year. He was cheerful. He was soon to be a father. He and his wife had moved to a nice apartment in Queens. And he was pleased with his performance. The firm had given him a $20-a-week raise. "This is a great opportunity here," he said. "This is a company that designs doors. I draw them—with the help of Fred, who's the boss here. Things are moving up for me."

Michael Mathews, who had got a job as a delivery dispatcher with the D'Agostino supermarket chain, was making $150 a week, $25 more than he had earned in 1971, before going to prison. He held the job until November 1980, when he was dismissed for undisclosed reasons. Mathews later said he quit. "I didn't exactly like the job," he says. "It was too much pressure for me. I couldn't trust the guy I was working for. He was on the shady side. I just left. I was getting into a CETA program." But before this happened his home telephone was disconnected, and Wildcat's job developers lost track of him. In December, Leon Harris reported that he occasionally saw Michael on the streets of Brooklyn, and he thought that he had returned to hustling. A close friend from Wildcat thought that he had returned to using and selling drugs. "He seemed like a nice person," this classmate said. "But then when you got to know him you saw he had things in his past, was a wanderer, was disorganized." In early 1981, however, Mathews did get a CETA job, and he began work as an office aide with a city agency. "I type. I file. I use a Dictaphone. I use the calculator. I answer the phones. I'm trusted with confidential material," he explained. (A friend, asking to remain anonymous, said Mathews was in fact only a messenger.) Mathews added, "But my job is being cut by the Reagan budget cuts." However, Mathews says he was told that the city agency planned to keep him on as a "provisional" after federal CETA funds were terminated.

Pearl Dawson, the Wildcat class's "outstanding academic student," spent several months searching for the right job. She got nervous. She had survived alcoholism, a manslaughter conviction, and a stay on welfare. She began to worry about losing her confidence again. But finally a Wildcat job developer arranged an interview that paid off. In August 1980, Pearl Dawson was hired by the City University as a financial aide, earning $209 a week. Her job includes typing, filing, and using a computer terminal. Within two months, her weekly salary jumped to $250. Her voice brimming with pride, she told me in early 1981, "Truly, I enjoy it."

Ivy Ford graduated from the Wildcat program, but her first several months in the job market were not encouraging. In August, she was fired from a $175-a-week job as a secretary with a small manufacturer in the Bronx. She says she was told that the employee she had replaced decided to come back. Wildcat records show that her next job was as a typist with a plumbing company, at $135 a week, and that she was fired again. She says that it was only a temporary job. In

October, she started as a clerk with a city agency, at $159 a week. She was also pregnant. In December, Ivy entered a hospital for an operation, and later lost the baby. By the end of the year, she was back at work, her pay had been raised to $175 a week, and she had been given new responsibilities—keeping time records and making out payroll checks. "It's nice. It's more money," she told me. She had moved to an apartment in Manhattan, and said she no longer received a daily methadone dosage. Ivy said her sights were now set on becoming a legal secretary.

Timothy Wilson, the youngest member of the Wildcat class, found job-hunting difficult. With assistance from a Wildcat job developer, he started work as a clerk-typist for a small firm on June 30, 1980, but before he could build up any seniority or benefits bad luck intervened. "I got sick," Wilson told me, explaining that he was in a hospital for two weeks. Someone else had been hired to fill his job by the time he came out. On his own, Wilson got a job sweeping and making sandwiches at an Arby's fast-food restaurant. He left after three weeks, when a vocational firm put him in touch with the New York Telephone Company. Timothy recalls how he used what he had learned in life skills for his first interview there. "I learned how to look for a job, how to mail in for a job, how to present yourself, and how to keep a job," he says. "When I went for this job, I had no problem. I always had problems on how to do interviews before Howard taught us little things like how to shake hands, how to sit down and cross our legs and put our hands together." Wilson started as a clerk and word processor in October, at a salary of $180 a week. By the end of the year, he said, he was typing eighty-five words a minute, expecting a raise, and getting along well with his supervisor and his fellow employees. "The job I got a lot of people wish they had," he said. But his real goal was to become a comedian-mime. "In the summer, I'm going to get me a job from four to ten or twelve, and take my act to the streets. At first I started it as a hustle. Now I'm perfecting it as a professional. I do Bruce Lee in slow motion. No other pantomime does this." On weekends, Timothy Wilson and Stephanie Long, a former addict whom he met at a drug-rehabilitation center and to whom he is now engaged, entertain pedestrians along Manhattan's Sixth Avenue.

The nervousness and insecurity that Hope Parker expressed on graduation day persisted until August, when she joined a city agency as a typist. At the end of 1980 she was still working there, in an office with seven others, typing, filing, handling financial records, and answering the phone. She had yet to receive a raise from her starting salary of $135 a week, but she expected one and was content. Al-

213

though Hope had rarely spoken in life skills, she had now become outgoing and enthusiastic. "Knowing I can do something for myself besides welfare has given me a lot of motivation," she said. She has moved from the Coney Island apartment she shared with her grandfather to a three-room apartment in Flatbush. And though she still did not look back fondly on the life-skills class, which reminded her of group therapy, Hope thought that the training she had received at Wildcat was invaluable. "I was down in the dumps," she said. "It was a period when I felt I had nowhere to go except Wildcat." Hope plans to stay with the city and grow, "so I won't have to go back to drugs or go on welfare."

William Block, who strove to overcome ill health, alcoholism, and fears that employers would blackball him as a former convict, got a job—with the help of a Wildcat job developer—at a dry cleaner's, in Manhattan. The weekly salary was $124, or $9 more than he had been earning at Wildcat at graduation. According to Wildcat's records, Block worked there just under two weeks. One day, he simply didn't appear for work—didn't call, didn't pick up his pay. Wildcat's job-development office sent Mailgrams to his home. They went unanswered. He had no telephone to call. "We don't know where he is," Mel Rosen said at the end of 1980.

Sixteen members of the class did not graduate, and they, like the others, have had varying degrees of success. Phillip Rivers, after being absent 32 percent of the time, was dismissed from the program in January 1980. Wildcat kept track of him, and records show that at the end of 1980 he was earning $128 a week as a messenger for a private firm.

Earl Billings was late 66 percent of the time, according to Wildcat records, and he was dismissed from the training center after one month. Wildcat tried to find him, but Billings, like many poor people, was not listed in the telephone book or with credit agencies, and shifted residences frequently. Wildcat officials do not know where he is.

Larry Pearl was dismissed from Wildcat for poor attendance and a surly attitude. Wildcat's records indicate that he earned $3.75 an hour as a mail clerk with the city's Department of Social Services through June 1980. He left that job on July 3. A Wildcat job developer arranged an interview for him for another position, but Pearl did not appear. He did not respond to Mailgrams.

Liza Lance quit the class. At the time, Howard Smith said, "She doesn't feel she can make it. She feels that everyone in the class is smarter than she is." At the end of 1980, Wildcat's records show, she was earning $130 a week working for a company that manufactures dolls.

Ronald Brooks left Wildcat because he was arrested and had been absent a quarter of the time. Mel Rosen reported that Wildcat found a job for Brooks but that he turned it down. Rosen said Brooks lacked motivation. Wildcat records show that at the end of 1980 Brooks was working as a shipping clerk, at $125 a week.

Stanley Lawrence was dismissed for poor attendance. Wildcat pursued him, and finally arranged an interview with one of its job developers for 9:00 A.M. on June 24, 1980. At 12:45 P.M., Lawrence was found wandering the halls of the main office, claiming that he had slept late. Another appointment was scheduled for the next day; again he did not show up. His Wildcat record is blank until September 8, when he was hired as a clerk by a sportswear store. He left after one week. On September 15, Wildcat found him another job, this time as a stock clerk. He was fired the first day. On October 7, he began work as a messenger, but he left after a few days. Wildcat lost touch with him after that.

Herbert Washington, who had not worked steadily since 1970, simply stopped coming to the class after a few weeks. Wildcat sent Mailgrams to his apartment inviting him to come in for job counseling. They were returned unopened, with the message that no one of that name lived there. Wildcat does not know what became of Washington.

Aubrey Powers was sent back to Wildcat's main office in March, for psychiatric help. He was judged to be a paranoid personality and potentially "very dangerous." Wildcat's psychological counselor met regularly with him and, in April, reported that he was working in the office and "doing fine." Soon thereafter, however, Powers was referred by the counselor to Bellevue Hospital for mental observation, but he did not keep the appointment arranged for him there, nor did he return to Wildcat. His whereabouts are unknown.

Gladys Miller, frustrated and bored with the drudgery of classroom work, returned to her supported-work job as a messenger with a city agency. When her year of supported work was up, the agency gave her a full-time job. At the end of 1980, she remained a messenger but had hopes of moving up to a better position. "I'm taking a test in March for an office-aide position," she said.

Ramon Lopez, who, like Gladys Miller, decided to leave the training center in the spring, because he was bored, and "nothing was moving there," and who had hated public school because teachers made him feel "dumb," returned to his supported-work job, as a printer for a city agency. In August, the agency put him on its full-time payroll, at $154 a week. "I'm doing okay," he said at the end of the year. "I duplicate copies. It's a job."

Henry Rivera, unlike his friend Ramon, did not survive the first ten

215

weeks at the training center. Nor did he succeed after returning to his supported-work job, as a filing clerk with the city's Human Resources Administration. Rivera was fired for poor attendance on May 15, 1980, the day after his thirty-seventh birthday. Henry had trouble understanding and speaking English. He had also never ended his dependence on drugs. The two factors may explain why, in the course of his thirty-seven years, Rivera had never held a regular job. After he was dismissed from his supported-work job, Wildcat called him in for a job interview. Wildcat records indicate that they sent Mailgrams to Henry's home. They went unanswered. Wildcat lost track of him. At least two former members of BT-27 claim to have seen Rivera on the streets of Brooklyn, and say he is now a numbers runner. They think he is secretly living with the mother of his child, who receives welfare.

John Painter, who was suspended from the training center in April, after repeated admonitions about attendance and lateness, started work as a typist with an employment agency on April 29, earning $135 a week, but he quit before the week was out. As often happens to those on parole, he was soon arrested for suspicion of committing a crime. He was later found not guilty and was released. But no doubt this incident reinforced his cynicism and his impression that cops were "punks." Painter hung around the house of his adoptive parents, in Jamaica, Queens, ignoring Wildcat Mailgrams and calls from his parole officer. In June, he got a job with a caterer at John F. Kennedy International Airport. "He seemed to like it," I was told by Dolores Painter, whose husband is a superintendent in the Postal Service and was the brother of Painter's natural mother, who died when he was an infant. In any event, Painter continued to ignore his parole obligations. The parole officer, a woman, was nice, Dolores Painter said. What I didn't know at the time was that while Painter was at Wildcat, he was arrested for armed robbery. Instead of sending him back to prison, Dolores Painter said, the parole officer gave John a break and let him continue at the training center. Mrs. Painter warned him that his parole officer's patience was wearing thin, but he laughed it off. "He just didn't follow rules and regulations," she said. In August, the parole officer had Painter arrested and sent back to prison, in Virginia, where he has another year and a half to serve.

In January of 1981, Dolores Painter, who had just returned from Virginia, where she visited John Painter in prison, said, "I said to him, 'Honey, you'd be surprised how many people would be jealous you had this chance. Your parole officer turned the other cheek.' I told him I was surprised she didn't clamp him in the clinker sooner. He just laughed. This was his second chance at life. I said, 'Make the most of it.' He didn't. One teacher summed it all up one day. Said he was 'too smart, and one day he's going to outsmart himself.' I told him, 'You are back in jail because of what you did. Don't blame no one else.' "

When Leon Harris left the training center, in May, he was hired by his brother as a builder's helper for a real estate company, at $150 a week. Harris worked there for two months. In August, his Wildcat mentor, William Mason, hired him as a private security guard, starting at $3.10 an hour. By the end of 1980, Harris had received a raise and was working the four-to-midnight shift under Lieutenant Mason. Of the job, he says, "It's pretty nice." Of Wildcat, he says, "It taught us a lot. To deal with myself. To deal with society and learn society." He says he no longer hustles on the side and still has the same career goal. "I really want to be a counselor, dealing with people," he said. "I'm scouting around to see if I can find a place in a hospital or a school."

John Hicks, who was suspended from the training center in early March, returned to his supported-work site, with United Neighborhood Houses, on East 15th Street. Instead of taking the civil-service exam or going to college, as he had vowed to, Hicks told a Wildcat job developer that he wanted to become a carpenter, and Wildcat helped place him in a carpenter-trainee program in June. John quit after three weeks, complaining that the sawdust was getting in his lungs. Wildcat checked, and found that, according to Hicks' supervisors, his attendance had been undependable. Wildcat's records show that Hicks then applied for welfare. "The last we heard was that he went to welfare and said we did not give him a job," Margre Torres, of Wildcat's job-development staff, recalled early in 1981. "We did give him a job. Welfare called here and we told them." She assumed that Hicks had been turned down by welfare. Wildcat subsequently sent Mailgrams to his home, in Queens, but received no response. By the end of 1980, his phone had been disconnected.

William Penn, after being dropped from the training center for excessive drinking and poor attendance, returned to his supported-work job—building parade barricades for the Police Department. He worked there until August 29, 1980, when his year of supported work came to an end. Penn started work on October 17 with a messenger service, earning $124 a week. By the end of the year, he no longer worked there, and could not be located. One member of the class said she had seen him on the streets of their Brooklyn neighborhood hawking what she assumed were stolen goods—clothes, jewelry, gloves, incense. Willy Joe, a close friend of his, said, "I don't think he's doing too good. He's going through pressures right now. He's not treating himself right. His attitude has changed. He's getting colder and bitter." Another friend said that Penn was not living at home with his parents but that his father, who retired recently from a private sanitation job, was "probably helping him out." The friend said that Penn also was supported by the woman he lives with, who receives welfare.

When Willy Joe failed to receive a ten-week Wildcat certificate, he was sent on to a supported-work site—building police barricades alongside Penn. He had several interviews scheduled for a possible job in a restaurant kitchen, his stated goal, but did not keep them. On June 27, Joe started work at a branch of Nathan's in Brooklyn. He was paid $124 weekly, and in January 1981 he told me, "I worked as a grill man. But I got fired 'cause I missed one day. I overslept that day. See, we had a new general manager." Wildcat's records show that Willy was fired in August because of repeated absences. Soon afterward, he was mugged, for the second time in 1980, and required three stitches to close a head wound. Rage began to build. He said he could feel himself becoming "a cold person again," and went on, "I said, 'Damn. I'm out here to earn a living.' I thought of putting a pistol in my hand and sticking up something and getting a thousand dollars and just laying back. Or just having a pistol to protect myself and take a life. But I thought, 'No, that's thinking wrong.' I think the Lord helped me." Willy Joe was studying the Koran. Striving to improve himself, he left the young woman who was so dependent on him, and moved from East New York to Crown Heights in Brooklyn. Soon afterward, in the fall, he started hawking hats and gloves from a small cart that he wheeled around downtown Brooklyn. The goods he sold were bought wholesale in the garment district by his boss, Willy said, and he earned $150 weekly in this off-the-books business. Partly because he worked in the underground economy, he continued to feel outside organized society. "I don't have no birth certificate," he said. "So I don't have no Social Security card." Willy said he had tried to get a birth certificate, but had been unsuccessful so far. Without identification, he can't cash checks.

At the end of 1980, Willy was still working the cart. And he was contemplating a reunion with the former girlfriend who treated him "like her god." He said, "I was with her today. She seems like she's ready to change." As for their daughter, he said he had not seen her "in a long time," and that she was still staying with her grandmother. Willy also said he had still not seen or heard anything about the woman somewhere in Trenton who is the mother of his son.

Despite these concerns, Willy said he no longer felt "crushed." Religion provided greater inner peace. He went on, "I got my thinking together. I now got my mind on what I want to do and how I'm going to do it." He said he hoped to become a male nurse. Just a few days before, a friend had told him that the job paid well and provided ample benefits. Willy said he had a lead for such a position. "I wrote down the phone number. I didn't have a chance to call them today." Becoming a nurse was a means to an end. His true dream, Willy said, was to save money and buy some land down South. He added, "I want to build a house and do some farming down there."

17

MDRC and Supported Work: Results of a National Experiment

For Willy Joe, a former drug addict and street criminal, the program known as supported work failed; for Pearl Dawson, a longtime welfare recipient, it succeeded. For the twenty-four other members of the underclass who enrolled in the Wildcat Skills Training Center's BT-27, the results were similarly mixed. But the program brought several questions into focus. What works for the underclass and why? Is the public subsidy, averaging $5,700 for each supported worker, justified? And what of those people, like Willy Joe, who fail? Should there be some other social program that attempts to assist them? What would this cost? Could any program supply the self-confidence and the motivation that Willy lacks? Can a program be devised to reach and calm traumatized people like Aubrey Powers, who suddenly flare up and attack instructors? Could any social program pay its participants enough to divert someone like John Painter, who found he could earn more than his Wildcat salary through hustling and crime? Or temper the hostility of someone like Cecil Breeden, in the West Virginia supported-work program? Are we willing to accept failure? Or, to put this question another way, how do we define success?

Some of these questions have no clear answer. Others were asked, and to some extent answered, in what the MDRC called "one of the largest social experiments ever conducted in the United States." The experiment focused on the underclass, a group of perhaps 9 million Americans who are chronically poor. While students of poverty differ on the size and origins of the underclass, they generally agree that this group experiences both income and (usually) behavioral difficulties. It is made up of street criminals and hustlers (who may not be poor), people for whom welfare has become the only known way of life, traumatized ex-mental patients and alcoholics—people who are cut off from organized society and the world of work. The twenty-six members of BT-27 were part of an $82 million supported-work program stretching over five years at fifteen locations around the nation. (Six more sites were eventually added.)* Eleven million dollars of this sum was earmarked for research, most of it in the form of contracts with Mathematica Policy Research, a social-science research corporation in Princeton which adopted the research design of Hans Zeisel of the University of Chicago, and the Institute for Research on Poverty, at the University of Wisconsin. Between 1975 and 1978, 10,043 people enrolled in the national program. The researchers kept track of 6,616 members of the underclass, half of whom were enrolled in supported work, and half of whom were eligible for it but were used as a control group. The reason for this elaborate research design was explained by the MDRC in a five-year summary of the supported-work experiment published in February of 1980:

> Too many costly federal programs had been established and expanded without adequate information about their effectiveness. Supported work sought to change this process: to acquire knowledge before legislators had to decide whether a demonstration should be expanded into a national program.

The mixed results of the Wildcat class mirror those throughout the country. About a third of the welfare recipients, ex-addicts, ex-offenders, and young people who entered the twelve-month support-

*In addition to the Wildcat Service Corporation and the AFL-CIO's supported-work project in West Virginia, the nineteen sites were: the Atlanta Urban League, Georgia; Options, Inc., in Chicago, Illinois; the Supported Work Corporation in Detroit, Michigan; the Maverick Corporation in Hartford, Connecticut; the Community Help Corporation in Jersey City, New Jersey; Transitional Employment Enterprises in Massachusetts; the Newark Services Corporation in Newark, New Jersey; the Peralta Service Corporation in Oakland, California; the Impact Service Corporation in Philadelphia, Pennsylvania; the St. Louis Housing Authority in Missouri; the San Francisco Phoenix Corporation in California; Pivot, in the state of Washington; and six sites in Wisconsin. Three of these sites—Detroit, San Francisco, and the state of Washington—closed during the demonstration and were replaced by three sites in New Jersey: the Bergen County Supported Work Corporation, the Trenton Supported Work Program, and the Atlantic County Supported Work Program in Atlantic City. All of these sites were counted in the original nineteen. The two additional sites added in 1980 were in Cincinnati and Wisconsin.

221

ed-work program went on to unsubsidized jobs or returned to public school. People find that result either good or bad, depending on their standard of measurement. In any case, an accurate assessment of such data requires an awareness of the traps involved in making sociological measurements. For instance, Richard Harris, Wildcat's assistant vice-president for operations, told me, "Our placement rates in December of 1979 were seventy-eight percent." That is true if the figure includes only the placement of those who completed a year of supported work. Since the average stay in supported-work programs was under seven months, the majority of those who enroll are obviously not placed in jobs. Another way to look at the data is to say that the high per-capita cost of the program and the program's national dropout rate of seventy per cent represented failure, as such a percentage would if one were grading ordinary students; or one could say that these are not ordinary students, and that a different definition of success and failure is therefore required.

The MDRC naturally favors the broader definition of success. The corporation came to believe that such a one-year intervention program was unlikely to alter lifelong habits, attitudes, insecurities, and patterns of behavior. "Given its experimental purpose and the severe handicaps of the groups to whom the program addressed itself, it was not expected that supported work would be successful with all or even a majority of its target groups," the MDRC's five-year summary said. The program was designed, the summary pointed out, not just to produce the best numbers but to "learn which group benefited more, which less, and which not at all." The quest was for information as well as for results. After five years, the MDRC found that for two of the four target groups—ex-addicts and mothers receiving AFDC payments—"the benefits exceed the costs." The benefits include a reduced reliance on welfare, reduced crime, and the conversion of some people from tax-consuming to taxpaying citizens. The results among ex-offenders were "inconclusive"; that is, there was no measurable benefit. For youths who had dropped out of school, supported work failed, with the costs clearly outweighing the benefits.

Of the four targeted groups, it was the AFDC mothers who benefited most from supported work. The typical mother enrolled in the program was thirty-four years old and unmarried (only 3 percent had husbands during their time in the program), was a school dropout (fewer than a third had completed high school), had not held a full-time job in at least two years (only 25 percent had), had been on welfare an average of eight and a half years, and was black or Hispanic (only 5 percent were not). To be eligible for supported work, a mother was required to have been on welfare for thirty of the past thirty-six months, to have no children under six, and to have limited or no work experience. About 40 percent of these mothers finished the training program and went on to regular employment. Their average attendance in the program was almost 90 percent, compared with about 80 percent for the three other groups; only 12 percent were dismissed from the program for poor performance—compared with 38 percent of other groups. The employment rate in the two years or so following participation in the program was about 20 percent higher for those enrolled than for those in the control group, and their earnings were almost 50 percent greater. By extrapolating future earnings and reduced dependency, the MDRC concluded that over the mother's working life "supported work generates an estimated $8,150 more in resources per participant than it uses up."

Among AFDC mothers, the biggest impediment to success was a lack of self-confidence. Howard Smith made this point when he observed of Denise Brown on graduation day, "She became afraid. She suddenly realized how comfortable the training center was." Gary Walker, the MDRC's senior vice-president, testified before a Senate subcommittee in March of last year that 25 percent of the AFDC mothers in supported work "could or would not go to a regular job." This fear is not hard to fathom when one meets women who have rarely worked, have rarely left their homes, and are accustomed to having their lives organized by welfare. Such a person was Marilyn Lawson, a participant in the Peralta supported-work program in Oakland, California. A mother at fourteen, Marilyn Lawson had been on welfare since her husband abandoned her fourteen years earlier when she was pregnant with their second child. She had no high school education, no job experience, and no means of financial support, and she was scared. Nevertheless, she struggled and succeeded at supported work, and afterwards looked back and described her fears, her earlier life, and her current success to an MDRC interviewer:

> I used to be withdrawn because of the lack of confidence I had in myself. . . . I wasn't positive about myself or anything. I didn't think I could do it. When I started the clerical thing in the office I couldn't spell, put punctuation into my typing. Many times I wanted to give up. Sandy Warren [a supervisor] always talked to me and told me to keep trying, that I could do it. Finally I started building up my confidence. . . .
> Q: That fear made you kind of withdrawn—did you not see people?

223

A: Yes. I didn't know how to communicate with people. I would put my head down when people spoke to me. . . . It was a different feeling going to work every day. After a while I felt like it was part of what everyone was doing, instead of just sitting around doing nothing. It made me feel good that I was doing something for my children, too. Before I didn't know anything.

Q: So you think it helped the children too?

A: Yes, I feel it did and it will help me when they grow up, too. Building confidence in me enabled me to build confidence in them. Peralta helped me do that. I didn't feel good about myself before.

Q: Can you think of a specific example of that? Where you paid attention to something where you might not have before?

A: With me and my children talking, I was unable to communicate with them. I have one boy who asks a lot of questions and wants answers and I would even withdraw myself from him. They had friends whose parents worked and I was on welfare and they wanted to know what I was doing, why I wouldn't go back to school, and things like that. Even now my boy wants me to go back to school. . . .

Q: When you were growing up did your mother work?

A: My mother worked. She did day work on the side. My father worked also. My mother never had much time for us. She was always out working. She was limited too, and uneducated. She felt very frustrated within herself also. If we came to her with a problem she would just tell us to go somewhere and sit down. She was hurt lots of times because she didn't know how to help us. She didn't know how.

Q: Did you feel deprived as a child?

A: Yes. I cried a lot. That's the very reason I winded up pregnant. I didn't understand anything. I had no one to talk to. . . . My kids were always depressed when I was on welfare because I was totally out of it.

Q: When you were always depressed before, were you trying to escape?

A: I wanted to escape but I didn't know how.

Q: What was your life like at that time?

A: I would wake up in the morning and do nothing. The people I knew then couldn't help me deal with my problems. I would watch television. I knew every program on TV. I watch TV now but I don't spend the whole day in front of it. I don't have the time. The way I do things now is totally different.

Q: What do you do for fun? Has that changed?
A: I do many things with my children where before I didn't do anything. My boys and I go skating now. Before there were many things I didn't do. Now I'm not afraid to do things.

To try to understand why the program worked best for AFDC mothers, the MDRC sent a team of interviewers in late 1979 to talk to women who had been enrolled. Why, they wanted to learn, did some of the women give up, while others did not? Martha Ritter, one of the interviewers and an MDRC consultant, concluded that AFDC mothers fell into four general groups. The most successful group, she wrote in a summary of her impressions, was made up of women who "made a conscious decision to break out of a day-to-day existence and were doggedly determined to develop a skill or at least to acquire the work experience they knew was necessary to enter the regular job market." For them, money was not the key aspect of a job. What mattered more was the sense that others counted on their work— that they were helping people. Supported work allowed them to "gradually defeat the frequently paralytic fears of entering or reentering the labor market." Such a woman was Pearl Dawson, who successfully completed the Wildcat program. A second group, Martha Ritter wrote, had similar desires, but luck was not on their side: "Misfortune befell them as soon as they hit the regular job market. Some faced intolerable working conditions. Straining physical labor produced incapacitating injuries; age, sex, and race discrimination wiped out others." For instance, until her luck changed, bad health and luck pushed Susie Haun of West Virginia into a life of welfare. A third group was motivated primarily by a desire to earn money, Martha Ritter said. Constantly searching for higher pay, they cared less about their job performance or their pride and tended to "roam from job to job—usually with no benefits—always looking for higher wages." She went on, "They find dependence on welfare generally acceptable as a tolerable resting place between more remunerative activities." These women sometimes encountered obstacles beyond their control, but they differed from the second group in that "they, themselves, also serve as obstacles to a secure job," she wrote, adding, "An exaggerated sense of victimization, along with health problems, a general disdain for supported work, and an acceptance of welfare all contribute to the fluid character of their working lives." Gladys Miller, an ex-addict in the Wildcat program, had such an "exaggerated sense of victimization." The final group was made up of women who remained on welfare. "They seem overwhelmed by the everyday workings of the world," Martha Ritter wrote. "Their homes reflect the disorder of their lives and their removal from daily affairs. They often fear for their lives and those of their children. They are deeply passive and accept welfare as a stable feature in their lives." Such a person was Jean Madison, an East Harlem mother with twenty-nine children who has been on welfare more years than she can remember, and who said, "You get used to it."

Wildcat and the supported-work program in general tried to offer these mothers work skills and new habits along with counseling and the support of their classmates. But as Eric Lax, another of the interviewers, noted, participants needed to have the right attitude. "If there is one word that can summarize what got those supported workers who are now working through the program and into the work force, it is 'responsibility,' " Lax's report concluded. "Dozens of people we interviewed said virtually the same thing a young man in Newark told me: 'If you want to work, the program is there for you. But you've got to want to do it for yourself.' I do not think it is oversimplifying matters to suggest that AFDC mothers had the highest placement rate in large measure because they wanted something better for themselves and for their children. . . . Supported work works for those people who want to change their lives, are willing to work at it, and who get a couple of good breaks along the way. It is quite possible that the most important of the three, in the long run, is the breaks: a good supervisor; a job on a crew doing work that is enjoyable; a chance for a good job after leaving the program."

The second target group that the MDRC judged a success was made up of ex-addicts. The typical ex-addict was twenty-eight, unmarried, male (20 percent were female), a school dropout (fewer than 30 percent had finished high school), had worked ten weeks the previous year, was on welfare when he enrolled (80 percent), had been arrested (90 percent), had served an average of 129 weeks in jail, and was black or Hispanic (only one out of seven was not). To be eligible for supported work, the ex-addict had to be currently enrolled in a drug-treatment program or to have been enrolled in one during the previous six months. The MDRC's five-year summary concluded, "During and after the time when the ex-addicts were in the supported-work program, they were involved in substantially less criminal activity than the control group." Their public-assistance payments went down and their employment went up. Although only 23 percent of the ex-addicts went on to full-time employment—the lowest percentage among the four target groups—they were judged a success compared with the poor performance of their control group, which trailed the three other control groups. In all, over the ex-addicts' anticipated working life the benefits—reduced crime, re-

duced welfare, and increased employment—exceeded the costs by
$4,345 per participant. There were disappointments, however. The
experiment "did not have a significant influence on the ex-addicts'
use of drugs," the report noted. "The unemployed members of the
sample show only a slightly higher use of drugs than those employed,
and in the final nine months of the study this is actually reversed."
Thus, as was true of Wildcat's Henry Rivera, it may be wishful thinking to call them "ex-addicts."

Obviously, the nation's economy played a part in determining the
success not only of ex-addicts but also of all other members of the
underclass and the much larger number of those who live in poverty.
In the 1970s, for instance, the official poverty count shrank impres-
sively (except in two periods of recession, 1974–75 and 1979–80). A
recession coupled with a rising inflation rate drove 4 million more
Americans into poverty in 1980. And President Reagan's sizable cuts
in federal income-transfer programs—along with a lagging economy
that may not respond to his tax-cutting plans, and may force deeper
budget cuts—could increase the number of poor people still further.
But among ex-addicts in the supported-work experiment—as among
the underclass in general—the effects of the national economy
should not be overstated. Failure, the MDRC found, often resulted
from bad attitudes, rather than just from constricted job opportunities.

This finding buttressed Howard Smith's argument that addiction
is mental as well as physical. In Smith's judgment, Henry Rivera
would be capable of holding a regular job if he could stop leaning on
drugs. Paul Weber, who was a white supported worker with Jersey
City's Community Help Corporation, told me in an interview that his
heroin intake rose while he was enrolled in the program, "because
I was earning more money." Weber talked of having been a hustler,
of once making an easy living on the streets. Other addicts and
members of the underclass are simply traumatized—too far gone to
reach—like Aubrey Powers.

Still others completed the supported-work program, got jobs,
seemed on their way to a new life, and then slipped back onto heroin.
Sam Aiken, forty-three, was one of those. At the Oakland site Aiken
won attendance awards and was made a crew chief. Yet his first
encounter with adversity drove him back to heroin. Like other members of the underclass, Sam had a behavioral—in his case, psychological—problem. Eric Lax writes:

> "Why did I start again?" he asked me with a sardonic grin. "If
> I could answer that question I'd be one of the wealthiest men

in the world. You just have to take it one day at a time. Sometimes you think, 'This is it, I'm clean,' and then, phew, something hits you in the back of the head and there you go."

But supported work was deemed a success for ex-addicts primarily because, although their reliance on drugs did not abate, the program did provide a regular income, and so lessened their need to commit crime. In short, the program resulted in a trade-off: to achieve a lower crime rate, society was in effect exchanging money for drugs. This raises several provocative policy questions. The results of supported work suggest that society can marginally reduce drug-related crime, but can government afford the billions it would cost? If the money were available, would the public be willing to subsidize the drug habits of addicts? If the public were willing to dispense drugs freely, should government any longer classify them as illegal? And if they were not illegal, would government be putting its stamp of approval on the use of drugs? Whatever the answers, the most important lesson of the supported-work experiment among ex-addicts is that addiction is a behavioral as well as an income problem. Guaranteeing an addict a job does not necessarily reduce his use of drugs. Local program administrators frequently attribute whatever success they had with this population to the generally passive personalities of addicts.

Ex-offenders, on the other hand, are often hostile. For this reason, among others, the five-year summary judged supported work to be only a "marginal" success among them. The typical ex-offender was an unmarried black or Hispanic male, was twenty-five years old, had not completed high school (25 percent had), had rarely worked (39 percent had not held a full-time job within the previous two years, and 11 percent had never worked), had been arrested nine times, and had averaged two hundred weeks in prison. To be eligible for the program, the ex-offender had to have been imprisoned as a result of a conviction in the six months before his enrollment. Twenty-nine percent of the ex-offenders went on to regular jobs, but, the MDRC reported, "while supported-work participants had a somewhat better employment and earnings record after twenty-seven months than the control group, the difference was not statistically significant. And, unlike the ex-addicts, the ex-offenders who had participated in the program did not show any reduction in criminal behavior." The benefits did not outweigh the costs. Welfare payments decreased among ex-offenders, but their crime and their drug use did not. They stayed in the program the briefest average period of the four target groups—five months and six days—and this drove their average per-capita cost up.

The ex-offenders' brief stay in the program highlights another reason for their disappointing results. "This most likely reflects unmet expectations with regard to work assignments, work settings, and wages, especially in comparison to the returns from criminal activity," the MDRC reported. For instance, John Hicks made more money selling narcotics outside Madison Square Garden than he could make attending Howard Smith's class. And many ex-offenders, like many AFDC mothers, were terrified of the everyday world—did not comprehend its workings. The MDRC report declared, "Perhaps most important was the uncertainty of this group that after completing the program they could find a permanent job and thereby have the option of breaking away from a life of crime." Like dependent mothers, ex-offenders often lack confidence, but it is usually a lack of confidence in society as well as in themselves—a feeling that they are permanently branded as outcasts. William Block, recalling the time he got out of prison, once told the life-skills class, "They offered me a security-guard role. I said, 'I'm on parole.' They said, 'Next.' " Gary Curtis, a white ex-offender and addict, entered Oakland's supported-work project in 1977. He rose to crew chief, graduated in 1978, and found a job with a waterbed manufacturer for $5.70 an hour, which was soon hiked to $7.30. And he was off drugs, as the short-sleeved shirts he proudly wore revealed. Yet to an MDRC interviewer he spoke bitterly of his experience in supported work:

> We had a lot of trouble with the police harassing the crews. They knew we were all ex-offenders and they didn't let us forget it or get comfortable. They'd drive by several times a day. . . . One day I let a guy go to make a phone call and he got arrested. They just stopped him and checked him out and found that he had an outstanding traffic warrant. When I complained to them that they couldn't just take him in, they threatened to take me, too. It's one of those things ex-offenders have to put up with. People on a regular painting crew wouldn't have these problems. They're just waiting for you to do wrong. They don't think we'll stay straight. Their attitude is, It's just a matter of time before we get you again.

The supported-work program clearly failed with the fourth group, school dropouts seventeen to twenty years old, half of whom also had a record of crime or delinquency. The typical youth was an eighteen-year-old male (males outnumbered females six to one) who had dropped out of school and run afoul of the law. Only 26 percent moved from the program to a regular job—a number deemed inadequate in comparison to the control group, which got jobs at about the same rate without supported-work training. The MDRC's conclusion was unequivocal: "Supported work had no significant long-term impact on the earnings, employment, criminal activity, or drug abuse of the youth group. The program's benefits for youth fell short of its costs." Of the four groups, the most severe lateness and discipline problems were among the delinquent youths, and their attendance (averaging 76 percent) was the worst.

Not surprisingly, the chief reason for their failure was found to be immaturity. Many of these young people were not searching for steady employment or careers, and they resisted discipline and regulations—one reason they may have left school. They were teenagers —preferring to hang out, escape responsibility, say and do what they wanted when they wanted. But unlike most teenagers, the majority of these young people did not have two parents to rein them in, did not have a working male at home to emulate, and did not know how to accept supervision or orders. On the streets, they were their own bosses. Their failure represented a typical teenage aversion to authority, but it also reflected poor teachers, and supervisors who didn't seem to care. As the MDRC summary stated, "many of the respondents claimed that the supervision was too lax."

One reason that the majority of those in all four targeted groups who entered the program failed to go on to self-supporting employment is that the habits of a lifetime are difficult for many to overcome. But William Grinker, president of the MDRC, also thinks that the absence of a guaranteed job at the end of the training undermined the effort. "They wonder where this is going," he said. "It may seem like another ripoff"—as it did to Wildcat participants like Leon Harris, John Hicks, Gladys Miller, and Ramon Lopez, among others. Grinker says that most of those who enrolled would prefer jobs in the private sector, because then they would not feel as if they were receiving a government handout, but he adds that private jobs in a free economy cannot be guaranteed. And such a guarantee might undermine the drive and determination that supported workers need to succeed.

Government was also a culprit. The welfare system, for instance, was a deterrent for some of those enrolled in the program, because under federal law benefits drop as earnings rise. In West Virginia, supported workers received twice as much as they would have received on welfare, but in New York the members of BT-27 received only fifty dollars a month more from supported work than they would have from welfare. And under President Reagan's welfare "reform" policies, that gap has narrowed. The MDRC study said that this was "bound to reduce the incentives of members of this population to seek employment." Similarly, the MDRC found that the shortage of child-care services available to the poor probably prevented some mothers from working. Nevertheless, the study played down these factors, claiming that the highly motivated mother overcame the welfare disincentive, and saying that she arranged for child care in her own or someone else's home rather than rely on formal day-care programs.

Local mismanagement played a major role in the failure of some of those enrolled. Chaotic discipline and fistfights between supervisors and supported workers in the MDRC's Oakland program chased promising recruits away. "You almost had to murder someone to get kicked out," complained Dorothy Lomack, a welfare mother, who protested what she said was the open use of drugs and alcohol on the job, and sex between supervisors and workers. Unheated classrooms at the Wildcat training center competed with Howard Smith for the attention of the class members. Poor management and scarce local resources forced the MDRC to close the supported-work program in Seattle, Detroit, and San Francisco. The program in Chicago was not as effective as it should have been, partly because its first two directors were deemed unsatisfactory.

As weak management can turn people off, so strong management can rescue them. Jim Carter, a black ex-convict who was the job developer for the Peralta Service Corporation in Oakland, was a strong manager who has rescued his share of people. Through February 1978, eighty-seven people graduated from his supported-work site. And, according to an internal 1978 MDRC audit, "Only five did not have jobs when they left the program (four did not *want* to work, the other simply disappeared)." The average starting wage for these graduates was $5.12 per hour, and more than 70 percent were still on the job a year later. The MDRC's analysis of this program left no doubt as to the reason for this startling success:

> These figures may appear magical compared with other supported work site figures, but they were accomplished by two very unmagical means: hard work and good preparation. The hard work goes into selling Peralta to companies with high entry level wages, the good preparation is what the Peralta workers get in their job development classes, and Jim Carter is responsible for both.

Carter's better way of lining up employers includes carefully going through two books: the *Oakland Chamber of Commerce Directory,* which lists 2,500 or so businesses in Alameda County that employ twenty-five or more people, tells where the company is located, what it makes, as well as who to contact; and the *Wholesalers' and Manufacturers' Directory*, which offers the same sort of information. . . . Then he calls the appropriate person. Instead of eliciting interest from one in thirty, he now gets it from about one in four. Carter makes out a five-by-eight-inch card for every company he calls, notes the date and the reaction, and tries to set up an appointment within a few days to go in and talk some more about Peralta. He also rates each company a 1 (want to hire graduates), a 2 (definite possibilities), or 3 (forget it). And he takes the personnel managers at their word. If one says call back in two weeks, Carter calls back in two weeks. He is persistent without being obnoxious and will spend months lining up an employer he thinks might take several graduates over time.

On July 28, 1976, Carter phoned the personnel manager of the Container Corporation of America, who explained that the company had recently laid off workers and planned no new hiring until the following April. Carter rated the company a 2, and forwarded material about Peralta. In the spring of 1977 Carter phoned again and learned that the company had a new personnel director, Bill Brown. Once again Carter explained the purpose of Peralta, and once again the personnel director replied that there were no openings. However, this time Carter learned there might be an opening in June.

Carter called on June 14. Nothing. On June 20, his call went unreturned. Carter persisted. In July, personnel director Brown said there was an opening for an electrician paying $8.25 an hour. Carter confessed that he had no one at Peralta with those skills. He wrote on his file card: "A good sign, even though we couldn't send anyone."

The file card continues:

8/30   appointment made for 9/8 at 2:00 with Bill Brown (bro.) [a black brother]. Very receptive, strong possibility. Entry level $5.93. Three shifts, Call 9/26 when he returns from reserve duty. Appointment on 9/22 at 2:00 to tour plant.

10/4   Brown will attend employer's conference on 10/11.

10/11 Brown called to cancel appointment.

10/25 Brown will no longer be with the company.

Carter then called Brown's replacement, Kathy Kooski. She said nothing was available. He sent her material. Some weeks later Carter phoned and made an appointment on February 8, 1978. She canceled because her baby was sick. Carter made another appointment for February 14. This is how the MDRC evaluator described the meeting:

> In the meeting with Ms. Kooski he explained the concept of supported work and what PSC has done in the last two years. He stressed that Peralta tries to instill good work habits: attendance, punctuality, productivity, and an absentee rate of 5.5 percent or less. Then he put a loose-leaf photo album on her desk, flipped [it] open, and showed her before and after pictures of Peralta projects. . . . "This is very impressive," Ms. Kooski marveled halfway through, and Carter told her, "I'm showing you these because I want you to be impressed." . . . Ms. Kooski said she would like to interview some Peralta graduates when she started to hire in March. Carter, after a year and a half of trying to get a commitment from the company, did not want to leave anything to chance. "When can I call you? Will you let me know when you have an opening?" She smiled as he added candidly, "I'm trying hard to get a commitment from you before you get away from me like the others." She told him not to worry: "I plan to stick around."

Because he stuck around, Jim Carter induced the Container Corporation of America to hire Peralta graduates. Sandra Walton, a personnel manager with a corporation that does business with Peralta, says that "the persistence of Jim Carter is what sold us—his calling, checking, and believing in his people."

Like Howard Smith of Wildcat, Jim Carter also taught a life-skills class. Peralta supported workers could take this class after they had been at a job site for six months if they had an absentee rate below 5.5 percent. In class, a different Jim Carter appears. Instead of the suits he wore for meetings with personnel officers, his class uniform consisted of jeans and polo shirts; he spoke the language of the streets. Like Howard Smith, he could communicate with supported workers because he's been where they've been. Born in a housing project in Chicago, Carter had served time in jail. The dialogue in his life-skills class is remarkably like the dialogue in BT-27:

"I just want a good-paying job, it doesn't matter what I do," says a twenty-six-year-old ex-offender.

"I want to reverse your thinking," says Carter.

"My philosophy is to look for the worst and hope for the best," the ex-offender says.

"Have you had a positive life to date?" asks Carter.

233

"Not really."

"I suggest it's because you're not looking for the positive," counters Carter, sounding like Norman Vincent Peale. "You can get what you want. You can make it happen."

When the five-year supported-work experiment was completed, the MDRC's board of directors formally recommended to the Ford Foundation and to the five federal agencies that helped underwrite the experiment that supported work be expanded for the two most successful target groups, AFDC mothers and ex-addicts; that experimentation and testing be continued, in an effort to devise a formula that might work for ex-offenders and delinquent youths; that "supported work for new groups, such as the mentally retarded, former mental patients and other hard-to-employ groups, should be assessed"; that research to keep track of those individuals who completed and dropped from the program should continue. The MDRC also recommended its own removal from the program. The board members, to free the corporation to conduct additional experiments, called for a new agency to "assume the oversight and management responsibilities carried out so far by the Manpower Demonstration Research Corporation." The reason for this recommendation, Grinker said, was that "we're not in the business of running programs forever, we're in the business of testing out ideas."

Some changes were made in 1980 and early 1981. The number of welfare mothers in the program was expanded from 25 to 40 percent of total enrollees. Because of cutbacks in funds to federal drug rehabilitation programs, there were fewer treatment centers to which to refer participants, as is required, and thus the number of enrolled ex-addicts declined to 9 percent. Although MDRC wished to pare the number of ex-offenders, cities like Chicago, Oakland, and Newark insisted they could be successful with this population, and that because of their criminal propensity this was the critical group for them to reach. No cutbacks were made. The percentage of youths in the program also remained at 25, although the training regimen for youths was altered. Starting at four sites, these youths were now provided with a counselor and were required either to return to high school or to receive remedial education help, which was also provided. Pleased with the initial results, in January 1981 MDRC extended these youth requirements to all sites. The number of sites grew from nineteen to twenty-one. Supported work for the mentally retarded was also being tested. And finally, after much wrangling, in the last months of the Carter administration the MDRC got the green light from the Department of Labor to spin off oversight responsibility for the entire supported-work demonstration. A new nonprofit corporation was to be created. This new corporation's sole function would be the management of the national supported-work program, leaving any research questions to the MDRC or to another organization.

However, by late in the summer of 1981, the twenty-one supported-work sites and the MDRC itself were fighting for their lives. Ten of the sites were forced to close by December of 1981. And that month the MDRC ran out of funds to finance the remaining eleven sites. The Reagan administration disapproved the creation of a "new instrumentality" to run supported work. In a series of meetings with Reagan administration officials, MDRC officials pleaded with them to continue to provide a third of the $36 million needed to keep the national supported-work program going, but their plea was rejected. In a letter to former Senator Jacob Javits on June 23, 1981, Secretary of Labor Raymond Donovan wrote, "We would . . . foresee no need for further funding of a nationally directed effort." Although the letter praised the MDRC and supported work, the Reagan administration insisted that state and local governments pay for any such program. If the nonprofit corporations that ran the twenty-one sites wanted federal funds to continue, they would have to compete with more politically powerful local training programs for revenue-sharing funds.

MDRC officials estimated that perhaps three to eight of the local corporations would be able to raise enough money to keep their supported-work programs alive, but with fewer participants. Amalia Betanzos, the president of Wildcat, told me in August, "We may have to scale it down." But she was confident that Wildcat could raise the necessary private, foundation, and local-government funds to keep going on a smaller basis. As for the MDRC, which could be viewed as a model of President Reagan's "new federalism" and his devotion to testing new ideas rather than throwing money at social problems, it was pushed to the brink of bankruptcy. In June, the corporation laid off forty-two people—almost half its staff. And by the end of 1981 supported work—a program that worked for Pearl Dawson, William Mason, Denise Brown, and other members of the underclass—lost its federal support.

18

A Guaranteed
Job for Youths:
The National Results

They are like refugees of war, the post-industrial age's street arabs. Waves of nomadic teenagers engulf city streets—out of work, out of school, out of hope, often deprived, sometimes depraved. These unemployed nomads are often choking with rage, which finds expression in broken windows, torched buildings, and acts of unimaginable violence.

And yet these nomadic youths are the survivors of neither a war nor a famine. In truth, chroniclers of their plight and plunder are not sure who or what is to blame. What we are sure about is that one-third of all violent crimes in America are committed by youths. And that teenage unemployment spiraled out of control beginning in the late sixties. Throughout the fifties, the gap between white and minority youth unemployment was narrow. But over the past two decades youth unemployment has tripled. In the final quarter of 1980, for example, the Bureau of Labor Statistics reported that 17.8 percent of American youths under age twenty were unemployed. Among blacks and Hispanics the figures are dismal—39.6 percent of black youths were unemployed and 21.5 percent of Hispanics. These numbers become more ominous when placed against the backdrop of two other facts: school dropout rates that in many cities claim one black and Hispanic teenager for every one that graduates; and the absence of employment opportunities for these youths, particularly in cities where most reside. In 1980, for instance, 47 percent of American teenagers held jobs, yet only 39 percent of those living in central cities worked. In New York City, only 22 percent of teenage youths were employed.

Since teenagers constitute such an important part of the under-class, the MDRC's work with teenagers merits scrutiny. To try to comprehend and curb youth unemployment and hostility, in 1977 the MDRC and the U.S. Department of Labor devised a joint national experiment—the Youth Incentive Entitlement Pilot Project—to test whether the guarantee of a job would keep youths in school. To be eligible for what was called "the nation's first guaranteed-jobs program," a youth need be between the ages of sixteen and nineteen, come from a family on welfare or in poverty, and reside in one of seventeen designated poverty areas.*

Unlike previous jobs programs, which often had the unintended effect of luring teenagers from school, the entitlement program awarded youths part-time jobs for ten to twenty hours per week during the school year and full-time summer employment—on condition that they remain in or return to school. Between February 1978, when the experiment commenced, and August 1980, 81,000 youths enrolled. The cost over this period was $230 million, 61 percent of it earmarked to subsidize the minimum wage and fringe benefits paid the youths by private and public employers. The cost of providing a full year of this program averaged $4,749 per youngster, and the youngster remained eligible until graduation from high school. As was true of supported work, this experiment set its sights on the underclass. Fifty-five percent of enrolled youths lived in homes receiving welfare assistance; 56.2 percent lived only with a mother; the average parent had a ninth-grade education; and one of every six youngsters enrolled was already a parent.

MDRC's final 175-page report, issued in November 1980, attributed rising youth unemployment to "multiple" factors. The unemployment numbers were somewhat exaggerated, they cautioned, because it was normal for youths to shop around in the labor market to sample various jobs, or not to want steady work. Employer preferences to hire more mature workers contributed to youth unemployment, as did "the need to pay the minimum wage for entry-level young unskilled workers" (although this was said to only play "a small negative role"). Sometimes employers discriminated against youths because of the color of their skin. Sometimes "the

*These were located in sections of the following cities or states: Baltimore; Boston; Cincinnati; Denver; Detroit; Albuquerque, New Mexico; King-Snohomish Counties, Washington; rural Southern Mississippi; Alachua County, Florida; Berkeley, California; Dayton, Ohio; Monterey County, California; Nashua County, New Hampshire; Bedford-Stuyvesant, New York; Steuben County, New York; Syracuse, New York; Philadelphia, Pennsylvania.

movement of jobs from central cities to the suburbs" was a factor, reducing job opportunities.

But these "demand-side" factors, as MDRC called them, offered a one-dimensional diagnosis. To fully understand the problem, three "supply-side" reasons had to be taken into account. The first of these had to do with population differences. The report cited "the relative population increase of young persons which has led mainly to increased competition among, and depressed wages for, younger persons." Wages for black and white youths were "comparable," but their relative numbers were not, since the birth rate and the size of black and Hispanic families was larger. "A second set of factors," the report continued, "is related to the inadequate education, skill and motivation levels of young people, as well as broad socioeconomic problems associated with life in the inner cities. . . . It is clear that drug and alcohol abuse, youth crime, broken homes, out-of-wedlock births, poor schooling and ineffectual work habits contribute, in the aggregate, to the youth joblessness problem and to its concentration among blacks and some white groups, particularly in the cities." The final supply-side factor was the "increased level of welfare payments," which contributed "to the problem by lowering the incentive to work at current wage rates." Their complex diagnosis: the youth unemployment epidemic was both institutional and behavioral, caused by both demand- and supply-side factors, and in combination produced a "structural problem," especially for minority youth.

Yet the MDRC, in its final November 1980 report reached a hopeful conclusion: "Youth Entitlement is a strategy with promise." A summary of the first eighteen months of the program—contrasting the youths at the seventeen sites with a control group—revealed these results:

· Fifty-eight percent of eligible blacks and 48 percent of eligible Hispanics in the seventeen locations enrolled. However, only a disappointing 17 percent of eligible white youths joined. As we saw in Mississippi, too many whites viewed Entitlement as a minority program.

· The program was more successful recruiting in-school youths than dropouts. Fifty-seven percent of the participants were unemployed teenagers attending school; 29 percent were unemployed dropouts (the remainder were youths already employed).

· Entitlement "significantly affected the rate of return to school for out-of-school youths, and the retention in school of in-school youths." In the fall of 1978, 36.4 percent of the former dropouts returned to school. "Based on the behavior of youths at the control sites, only an estimated 22.4 percent would have returned without the program, a difference of 14.0 percentage points. Thus Entitlement resulted in a large 62.5 percent increase in the rate at which former dropouts returned to school. Of those previously enrolled in school, 79.8 percent of the participating youths remained in school—an increase of 3.7 percentage points over estimated school retention in the absence of the program."

· Entitlement had "a large effect on the level of youth unemployment." For example, 48.3 percent of the eligible youths were employed by the program. This contrasted with an estimated 25.4 percent of the control-group youths who would have been employed under normal circumstances. Thus it was said that entitlement "led to a large 90 percent increase in the employment rate of disadvantaged youths in the demonstration sites."

MDRC President William Grinker, somewhat surprised that the research findings were more positive than their early soundings, told me: "At least in terms of short-term impacts, this program had an effect. The most surprising effect is that it encouraged the return to school. I thought when we got into this it would have some decent effect on kids in school. I didn't think it would affect kids not in school. It does."

But like so many of MDRC's efforts with the underclass, these results are comforting or disappointing depending on your definition of success. Looking at a half-full glass, Grinker said, "It works." But he implicitly acknowledged that the glass could be described as half-empty: "we're still only getting one-third of the dropouts compared to what we would have reached without the program. Which is just one-fifth of all dropouts. And what does it mean to go back to school? That we don't know yet."

Youth Entitlement provided valuable lessons for any future youth programs, including a lesson or two in Parkinson's Law of bureaucracy. Vast city sites were generally slower to organize and match people with available jobs. Some sites did not wish to terminate youth they should have in order to "maintain the appearance of high program enrollment to enhance a local or national reputation." Others feared that a high termination rate would hike their cost ratios, and thus weaken future funding potential and perhaps "lead to a cut in participant expense and, in turn, to a cut in management funds, probably in staff." Several local staffs viewed "entitlement as a 'hard,' unforgiving program because of the standards, and there was frequently a desire among counselors to keep poorly performing youths in the program in an effort to help them, an understandable but vexing position in a tightly conditioned Entitlement program."

239

As we saw in supported work, mismanagement hindered many youths. A March 1980 draft audit of three sites by the Government Accounting Office (GAO) lamented that Denver's program had gone through five coordinators in two years and that a thousand youths awaited job assignments that were being made at the glacial pace of fifty per week. There were also frequent management clashes between MDRC and the community-based organizations, stemming in part from their different roles. Local program operators viewed Entitlement as a work experience program that should serve as many youths as possible. The MDRC and its chief funding source, the Department of Labor, viewed Entitlement as a laboratory to test ideas. The March 1980 MDRC report on Entitlement acknowledged the program's "dual purpose," saying, "the difference between the two points of view was not one of contrary principles but of emphasis."

Recruitment difficulties had tangled roots. Dropouts, said a March 1980 MDRC report, are "less likely as a group to want to return to school than youths who are already in-school are prone to leave." Not surprisingly, dropouts wanted full, not part-time, employment. Nor were many inclined to return to schools they had already left in order to attend classes with younger teenagers. There was also evidence that some youths rejected working for the minimum wage, preferring the more plentiful money made on the street. The deep hostility of some youths was a major recruitment impediment. "Students see themselves as poor, as powerless, and as manipulated by the forces around them," anthropologist Barbara Joans wrote in July 1980, after extensive interviews with teenagers for the MDRC.

The Entitlement Program, in this instance, becomes one of the forces of that manipulation. The boys talk tough. They pride themselves on being aware of their circumstances. They see themselves at odds with their environment. They articulate this awareness.

"If I had money you could take this program and shove it."
"You could shove it anyway."

I think the gender split is, again, important. I do not know if the girls feel the hostility as keenly as the boys, but, because of female socialization, suppress it, or whether they truly do not feel it. It is possible that male training incorporates models of hostility as part of the male ethos. From images of street toughs to punk rock, the sullen, resentful, angry young man is seen as the approved and appropriate model to emulate. In short, they are expected to be hostile. It is one part of being male in America.

Because the image of hostility is so appealing to so many men in American culture it is difficult to assess how much of student hostility grows from their views of themselves as poor and powerless and how much of it arises from their desire to be cool.

The mix of factors that go into a youngster's success or failure in the program became more vivid to me when I visited Entitlement projects, including one in the Bedford-Stuyvesant section of Brooklyn. There, in a three-story yellow brick building at 85 Lexington Avenue, a staff of forty-seven, including seven counselors, supervise 450 mostly black and Hispanic youngsters. Many of these youngsters, says Ramona De Leon, who was born in Spanish Harlem and is the director, suffer from a feeling of "rejection." "There are many young black or Hispanic students who graduate and can't get a job downtown. White kids get the job. It's basic racism."

The youngsters are victims of the education system and its attitude that minority kids can't learn, says Alice Boyce, the supervisor of counseling at this Entitlement project. "A lot of failure is caused by students who have been inadequately educated. Some of the students really wanted to be helped. They really try. And yet they are unable to overcome educational inadequacies. It's frustrating to see a nineteen-year-old with a fourth-grade reading level. It's sad that they were just passed along over the years."

Cleveland Miller (the students' names have been changed), a muscular sixteen-year-old who attends Boys' High School and receives special tutoring at the Entitlement center, complained, "I can't learn anything in school. Too many people influence you not to learn anything." In school, he says, it's "every man for himself. You got people who don't want to learn."

Cleveland's older brother Melvin, who is eighteen, sees it from another angle, blaming more than peer pressure. He thinks the feeling of rejection is what prompts kids to leave school and the Entitlement program. "See what it is, a lot of us blacks have given up. It's hard as hell for a black man to get a job. They go out and rob and steal. Me, myself, I don't fault a black man who goes out and robs and steals. You've got all these foreigners coming in here. They got all these businesses. Haitians and Koreans and Puerto Ricans—they're taken care of."

"They work for less money," interrupts Cleveland. "We're not willing to work for less money."

"I know brothers who finish high school and just sit home," continues Melvin. "He can't get a job. Everywhere he go they say, 'Don't call me. We'll call you.' There's plenty of money in this country. A lot of these black guys when they get to be twenty-five they'll be lost on the sauce. A lot of time I see young brothers and say, 'Hey, man, go to school. Stop snorting coke and standing in doorways.' It goes in one ear and goes into another. I used to be out there stealing and robbing. I found myself. Problem is a lot of brothers don't sit down and find themselves. Only thing leading them is to death, hard time, or the penitentiary." Religion, say Melvin and Cleveland, who come from a broken home and used to snatch necklaces and commit street robberies, is what saved them from a life on the streets.

Many youngsters drop out of school or Entitlement because they can't compete with the streets, says John Kiser, a counselor in the program. "The peer pressure is that a lot of students don't go to school. They hang out. They're not doing things productive. It has an effect. Other students don't want to look bad, they want to be accepted by their peers. So they do negative things. They also have a certain lack of motivation. That's caused by the parents. A lot of the students' parents are not professional, they make little income, and in terms of role models there are not enough positive role models for the student in the community or at home." Kiser, who is black like the majority of the Bedford-Stuyvesant staff, dismisses the idea that the youngsters feel defeated and lack confidence. "The kids feel they will be a great success," he says. "They have TV and the movies. They feel that if they get over high school or 'Get my G.E.D., I've got it made.'" Some dream of being a basketball star, as John Painter of BT-27 did; others of owning Cadillacs and mink coats. "Some of the kids feel the world owes them something. They don't come right out and say it. They say, 'If I don't like the place, I don't have to be there.'" Kiser thinks welfare bears a large responsibility for creating this unreal world because it creates a sense of entitlement—"I'm entitled"—that undermines the work ethic and fans resentments.

Director Ramona De Leon thinks it often comes down to simple economics. "It's difficult to compete" with hustling on the streets, she says. "A lot of these kids can make a hundred dollars a night on the street." For some, she believes, crime does pay.

Alice Boyce, the supervisor of counselors, disagrees with John Kiser's belief that the youngsters inhabit a dream world. "What I find mostly is students not thinking that far ahead," she says, echoing the views of Edward Banfield. "It's typical of all teenagers. They don't know what they want to do. They don't think about tomorrow. Unfortunately, rather than living in a dream world, many of our students suffer from lower expectations." But she, too, blames dependency. "That's the welfare syndrome. You know, 'I'm not going to do any better than my parents.'"

"So many of them have a welfare syndrome," says Ramona De Leon, a middle-aged widow who lives with her three children in the Bronx and has worked in antipoverty programs since the early sixties. "You come from a welfare home and you have no sense of what the real world is. You have clothes and food and shelter. It's not good, but you still have it. These are just youngsters or people who become trapped in the welfare system and they just lose hope." Welfare becomes a habit. "We're talking about kids who wake up early," she continues, "and at 11:00 A.M. their mother is still in bed. Why? Because she doesn't want to get up today. So at each age the kid sees this. On TV he sees Mommy and Daddy go to work. Yet at home Mommy or Daddy sleeps or drinks. They assume that's what life is supposed to be like. I have kids, and they imitate their parents."

"You have young girls who want to become pregnant to get on welfare," Vergie Foster, the program's assistant director, told me. She says she constantly runs into this syndrome: "If your mother has been on welfare fifteen years and is sick—a lot of these people are ill—there's a sense of loss in that home. And the only time the kid gets away from it is in school. And in school he's just a piece of meat."

De Leon outlines the home-life barriers Entitlement seeks to overcome: "There's often an alcohol problem. Sometimes an addiction problem. Sometimes a mental deficiency problem. Sometimes the parent is too strict. Often they're on welfare. Could be a feeling they're imprisoned in their own home. A lot of kids say there are too many kids in the home. No space. They want to break out. All this leads to frustration."

"Here's a person who's up against the wall, and to protect himself he's impervious," says Vergie Foster. "That's the blank stare people see. It's self-preservation. They're reduced to being animals. We've had people who were that way. We reached them. The key thing is reaching them before they're hardened."

"The key thing is caring," interrupts De Leon. "Giving them a sense we care." Also, a sense of pride, which she believes comes from knowing you earned your way. De Leon, like Charles Bannerman in Mississippi, pushes for private, as opposed to government jobs, for her 450 youths. Why? Because, she answers, "When you have to compete for your job within your job, it's a driving force. You tend to think better of yourself. In a government job you don't have that. People tend to be lackadaisical in government-type jobs. We have government jobs where the supervisors say, 'Okay, sign the kid in!'—even if he doesn't work. But when the money is coming out of your pocket, there's more interest." Like so many people I interviewed who work with the underclass, she believes government jobs and welfare often undermine pride and the work ethic: "We have a large number of Haitians and West Indians. They tend to work. It has to do with pride. Maybe it also has to do with being an alien."

"They refuse welfare," says Vergie Foster. "They'd rather work at three jobs. They come here from a country and are happy just to have an opportunity to have a job they couldn't have there."

De Leon agrees: "They come here looking at the American dream. They come from a poor island, with no clothes. Foreigners still have the American dream—'I can become a millionaire.' Unfortunately, Americans don't have it any more. The American kid is born into poverty in a land of milk and honey, and there doesn't seem to be any light at the end of the tunnel."

The national Youth Entitlement experiment, which was to light the tunnel, was scheduled to conclude in September 1980. By then the MDRC was supposed to have completed its research, to have deciphered what works and why. As originally planned by the Carter administration, which earmarked 11 percent of its 1980 youth manpower budget to the Entitlement experiment, the program was then to be merged into an omnibus $2 billion jobs-and-education effort for 500,000 additional youths. The MDRC recommended to the Labor Department that Entitlement be slowly expanded starting in 1981, and that a closer link be forged between the school system and Entitlement to better monitor school performance. "We want to look at targeting—whether we should target in or out of school kids more," said MDRC President Grinker. "Or limit their time in the program. Or change the eligibility. We know the strengths and weaknesses of our program. But since we don't know everything else that's going on out there in youth programs, we're not sure what to recommend."

By the winter of 1981, Grinker—and the seventeen sites—were not sure what the incoming Reagan administration planned. They knew of Reagan's commitment to slash the federal CETA program, which funded Entitlement. And they knew that in 1981 the Labor Department pared the number of enrollees in half, to 14,000. But they didn't know whether the new president would consider "the nation's first guaranteed-jobs program" a success, or a failure. The answer came in the summer of 1981, when the Reagan administration and the Congress decided not to extend the Entitlement program. On August 31, 1981, the seventeen Entitlement sites officially shut down. In their place, no new youth-unemployment initiatives were begun by the Reagan administration. Government was getting out of the way, consigning these youths to the mercies of a private job market that in years past either feared or deemed them superfluous.

19

Other MDRC Experiments and Lingering Questions

MDRC's experiments and the information gleaned from them are tiny planets within the vast, largely uncharted universe of the underclass. Inevitably, they generated more questions than answers. But something was learned from each of MDRC's exploratory programs.

Their Tenant Management Demonstration was designed to empower tenants in public housing to actually manage the buildings themselves, determine their own rules and priorities, decide how monies could be spent, hire and fire building personnel, screen applicants, and weed out those who refused to pay rent or threatened the safety of their children.

The Ford Foundation and the federal Housing and Urban Development (HUD) agency in June 1975 approached the MDRC and asked it to select the sites, provide or arrange training and technical assistance, monitor the local organizations and prepare a research plan to evaluate the results. The MDRC selected seven locations in six cities.* With grants of $20.2 million from HUD and $1.5 million from the Ford Foundation, the demonstration commenced in 1977. The research component, designed by the Urban Institute in Washington, asked four questions: How did tenant management in general compare with public management? Were the costs comparable?

---

*A Harry Moore and Curries Woods in Jersey City, New Jersey; Iroquois Homes in Louisville, Kentucky; Que-view in New Haven, Connecticut; Calliope in New Orleans, Louisiana; Sunrise Acres in Oklahoma City, Oklahoma; and Ashanti in Rochester, New York.

Did tenant management improve operating performance and increase tenant satisfaction? How could the results of tenant management be measured?

These questions were answered in a 273-page draft report submitted to MDRC's board of directors at a quarterly meeting on April 18, 1980. Their conclusion was less positive than it was for either supported work or Youth Entitlement. Although tenant management was deemed "at least as effective as previous management" at most sites, it did cost more. The program, they found, works in some places and not in others, and therefore "it would be unwise to mandate any universal approach to tenant management—either requiring it everywhere or prohibiting it." Therefore, the MDRC report said: "We do not believe HUD should regard widespread implementation of tenant management as a high-priority objective."

With its report issued, MDRC judged its work done. HUD took over the supervision of the seven tenant-managed sites and extended funding through June 30, 1981. Peter Kivisto, the HUD research analyst who oversaw tenant management from Washington, said in January 1981 that he basically agreed with the MDRC's lukewarm endorsement of the program. "The sites do seem to perform as well as Public Housing Authority management. But that's a whole other question since few are pleased with Public Housing Authority management." The incoming Reagan administration allowed federal support to lapse, as scheduled, in the summer of 1981.

Of the four national experiments MDRC policed through 1980, the WIN Research Laboratory was the least ambitious. WIN—the Work Incentive Program—was enacted by the Congress in 1967, and required that all mothers receiving welfare who were in good health, with no children below the age of six, register for job training and supportive social services. The program aimed to coax these women, who comprise 75 percent of those adults receiving AFDC payments, into jobs and a life independent of welfare. A decade later, in 1977, the U.S. Department of Labor and the then Department of Health, Education and Welfare, which jointly administers WIN, invited the MDRC to test techniques to assist these mothers. The Ford Foundation gave a grant, and in 1978 the MDRC selected four local WIN offices to serve as laboratories: Denver, Colorado; Louisville, Kentucky; Madison and Racine, Wisconsin; and St. Louis, Missouri.

Each site designed its own experiment. Denver's laboratory tested whether young mothers with children under six could be encouraged to seek employment. Louisville examined whether more mothers were reached if child-care and support services, such as transportation, were provided. Madison and Racine explored whether they could steer women away from clerical positions into higher-paying jobs if the mothers were offered special training and the employers a 100 percent on-the-job training subsidy. St. Louis tried shortcuts to circumvent employer resistance to hiring welfare recipients. For two years these four ventures were placed under MDRC's microscope.

In April 1980, the MDRC issued its "Preliminary Research Findings." Like tenant management, the results were, at best, deemed a modest success. MDRC came away from the experiment disappointed. "While we got some significant information out of the program," Grinker said in early 1981, "if you want to run something like this successfully you have to generate program ideas and institutions at several places simultaneously." Four sites were too few. And the local program coordinators were too timid. "The little things we tried were not of great importance," Grinker concluded sadly.

New MDRC Programs

With its four national experiments winding down, the MDRC spent 1980 scouting various program ideas to assist the hard-to-reach.

One idea was to test whether supported work could assist the mentally retarded, the most custodialized group in American society. The Carter administration's U.S. Department of Labor tentatively agreed to put up $10 million, with the remaining $5 million to be raised locally. The three-year Structured Transitional Employment and Training Services program, as it was billed, was to commence at six locations in the autumn of 1981. The Reagan administration's Labor Department, however, cut back its funding to only one year; by early 1982, MDRC officials were still uncertain whether the Reagan administration would underwrite a three-year test at an annual cost of $2.8 million.

The second new project initiated by the MDRC in 1980 focused on teenage mothers. Impressed by the work of organizations such as the Little Sisters of the Assumption in East Harlem, the MDRC designed an experiment to provide counseling and assistance to teen mothers trapped at home with infants. Calling their proposal Project Redirection, the MDRC raised $2 million from the Ford Foundation, WIN, and the Labor Department to finance a surrogate-mother test for 550 teen mothers. Over a period of eighteen months, adolescents in five cities were to be paired with an elderly work-oriented woman who was a mother herself. The older woman would become a combination mother, counselor, companion, and babysitter. The purpose, the MDRC proposal said, was to "intervene judiciously in the family lives of the teenagers."

Five organizations were selected to operate the laboratories: the Cardinal Cushing Center in Boston; the Detroit Urban League; the New Harlem YWCA in New York; the Chicanos por La Causa in Phoenix, Arizona; and the Children's Home Society in Riverside, California. Mississippi's MACE was not selected; their proposal did not conform to MDRC's guidelines, since they preferred their own to the MDRC's approach. The National Council of Negro Women was retained to develop a technical assistance and training package for the five sites.

Project Redirection commenced in July 1980. By January 1981, 270 teenage mothers were enrolled. The first interim research reports on the surrogate-mother program were due in the latter part of 1981. MDRC officials were cautiously hopeful that the Labor Department would fund the experiment through 1982, as originally planned; however, they were aware that untested programs with weak political constituencies might be the first casualties of further federal budget cutting. On December 31, 1981, the MDRC learned that the Labor Department had decided not to fund the program through 1982, as originally planned. It was the MDRC's hope that with additional Ford Foundation and other grants, the test could be completed.

To test-market fresh approaches to dropouts and to build on the lessons of the Youth Entitlement Project, the MDRC in 1980 devised another demonstration. The general target was teenage unemployment, but this test was to aim as well at the 45 percent of Hispanic youths and 35 percent of black youths who drop out of school annually. Called the Comprehensive Opportunity Project (COP), out-of-school as well as in-school youths would be eligible, and a broad range of educational, employment, training and counseling services would be offered.

Secretary of Labor F. Ray Marshall in 1980 agreed to provide, over a three-year period, $1.5 million from his discretionary budget. Two locales were selected—Opportunities Industrial Center (OIC) in Philadelphia, and the Mexican-American Unity Council in San Antonio. Beginning in November 1980, these organizations were to open their doors to a total of 1,000 youths. By the summer of 1981, only 450 were enrolled. Because of local problems, Philadelphia was dropped. The Reagan administration's Labor Department agreed to fund the San Antonio experiment for one year, rather than the three originally planned. Federal funding for research was all but eliminated. What would happen after year one remained up in the air.

By the end of 1981, the MDRC scorecard read as follows: of the four initial national experiments—supported work, youth entitlement, tenant management and the WIN research laboratory—three of the demonstrations were over, and supported work had been shrunk drastically. Of the new projects, supported work for the mentally retarded was underway; the Comprehensive Opportunity Project (COP) to provide employment and counseling for youths was open in San Antonio; and Project Redirection for teen mothers was halfway toward completion, although it had lost its federal benefactor.

MDRC's plate was, by the summer of 1981, almost bare. They were, essentially, no longer in the long-term research business. The MDRC was a casualty of federal budget reductions, of President Reagan's "new federalism," which returned problem-solving functions to state and local governments. But since these governments lacked resources, and since the MDRC and the clients they served lacked political clout, prospects for new experiments were dim. The organization scurried about and vied for possible state contracts to design employment programs for the underclass. Morale plunged. In late 1981, William Grinker, the MDRC's original president, announced that he "had had enough" and would leave in early 1982; the chairman of the board, Eli Ginsberg of Columbia University, also stepped down, and was replaced by Richard P. Nathan, a professor of public and international affairs at Princeton University. The staff was cut. Without new government support, President Reagan's scorched-earth policy of warring against waste was likely to claim some innocent victims.

All the projects of the MDRC have provided "data about the *what* question," says Richard P. Nathan. "But we don't have any answers to the *why* question." In other words, the MDRC learned what sort of program might help members of the underclass, but not always why the program succeeded. The questions that one might ask are inexhaustible.

Why does one member of a broken home—for instance, Willy Joe of BT-27—feel "crushed," unable to cope with organized society, while his brother becomes part of the world of work? Why does one brother go to prison while Charles Bannerman went on to build a successful community-based organization in Mississippi? Why did Pearl Dawson and William (Akim) Penn, both of whom grew up in comfortable homes with two parents, go to prison and end up on welfare? Why did Pearl develop an unquenchable desire to escape welfare and finish Wildcat, while Akim did not? If each was not born with so-called lower-class values, is it possible to acquire these like a common cold? If those on the left like Kenneth Clark and William Ryan are correct that society and racism are to blame for the underclass, then why don't *all* minority kids fail? Conversely, if conservatives like Edward Banfield and Thomas Sowell are correct in claiming that lower-class culture and broken homes are to blame, why don't *all* children from broken, welfare-dependent homes remain mired in poverty? When does a traumatized individual's mind snap? Why?

The mysteries abound: Why is the black native American family so much more fractured than the black West Indian family, although both were victimized by slavery? Why were 41 percent of Puerto Rican families headed by a female in 1978, compared to only 16 percent of Mexican-American families? If poverty explains the dissolution of families, then why are families generally more stable in many (not all) of the more impoverished nations of Latin America, Africa, and India? If racism is not a major cause of fractured families, then why are family dissolution rates so much lower among poor whites, who outnumber poor blacks and Hispanics? Do cultural and historical traditions of different groups play a part, as economist Thomas Sowell argues? Does the pressure of living in an unequal society of abundant, flaunted wealth undermine the family? Do high tax rates and the pressures these generate weaken family ties? Is historian Herbert Gutman correct to believe that the massive migration North from the rural South and Puerto Rico was a major factor in loosening family ties? Does the man-in-the-house rule imposed by many state welfare departments prompt families to dissolve in order to receive welfare? Do years of dependence on welfare corrode family life? Are children, particularly young males, harmed growing up in female-headed households? How much does the extended family of relatives and friends compensate? Or a caring teacher?

Why did the welfare caseload explode in the sixties when the national economy was expanding and unemployment was relatively low? And do more stringent eligibility requirements alone explain why the welfare caseload shrank in the seventies when the economy slowed and unemployment rose? Why do more recent immigrants—Haitians, Dominicans, Koreans, Vietnamese, Cubans, Jamaicans—generally seem to be doing better than their black and Puerto Rican predecessors? Is it because they possess a greater work ethic than many poor Americans on welfare? Is it because they are more willing to be exploited and will work for lower wages? Or will those without job opportunities also in time become part of the underclass? Why does Japan, with a more extensive corporate and government welfare state, enjoy a 2 percent unemployment rate? If so many ghetto residents are without drive, how explain the thriving underground economy of many poor communities with their enterprising street vendors, numbers runners, three-card-monte hustlers, and drug pushers? Why did Joyce Leroy, a teenage mother in Belzoni, Mississippi, surrender to a life on welfare, while Barbara Harrison, who lived just a few blocks away, refused to?

If dependency on welfare and government support causes violence, as Daniel Patrick Moynihan once suggested, why do West Germany, Great Britain and Japan, more advanced welfare states than our own, have so much less violent crime? If poverty is the cause, why is random violence so much more widespread in affluent America than it is in many more destitute nations? Why does Mexico have one of the highest murder rates in the world, while India does not? If governmental neglect and unemployment are the sole cause, why did crime rise in the sixties when federal aid to the poor rose and unemployment dropped? If racism produces crime, why aren't all blacks criminals? Is crime a form of protest? Does it stem from a sense of hopelessness? Is the growth of random violence linked to neurological disorders, and can these be curbed with drugs or treatment? Do lenient laws and uncertain punishment promote crime? How many are criminals because they conclude that the gains outweigh the risks? What role does television and film violence play? Or the absence of male role models? Or the cynicism fanned by welfare? Or the pressure of the American success ethic? What role do values play, and from whom do they derive? What role does genetics play? Or diet? Is underclass behavior learned or inherited?

Is the minimum wage too low, discouraging many from working? Or is it too high, discouraging employers from hiring the poor? What has become of the roughly one million people who, the Bureau of Labor Statistics reports, have dropped out of the labor market and are no longer looking for work? Why has youth unemployment risen so sharply? Is poverty overstated? How many of the 29 million citizens officially counted as poor in 1980 are actually making ends meet through in-kind benefits like food stamps, or are making a decent living in the subterranean economy and in street crime? On the other hand, is poverty understated, with many poor people and undocumented aliens not counted?

Why are the incomes of West Indian blacks equal to those of American whites, while those of American blacks are not? If the richer cultural traditions of West Indians is a major factor, as Thomas Sowell believes, then why do West Indians generally fare poorly in Great Britain? Why is the median income of Puerto Rican Americans well below that of Cuban Americans? Why do resource-poor nations —Japan, Taiwan, South Korea, Hong Kong, Israel—suffer relatively little poverty, while resource-rich nations or states like Syria or West Virginia suffer much? How big is the American underclass, and who should be included? How do you objectively measure "deviant" behavior?

The questions are endless. Yet students of poverty say that the questions are too rarely asked, that research is too often primitive, and that the answers are usually debated—if at all—only in esoteric academic journals. Professor James N. Morgan, the coordinator of a study at the University of Michigan's Survey Research Center which started tracking five thousand families beginning in the late 1960s, asks, "Why in this wealthy nation [do] we have such a huge backlog of undone crucially important behavioral research even though we know how to do it and it is necessary for policy decisions?" Morgan places most of the blame on "the absence of financial support." Richard Nathan blames researchers for too often asking the wrong questions. "Instead of asking, 'Do you want to work?' and getting a predictable 'Yes' answer," Nathan told me, "the better question is 'Will you take a job for $2.84 an hour?' "

Liberals complain that questions are not asked because the poor are less in fashion these days than they were in the early sixties, when Michael Harrington wrote *The Other America;* they say that most Americans, or at least their leaders, no longer believe that government can make a difference. Conservatives say that researchers are often afraid to ask behavioral questions, because they are fearful that they will be called racists. Some liberals are worried that focusing attention on pathology, on an underclass "separate" from society, would relieve pressure on government and society to correct injustice, and would create the misleading impression that all poor people have behavioral problems.

Before America can begin to deal more effectively with its underclass, it must ask questions and try to agree on the nature of the problem. If policymakers assume that the underclass results solely from racial and economic discrimination, then only sweeping social and economic changes can cure this injustice. If the policymakers assume that the underclass results solely from a "culture of poverty" and from ingrained behavioral disorders, then there is little that can be done. If they assume that the causes are varied and complex, then they arrive at a position midway between revolution and resignation.

Has There Been Progress in the "War on Poverty"?

The question of whether there has been progress in relieving poverty elicits various responses. It is like the Japanese movie classic *Rashomon,* in which four people witness the same killing, the same victim, the same weapon being used—yet offer four conflicting opinions of what they saw. What are the "facts"?

What "facts" you see depends in part on the angle you view them from. For instance, from the point of view of most civil-rights leaders, America has made too little progress. They see that whites are still twice as likely to attend college as blacks. From the viewpoint of optimists, there is reason to celebrate the progress American blacks have made. They see that the percentage of black college graduates increased from 2 percent in 1940 to 11 percent in 1975. Which "fact" you see depends partly on your politics.

Those who assume that poverty is best defined as relative inequality reasonably conclude that as long as the few are wealthy and the many are not, scant progress will be made in eradicating poverty. Yet those who assume that poverty is defined by an absolute income cutoff—the federally defined ceiling is now just over $8,400 for an urban family of four—see that the number of Americans classified as poor dwindled from 22.4 per cent of the population in 1959 to 11.4 per cent in 1978, or 24.5 million people.* Naturally they feel that progress has been made.

*Largely due to a recession and inflation, the number of poor jumped to 29.3 million in 1980, or 13 percent of the population. But the steady trend for the past two decades has been for the official poverty population to shrink.

Those subscribing to the somber view can marshal a depressing array of facts. Black Americans are three times as likely to be poor as whites, and Hispanics more than twice as likely. In the introduction to the National Urban League's annual assessment, *The State of Black America 1980*, Vernon Jordan, the league's president, wrote, "Black income, which was over 60 percent of white income in 1969, fell to only 57 percent by the end of the decade. More blacks were poor at the end of the seventies than at the beginning. The black middle class, described as rapidly expanding by some so-called experts, actually declined from 12 percent to 9 percent of all black families during this period. . . . On balance . . . the seventies were not a time of progress within Black America." According to the National Puerto Rican Forum, the family income of Puerto Ricans dropped from 71 percent of the national average in 1959 to 47 percent in 1979.

A black child, according to the Children's Defense Fund, in Washington, is about twice as likely as a white child to die before reaching the age of one, is more than twice as likely to be suspended from school, and more than four times as likely to be murdered between the ages of one and four, and one black child drops out of school for every two who graduate. The National Advisory Council on Economic Opportunity, which was established by the Economic Opportunity Act of 1964, in its thirteenth report, issued in September 1981, warned that it was a "myth" that poverty had been abolished within the past ten years, as some economists and social scientists have claimed. Taking into account "an expanded estimate of the needs of the poor," the council said that the number of those classified as poor in 1978 should be not 24.5 million but 45 million, or almost 21 percent of the population. A more explicitly egalitarian argument—for equality of result as opposed to equality of opportunity—is put forth in Richard H. deLone's book *Small Futures,* which was sponsored by the Carnegie Council on Children and was published in 1979. Pointing out that in 1976 only 5 percent of all American families had annual incomes of more than $37,000, deLone wrote that as long as America adopts incremental reforms, liberal or conservative, and denies itself a more radical form of democratic socialism—as long as it doesn't strive for equality of result—poverty can never be eliminated.

Those who believe that America has made important progress also use a relative measuring stick—one that is relative to a government-defined income standard and to where we were in the past. They demonstrate that this income standard shows that the percentage of the population living in poverty was reduced by half between 1959 and 1978. (These analysts attribute the 1980 increase in poverty to temporary economic conditions.) The percentage of black individuals who were poor fell from 56.2 percent to 32.6 percent. In addition, the poor appear to be more economically mobile than was commonly assumed in the sixties. The University of Michigan study found that only one out of five people who were considered poor in 1975 had been poor in every one of the preceding nine years. Moreover, the notion of a static America—one in which individuals are locked into an economic and social caste system from birth—ignores the considerable social and economic mobility of Japanese, Jewish, Irish, German, Polish, Italian, West Indian, Cuban, and other recent immigrants, many of whom arrived poor but did not stay that way.

It ignores as well what at least until early 1981 seemed to be the dominant view of American blacks. In a 1981 *Washington Post*–ABC News national survey, by a three-to-one margin blacks took the view that conditions for American blacks had improved in the past decade. Although the incomes of blacks, Hispanics, and whites are still not equal, the Census Bureau has found that the gap between them has narrowed. In 1978, the Census Bureau reports, the median income of Hispanic males was $11,943, of black males $12,530, and of white males $16,360. The gap was considerably narrower between women. Hispanic females had a median income in 1978 of $8,331, black females $9,020, and white females $9,732. For college graduates, the gap was narrower.

Other people see the official poverty figure as inflated, and are optimistic. Their argument is that most poor Americans now receive some form of government support—not only AFDC and Supplemental Security Income (SSI) payments and Social Security checks but such nonmonetary aid as food stamps, free or subsidized school lunches, child care, and Medicaid and other health support—yet the official poverty figures are based on only the direct income-transfer payments that the poor receive, such as AFDC, SSI, and Social Security checks. Other government support—called in-kind or non-cash benefits—is excluded. Yet these in-kind benefits have risen by more than 60 percent since 1976 alone, and, according to the Congressional Budget Office, in-kind benefits to all Americans cost about $60 billion in 1980. In a typical recent year, the federal government spent more on food stamps ($11.3 billion), which went to 22.5 million Americans, than on AFDC payments ($6.9 billion), which went to 10.8 million Americans. Admittedly, not all the money spent— whether on direct or indirect aid—went to the poor. Medicare and hot lunches and subsidized housing can and do assist middle-income families; and it is novel logic to claim that a family is no longer poor because ill health increased its Medicaid support, which then carried it over the poverty threshold. Still, Sar A. Levitan, the director of the Center for Social Policy Studies at George Washington University, wrote in his book *Programs in Aid of the Poor for the 1980s,* that "during the seventies, the programs in aid of the poor reduced poverty by about a third, from 25 million people to about 16 million."

There are those who believe that the figure of 16 million is also inflated. Counting in-kind benefits and correcting for underreporting of income, the Congressional Budget Office estimated in mid-1977 that in fiscal year 1976 15.5 million Americans were in poverty —which is to say, only 7.4 per cent of the population. For 1975, Morton Paglin, a professor of economics at Portland State University, in Oregon, put the figure as low as 7.8 million people, or 3.6 per cent of the population; and in 1978 Martin Anderson, now President Reagan's chief White House domestic adviser, claimed in his book *Welfare: The Political Economy of Welfare Reform in the United States* that poverty had been "virtually eliminated."

Whatever the number of poor people, from a historical perspective there has been progress, though how much is unclear. Because of government income supports, says Harlem Congressman Charles Rangel, "No one is starving today like years ago." Certainly it is different now from the late nineteenth century, when one-third of New York City's residents begged for food or survived on charity; then, only one American child in fifteen went beyond elementary school. As miserably as far too many Americans live today, their living standards are often luxurious compared to those who slept on ashes to keep warm in Hogarth's eighteenth-century London, or to the 1.1 billion people in the world who the World Bank says subsisted on per-capita incomes of $220 or less in 1980. We have come a distance from Henry VIII's Poor Laws, when beggars were whipped the first time they were apprehended, had their right ear cut off the second time, and if convicted a third time were summarily executed.

Applying this relative historical measure, economist Thomas Sowell views with considerable calm the gap between the incomes of white and minority Americans. As it took earlier immigrant groups two or three generations to climb from poverty, Sowell says, so it will take a little more time for blacks and Hispanics to catch up. Blacks, he goes on, have been free for just one century, and have populated urban communities for only two generations; Puerto Ricans and Mexican-Americans are even newer to urban America. And since their average age is younger, it should be no surprise that their average income is lower.

One of the most baffling things about the poverty debate is that serious people seem to be arguing over facts that should be susceptible of adjudication. Has black income gone down, as the Urban League argues, or up, as others argue? Are the Urban League and its opponents looking at the same facts?

As it turns out, they are not. The Urban League and others who take a pessimistic view are comparing *family* income of blacks and whites, and here the gap has widened—the median black family income dropped from 61 percent of the median white family income in 1969 to 58 percent in 1980. Those who take an optimistic view compare *individual* income of blacks and whites, and here the gap has narrowed: between 1948 and 1978, the median income of black individuals rose more rapidly than that of white individuals. A similar pattern is found among Hispanics.

The relative drop in family income and relative rise in individual income can be explained by the changes taking place in the structure of black families and, to a somewhat lesser extent, in Hispanic ones. Two sets of statistics mirror this change: the explosion of out-of-wedlock births and the growing number of poor families maintained by women. In 1940, the Department of Health and Human Services' National Center for Health Statistics has estimated, about 15 percent of all births to black women were out of wedlock; by 1979, that number had more than tripled, to almost 55 percent. (The National Center for Health Statistics does not keep comparable figures for Hispanics, because not enough states make the necessary information available.) In 1980, 47 percent of all black families with children under eighteen were maintained by women, as opposed to 30 percent in 1970; among Hispanic families, 22 percent were maintained by women, as opposed to 15 percent in 1970. (Among mainland Puerto Rican families, over 40 percent were maintained by women in 1980.) The number of white families with children under eighteen maintained by women did not rise rapidly in the decade, and in 1980 only 14 percent of white families were maintained by women.

The social consequences of the increase in the percentage of families maintained by women are a subject of sometimes intense debate; the economic consequences can not be. There is a direct correlation between poverty and whether a family is maintained by one wage earner or two. The majority of the poor today live in families maintained by women—a rise of 25 percent in a decade. This "feminization of poverty" means, according to the 1981 report of the National Advisory Council on Economic Opportunity, that of families maintained by women one in three is poor, compared to one in ten maintained by males and only one in nineteen maintained by two parents. The single mother often has young children to look after, and is usually without skills or education. Salary levels for females are invariably below the salary levels for males. (The median income of males who worked full time in 1980 was $19,173, compared with $11,591 for females.)* And in the majority of today's two-parent homes both adults work. It comes as no surprise, then, that in 1978 the median income of a black household maintained by a woman was $5,888, compared with $15,913 for a two-parent black home; among Hispanics, the figure was $5,578 for a single mother, and $14,720 for two parents. Among families where both parents work and the head of the household is employed full time, the white family's median income is $24,627, the black family's $22,125—a gap of only 10 percent. "The decline in poverty during the past decade has been almost entirely in male-householder families," the 1981 National Advisory Council report said.

Thus there are at least two distinct minority communities—one, consisting mainly of female-headed households, slips more deeply into poverty; the other moves forward, albeit too slowly, toward the economic middle class. Within these female-headed households poverty multiplies, as does the pathological behavior that affects everyone. With the exception of Pearl Dawson and Akim, the members of BT-27 were raised in divided homes. Willy Joe, John Painter, and Mohammed never knew their fathers. Ramon Lopez knew his father, but he also knew that his father was perpetually unemployed and often drunk. Leon Harris felt that he was in competition with his father. Denise Brown was raped by her stepfather. Hope Parker, William Block, and Carlos Rodriguez were abandoned to the care of relatives. Timothy Wilson was deposited in foster homes. Many of Appalachia's poor experienced family problems.

On the other hand, the group that seems to be improving itself financially usually lives in two-parent households. This economic middle class expands. For instance, in 1978 there were 300,000 more black families earning the equivalent of $25,000 annually than there were in 1970. This is the "deepening schism" former Federal Reserve Board member Andrew F. Brimmer, who is black, spotted as early as 1970:

> Within the Negro community, there appears to be a deepening schism between the able and the less able, between the well-prepared and those with few skills. This deepening schism can

---

*Admittedly, more women work part-time, depressing the overall average pay of working females. But women are disproportionately represented in clerical positions.

be traced in a number of ways, including the substantial rise in the proportion of Negroes employed in professional and technical jobs—while the proportion of Negroes employed in low-skilled occupations also edges upward; in the sizable decline in unemployment—while the share of Negroes among the long-term unemployed rises.

It is this schism which prompted NAACP President Margaret Bush Wilson to tell that organization's 1980 annual convention:

> Over the last fifteen years in many urban black communities, there has been developing a widening income gap. For example, the number of middle-income blacks has doubled during this period so that some 25 to 45 percent of all black Americans have middle incomes. However, the size of the black low-income group has hardly changed.

Thus it turns out that one cannot talk about poverty in America, or about the underclass, without talking about the weakened family structure of the poor. And yet most news accounts and political speeches tend to characterize the minority community as one homogeneous, undifferentiated mass. After the 1980 Miami riots, for instance, the *Times* and the Washington *Post* carried major articles about American blacks. Each recited dismal economic data about blacks, using only family-income figures. Neither paper recited the progress made by individuals reared in two-parent black families.

The struggle to overcome poverty has entered a new phase, and one of the most significant problems that has emerged is family structure. An unpublished memorandum prepared in March of 1980 for the federal government by Steven Sandell, an assistant professor of economics at Ohio State University, who served for a year as a policy fellow at the Department of Health and Human Services, tells why. "The single most important reason for the deterioration in the black-white income ratio between 1970 and 1978 is the substantially faster growth of female-headed families for blacks than whites," the memorandum said. It went on, "In fact, if the pattern of family composition that existed in 1970 were present in 1978, the black-white income gap would have narrowed by six percentage points." Sandell found that "about one-third of the 1978 black-white income gap is attributable" to the vastly larger percentage of black families maintained by women. He was careful to note that even without differences in family composition a gap between black and white income would remain. Racism, he said, was obviously a factor. But "other factors contribute substantially to the black-white income gap," and chief among these was that black families are almost four times as likely to be maintained by women as white families are.

The family issue is hardly new. In the thirties and subsequently, for instance, the sociologist E. Franklin Frazier warned that "family disorganization" was handicapping black Americans. In 1965, psychologist Kenneth Clark wrote about it in his book *Dark Ghetto*. These black scholars were quoted at some length by Daniel Patrick Moynihan in his 1965 report *The Negro Family: The Case for National Action*. Moynihan, then Assistant Secretary of Labor, expressed alarm that "the racist virus in the American bloodstream" and "three centuries of sometimes unimaginable mistreatment" had "taken their toll on the Negro people," and he went on, "The fundamental problem, in which this is most clearly the case, is that of family structure. The evidence—not final, but powerfully persuasive —is that the Negro family in the urban ghettos is crumbling. . . . So long as this situation persists, the cycle of poverty and disadvantage will continue to repeat itself."

The Moynihan Report, as it came to be known, provoked considerable hostility. Moynihan was accused of providing "the fuel for a new racism," of assuming that "middle-class American values are the correct ones for everyone in America," of "blaming the victim," of being a "sexist"—or, worse, a "racist." President Lyndon Johnson's White House Conference on Civil Rights, in June of 1966, which was to discuss the Negro family, among other topics, changed its agenda after sixty representatives of churches and civil-rights groups petitioned Johnson to strike "family stability" from the agenda. The subject eventually faded from public view, even though a number of national civil-rights leaders thought Moynihan had been treated as if he were one of Senator Joseph McCarthy's alleged Communists. Clark, who later became a bitter opponent of Moynihan, said at the time, "Is a doctor responsible for a disease simply because he diagnoses it?"

After the furor died, two scholars, Lee Rainwater and William L. Yancey, authored a dispassionate 493-page volume about the Negro family and the uproar over the Moynihan Report. They concluded that the subject required discussion. They assumed that one could be an opponent of racism and still recognize the economic disadvantage of female-headed families; that one could call for "equality of result" for blacks—as the Moynihan Report did (and many today do not because they oppose quotas)—and still recognize the "tangle of pathology" created by many poor, female-headed families. They believed that this pathology was an *effect* of poverty and racism, not a *cause* of it. But in any case it was real, and would not disappear because people refused to discuss it. They conclude their 1967 book this way:

> While the issues raised by the Moynihan Report are overshadowed for the moment, at some future time they will be raised again, debated and fought over, and, hopefully, bear fruit in meaningful programs to provide the kind of social and economic resources that must exist if Negroes are to have the chance to climb out of the degradation into which white society has forced them.

Sixteen years after the Moynihan Report appeared, few local or federal efforts have addressed the role of family structure in perpetuating poverty. As a candidate in 1976, Jimmy Carter vowed to adopt measures to engage the problem, but it wasn't until 1980 that a series of White House Conferences on Families was convened. These conferences did not focus on poverty and the family, however; the agenda gave equal weight to such unequal topics as "lifestyles" and gay marriages, and delegates even disagreed over the definition of "family." The issue of family structure is too rarely discussed. Although the federal government paid Steven Sandell's salary for one year, for instance, the Department of Health and Human Services has not yet published his findings concerning family dissolution and its effect on poverty. In the summer of 1980, Sandell explained in a telephone interview that his report was "an internal document" inspired by *The State of Black America 1980*, and merely attempted to give an accurate comparison of white and black income. Sandell's response when he was asked if his report had caused internal debate, and if there had been demands that it not be published, was that the report was not suppressed. Asked to explain why conclusions such as the ones he reached were not more widely circulated, Sandell admitted, "With the background of the Moynihan Report, one has to feel a little inhibited."

Increasingly, however, some leading black officials have become less inhibited on the subject. Of the Moynihan Report, Eleanor Holmes Norton, who headed the federal Equal Employment Opportunity Commission from 1977 until February 1981, told me, "That it had to come from a white man tells you about the failure of black leadership." Robert Hill, the director of research for the National Urban League, said in a 1980 interview, "I believe Moynihan was sincere." Hill claims that the family issue is being discussed, but only among blacks. "If you're speaking to blacks, it comes out. To go before a predominantly white audience and speak about the breakup of homes? No. When you talk to whites, you talk about the things they can do something about." Eleanor Holmes Norton, for one, sees the question more broadly. As a speaker at the Urban League's national convention in July of 1975, she raised it in the form of an open letter "from a black woman to a black man":

> My subject this evening is not an issue at all. It is at best a whisper. I believe it should become, if not an issue, a decided focus for us as a people and for the government as well. . . . The repair of the black condition in America disproportionately depends upon the succor of strong families which can defend against the forces that prey most menacingly on unprotected black men, women and children. . . . Raising black children in today's cities, fraught with social danger, requires the maximum in physical and psychological support. Particularly in the nation's ghettos, where blacks are increasingly concentrated, it is simply too much to ask what amounts to an increasing number of black women to raise the children of the black nation.

The problem that Norton spoke of and Moynihan wrote about in 1965 has "shot up like a rocket," Moynihan observes today. It has become, he says, "a self-generating phenomenon not controlled by the economy." Since Moynihan wrote his report, black out-of-wedlock births have risen from 23.6 percent of all births in 1962 to 55 percent in 1979, and over 70 percent in many urban ghettos. (White out-of-wedlock births have also risen, but these total just 9 percent of all white births.) The proportion of black and Puerto Rican families headed by women doubled. AFDC rolls swelled from 3 million in 1960 to 10.8 million in 1980, and the number of black children supported by welfare rose from 14 to 36 percent.

The reasons that this issue has remained submerged are varied. Understandably, many people fear that pointing out family weaknesses will ease the pressure on government to do more to help the poor. Or as Martin Luther King, Jr., who agreed with Moynihan that the condition of the black family was a "social catastrophe," said at the time of the Moynihan Report, "the danger will be that problems will be attributed to innate Negro weaknesses and used to justify neglect and rationalize oppression." Thus those who oppose further government and societal efforts will cite evidence that the "solution" to poverty must come from the individual, not from society. Civil-rights leaders face a dilemma: they are torn between their desire to condemn inequality in order to get government action and their

263

need to applaud "progress" in order to convince society—and poor people—that government works. This dilemma has been heightened by the election of a conservative president and a Congress less sympathetic to their needs.

A related worry has been expressed by Dr. Bernard Gifford, professor of political science and vice-president for student affairs at the University of Rochester. If the problem of black and Hispanic poverty seems "impenetrable," he says, white people will "withdraw." Moreover, if civil-rights leaders are thought not to be speaking for the overwhelming majority of blacks and Hispanics, their power declines. Bernard C. Watson, vice-president of Temple University, in Philadelphia, writing in *The State of Black America 1980,* implicitly acknowledges this: "Arguments about two classes of blacks are ultimately self-defeating and only serve to give credence to arguments and strategies designed to divide blacks in their continuing struggle to achieve equality." Civil-rights gains in the past, he says, were achieved only "by the unity of all classes of blacks."

The *Washington Post* columnist William Raspberry, who is black, sees this matter differently. Black leaders believe that "white guilt is the driving force for progress for black America," he writes. "Anything that reduces that guilt is seen as crippling the engine." He also observes that many middle-class black leaders suffer from a form of "black guilt," fearing that they will be accused of being élitists, different from the poorer blacks they represent. In October 1980, Carl Gershman, former vice-chairman of Social Democrats, U.S.A., and now special counselor to the American ambassador to the United Nations, in a *Times Magazine* debate with Kenneth Clark—"The Black Plight: Race or Class?"—made this point less gently:

> The myth that all blacks are equally the victims of racism serves a dual purpose, justifying the claims of the most successful blacks to racial entitlements and, by allowing such claims to be made in the name of all blacks, concealing the specific class interest that is served.

The class-versus-race controversy that gave rise to this debate—the question of whether the poor are victims of racism or, broadly speaking, of class—is vastly oversimplified, because one can simultaneously believe that both are factors: that Wildcat's Willy Joe had suffered discrimination and also suffered from his own lack of skills and drive; that one individual is denied decent housing or a job because he is black or Hispanic and another because of chronic alcoholism; that one child fails in school because the teacher has "low expectations" for minority youngsters, and another fails because he thinks school is for squares and wants to hang out with his friends. One can simultaneously advocate a policy to strengthen the poor family *and* a policy to eradicate racial injustice. Unfortunately, most civil-rights leaders—even those who are deeply troubled about family dissolution and pathology and what to do about it—publicly suppress these concerns and stress racism or economic discrimination as the chief affliction of black and Hispanic Americans. Conservatives tend to ignore such causes; they prefer to stress class factors as the reason for the existence of the underclass.

Who's right? On the larger philosophical question of race versus class, society versus individual responsibility, determinism versus free will, retrenchment versus progress, Friedrich Nietzsche supplied perhaps the best answer when he said, "There are no facts, only interpretations."

But that won't quite do. Some facts about poverty and the underclass are undebatable, and unavoidable, and bring with them important policy implications. Among these facts, as we have seen, are the following:

(1) Poverty has become feminized. The number of families maintained by women has jumped 62 percent since 1970, and 3.1 million poor families are maintained by women today. Increasingly, the division between those who rise into the middle class and those who are poor can be viewed in terms of two-parent families versus families maintained by women. For instance, almost three-fourths of all poor black families are maintained by women. In 1980, about half of all poor families were maintained by women, and their poverty rate was 32.7 per cent, compared to only 6.2 per cent for two-parent families.

(2) Whether family dissolution is a cause or an effect of poverty, it unquestionably cannot be overlooked. As Andrew Hacker, a professor of political science at Queens College, has shown, family dissolution largely explains why black Americans now constitute "an even greater share of the poor than they did at the outset of the seventies." He continues, "In 1970, black families accounted for 22 percent of all low-income households in the country; in 1978, they made up 28 percent." Put another way, female-headed families are five times as likely to be poor as two-parent families are.

(3) Contrary to a widespread belief, many poor Americans are not locked into poverty. Frank Levy, an economist at the Urban Institute, in Washington, basing his estimates on his analysis of the University of Michigan Survey Research Center study of about 5,000 families, says that three out of ten poor adults are poor only temporarily. "Children did better than their parents," he wrote. "Most new

households formed by poor children—about four out of five—had incomes well above the poverty line."

(4) While poverty may have declined, an American underclass has grown. Levy estimates that about 9 million people are "the long-term poor." Half of this population is drawn, he found, from families maintained by women. (Whether this is an accurate number or not depends on one's definition of the underclass. If the definition includes what some refer to as "deviant behavior," no one can do more than guess at the size of the underclass.)

(5) The underclass represents a minority—not a majority—of the poor.

(6) An underclass threatens to become permanent. In 1968, the National Advisory Commission on Civil Disorders warned that "our nation is moving toward two societies, one black, one white—separate and unequal," and this warning could be applied to the underclass and the rest of the population today.

(7) Increasingly, poverty and the underclass are urban phenomena. The majority of the poor once resided in small towns and rural areas, but by 1977 60 percent lived in metropolitan areas, and three of five people in that group lived in central cities. As George Sternlieb and James W. Hughes of Rutgers University have ominously noted, while blacks made up 23 percent of the population of central cities, they made up 46 percent of the cities' poor. The official poverty population declined by 2.2 million between 1970 and 1977, and the population of central cities shrank by 4.6 percent, but during that same period the number of poor people living in central cities grew by 2.5 percent. This rise in city poverty is traced to the growth in the number of poor families headed by women, which swelled 44.7 percent in the period.

(8) More and more, poverty is linked with welfare. There was a time when poor people starved, but today few do; now most poor people receive some form of government assistance. The AFDC program, enacted as part of the New Deal, was designed as a small effort to assist children whose fathers had died. More than four decades later, the AFDC rolls had swelled to 10.8 million people, receiving almost $7 billion from the federal government (the 1936 figure was just over $21 million for 534,000 people), and more than 80 percent of the enrolled children received benefits not because their father was dead but because they were born out of wedlock (37.8 percent) or their parents were divorced (20.3 percent) or separated (24.4 percent). Of all children born in 1940, fewer than one in ten were supported by welfare at some point before reaching adulthood; about one in three of the children born since 1970 are. And in

1979 more than 40 percent of the families receiving welfare had been receiving it for three years or more.

(9) The individual income of blacks and Hispanics still lags behind the income of whites. There has been undeniable economic and social progress, but numerous indicators, including school-dropout, infant-mortality, and unemployment rates and mental-health disorders, still show wide disparities. Blacks are three times as likely to be poor as whites, and Hispanics more than twice as likely.

(10) Whether it is a cause or an effect of poverty and unemployment, the underclass often exhibits abnormal behavior—hostility, poor work habits, passivity, low self-confidence, alcoholism, drug addiction. This is true among the poor of white Appalachia, black rural Mississippi, Spanish Harlem, or Oakland, California. Bernard Anderson, an economist and one of three black members of the MDRC's board of directors, wrote in *The State of Black America 1980,* "Race discrimination alone is not the only barrier to greater economic opportunity, and little will be gained by failing to confront the issues raised by the changing domain of opportunity for the better prepared black workers, as compared with others who because of persistent unemployment, poor education, poor housing, negative attitudes toward work and toward society at large have become increasingly isolated from economic progress."

(11) The poor in America today are unlike the immigrant poor of the nineteenth and early twentieth centuries. Today's poor often lack the protection of a strong family and often carry the badge of their color. Society is more calcified. There are fewer manufacturing and low-skilled jobs, for the economy is increasingly service-oriented. The obstacles to entering society are more difficult to overcome—rigorous civil-service exams, enrollment qualifications to join unions, urban neighborhoods divided into a checkerboard of white and black sections—and inflation wipes out savings and ruthlessly kicks people right back down the ladder.

(12) Because of inflation and slowed economic growth, it is harder for Americans to climb that ladder. Basic welfare payments have rarely kept pace with inflation, although in-kind benefits, such as food stamps, Medicare, and Medicaid, have. More Americans hover just above the poverty line. In 1980, the typical American worker earned more than twice what he or she did a decade ago, according to the nonpartisan Washington-based Tax Foundation, but real income after inflation and taxes was 5 percent less than it was then. And a recession, coupled with rising inflation, drops many more Americans into the poverty category, as was the case in 1974 and 1975, and again in 1979 and 1980. For instance, according to Census

267

Bureau data, the official poverty population shot up from 25.2 million in 1979 to 29.3 million in 1980, with 2.5 million more white Americans classified as poor.

(13) The arguments of both those who claim that American poverty has worsened and those who claim that it has improved are usually overstated. Pessimists would be less gloomy if they would simply acknowledge the economic progress made by minority *individuals*; optimists would be less cheerful if they calculated the income of *families*.

In any case, it is fair to conclude that the face of poverty has been altered and that poverty is still too little talked about. Today, perhaps for the first time, America has a sizable, and so far intractable, intergenerational underclass. Moynihan, who, it turns out, was prescient about the changing structure of American poverty, wrote an essay in 1967 explaining the danger of hiding from this reality. Both the left and the right, he wrote, seemed eager "to establish *guilt* instead of to deal with a problem." He continued:

This is terrifyingly reminiscent of Stanley Elkins' abolitionists who seem never to have seen slavery as a social problem for slaves, but only as an ethical problem for slaveholders. Once legal bondage was at an end, the subject was closed so far as the Northerners were concerned. The fact that the slaves lived on, and the child is born—and needs help—is a matter somehow to be passed over. This is the crux of it. Typically, the refusal of the liberal Left to accept the unpleasant facts of life for the poor— there is delinquency in the slums, but those kids in the suburbs are just as bad and don't get arrested, etc. etc.—leads to the same position as does the insistence of the extreme conservatives on just such facts: namely, to do nothing. The liberal Left will acknowledge the relevance of these facts only to the extent that they serve as an indictment of American society; after that it loses interest. The extreme conservatives harp on these facts in order to indict the poor; after that, *they* lose interest.

Possible Solutions:
The Wholesale Option

It is difficult to reach a consensus on what to do about the underclass, because there is no agreement on the cause and the scope of the problem. In broad terms, opinion on these questions can be grouped into three categories. Those who favor what might be called the wholesale option from a left, or liberal, perspective are optimistic that government money and compassion and effort applied on a large scale can cure the problem; proponents of that approach on the political right are optimistic that reducing taxes and government will liberate private enterprise to generate jobs, and that "getting tough" will end welfare-dependency and crime. At the other end of the spectrum is the laissez-faire option. Those who favor this option are generally pessimistic, believing that neither government nor private philanthropy is likely to alter what is often innate "lower class" behavior. In between are those who adopt a retail approach. Retailers are skeptical about quick fixes, yet abhor the thought of doing nothing, so they tend to favor incremental solutions. Merit may be found in many of the proposals put forth by each, but, predictably, the position one advocates has as much to do with judgment and values as with facts.

The Wholesale Option

Before Vietnam and Watergate and public fatigue with government bureaucracy and taxes, the public and its leaders seemed to possess boundless optimism. Their expectations were expressed by President

Johnson in March of 1964, when he said, "I have called for a national war on poverty. Our objective: total victory." Yet despite what the federal Advisory Commission on Intergovernmental Relations said was the growth of income transfer programs from $77 billion in 1965 to $394 billion in 1978, those on the political left who favor large-scale reforms sincerely believe that the war on poverty failed because the efforts were too timid. In the opinion of Michael Harrington and others, the efforts did not address the structural causes of poverty, did not truly redistribute wealth from the haves to the have-nots. From this point of view, the underclass is primarily an economic problem; the psychologist William Ryan writes in his book *Blaming the Victim* that "poverty is most simply and clearly understood as a lack of money." To achieve the necessary redistribution of money requires a major commitment to economic as well as political democracy—in other words, not just equality of opportunity but equality of result. What counts, according to the Carnegie Council on Children, is not incremental liberal reforms or the efforts of individuals but a fundamental economic redistribution.

These major structural changes would require the federal government to take from the rich—through public ownership, taxes, profit ceilings—and give to the poor. Such a redistribution of wealth might also be accomplished through companies owned and managed by employees. These, it is assumed, would be more profitable (with profits going to the public), would improve employee morale, and would guarantee wise investment decisions. Investments presumably would be earmarked for labor-intensive industries that perform a public good—making subway cars and buses, creating solar technology, constructing schools and public housing. These changes might be accomplished through a form of radical democratic socialism, such as the Carnegie Council and Marcus Raskin of the Institute for Policy Studies in Washington, have urged, or through an Economic Bill of Rights, such as Martin Luther King, Jr., proposed in the last days of his life, or through a domestic Marshall Plan, such as many civil-rights leaders have advocated. A domestic Marshall Plan would not necessarily mean socialism, but it would mean a vast increase in federal funds spent on public jobs, subsidized housing, and other entitlements for the poor.

Such a plan would have many parts. One part might be that the federal government would provide a guaranteed annual income to all citizens—a floor below which no income could fall, whether people worked or not. Such a guaranteed income exists in about sixty-five industrialized nations. In the late 1960s, Moynihan, then a White House aide, persuaded the Nixon administration to propose legislation conforming to the European model, but this proposal, the Family Assistance Plan, was defeated by the combined efforts of conservatives who worried that it would undermine initiative, liberals who felt its income floor was too low, and bureaucrats and social workers who feared that they would lose their jobs. If the income floor was high, the political left would generally favor a guaranteed income to replace welfare, thereby getting rid of welfare's steep administrative costs, removing its "demeaning" regulations and interviews, and, above all, disposing of the notion that welfare is a privilege, not a right.

Patricia Roberts Harris, who was Secretary of Health and Human Services in the Carter administration, says, "The debate today is not about whether we have a guaranteed income but about the level. People today can be assured of certain payments." Or at least most can. Single people without children are usually not eligible, and neither is an able-bodied married couple. Nor are those—like Willy Joe—who fail in a training program. Harris believes someone like Willy should be supported by the government even if he doesn't work. But what of hustlers like Henry Rivera of BT-27, who chooses a life of drugs and crime? "I'd make life more difficult for him," says Harris. "That guy I'd slam in the pokey. Those people who make a rational judgment that they can make more money by not working, that is a different group. It may be a hopeless group." It is also, she and most liberal wholesalers are convinced, a very small group.

Those who believe that a guaranteed annual income for all Americans is politically unrealistic sometimes substitute a call for the "federalization" of welfare. Under this plan, the federal government would assume all welfare costs and provide a minimum national income, which would be linked to the cost of living. Thus citizens of Texas, which in 1979 provided a family of four with a monthly welfare allowance of $134, and citizens of Mississippi, which furnished 90¢ a day for a family of three, would no longer be penalized because of where they live.

The concepts of a guaranteed income and a decent national welfare standard are seen as two large-scale ways of attacking family dissolution and other ills associated with poverty. A guaranteed job—government as the employer of last resort—is seen as a way of combating unemployment; 9.5 million Americans were officially unemployed in January 1982. A guaranteed income and a guaranteed job differ in that the latter has a work requirement, but they are alike in that both assume an adequate income to be a right. "In principle, there are two ways of dealing with relief explosions and the underlying economic and social dislocations which they reflect,"

Frances Fox Piven, professor of political science at Boston University, and Richard A. Cloward, professor of social work at Columbia, wrote in their book *Regulating the Poor: The Functions of Public Welfare.* "One is by reforms in economic policy that would lead to full employment at decent wages, and the other is by relief reforms. If jobs were created on a large scale, whether by public or private investments, and if the wages paid were adequate, many AFDC mothers would immediately take jobs."

A federal jobs program would undoubtedly mean a large-scale effort—one that might dwarf the programs passed during the New Deal era. This could be accomplished through public-works projects or it could be accomplished through "reindustrialization," a notion in vogue today—investing public money in useful public and private industries. A common assumption runs through both: if there were an adequate number of jobs, members of the underclass would readily take them. There is some evidence to support this view, including people named Pearl Dawson, Denise Brown, William Mason and Hope Parker. To cite another example, in September of last year at least 26,200 mostly unemployed men and women in Baltimore—some of whom undoubtedly would be classified in the underclass—rushed to get job applications when they learned of seventy-five entry-level job openings with the Social Security Administration. Some of the job seekers waited in line for three hours to get applications for jobs that paid $7,000 to $11,500 a year.

To combat youth unemployment, which is officially reported at about 40 percent for blacks and 25 percent for Hispanics, a variety of wholesale ideas are offered. Franklin Thomas, the president of the Ford Foundation, endorses compulsory national service of some kind for every young person, male or female. Some of the young people would be drafted into the military, others into public-works projects. "It seems to me that one of the things that are right in front of us for the fourteen-to-twenty-three-year-old group is to rethink the idea of national service, particularly the voluntary armed forces," Thomas told me. "Instead of treating it as a dumping ground, think of it as a source of national honor. For a youngster growing up in the South Bronx, it would provide self-discipline, provide education, provide the certainty of expectations—you've got to get up at a certain time, perform certain chores, achieve certain things." Teenagers could perform public-service tasks in an expanded Jobs Corps, says Eleanor Holmes Norton. "It may be that the Job Corps is more successful than many programs in the ghetto. It takes possession of the whole kid." The Job Corps, one of the many antipoverty initiatives of the Johnson administration, moves school dropouts from poor families away from their neighborhoods to camps, where they are taught skills. This program has had some success, but it is expensive—the Job Corps budget is about $13,000 annually for each of 41,500 youngsters.

The most serious and sustained criticism of these wholesale efforts to assist the underclass centers on cost. Where would the money come from? At the moment, the federal deficit for fiscal 1982 is conservatively pegged by the Reagan administration at $109 billion. The Reagan administration has officially acknowledged that its pledge to achieve a balanced budget in 1984 is unattainable; and if the President's optimistic assumptions about economic growth and lowered inflation and interest rates and a burst of support from the financial community for his tax cuts prove false, the deficit will mushroom. That leaves too small a treasury to launch a domestic Marshall Plan. Those on the left may dispute this, noting that deficits are not the sole, or even the largest, contributor to lagging growth and rising inflation. They claim, accurately, that Japan and West Germany run proportionately larger deficits and yet have enjoyed expanding economies and lower rates of inflation. No matter. As long as the investment community and the rest of the public believe otherwise and endorse efforts to balance the federal budget, liberal wholesalers will remain isolated.

There is also a problem of interpretation. Contrary to the view espoused by many liberal wholesalers, a great many people do believe that federal efforts to eradicate poverty were not so timid. There is some evidence to support this argument. Beginning in the Kennedy administration and continuing through the Johnson, Nixon, Ford, and Carter administrations, dozens of federal initiatives were born, including Head Start, manpower-training programs, the Job Corps, community-action agencies, subsidized housing programs, Medicaid, food stamps, the Comprehensive Employment and Training Act, hot lunches, energy supplements for the poor, subsidized legal aid. The magnitude of this growth is better understood if we consider that in the federal fiscal year beginning October 1, 1981, entitlement programs—including Social Security payments, Medicare, food stamps, and veterans' benefits—were expected to climb by $50 billion. This one-year rise in spending equals nearly half the size of the entire federal budget in 1962.

These expenditures swell the deficits. In fiscal year 1981, about 15 percent of the federal budget—almost $100 billion—went for interest payments. This sum is eight times what the federal government spent for food stamps in 1981, and was more than it spent for education, nutrition, and medical programs combined.

Faced with these facts, a liberal may respond that money to finance a war on poverty can be found by cutting the military budget and "reordering national priorities." But this response ignores still another reality: the voters, as the 1980 elections showed, favor larger, not smaller, military expenditures. And most public officials agree with them, believing that American military strength has dangerously atrophied.

The final alternative pot of gold, say some wholesalers, is to be found buried in corporate boardrooms. Here the arithmetic offers no comfort. Corporate profits after taxes totaled $163 billion in 1980—equal to what we spend yearly for Social Security. Of course these profits do not all go into people's pockets as dividends. A good share of these profits are plowed back into the corporations for expansion. And those who do receive dividends might fairly ask why they should risk their money without the promise of a return on their investment. If investors won't risk their money for the good of the state, where would the government get its funds?

If we could set aside the question of scarce financial resources, we still could achieve no consensus, because many on the left as well as on the right believe that some wholesale ideas can be harmful. A guaranteed income or too generous welfare payments, for example, are opposed by Kenneth Clark, who favors a domestic Marshall Plan. Clark told me that he had objected to Moynihan's proposed Family Assistance Plan. "I thought it would reinforce dependency," he said. "Every individual needs some sense of personal achievement. I would not oppose a guaranteed annual income if it was tied to achievement."

Even Moynihan has subsequently backed off his proposal. "Our proposition was that a condition that was normal and universal would not have the effect of creating dependency," he said in an interview. "Experiments have cast doubt on this." He cited federal pilot programs in Seattle and Denver which suggested that a guaranteed income reduced initiative, reduced hours worked, encouraged family dissolution, and increased dependency. "Current research, as I understand it, says it creates more problems than it solves," Moynihan told me. Martin Anderson summed up the opposition to these welfare changes when he wrote, "Radical welfare reform or any variety of a guaranteed income is politically impossible," because no "plan can be devised that will simultaneously yield minimum levels of welfare benefits, financial incentives to work, and an overall cost to the taxpayers that are politically acceptable."

This dilemma is not new. Although he was an advocate of the poor, England's Henry Mayhew wrote in the nineteenth century: "It becomes almost a necessary result of any system which seeks to give shelter and food to the industrious operative in his way to look for work, that it should be the means of harbouring and fostering the idle and the vagabond." Wholesalers tend to ignore this Hobson's choice: how provide a decent standard of living without encouraging dependency? Conservative critics of a guaranteed income tend to fear more the idleness and the potential harm done individual initiative by benefits and tax policies that make it too easy to be dependent. They fear also that such a free lunch fans hostility, creates a feeling that society owes the individual a living. A guaranteed job is thought to have many of the same defects. The federalization of welfare costs is unlikely in the near future, since an opposite course was advocated by the 1980 Republican Party platform and by Ronald Reagan (although Reagan has now come out for the federalization of Medicaid costs).

Well-meaning advocates of the wholesale approach tend to ignore the stubborn reality of the underclass—a reality brought home by the MDRC experience. The MDRC found, in its seventeen Youth Incentive Entitlement Pilot Projects, that even the promise of a guaranteed job did not guarantee that every young person would want to work. Some young people preferred to hustle. Some of those listed as unemployed were in fact earning a living in the underground economy. The notion that a job automatically equals less drug use and less crime is dismissed as naive; the MDRC found, for instance, that a guaranteed job for a year in supported work did not reduce drug use—though it did reduce crime. But crime is caused by more than just unemployment. For the career criminal, crime becomes a way of life—a calculated business decision. The necklace snatcher rarely has the basic skills needed to land a white-collar job, and earns more on the streets than he could on the assembly line. Leon Harris, a former stickup man in the Wildcat program, said he used to think that the cost of punishment paled in comparison to the profits.

Interestingly, the political left no longer monopolizes wholesale ideas to attack persistent poverty. Supply-side conservatives suggest generous tax cuts, rather than massive government spending, as a means of engendering economic opportunity. Slashing taxes and reducing government spending and government regulations, they say, will allow the market to perform its miracles and free the nation from the cannibalizing effects of liberal doctrine. "Jimmy Carter is not the major problem," Ronald Reagan told the annual convention of the National Urban League in August of 1980. He went on:

The philosophy he believes in and the policies he promotes are. Replace him with someone more competent, but who believes

275

in the same philosophy, and things won't get much better. The problem is, that economic philosophy is based on the mistaken belief that for some people to benefit, others must suffer. We are told the following: that people must lose their jobs; that to help the cities, we must increase taxes on other areas of the country; that to find more jobs for blacks, we must deny jobs to non-blacks. . . . There is a better answer. We must get the economy moving again. Instead of fighting over who gets the last piece of a shrinking economic pie, let's help America produce a bigger pie so that everyone will have a chance to be better off.

George Gilder, an intellectual favorite of President Reagan's, goes a step further, arguing that most government programs aimed at the poor achieve the opposite effect from that intended. In his book *Wealth and Poverty,* published in 1981, Gilder writes:

When government gives welfare, unemployment payments, and public-service jobs in quantities that deter productive work, and when it raises taxes on profitable enterprise to pay for them, demand declines. In fact, nearly all the programs that are advocated by economists to promote equality and combat poverty—and are often rationalized in terms of stimulating consumption—in actuality reduce demand by undermining the production from which all real demand derives. . . . Government cannot significantly affect real aggregate demand through policies of taxing and spending—taking money from one man and giving it to another, whether in government or out. All this shifting of wealth is a zero sum game and the net effect on incomes is usually zero, or even negative.

Consistent with these ideas, President Reagan induced Congress in 1981 to impose $475 billion in federal budget cuts over the next five years, and to cut taxes over that period by $750 billion. Reagan, too, believes in redistributing income—from government back to the rich, the assumption being that the new wealth generated by his economic programs will eventually provide jobs and opportunities for the poor. This philosophy is now supported by a number of black and Hispanic leaders, among the most prominent of whom is Thomas Sowell. In December 1980, shortly after Reagan's election, Sowell and nearly a score of other black social scientists, journalists, and corporate executives were invited to attend a Black Alternatives Conference in San Francisco sponsored by the Institute for Contemporary Studies, a nonprofit public-policy research organization. "It is clear to most sensitive people that the old dependency-encouraging approaches to social policy have failed," read a statement of the conference's purpose which was circulated to participants. "Unfortunately, great numbers of those programs, often involving dead-end jobs and other forms of handouts, remain on the books, subsidizing a major portion of the old civil-rights black and Latino leadership class, which the media and others take 'to speak for blacks and Latinos.' . . . Reagan's election creates an opportunity, if seized, to make a whole new start—to fashion a whole new approach to the race problem, developing new approaches and policies."

In general, those who favor the wholesale approach, both on the left and the right, tend not to distinguish between the poor and the underclass. Both assume that their prescription, whether it is for a resurgent free-enterprise system or a large increase in government spending, will reach those in need. One of the few targeted approaches endorsed by President Reagan and some other supply-siders is a bill that was introduced in June of 1980 and again in June 1981 by Representative Jack Kemp, a Buffalo Republican, and Representative Robert Garcia, a South Bronx Democrat. Under the original bill, the federal government would designate certain depressed areas as "enterprise zones." Each year for three years, it would select, from a list of proposed sites, ten to twenty-five, both rural and urban. In these zones, the government would reduce certain business and individual taxes and in return businesses would be required to hire forty per cent of their new employees from workers eligible for CETA benefits. When discussed at the White House in late 1981, other advocates urged that minimum-wage laws be suspended in these zones. Kemp opposed this. When Kemp introduced this bill for the first time, he told the House:

> Today a segment of our population is trapped in a cycle—a poverty trap which has no beginning and no end. Without government help, some 43 million Americans—20 percent of the population—would be classified as poor. Why has this percentage remained the same for the past dozen years, despite creation of millions of new jobs and rising nominal wages?

Kemp's answer is consistent with his economic philosophy: "A person today who gives up welfare or unemployment benefits to take a job that provides scarcely more, if any, in after-tax income than those benefits provide is just not being realistic. But that is exactly what we ask of our inner-city poor. . . . I would make the case that the poor are motivated by exactly the same things as all other people: incentives, rewards, jobs that bring dignity, not despair." Similarly, Kemp argues that entrepreneurs flee the high taxes and other disadvantages of aging cities. The enterprise zones are supposed to supply the missing economic incentives for both poor people and entrepreneurs.

To avoid the pitfalls of the welfare system and also its huge bureaucratic cost, some conservatives have endorsed the idea of a negative income tax. This idea, which was first proposed in 1962 by the economist Milton Friedman and was later embraced in principle by a number of conservatives and liberals, including Richard Nixon and George McGovern, is fairly simple. Basically, the negative income tax would use the tax system to reward work. Because of graduated income-tax rates, the poor whose incomes fluctuate from year to year wind up paying higher taxes than those who earn the same amount over time from steady employment. The negative income tax would remove this deterrent to working by requiring that the worker pay taxes in a good year but that in a bad year the government pay taxes to the worker. And for those citizens who did not work, welfare payments and other government income supports would be replaced by one direct federal subsidy, similar to a guaranteed income. At worst, money would be saved by providing those on welfare with a direct cash grant and eliminating a costly middleman. At best, there would be a financial incentive for people to get away from welfare, because their taxes would drop as they worked. Of course, as was true of the Family Assistance Plan proposed by the Nixon Administration, there would be fierce disagreement about whether the income-cutoff eligibility level was adequate. Public-employee unions would protest the necessary layoff of social workers. And taxpayers and public officials would resist the idea of a permanent dole for those who did not work.

Traditional conservatives and conservative wholesalers usually agree that the minimum wage serves as a deterrent to hiring the poor. The minimum wage (now $3.35 an hour) "prices people out of the market," Thomas Sowell says, adding, "I imagine that we could absorb every unemployed person as domestics or babysitters" if it were suspended. This belief is shared by the economist Walter Williams, who, like Sowell, has been influenced by Milton Friedman. As a start, they would lower the minimum wage for young people. Sowell proposes a rate of $2.00 an hour for those under twenty. As a presidential candidate, Reagan endorsed a lower minimum wage for young people, without specifying a rate. Because the idea was strenuously opposed by organized labor and because he was unwilling to risk losing support for his budget and tax-cut proposals, the president decided in March 1981 to postpone sending a specific legislative proposal to Capitol Hill.

Unknown to many of its advocates, such a sub-minimum wage has already been tested in the MDRC's Youth Incentive Entitlement program. The MDRC estimated in 1977 that 45.3 percent of those who were then enrolled in the program and working in the private sector were at or below the minimum wage. There are two ways by which government could reach this goal without actually lowering the wage. It could decide, as the MDRC Entitlement Project did in some cases, to subsidize the difference between the actual minimum wage and the wage paid by private industry; or, as Dan J. Smith, a management consultant and a member of the California State Commission for Economic Development, suggested at the Black Alternatives Conference, it could offer business a "youth-employment tax credit" to bridge the difference.

But the MDRC's actual experience with a lower wage, its president, William Grinker, says, suggests that "any evidence we have does not indicate that lowering the minimum wage would significantly affect this youth population." When the MDRC's Youth Incentive Entitlement Project offered a total wage subsidy, only one in ten private employers accepted it. "So what the hell difference would it make with a ghetto kid who can't hook up with the labor market and whom private employers don't want if the minimum wage is $2.85 or $3.35 an hour?" Grinker says. Sowell retorts that firms boycotted the program because small businesses don't want to become entangled with government. Grinker counters that many of these employers simply do not want to hire minority youngsters. Grinker foresees another practical problem: lowering the wage for school dropouts would worsen matters. "They have to make enough to live," he says. "How can they live on $2.85 an hour? If you make the wage less, they'll be less interested."

While those on the left and the right who advocate the wholesale approach usually disagree about the causes of persistent poverty and about how to eradicate it, they do share one assumption: that the root of the problem is economic. Offer a government job or a guaranteed income, those on the left say, and alienation, crime, family dissolution, discrimination, and welfare dependency will decline. Offer economic incentives to business and the poor, those on the right say, and cities will be rebuilt. Representative Kemp is a member in good standing of the so-called new right. He is also an economic determinist. "Seventy-five to eighty-five per cent of the social problems of the country are being caused by the shrinking of the economy," he said to me in an interview in his Capitol Hill office. "I've changed.

279

I was brought up as a Calvinist. I used to think that people create their own environment and that blaming the 'environment' was not much of an excuse. I now realize that crime and social problems, to a larger extent than I thought, result from economic problems. If you ain't got no boots, it's tough to lift yourself up by your bootstraps."

Generally speaking, the old left and the new right play down or perhaps do not know about the kinds of vexatious behavioral habits that have haunted the MDRC's experiments with the underclass. "There's no program on earth that's going to take this kind of group and within a year or two, no matter what the program, turn their world around," Grinker says. Take President Reagan's economic quick fix—the one he presented to the 1981 convention of the National Association for the Advancement of Colored People as a better alternative for the poor than government-funded programs. Under his own economic assumptions, this plan would create 3 million new jobs by 1986, in addition to the 10 million new jobs already envisioned. These 3 million new jobs represent growth. But they would not be nearly enough for the entire underclass. More important, they do not represent opportunity for people without job skills or the social skills and habits of knowing how to get up on time, how to look for a job, how to act in an interview. Training funds were one of the first casualties of Reagan's budget.

In a sense, Atlantic City, New Jersey, already has a "free-enterprise zone." With the passage of the Casino Gambling Referendum in 1976, businesses were invited in. Billions of private dollars were spent in Atlantic City. Old buildings were razed. Thirteen thousand new jobs were created. "But despite the city's vastly expanded economic opportunity," a 1980 report by the Governor's Task Force on Unemployment in Atlantic City stated, "local residents have benefited the least. For the first quarter of 1980, local unemployment stands at over 13 percent, far exceeding the state average." Why were local residents not hired? "In general, the Task Force found that in competing with outsiders for casino-hotel jobs local residents are adversely affected by problems related to education, training, discrimination, health, housing, transportation, child care and other specific concerns." True, free-enterprise zones differ because they insist that employers hire at least 50 percent of their workers from residents of the zone. But if the residents are unskilled or lack child care, will the employer be able, or willing, to overcome this obstacle? Again, a panacea collides with reality.

Economic determinists of the right and left are frequently unaware of the crippling insecurities of many welfare recipients. Among poor whites in the hills of West Virginia, for instance, the

MDRC found that a sizable number of long-term welfare recipients rejected supported work. Some were lazy; many were just scared. Or as Nicholas Lemann reported in a series on a welfare family that appeared in the *Washington Post* in 1980:

> A welfare check is, indisputably, reliable money. A job can end, and in North Philadelphia, unless it's government work, it usually does; a welfare check always comes. It is this point that the people who make welfare policy in Washington don't understand. When they talk about there being a tradeoff between welfare and working, they mean it as a weighing of greed against laziness. In real life, it's usually a little money that's secure versus a little bit more money that's not.

Beyond all the talk about programs, there is the question of whether some members of the underclass are even reachable. Former Bronx Representative Herman Badillo guesses that perhaps 2 percent of the people in the underclass are beyond hope—so twisted and hostile that no program, no amount of compassion, no economic incentives can reach them. But, just as many traditional conservatives err on the side of caution, Badillo and other liberals want to err on the side of trying. "Because you can't reach two per cent doesn't mean you don't go after the ninety-eight percent," he says. Is it, however, only 2 percent of the underclass who can't be reached? Dr. Hugo M. Morales, the medical director of the Bronx Mental Health Center, suspects that a majority of the underclass may be unreachable. He divides the underclass into those who are passive and "traumatized" and those who are "anti-social" and lack a "strong superego"—who "have no conscience, no remorse, no guilt." He includes "hustlers" in the latter group. Of this group, Morales says, "The damage is already done in many of these cases, and no matter how much we spend I don't think we'll do much. The key is prevention."

There are many ideas about prevention. If crumbling families are the seedbed of the underclass, the Harvard political scientist Edward Banfield has asked, how can society not take the child away from the destructive influence of its mother? "The child should be taken from its lower-class parents at a very early age and brought up by people whose culture is normal," Banfield suggested in his book *The Unheavenly City*, published in 1970. However, Banfield recognized that taking a child from its parents might not be advisable; such a practice smacks of totalitarianism to many Americans. Further, it assumes that children born to single lower-class mothers are destined to become criminals or a burden on society. Another variant of Banfield's idea is for government to intercede by preventing many of these births. In a 1967 essay that could prove embarrassing to a Democrat striving to replenish his "liberal" credentials, Daniel Patrick Moynihan suggested that the abolition of mass welfare dependency might require "a sharp curtailment of the freedom now by and large enjoyed by low-income groups to produce children they cannot support." China, to control a population that is pushing one billion, has been debating compulsory birth control. According to the *Washington Post*, proponents of the idea there urge laws to prevent "imbeciles, lunatics, hemophiliacs, and those who are color blind or carry hereditary diseases" from having children.

However, many conservatives fear any government birth-control intrusion. Chastity, says Republican Senators Orrin Hatch and Jeremiah Dent, is the answer. "The most effective oral contraceptive yet devised is the word 'no,' " the Senators jointly wrote to the *New York Times* on June 15, 1981. "It costs nothing, has no harmful side effects and is a hundred percent effective."

Less drastic approaches to shoring up the family have been proposed. Martin Anderson has supported a requirement that absent fathers provide child support—a move that he believes would lower welfare costs. To strengthen family ties, President Reagan urged Congress in May 1981 to consider the income of stepparents, for the first time, in calculating a child's need for welfare benefits and to strive to collect alimony and child support from absent fathers. To break the cycle of dependency and to reduce the 10.8 million people on the AFDC rolls in 1980, wholesalers on the right have urged a crackdown on many recipients of welfare. Thomas Sowell says he would prohibit welfare for all but those in "distress"—the old, the sick, the infirm. In *Wealth and Poverty,* George Gilder, who takes exception to the "fake" reforms proposed by liberals and conservatives alike, wrote, "Neither side is willing to tolerate fraud, both sides advocate largely fraudulent work requirements, and neither side understands the need to permit a gradual lowering of the real worth of benefits." To purge the welfare rolls, he would simply lower or freeze benefits. Gilder believes that true poverty is the best "spur" to motivate the poor. Adam Walinsky, the former chief legislative aide to the late Senator Robert F. Kennedy, agrees that benefits, particularly in many Northern states, should not be permitted to rise, as they did in New York in 1981. But he believes that the welfare rolls must be purged in another way. "I absolutely believe it is outrageous and totally immoral not to require work in exchange for every dollar of welfare given out," he told me. He would exclude the sick and the infirm, but "work" would include "going to class and getting an education," he said. "It would be like the Israeli Army, which was used as an assimilation device. You don't go to class, you don't eat." What of the 560,000 teen-agers who became mothers in 1979? Walinsky (who drafted a well-received speech on the underclass given at a meeting of the NAACP in 1978 by Senator Edward Kennedy) said that he would provide day care, "but not in the sense of paying white teachers to come in at $25,000 a year." Recipients could work four days and rotate as babysitters the fifth day, he said. Was he not being callous? "I'd say the callousness is really on the part of those, whatever the nobility of their sentiments, who want to allow the present situation to continue," he told me not long ago. "The fact is —to take a simple example—if you're the parent or someone with any feeling for the lives these kids lead, you know they have to be disciplined and taught. And they've got to be taught the same lessons we teach our kids. Imagine my teaching my kid that it's all right to sit around on his ass, not to go to school, not to work, to get a girl pregnant!"

A work requirement for adults receiving welfare has been part of federal law for years. Because of a growing conviction that welfare produces the passivity or the resentment so prevalent among the underclass, many liberals today support more stringent work requirements. Carl Holman, president of the National Urban Coalition and a member of the MDRC's board of directors, says, "Welfare is deteriorative. Jobs help define who you are. The answer, I'm more and more convinced, is that welfare reform that simply brings benefits up to a uniform level is not the answer." Simply raising benefits ignores the growth of what might be called a welfare culture. Such a culture was described, repeatedly, by members of BT-27 and by the white supported workers in Appalachia. It is described by Michael "Junior" Antonetty, a thirty-seven-year-old janitor who was born in Puerto Rico and now lives in a Coney Island, Brooklyn, housing project: "I have friends. They're strong. Yet they're not going to work. No way. They get rent. They get food stamps. They get welfare checks. They say to me, 'What are you going to work for?' They're supposed to go to work like I do. I go to work at five o'clock in the morning. The guys don't seek. The problem is the government. They don't check it out. Right now I could send my wife over there and she could tell welfare, 'Junior left me.' She would get a check. I won't do it."

In 1981, President Reagan proposed a series of actions to reduce welfare dependency. He called for a national "workfare" program, asserting that 800,000 of the more than 3 million adults receiving

AFDC payments were employable. He urged Congress to count in-kind benefits such as food stamps in calculating whether an individual or a family was poor. Congressional conferees ultimately agreed to eliminate $6 billion in food-stamp benefits over the next three years. In all, 875,000 households would lose their food-stamp benefits and 1.4 million families would have them reduced. The President also moved to eliminate 300,000 CETA jobs, on the ground that these were "make-work" jobs. (Included in this cut were CETA funds that provided work for the MDRC's supported workers.) AFDC funds are to be cut by a billion dollars in fiscal year 1982, and this will remove 408,000 families, or more than 10 percent, from the welfare rolls and lower the benefits of 279,000 families; about three-quarters of a billion dollars more is to be cut in each of the succeeding four years. The federal Medicaid contribution, which would have amounted to 16.5 billion dollars in 1981, is to be reduced by a billion dollars for 1982, by 2 billion for 1983, by 3 billion for 1984, by 4 billion for 1985, and by 5 billion for 1986. Housing subsidies, unemployment-insurance benefits, energy-assistance supplements, subsidies for school meals, loans for college students, aid for elementary and secondary schools, training funds, and free legal assistance are to be reduced.

"These cuts sound like enormous sums—and they are—until one considers the overwhelming size of the total budget," Reagan said in a budget message to Congress on March 10, 1981. "Even with these cuts, the 1982 budget will total $695.3 billion, an increase of 6.1 percent over 1981." A prime reason for this increase is military spending, with Reagan proposing to more than double the Defense Department budget—to $368 billion—by 1986. In arguing for his proposals, the president said that he was preserving the nation's existing "social safety net," and that those "who rely on government for their very existence" would continue to be protected. However, a study by the Congressional Budget Office, which was able to evaluate the impact of only about a third of Reagan's proposed cuts, found that nearly half of all low-income families would lose spendable income if the plan was enacted, and that 41 percent of all families with incomes of less than half the official poverty threshold would suffer losses. A study by the University of Chicago's Center for the Study of Welfare Policy found that a federal formula change proposed by Reagan would have the severest impact on low-paid workers eligible for welfare, and so would unintentionally discourage people from working. For example, according to the study, in March 1981 a working woman on welfare in New York State with two children had a disposable income of $754 a month. This contrasted with $542 available to a nonworking mother—a difference of $212. If the Reagan changes were put into effect, the study concluded, the disposable income of the working mother would be reduced to $555 a month and that of the nonworking mother to $518—a difference of only $37. "We already have a disincentive problem, but this would worsen it," Edwin L. Dale, Jr., an official spokesman for the Office of Management and Budget, told David E. Rosenbaum, of the *New York Times.* Unavoidably, the Reagan administration ran into reality, and that reality is that welfare is like a seesaw: remove benefits and suffering goes up; add benefits and dependency goes up. Democratic administrations have tended to worry more about the sufferers, so they have treated welfare as an income-supplement program; Republicans tend to worry more about the ill effects of dependency, so they treat welfare as a safety net (though, apparently, an imperfect one).

To police the effects of the underclass, wholesalers advocate a "get-tough" approach to crime. In *The Unheavenly City,* Edward Banfield, who generally cannot be grouped among optimistic wholesalers, urged that those career criminals with a record of repeated offenses who are deemed by the courts as "likely" to commit violent crimes should sacrifice some freedom (preventive detention). The most serious cases, said Banfield, "would be confined to a penal village or work camp where he might receive visitors and support a family but from which he might not leave." Banfield conceded such measures might be politically difficult, and in any case probably violate the Bill of Rights. Nevertheless, he concluded:

> If abridging the freedoms of persons who have not committed crimes is incompatible with the principles of free society, so, also, is the presence in such society of persons who, if their freedom is not abridged, would use it to inflict serious injury on others.

Since Banfield wrote these words, the conviction has spread that for the career criminal—who commits the majority of violent crimes citizens most fear—crime does pay. In New York City, as noted earlier, the *New York Times* reports that 99 percent of those arrested for felonies never serve a state prison term, and 80 percent are not even prosecuted as felons. (*Newsweek* magazine, some months later, said, "the *Times* was wrong"—25 percent of all felony arrests led "to some incarceration." That's still an astonishing 75 percent who never serve a prison term!) Calculating the odds, the gains from crime may outweigh the risks, as Leon Harris of BT-27 reminded us. To combat this perception, various antidotes have been suggested and, in some cases, implemented. New York State two years ago imposed a juvenile-offender law to stiffen the penalties for children under sixteen who commit serious crimes. Washington, D.C. has experimented with preventive detention. Stop-and-frisk laws and permitting misdemeanor arrests for "probable cause" and mandatory life sentences, mandatory minimum sentences, decriminalizing certain crimes, and the reinstitution of the death penalty are but a few of the "solutions." Attorney General William French Smith's eight-member Task Force on Violent Crime, in August 1981, made a series of sweeping recommendations to combat violent crimes, including: evidence in a criminal case illegally obtained by a police officer should not be excluded from courtroom testimony if the officer has a "good-faith belief that it was in conformity" with the law; eliminating bail in certain extreme cases; and the curtailment of habeas corpus petitions. Some of these ideas may be judged extreme or unworkable. But above all else, their proponents wish to convey a new attitude. "They've got to fear the system," says Tom Fennell, a New York City cop. "If you tell them to move, they should fear you," says his partner, Roy Miller.

Such a get-tough approach is supported by more than conservative law-and-order types or those who are sometimes identified as enemies of the poor. "A short stick against somebody's ass that is about to go out there and mug old women—no question in my mind it is a deterrent," Harlem Congressman Charles Rangel told me. "I don't care what social workers tell you. They're full of shit!" Rangel's sentiments are consistent with a widening perception that poverty alone does not explain crime. "If violence was commensurate with poverty, we'd have anarchy or a police state," says Vernon Jordan. Of "mean kids" and career criminals, Jordan says, "what you don't do is parole them."

All this said, there are no miracle remedies for crime. Reagan administration officials may complain loudly about crime, but an estimated 94 percent of all crimes fall under state and local jurisdictions. The president can use the White House as a "bully pulpit" and push to reform the federal criminal code, curb the flow of narcotics into the country, and increase assistance to local law enforcement, but he has little authority over street crime. State legislation imposing mandatory minimum sentences and crackdowns on criminals presuppose more prisons to house felons. That costs money, more money than many cities and states have. According to New York City Corrections Commissioner Benjamin Ward, it costs $100,000 to build a prison cell. The state of New York has 22,000 jail cells, and they are filled to capacity. Attorney General Smith's task force recommended that the federal government spend $2 billion to help the states build prisons, but there was no clamor from the White House or the public to embrace this proposal. There is a constituency for getting tough; less visible is a constituency to pay the bill.

Similarly, to relax restrictions on police officers—to permit stop-and-frisk laws, for instance—might grant a license to people, some of whom are bigoted, to harass blacks and Hispanics almost at will. Such measures might be counterproductive in that they would exacerbate, not relieve, tensions and hostility. Only the U.S. Army might then be able to patrol the streets. Undeniably, preventive detention or stop and frisk laws alter the presumption of innocence that has been the bedrock of American jurisprudence. They assume that criminal behavior can be predicted. To grant that presumption and authority to police officers invests them with the power of both prosecutor and judge. Once the due process procedural wall is bulldozed, the American Civil Liberties Union and others say, what is to prevent the Moral Majority or outraged feminists from insisting on censoring certain books or magazines as pornographic. Better, they say, to err on the side of the Bill of Rights.

There's another reason that crackdowns on crime arouse ire. Such efforts are perceived as excuses to "blame the victim" and legitimize repression. Those on the political left want to fix society's attention on the causes of crime, not what they see as its effects. Society, not the individual, is to blame. Thus the National Urban League's 297-page report, *The State of Black America 1980*, contains forty-nine recommendations for combating social ills. Yet only two address themselves to crime: (1) "Alternatives to incarceration should be aggressively pursued as a method of rehabilitation"; and (2) "All political jurisdictions should initiate affirmative action in the field of criminal justice." A dwindling but still substantial portion of the American populace probably still agrees with the conclusion of President Johnson's National Crime Commission, chaired by Ramsey Clark: "Warring on poverty, inadequate housing and unemployment is warring on crime. A civil rights law is a law against crime. Money for schools is money against crime."

Again, two theologies war. The left starts with a more sanguine view of human nature. To give up on rehabilitation and write people off, they say, is to give up on the optimism and faith in the improvement, if not perfectibility, of man that is a pillar of democratic government. The street toughs cops and citizens alike think of as monsters, are thought of as misunderstood kids. There is no agreement

287

about reality; therefore there can be none about what to do about it. Some people look at a blank stare and see an animal; others see a victim.

Those advancing the get-tough approach to controlling crime, hostility, and dependency dismiss such "victim" arguments. A judge may have reason to grant lighter sentences or to offer low bail, they assert, but the cumulative effect of hundreds of individual decisions coalesce into a single impression of weakness. The whole is greater than the sum of the individual parts. Insistence on civilian review boards to check cops, on welfare "rights" or student and prisoners' "rights," undermines authority. Students feel they have a "right" not to obey dress codes; criminals that they need not fear punishment; welfare recipients that they need not work. Our ancestors abandoned their caves and joined tribes and, later, a civilization, in search of security, a security now threatened by rampant crime. In this view, only a wholesale change in attitude—and policy—can police underclass behavior.

In a parallel way, wholesalers on the left believe that only a wholesale change in government attitudes and policies can alter underclass behavior. The two views are poles apart—their assumptions, their facts, their view of the causes of the underclass, and their prescriptions are so different—yet wholesalers on the left and right often agree about three things: each is optimistic that they have the answer; each believes only a mini-revolution can provide a cure; and each is convinced that the root of the problem is economic.

The Laissez-Faire Option

While both liberals and conservatives who favor the wholesale approach are optimistic that their proposals can eradicate the underclass, subscribers to the laissez-faire approach are profoundly pessimistic about the idea that any government intervention can transform the underclass. Some of these conservatives are lineal descendants of Thomas Malthus, who argued in the eighteenth century that poverty and distress were unavoidable and often unalterable. Whether black or white, Hispanic or Asian, these people say, some segment of every population is infected by "lower class" behavior or a "culture of poverty," for which there is no known elixir. Their position is outlined by Edward Banfield in *The Unheavenly City*:

> So long as the city contains a sizable lower class, nothing basic can be done about its most serious problems. Good jobs may be offered to all, but some will remain chronically unemployed. Slums may be demolished, but if the housing that replaces them is occupied by the lower class it will shortly be turned into new slums. Welfare payments may be doubled or tripled and a negative income tax instituted, but some persons will continue to live in squalor and misery. New schools may be built, new curricula devised, and the teacher-pupil ratio cut in half, but if the children who attend these schools come from lower-class homes, they will be turned into blackboard jungles, and those who graduate or drop out from them will, in most cases, be functionally illiterate. The streets may be filled with armies of

policemen, but violent crime and civil disorder will decrease very little. If, however, the lower class were to disappear—if, say, its members were overnight to acquire the attitudes, motivations, and habits of the working class—the most serious and intractable problems of the city would all disappear with it.

Although Banfield does discuss large-scale measures to reduce and police the underclass, he believes that these measures are either unfeasible or unacceptable. Besides, he says, many ideas would only perpetuate what the sociologist Robert K. Merton, of Columbia, has called a "reign of error." Like Banfield, Thomas Sowell advocates several large-scale measures, particularly in regard to a market economy and ways of policing the underclass. However, Sowell, too, remains pessimistic, cautioning that every ethnic group transmits different traditions and different cultures, which, he says, affect the group's current behavior. "It may be unsettling to American ideology to believe that a man's current performance in a factory or classroom is related to how his ancestors lived thousands of miles from here and hundreds of years ago," Sowell wrote in his book *Race and Economics,* published in 1975, and he goes on to say that we are witnessing "an intergenerational *relay* race," with some ethnic groups starting farther back and therefore taking longer to catch up.

Sowell recites similar historical differences to explain why the underclass includes a large number of native American blacks but not of West Indian blacks. If racism is the cause, he asks, why do West Indians generally get ahead of American blacks and earn incomes comparable to those earned by white Americans? Both groups endured slavery, enforced illiteracy, the brutal destruction of family life. "Yet a hundred years later, the West Indian in the United States is not only more prosperous and better educated, but also has a much more stable and patriarchal family life," Sowell writes. He traces the reasons back to the different histories of the two groups. Under American slavery, blacks were rarely permitted to grow their own food. They were taught to be dependent on their masters. With no commercial supply of food in the islands, West Indians farmed or starved. In the American South, blacks were in the minority. This was not the case in the West Indies. There, because whites made up just 10 percent of the population, slaveowners had to permit some economic autonomy and self-sufficiency. They also had less control over slave escapes and slave rebellions. Thus, Sowell concludes, "the West Indian setting permitted and fostered more self-reliance, more economic experience, and more defiance of whites." American blacks start behind because slavery undermined their self-reliance,

Sowell says, and their new-found freedom suffered a further jolt with the mass migration of blacks from the rural South to the urban North.

According to Sowell, many Puerto Ricans experienced the same fate, moving, as they did, from a rural setting to an urban one. Unlike nineteenth- and early-twentieth-century immigrants, the new immigrants flocked to cities that were losing entry-level jobs. Lacking skills, language, and confidence, he says, these new immigrants could not compete for white-collar positions. What was available was welfare, which only reinforced dependency. There is no good solution except patience, Sowell says. Government attempts to buy cures will not attain the desired ends.

> Perhaps the greatest dilemma in attempts to raise ethnic minority income is that those methods which have historically proved successful—self-reliance, work skills, education, business experience—are all slow developing, while those methods which are more direct and immediate—job quotas, charity, subsidies, preferential treatment—tend to undermine self-reliance and pride of achievement in the long run. If the history of American ethnic groups shows anything, it is how large a role has been played by attitudes—and particularly attitudes of self-reliance.

Again, it would be a misrepresentation of the position of Sowell, Banfield, and other proponents of laissez-faire to suggest that they offer no policy recommendations except patience or resignation. Banfield has enumerated a variety of policies that might be effective. Sowell endorses President Reagan's emphasis on tax cuts to promote economic growth and reduce unemployment, favors a minimum wage of $2.00 for young people and a work requirement for most welfare recipients, and says that one of the crucial things President Reagan can do is appoint law-and-order justices to the Supreme Court. "You keep putting people on there from the turn-'em-loose category and the due-process types, and violence will be much cheaper, and we'll have more of it," he adds. However, their basic argument—and that of many traditional conservatives who favor drastic cuts in social-welfare spending—is that many people are beyond hope of redemption, and that society should beware of "solutions" and concentrate on quarantining the patient. Some people must be written off, with the government adopting what amounts to a triage policy, carefully directing remedial efforts only toward non-"lower class" people, who have a realistic chance of justifying the social investment. In the spring of 1980, Sowell said to me, "We should shift concern toward people who are trying to do the right

291

and decent thing, and make sure they don't lose. Stop kidding yourself that we can solve all problems. There are people whose problems we can't solve, but we can stop them from causing problems." To attempt to rebuild devastated areas like the South Bronx and the South Side of Chicago is, in his view, insane. As long as the underclass remains there in substantial numbers, new buildings will be burned, just as the old ones were. Assuming limited resources, government must concentrate on the doable, not the desirable. Unlike moderates who adopt this viewpoint, Sowell and Banfield and many traditional conservatives have a pessimistic view of the doable.

Liberal critics will assail this policy as "planned shrinkage," because it assumes that market forces will work their will without government interference and that the population of ghettos will dwindle as people search for job opportunities. Indeed, some progressives as well as conservatives say we should encourage people to move where the jobs have moved. President Carter's Commission for a National Agenda for the Eighties urged the federal government to step back and stop trying to stem the decline of aging cities.* "Contrary to conventional wisdom, cities are not permanent," the commission said in its report, published in January 1981. "Their strength is related to their ability to reflect change rather than to fend it off. . . . Growth and decline are integral parts of the same dynamic process in urban life. When the federal government steps in to try to alter these dynamics, it generates a flood of demands that may sap the initiative of urban governments because of the expectation of continuing support."

In a November 1981 interview with several print reporters, President Reagan extended his free-market faith to state governments, asserting that rigorous competition among states was healthy; dissatisfied citizens, he said, were free to vote with their "feet." President-elect Reagan's urban-affairs task force proposed a similar hands-off approach with regard to housing. This task force, headed by Mayor Pete Wilson of San Diego, said that the federal government should withhold housing grants from any city that had rent-control laws. Only if government gets out of the way and encourages the private sector will housing for the poor be built, according to this view. As President, Reagan has not taken a position on the proposal. But his administration has endorsed a basically laissez-faire approach to birth control and out-of-wedlock births. Within days of assuming

---

*The commission also urged such wholesale ideas as national health insurance, a guaranteed annual income for the poor, and the federal assumption of all welfare costs.

office, Secretary of Health and Human Services Richard S. Schweiker declared that his department should not be promoting sex education and that doctors treating poor, unmarried teenagers under the Medicaid program should not be allowed to prescribe contraceptives. Sex education, he maintained, was primarily the responsibility of parents, and he reiterated his support of a constitutional amendment—also supported by Reagan—to outlaw most abortions.

Proponents of these policies might not concur with the notion that some or all of them represent a laissez-faire approach. To encourage poor people to move where there are real employment opportunities, for example, shifts government attention away from assisting "places" to assisting "people," they would say; the goal is not to help New York and Detroit maintain their populations but to help poor people find jobs. Eliminating rent control is defended as a positive step—not a negative one—since it would induce private developers to build housing. Generally, however, these policies leave the poor to the fate of the marketplace, their own ambitions, their own free will, and reject the notion that government intervention helps. Or as President Reagan declared in his inaugural address, "Government is not the solution to our problem; government is the problem."

The Reagan administration seems to think that the federal government's role is not to interfere and help people escape poverty or to supplement the income of the working poor but, rather, to provide a safety net for the "truly needy," and Administration officials have a narrow definition of the "truly needy." The basic tenets behind this policy, as the president said, is that "government is the problem"; and that escaping poverty usually requires an act of will. If Reagan's wholesale budget reductions and supply-side economic policy works, jobs will be created and the poverty population will shrivel. But if it doesn't, and if the White House refuses the government helping hand that members of the underclass like Denise Brown or Hope Parker of BT-27 needed, then "new" conservatives like Reagan and Jack Kemp are unmasked as traditional conservatives with an essentially laissez-faire approach to the poor and the underclass. Or as Reagan's budget director, David Stockman, confessed to the *Atlantic Monthly,* supply side economics is really "a Trojan horse to bring down the top rate" and "get a tax policy that was really 'trickle-down.'"

Unavoidably, fewer government entitlements and intervention requires toned-down rhetoric from those who lead, and lowered expectations from those who are led. The message is that self-help, not government help, offers salvation. And of course this process takes time. Some poor people will succeed; many will fail. Realism dictates that one should be surprised by the successes, and not by the failures. The underclass is retarded, in the view of many conservatives, not primarily because its members are poor or are victims of racism or economic inequality but because of their own attitudes and values. James Q. Wilson, a professor of government at Harvard, does not believe that any attempt to address the causes of crime will work, because crime is "almost invariably 'caused' by factors that cannot be changed easily or at all." In his book *Thinking About Crime,* published in 1975, he goes on:

> This is because human behavior ultimately derives from human volition—tastes, attitudes, values, and so on—and these aspects of volition in turn are either formed entirely by choice or are the product of biological or social processes that we cannot or will not change.
>
> It is the failure to understand this point that leads statesman and citizen alike to commit the causal fallacy—to assume that no problem is adequately addressed unless its causes are eliminated. The preamble to the UNESCO charter illustrates it: "Since wars begin in the minds of men it is in the minds of men that the defenses of peace must be constructed." The one thing we cannot easily do, if we can do it at all, is change, by plan and systematically, the minds of men.

This emphasis on values is not the exclusive concern of conservatives and neo-conservatives. If the president of the United States asked him for a suggestion to assist the underclass, says Howard Smith, the Wildcat training center's life-skills teacher, who does believe in government intervention, his first priority would be "a program that would teach morals or ethics." Smith told me, "I see that as far more effective than dumping millions of dollars. That's what Johnson's Great Society did by dumping all that money into teaching 'marketable skills.' A lot of those people got those marketable skills and they're still out there. Skills are important. An ability to read and write is important. But ethics is key."

A growing number of those in the political center and on the left accept the importance of self-help, of encouraging the right attitudes. The argument on this question occurs over emphasis. Marian Wright Edelman, president of the Children's Defense Fund, charges that Jesse Jackson and others who preach self-help are "playing a simplistic game, suggesting it is solely up to the parents and the kids" to reform themselves. Parents obviously do have a role, and so do children. But one should not underplay the role of society, of racism, of forces beyond the individual. Possessing self-esteem may not help a teenage mother who is forced to leave school and have a baby, and who must stay home to care for it. Self-esteem is sometimes not possible in a child whose life is consumed by an economic struggle, whose father is unemployed or is not at home, who has few successful people to emulate. A healthy self-esteem may be retarded by uncaring teachers who assume that black or Hispanic children cannot learn.

Those who assert that federal social-welfare programs should assist only the aged and infirm, as Martin Anderson, Thomas Sowell, George Gilder, and others do, run the risk, it is said, of letting an abstract ideology shove aside the experiences of real people. People like William Block, the quiet, soft-spoken Wildcat student who had just been released from prison, would not be supported by welfare, even though such people, like him, might struggle to find a job and be turned down because of their records. Similarly, people like Pearl Dawson would be removed from the welfare rolls—even though such people, like her, might need a training-and-counseling program to help them overcome deep insecurities and become productive members of society. People are to help themselves, even though people like a number of those in the Wildcat class might have no idea how to get through an interview, dress for work, cash checks, or participate in society. Responding to the free-market theories propounded at the 1980 Black Alternatives Conference, Bernard Anderson, of the MDRC, told the audience, "A comment made by the late President Kennedy says that 'a rising tide lifts all boats.' That's true, but let us not forget that a rising tide does not do a thing for shipwrecks at the bottom of the sea."

The idea of writing off large numbers of people—triage—is offensive to many on the left and some on the right. Bob Woodson, a Fellow at the conservative American Enterprise Institute in Washington who has written a book about self-help organizations, describes a violent youth-gang member in Philadelphia who murdered his mother. The teenager was hostile, seemingly unreachable, before he was taken in by the House of Umoja. "Now if I were to impose that rigid criteria," says Woodson, who is black, "he'd be a throwaway. Yet the House of Umoja picked him up and he has blossomed. He went on to write a play." Mohammed of BT-27 was the war lord of a Brooklyn youth gang, a self-proclaimed "racist" who says he committed "bad" crimes. Today he is an architectural draftsman. Alvia Y. Branch rejects the notion of freezing people into an underclass category. A tall black woman who grew up poor in Chicago in a female-headed family, she went on to receive a Ph.D. in social

295

psychology from Harvard, and is today a senior research associate at the MDRC. She says: "Even if a person has a criminal record, you don't say the person is devoid of redeeming values." While conceding that some may be unreachable, like most liberals she thinks the number is "minuscule." Besides, she believes it is immoral not to make the effort.

Liberals turn the practicality argument around and charge that people like Sowell and Banfield are the impractical ones. If the government does not rebuild a ghetto like the South Bronx, says Herman Badillo, society is encouraging the members of the underclass who live there to move into other neighborhoods. Without hope, he says, people will become more hostile, not less. Try to quarantine them and there will not be enough police, enough armies, enough jails to contain them. Encourage members of the underclass to move to the Sun Belt, as the Commission for a National Agenda for the Eighties urged, and they will still be without the skills and the experience to get good jobs. Robert C. Embry, Jr., and Marshall Kaplan, officials in the Department of Housing and Urban Development in the Carter Administration, noted in an article they wrote for the Op-Ed page of the *Times* that "merely to go with the market tide, as the commission suggests, would reflect premature submission to the new conventional wisdom that the cities' decline is immutable and that the government is impotent."

In fact, critics of laissez-faire believe there is ample evidence that government does perform. "It is the big lie that federal and social programs don't work," Vernon Jordan said after Reagan's election, thus shifting his emphasis to defend rather than attack government efforts. "In fact, they do work. Food stamps have just about wiped out hunger in America." In 1980, food stamps stood between hunger and about 20 million Americans. Head Start aids 375,000 preschool children and prevents later scholastic failure, a recent Carnegie Corporation-sponsored study suggested. Since 1959, Social Security has helped to more than halve poverty among the elderly, reducing it from 35 percent to 15.7 percent. Automotive safety regulations have saved lives. In just one year, the Voting Rights Act of 1965 doubled the number of blacks registered to vote in five Deep South states. Government has succeeded in outlawing child labor, relieving pollution, providing low-cost home mortgages, constructing roads, subways, dams. Supported work led to productive jobs for a third of those who enrolled. And for 1980–81, the Wildcat Service Corporation reports an overall job placement rate of about 60 percent. Ironically, in making the argument that the war on poverty has been "won" Martin Anderson implicitly acknowledges that this was accomplished by the federal government's income-transfer programs —programs that President Reagan wants to reduce or eliminate.

To accept the premise that cultural deficiencies render the underclass hopeless, critics charge, is to flirt with views similar to those of racists who claim that blacks or other groups are genetically inferior. There is an unintentionally parallel line of reasoning. Each is saying that the poverty is in the individual. No amount of compassion, concern, or philanthropic or government intervention can overcome their cultural or intellectual defects.

Inevitably, critics charge, their grim description becomes a prescription for doing nothing. They might quote something Sancho Panza said to Don Quixote, "A good hope is better than a bad holding." Pessimists would no doubt counter with the advice proffered by the Duke of Omnium to the Prime Minister in one of Anthony Trollope's Palliser novels: "I have never been a friend of great measures, knowing that when they come fast, one after another, more is broken in the rattle than is repaired in the reform."

The Retail Option

Between the optimists and the pessimists are the skeptics: too optimistic to accept the laissez-faire theory and too pessimistic to embrace wholesale government solutions. If an epigram captured their ambivalence, it might be Lewis Mumford's: "I am an optimist about possibilities and a pessimist about probabilities." If a program mirrored their cautious compassion, it might be the MDRC's test-market approach to the underclass. Usually, in the eyes of those who take this "retail" approach to social programs, an issue has at least four sides. Retailers worry about trade-offs and "zero sum" solutions—about how to increase government spending without also increasing inflation, how to improve welfare benefits without also encouraging dependency, how to crack down on muggers without also doing violence to the Constitution. Though they are wary of grandiose rhetoric, they do wish to communicate hope. They believe in government intervention but oppose big government; they think that the underclass usually has behavioral deficiencies but also income deficiencies; they think that racism can be a cause of social problems but also a crutch. They do not believe that more money or more compassion or more commitment or more brains alone will solve the problem—yet they believe that all are sometimes necessary.

"If we reduce this problem by one or two percent a year, that's a lot," says Mitchell Sviridoff, a former Ford Foundation vice-president who helped devise the supported-work experiment. Proponents of large-scale solutions would dismiss such small progress as mere tinkering. But Robert Schrank, a radical in the thirties, a union leader, plant manager, and government anti-poverty official who retired from the Ford Foundation in early 1982 to teach and write, says, "The assumption that there is a single answer to a complex question is the Fascist solution. I mean, the Soviet Union has one answer to a lot of problems. It's called labor camps. One of the major lessons of the sixties is 'Watch out for quick answers.' You create real social upheaval with promises that can't be fulfilled."

Big promises, the MDRC experience suggests, often mean big bureaucracy. Giant youth-incentive programs were almost uniformly slower to recruit eligible youths and to find them jobs than smaller programs were. "The basic fights of the eighties will be resource fights," says Marian Wright Edelman. "The tradition we come from in the civil-rights movement of addressing big issues won't work now. Today, most of our victories you just don't hear about." Instead of general goals, Edelman said shortly before the election of Reagan, she now sets specific ones. "If we get a hundred million dollars each year for Head Start, in ten years we'll have a billion-dollar program. You aren't going to grandstand or preach your way through children's issues in the eighties. It's hard, challenging, and not exciting stuff. But that's the way you change things in this country."

In addition to learning more about the limits of the political system, Edelman has come to believe in other limitations, including the notion of a "culture of poverty." She has always known that some people are victims of society, racism, or economic disadvantage; now, she also believes some are victims of growing up in fatherless homes, of not being taught the value of an education. Although she disagreed with the weight Jesse Jackson gives the old-time religion, and is a wholesaler on some issues, Edelman believes that poor values, as well as constricted opportunity and government assistance, help determine individual success—as they did for, say, Henry Rivera of BT-27. Edelman's father, a Mississippi minister, instilled values. He always insisted that there be books in the house and that they be read, she recalls. He treated boys and girls the same. "Daddy used to take us around—I was named for Marian Anderson—and if she was in the South we'd drive to see her and other black folk. We had all of Mark Twain and Abe Lincoln. In the ambulance on the way to the hospital the last word I heard—he knew he was going away—was, 'Listen, don't let anything get between you and education.' There was never a time any of the five of us did not know we were going to college. It never occurred to us. Just as it never occurred to us to accept segregation. Education was a creed. I grind it into my children. The family is important. It protected us against internalizing segregation."

Pride, faith, lust for learning, self-confidence, ambition—complex, hard-to-quantify *values*—and the intervention of a caring person emerge as melodies running through the testimony of many poor people who are now successes. Charles Hamilton, Wallace Sayre professor of government at Columbia University, grew up in a fatherless home on the South Side of Chicago. His father deserted them, leaving the family on welfare. But an extended family of aunts and uncles steadied Hamilton, helped communicate "ethical and moral values." Unlike many youngsters growing up today, Hamilton says his uncle Zeke provided him with a male role model. Frank Thomas, president of the Ford Foundation, was raised in a broken home. His father died when he was fourteen. His mother was a domestic. Yet she inspired him to believe "you could be anything you want." Congressman Charles Rangel, who grew up on welfare in a fractured Harlem home, credits the military and its peer pressure for straightening him out. Thomas Sowell—who never knew his parents and moved to a cold-water Harlem flat with his foster parents and later dropped out of high school—credits the Korean War and the discipline that the Army imposed on him. Susie Haun, the white former welfare mother in West Virginia who finished supported work and now manages a public housing project, credits a strong, caring supervisor for getting her over the hump. Howard Smith, the life-skills teacher, credits religion. The late novelist Richard Wright said books gave him landmarks to "guide my daily action." Amalia Betanzos, president of the Wildcat Corporation, acclaims the value of pride. "We were hungry, but we would have died before going on welfare," she says of her mother, who brought them up in the South Bronx. "Today welfare is socially acceptable."

Bernard Gifford, former deputy chancellor of the New York City Board of Education and currently vice-president for student affairs at the University of Rochester, lauds a strong teacher. "I was saved by a teacher—Pearl Nyefsky—who took an interest in me and held me together for a year," he says of the time he was attending Brooklyn Tech and his home was devastated by a fire. "She called me in the office, checked my homework, called my mother." At sixteen, Gifford became frustrated with school, forged his mother's signature, and enlisted in the Navy. "Pearl Nyefsky was talking to my guidance counselor and he casually mentioned it. Pearl said, 'Daisy would never allow Bernard to join the navy.' She called my mother and asked if it was true. It was the first my mother ever heard of it. Needless to say, I didn't go into the Navy. But the guidance counselor never questioned it. He saw another black kid punching out of Tech." Gifford honors the memory of Pearl Nyefsky, but also that of his mother, who died just days before he received his Ph.D. "My mother was always ashamed to be on welfare. My brother was ashamed. I was ashamed. And though we grew up in a neighborhood where it was prevalent, we never accepted it. And what is different now is that I see lots of people accepting dependency. No one ought to be ashamed to be poor. Yet I'm convinced that the shame we felt being on welfare made us get away and escape repeating this cycle.

"In many ways the kids today are victims of liberal victories," he continued. "One of the battles we fought in the 1960s was to take the stigma away from people who are poor and place it on society; to emphasize the structural barriers to poverty. That needed to be done. We were successful in saying to society: there are real structural impediments. We placed so much emphasis—how can I say this without sounding right-wing?—that government could do this, that government could remove barriers. The problem was that we shifted the focus of attention from local institutions—family, church, neighborhood organization—to government. We undermined those institutions and made it possible for people to accept welfare."

Robert Woodson, a Resident Fellow at the American Enterprise Institute in Washington, blames government for undermining the family and community institutions: "I grew up in Philadelphia. My father died when I was nine. My mother raised five kids by herself. She worked full-time. All of us succeeded. But we had friends who didn't succeed. I think my relationship to the group was as important as the relationship to my mother. There was mutual support. And there were always people around who helped—the guy who drove us around to play baseball. I cleaved to my best friend's father. There was a time when this extended family was natural. Now we look on these neighborhoods as cesspools of pathology. And once you see that you think that the only thing that can help is outside intervention."

Former Congressman Herman Badillo, who grew up an orphan, isn't sure why some make it and others don't. "If I knew, I'd patent it," he says. "You need luck and intelligence and motivation. How you get it, I don't know." Whether it be luck, motivation, pride, books, teachers, discipline, peer pressure, two parents or one, religion, role models, self-confidence—these successful individuals and others generally agree with Badillo that the answer cannot be reduced to boiler-plate formulas.

None of this fits into traditional liberal or conservative pigeonholes. To hear the Reverend Jesse Jackson, head of Operation Push, denounce "freedom without responsibility" and "our spiritual depression," or smoking and alcohol, one could think Jackson was a recruiter for the Moral Majority. Conservatives sound like liberals when they chant "community participation" and "growth." Ronald Reagan quotes Franklin Roosevelt. A Democratic president (Carter) endorsed the traditional Republican medicine of encouraging unemployment to relieve inflation. NAACP officials applauded the deregulation of oil prices. Many liberals and conservatives agree that a voucher system would strengthen public education, even if it weakened teachers' unions. (Or perhaps *because* it weakened unions!) "Law and order" is no less popular in the minority than the white community. On social, as opposed to economic issues, polls consistently show that blacks are often as "conservative" as whites. An April 1981 *Times*/CBS News poll, for instance, revealed that 78 percent of blacks favored a constitutional amendment to permit school prayers (77 percent of whites did). A "balanced budget" and "capital formation" and tax "incentives" to encourage "savings" and "productivity" are now widely accepted notions. In this post-ideological era, many retailers measure proposals not by whether they pass ideological muster, but by whether they might work, and can be afforded.

Increasingly, retailers have been shifting their attention from government programs to community-based self-help programs—from government institutions to business and to philanthropic institutions. Franklin Thomas, in his second annual report as president of the Ford Foundation, published in 1980, wrote:

> The nation would be better served in the years ahead if the private sector assumed a fuller role in the redress of social problems. My agreement is not based on ideological worries concerning the evils of the encroaching federal presence. Given the colossal scale of societal problems, I don't think that very much can be accomplished without the resources and legal powers of government. Government is not the enemy. But it is too often an ineffective manager of programs and deliverer of services.

Thomas went on to hail the American corporation as "the economic engine of our society"—a thought that was once alien to many Keynesians, who assumed that the government made the economy work, and so was the primary engine for social change. In this sense, and in their advocacy of expanded philanthropy and volunteer work, Thomas and other retailers share some common ground with President Reagan. They disagree over whether the private sector can close gaps left by Reagan's budget reductions, noting that corporate charity in 1980 equaled just $2.6 billion. All charitable contributions, most of them earmarked for the hard-core poor, equaled about $43 billion—far less than was sliced from the domestic budget.

There is also a disagreement with Reagan over the importance of government help. The kind of sweat equity President Reagan extolls when practiced by community groups who renovate homes is often not possible without a helping hand from government. Yet federal community development funds, which helped defray the large expense of renovation—interest costs, installing heating, plumbing and electrical wiring—have been sharply reduced by Reagan; the federal 312 loan program to reduce sky-high mortgage rates for multifamily homeowners has been hacked by two-thirds; the federal 235 loan program for one-family homes has been eliminated. Nor does it appear that volunteers can fill the gap. Despite the exhortations of presidents from Herbert Hoover to John F. Kennedy to Ronald Reagan, less than 5 percent of Americans, according to a recent Gallup poll survey, engage in any "social welfare" volunteer activity. Twitting the President, the *Washington Post* editorialized in the fall of 1981 that while volunteerism and charity should be encouraged, they "never did suffice to erase the horrors of the almhouse or the sweatshop."

Thomas draws certain lessons from ten years he spent as president of the Bedford-Stuyvesant Restoration Corporation, a much-acclaimed self-help organization. It worked, he says, because it had government as a partner and also forged a partnership with the private sector; because it was small; and because it pounded away at developing such values as pride and independence in addition to providing a good work experience. With a small budget supplied by government and private sources, the corporation began by recruiting youths to fix up the exteriors of buildings—paint façades, gates, fences—one block at a time. If there was no block association, families were encouraged to form one. After 60 percent of the families on a block had done so, there was a one-time fee of twenty-five dollars per building for the exterior-repair service, and at the same time each family had to commit itself to an equivalent program of interior repair and to using local labor in achieving it. Local residents now had an investment in those buildings, a reason for pride. The young people received green uniforms and jackets, learned to paint, and learned something of masonry repair, ironwork repair, and carpentry.

Thomas and the community corporation were criticized by both the left and the right. Thomas recalls, "Critics said of the corporation's program, 'It's cosmetic. It doesn't get to the root of the problems. The buildings will be destroyed. It doesn't have any long-term job potential for the kids.' But what about the kids? They had enormous pride. We said to every youngster, 'We're not going to make a painter or a carpenter out of you. What you'll get is a work experience. You'll learn a skill that will be with you the rest of your life. But the main thing is to get in the habit of coming to work on time, being prepared for the job, taking supervision, and seeing a product. To see improved conditions as a result of your labor. You'll know it.' For an awful lot of kids, this was their first successful work experience." Over ten years, the community corporation reclaimed entire blocks; induced banks and other lenders to invest $24 million in mortgage loans to local buyers of small homes and $29 million to renovate and construct apartment houses; cleared the path for a $13 million manufacturing plant and a $6.5 million shopping center; and helped to obtain $20 million in loans to small businesses. In view of the fact that Bedford-Stuyvesant has 300,000 residents and an area of more than five square miles, the community corporation's effort is perhaps comparable to filling a lake with pebbles a handful at a time. But Thomas, among others, believes that this is how success is usually achieved—slowly.

That is also the way in which the House of Umoja in Philadelphia advanced, says Robert Woodson, who was with the National Urban League before joining the American Enterprise Institute. To avoid losing one of their six sons to a local street gang, Falaka and David Fattah offered the fifteen gang members, most of whom were homeless, the opportunity to join the Fattah family, fix up and share their two-story row house on North Frazier Street, and set their own rules. In return, the gang members agreed to lay down their weapons, forsake violence, accept tutoring, and participate in community activities. "We felt that the reason for the gangs was the destruction of the family," Falaka Fattah told a reporter for the magazine *Parade*. "Our theory was that if the problem was the breakdown of families, then the solution was to rebuild one for them." During the day, civic organizations joined in and helped tutor the former gang members. By 1980 the House of Umoja had repaired twenty-one abandoned homes and taken in a total of five hundred gang members.

"Most social programs treat kids like clients," Woodson told me, in explaining why he thinks the House of Umoja works. "There are social workers, teachers, psychologists, job counselors, probation officers. All these people are external to the child, foreign to his culture, alien to his system of values, totally lacking in understanding of what he needs to survive on the streets. Also, they treat the child as a single individual, not in the context of a gang or a collective. The danger in this society, as Peter Berger, a conservative sociologist, said, is people who don't have a stake in our institutions. Jesse Jackson is a hell of a teacher. He says black kids are on the brink of educational collapse. You can't just offer jobs. There's a motivational question. There's ethical and spiritual values. These are influences that come only from the family or the surrogate family. That's where we get our values. Government doesn't give you values. There is nothing more important for these kids than reestablishing a sense of their own self-worth, the value of American institutions, and becoming reacquainted with the spiritual side of life. None of these can be accomplished through job training or anything governmental. These can only be imparted by local value-generating institutions—family, extended or surrogate families, or institutions that have some impact." Government should provide seed money and technical assistance for these local efforts, he says, and then get out of the way.

These principles—self-help, individual attention, reliance on community-based organizations—were the foundations of the MDRC's supported-work experiment. The program provided jobs, training, and counseling. Painstakingly, the program tried to rebuild the self-confidence of those enrolled, wean them from their anxieties, hostilities, and bad habits. As Ramon Lopez said to the members of BT-27 one day in class: an individual gets "used to so many years laying up and doing nothing. . . . He doesn't have a routine of doing things as other natural people do who have done it all the time." As national programs go, this was a relatively meager effort—it cost $82 million over the first five years, or one-seventh of one per cent of the manpower-training money spent by the federal government since 1962. But people like William Grinker favor a slow approach. After learning that supported work succeeded best with welfare mothers and ex-addicts, the MDRC recommended expansion of the program for these target groups and further experimentation to test how the program might work with other hard-to-reach groups, such as the mentally retarded. Pilot programs, not audacious federal ventures, were recommended to help reduce youth unemployment, dropping out of school, truancy, and the isolation of teenage mothers. To undertake a massive supported work effort, for instance, would be expensive. Assuming a target population of five million adults, and an average cost of $7,000, the bill would run to about $35 billion the first year. And after the program were in place, there would still be the question of what to do with the majority of those who abandoned supported work.

Critics on both the left and the right are united in dismissing incremental solutions as too timid. That the underclass should exist is an outrage, according to many on the left; the underclass represents a clear and present danger to society, according to many on the right. Those on the right usually favor across-the-board budget cuts. They focus more on aggregate costs than on individuals. To engage in piecemeal cuts as opposed to wholesale ones, they fear, is to risk getting sandbagged by swarms of special-interest groups, as President Carter's targeted budget-cutting proposals were. But to insist that Congress vote one budget-cutting package up or down, as President Reagan did, overlooks programs like supported work, which have saved people's lives.

The strengths—and weaknesses—of the retail approach are displayed when we come to one of the central problems of the underclass: how to strengthen families. "To reach them, you have to reach them early," Eleanor Holmes Norton says of the children. "That means getting involved in the family situation, and that's tough in a private society." Patricia Roberts Harris wants to walk the fine line between offering support to teenage mothers and dictating how a single mother should live. Child-care services are recommended by some, whether in the form of a major federally funded day-care program, of public subsidies to relatives or friends to serve as child caretakers, or of encouraging voluntary babysitting services. The goal is to free the mother from the home so she can get a job and escape welfare dependency. For example, it is seen as self-defeating for President Reagan to propose "workfare" for 800,000 adult AFDC recipients without providing some form of care for the children of these mothers.

Another preventive step pushed by retailers and others is to seek to end the practice followed by more than half the states of requiring that AFDC payments be awarded to mothers *only* if there is no able-bodied man in the house—the so-called man-in-the-house rule. Says Carl Holman, president of the National Urban Coalition in Washington, "We went through a decade where a man who didn't have a job couldn't live at home or we would cut off his welfare benefits. You encouraged the breakup of family. We, in other words, created the system. They didn't." Far better, he says, to earmark the money to the child, as some states do. Mississippi, for example, earmarks payments to the children, but the benefits are scandalously low. Critics on the right counter by saying that without a rigorous work requirement, raising benefits would encourage dependency. Critics on the left respond that without a decent payment level the system will be inhumane. Both sides talk past each other. We could extricate ourselves from this rhetorical quagmire if we simply admitted what common sense rather than doctrine dictated: Both sides are right.

Supported work was a program that recognized the horrors of dependency and also the importance of government help. It was not a large-scale government program but was run by local, community-based organizations. Funds came from private as well as government sources. There were standards to be met, and rigorous cost accounting, and the kind of research that conservatives have long clamored for. But underlying this structure was a belief that the federal government had a role to play and that some members of the underclass could be helped.

Thus, in the long run, programs that reduce dependency and unemployment constitute one method of stabilizing families. Another is preventing the birth of unwanted babies. Poor women, both because they cannot afford private abortions and because they may not be as aware of or knowledgeable about birth-control methods, don't have real freedom of choice. Either the government pays for their abortions and promotes the dissemination of birth-control information or society is likely to have more unwanted, hostile children and dependent mothers.

Where the left and the right might agree is in recognizing that government policies have an impact on family stability. In 1980, the Family Impact Seminar at George Washington University found that in 1976 there were 275 federal programs that could affect family life, sometimes adversely. In a paper prepared at the Urban Institute, the economists Maurice MacDonald and Isabel V. Sawhill singled out the tax and welfare systems as "primary family disincentives." For instance, they wrote, taxes go down and welfare payments go up as the number of children increases, and so people are encouraged to have more children. "At the same time, marriage and resource sharing among adults is discouraged," because "two-parent families are categorically denied welfare benefits available to similarly situated one-parent families." If a mother on welfare lives with an employed male or in an extended-family situation where someone in the household works, her benefits are usually reduced. And until 1982, when a change in the tax law becomes effective, if a husband and a wife are both wage earners they generally find themselves paying higher taxes than an unmarried couple with the same earnings.

MacDonald and Sawhill, however, saw several sides to the complex issue of the effect of the welfare system on the family. For the most part, they noted, this policy of penalizing marriage was not "irrational." They said:

It represents a compromise with other objectives, especially equity. While neutrality requires that the tax or transfer system

307

not influence family behavior, equity requires that individuals in similar circumstances receive similar treatment—more specifically that taxes and transfers be adjusted for the different economic "needs" of different households or families. Thus, children increase family "needs" and are considered deserving of support, but this necessitates rewarding adults for producing more of them, giving a strong pronatalist bias to policy. In addition, the per-capita economic needs of smaller units are generally considered to be greater than those of larger units because of the presumed economies of scale which come from resource sharing. This leads to a benefit schedule which . . . [creates] incentives for household fragmentation.

The dilemmas are real. The government saves money when families live together, but the individuals within the families lose money. Such trade-offs and sacrifices are usually ignored or challenged by wholesalers of the right or the left; they are a constant concern of those who favor the retail approach. Reality suggests that sometimes the government has to choose between saving money and encouraging family fragmentation. And, more fundamentally, it has to choose between the conflicting goals of providing an adequate level of welfare support and preserving incentives for work.

In truth, most retailers have no comprehensive cure for the problem of family dissolution. Their proposals do not get at the core of the problem. They assume that there is no quick fix. They embrace day-care centers or a surrogate-mother program and then worry that such expedients will supplant the role of the parent. They favor abortion and then worry about morality. They want the government involved but are concerned about privacy. They usually end up declaring that family dissolution, and its role in creating an underclass, at least cries out for public attention and debate.

Schools are another target for retailers. Many black and Hispanic youngsters would agree with Ramon Lopez of BT-27, who complained that his ghetto school taught him that he was "dumb." To correct deficient schools, many educators and parents would like to require that teachers, as well as students, pass minimum competency exams. The return to basics and away from "reforms" such as teaching what was "relevant" or of "practical use" to the child is now widely accepted. The order of a federal judge that an Ann Arbor, Michigan, school accept black English as a dialect so as not to damage the self-esteem of black students is today opposed by many liberals as well as conservatives because it may handicap black children when they become adults.

The back-to-basics approach finds eloquent expression in the Chicago classroom of Marva Collins, a forty-five-year-old black woman who insists on introducing Chaucer and Shakespeare and Dostoyevsky to her thirty ghetto students, ages four to thirteen. The nation was first brought into her private schoolhouse via the cameras of CBS's *60 Minutes* and the reporting of Morley Safer. "There are no frills at West Side—no art classes, no music, no gym, not even recess," Safer began. "There are also no discipline problems. The emphasis is on basic education, with an even stronger emphasis on literature and composition. The students must read one very tough book every two weeks, and they must write a composition every day." Why does Collins insist on teaching the King's English? "If children are going to go out into the world and command a job in our society," she told Safer, "they have to be able to speak standard English. No one wants to hire a secretary who cannot spell. No one wants to hire a president of a corporation who is not articulate."

Why does she unashamedly moralize and seek to imbue her students with middle-class values? Collins responded:

> Even when the four-year-olds begin to read *The Little Red Hen,* I point out the moral that if you don't work you don't eat. I never miss that opportunity. Children want structure. I think we've given them so much freedom that they really don't know what to do with it. I think they're really destroying themselves. . . . When I look at this area, I could really scream at all the monies that are being spent on programs, all the monies that are being thrown away, and not a doggone thing has changed in this area for the last seventeen years. . . . You pick up the children, you bring them to me, and you come back one month later, and I'll show you a different child; not through beating, not through screaming, not through yelling. . . . Through constant talking, through telling that child every day that his only hope is a good education; that in order to make it in this world, no one is going to give it to you, you have to earn it.

Those who may differ with Marva Collins' traditional teaching methods can still draw comfort from the lesson implicit in her school: a good teacher can make a difference. In a study of effective and ineffective ghetto schools for the October 1979 issue of *Education Leadership,* the former chief of instruction for the New York City Board of Education, Ron Edmunds, explained the importance of teachers' expectations:

Many professional personnel in the less effective school attributed children's reading problems to non-school factors and were pessimistic about their ability to have an impact, creating an environment in which children failed because they were not expected to succeed. However, in the more effective school, teachers were less skeptical about their ability to have an impact on children.

Marva Collins, like Howard Smith, emphasizes individual as opposed to society's responsibility. She is not afraid to fail someone, not afraid he or she will feel rejected, unloved. But of course there are those on the left and right who would think her message too simple. The Marxist view, as expressed by Martin Carnoy about American schools in general, is that: "Schools attempt to meet the needs of monopoly capitalist organizations . . . by teaching lower-class children to be better workers and middle class ones to be better managers in the corporate economy, and by reproducing the social relations of production in the schools to inculcate children with values and norms which reinforce the prevailing economic structures." Many conservatives, on the other hand, say some students are unreachable.

There is no consensus in our society about how to reform education. Some advocate busing to achieve school integration, believing that pupils who are not doing well will benefit from mingling with good students; a surprising number of black and Hispanic parents oppose busing because they say it assumes their child cannot learn without exposure to whites. Some push the three Rs; others emphasize vocational skills. Some promote bilingualism, saying it will prevent Hispanic students from losing self-confidence and guarantee that they receive an education; others say it will, like black English, guarantee that they cannot compete as adults.

There is broader agreement among educators that the problem of the disruptive student must be wrestled with. As is true with violent crime, a relatively small number of students seem to have a disproportionate effect. Abraham Lass, former principal of Abraham Lincoln High School in Brooklyn, New York, explains why. In order to achieve greater racial balance, the Board of Education began busing about three hundred minority students to Lincoln in 1969. Racial flare-ups and incidents of violence spread. "We became alarmed," recalls Lass. "At the beginning we assumed these kids were no different from ours. There was a big debate on that. We decided we didn't want them to feel different. Then when those things began to pop up we studied it and discovered that every time there was a racial incident or rumble, the same names came into my office. Maybe eight or ten kids out of four thousand. But it wasn't eight kids because you had to multiply each by eight. Why eight? Because you've got to take eight kids and multiply by eight periods. So what we really had was fifty-six explosive, hostile, nasty, disturbed, and disturbing kids." By keeping those eight to ten students under surveillance rather than by branding all of the minority students as disruptive or innocent, Lass says they were able to restore order to the school.

Retail ideas are also advanced for policing the relatively small number of violent criminals. One example is the New York City Police Department's Felony Augmentation Program, which was designed to track career criminals and make sure that when apprehended they do not receive low bail, plea-bargain the charge down to a misdemeanor, or get away with a light jail sentence. New York City Police Commissioner Robert McGuire recently announced that the pilot program was being expanded, and that 170 additional detectives would be assigned to track and gather intelligence on 6,000 violent career criminals. New York State has had a similar program since 1978, and through September 1980 the state disposed of 929 cases and had a conviction rate of 95.6 percent.

Stricter gun control laws and punishment for criminal use of guns is also promoted by many. There are an estimated 50 million handguns in circulation in the United States today—upwards of 2 million illegal handguns in New York City alone. And "Saturday night specials," as they are called, can be ordered by mail like flannel shirts. The growth of violence in the decade of the seventies is linked by many to the growth of guns—when was the last time someone robbed a bank with a knife or club? In Japan, where private ownership of handguns is essentially banned, there were but 48 handgun homicides in 1979, compared to 10,728 in the United States. More than half those killed in Chicago since 1970, for instance, were gun victims. And each day over 50 Americans lose their lives from handguns.

But, alas, as it is too easy to proclaim economic quick fixes for the underclass, so it is too glib to pretend that strict gun controls will stop the killing. Switzerland, it could be noted, has no gun controls and few murders; Britain and Italy have strict gun licensing laws and ample killings. How will the government round up the estimated 50 million handguns? Will it pay a bounty, and how expensive will that be? Will we be disarming shopkeepers and other law-abiding citizens who reside in high-crime neighborhoods and require guns for self-protection? Will liberal proponents of gun controls favor searches and seizures for illegal handguns? Or aggressive undercover operations and stop-and-frisk laws designed to target and round up likely offenders? Sadly, strict gun control promises no panacea.

311

Whatever the fate of gun control, a surprising number of opponents and proponents do endorse strict mandatory minimum sentences for those committing crimes with a gun. President Reagan, who opposes gun control laws as violative of the constitutional right to bear arms,* has said, "If somebody commits a crime and carries a gun when he's doing it, add five to fifteen years to the prison sentence." The states of Massachusetts and New York already have laws imposing a minimum sentence of one year in jail for possession of an illegal gun. And Mayor Koch of New York, for one, has campaigned for a state minimum penalty of five years for anyone using a gun to commit a crime.

Those who propose incremental solutions find the concept known as targeting to be an extremely compelling one. Deeply aware of limited resources, limited government capacities, and the limits of people, they advocate a limited, focused approach to social problem-solving rather than a broad, comprehensive effort. If the lifeboat will hold only twenty people, you can't save eighty. A retailer might say that it is better to guarantee the safety of twenty than to risk all. Instead of advocating general programs for blacks and Hispanics and the poor, as many civil-rights organizations and their allies do, they are more likely to target the underclass separately. It is "wrong tactically and factually to pretend we're all in it together," William Raspberry of the *Washington Post* told me. "We're all in it together as regards Bull Connors' police dogs. But we're not all in it together as regards the bottom of the barrel, and it strikes me as madness, to the point of dereliction, to pretend otherwise. There are blacks in a position to make things happen for those at the bottom of the barrel, and we ought to be doing those things rather than strike a psychological identification as if it does something for them."

People differ over whom to target. At the community level, some public-housing sites strictly limit the number of welfare recipients or screen out those they consider undesirable. "We don't refuse them," Lillie Howard, the black tenant manager of Montgomery Gardens in Jersey City, told me. "We just take somebody else over them." Robert Hill of the Urban League says that if he were forced to choose what group to target, he would take aim at "female-headed families," which in his view are the main cause of the underclass. Marian Wright Edelman of the Children's Defense Fund would aim at youths, seeking to break the cycle of poverty there. Perhaps the

*Reagan's 1981 Task Force on Violent Crime, however, did urge a tightening of restrictions on the easy purchase of handguns. At this writing, Reagan has ignored the recommendation.

greatest division occurs over whether to target the underclass or the working poor. Assuming limited resources, government or community-based organizations cannot do both. The dilemma is real, and rarely discussed. Does society focus resources on those who have the best chance of being reached (the working poor), or on those who most need assistance (the underclass)?

Targeting can take many forms. Representative Clarence Brown, a Republican from Ohio, has introduced legislation to target subsidies to businesses that train hard-to-employ people for actual jobs. President Carter's urban policy was designed to target "distressed communities in declining areas and regions," and to provide more federal assistance to those cities most in need. Affirmative-action programs are among the more controversial forms of targeting. "One way to overcome unequal history and a discriminatory present is through affirmative-action programs that will provide measurable goals and timetables to effectively help bring black people into the mainstream of American life," Vernon Jordan has said. Over the last two decades, affirmative-action "goals" have become the policy of the federal government and of many state and local governments. Businesses and contractors have been screened to determine whether they hire or seek to hire minorities, schools have been inspected for "racial balance," and police departments have been attacked for "biased" examinations—all in the hope of righting past wrongs and expanding equality of opportunity.

But President Reagan and others oppose compulsory affirmative action as a hidden quota system. To penalize a firm for hiring ten minority employees instead of fifteen makes the fifteen not just a target but a quota, they claim. Unavoidably, better-qualified people will be passed over because they are the wrong race or sex, and the races and the sexes will be further polarized. Affirmative action, like busing, is seen by a number of blacks as a patronizing policy. "I don't want it for me," says Charles V. Hamilton, Wallace S. Sayre Professor of Government at Columbia, and the co-author, with Stokely Carmichael, of *Black Power: The Politics of Liberation in America*, published in 1967. Hamilton recalls attending a conference at which affirmative action was discussed. He told the conference that officials at Boston College, where his daughter was studying, assumed that she needed special "minority aid." Informally, those attending the conference were polled on the issue. Almost all of Hamilton's black and Hispanic colleagues said they opposed such special aid for themselves or their children, because their financial situations made it unnecessary. Most of his white colleagues favored it, saying that the legacy of racism was a burden for Hamilton's daughter and for all

313

blacks. "I said, 'That's a lot of nonsense!'" Hamilton told me. "At some point, we have to assume responsibility for our own situation —in spite of racism." His daughter was offended, and she defiantly told the college officials, "I'm not one of your needy 'minority students'!" Hamilton beamed with pride at her defiance—a defiance not unlike that of sixties black-power advocates. "I saw it at Yale, where I taught a few semesters ago," he went on. "The regular students there wanted to be distinguished from the special-admissions students. They wanted it known that they were not 'special-treatment' students." Nevertheless, Hamilton does believe that equal opportunity is denied to blacks because of their race. His daughter, unlike many others, has the financial wherewithal to reject assistance, but he fears that his opposition to affirmative action could be used by foes of black advancement. "My very good friends will accuse me of blaming the victim," he says. "I understand that. It's a dilemma. I don't quite know how to deal with it. If I could talk to blacks and not be heard by whites, I'd say something different. And vice versa. When I am talking only to black students, I talk about assuming responsibility for yourself, but if I'm with a wider audience I know I'll be accused of blaming the victim."

Hamilton's dilemma deserves broader acknowledgment and discussion. Both quotas and affirmative action can be degrading to the black or Hispanic beneficiary and also an affront to the innocent white. But affirmative action need not become a quota system. A mayor who decides he wants to hire a black police chief or a Hispanic woman to head his city's housing agency or a handicapped person to work with the handicapped is not imposing a quota—unless, of course, one assumes there are no qualified blacks, Hispanic women, or handicapped individuals. President Reagan surely did not think he was imposing a quota when he insisted on appointing a woman to the Supreme Court.

President Reagan and supply-side conservatives like George Gilder stress the central importance of faith in restoring America's economic growth. An investor needs faith that his money will earn money, or he will not invest; without faith a smart entrepreneur will not borrow to expand; a citizen will not save without faith that inflation will not wipe him out. Helping restore this faith is a legitimate and important function of government. So is giving America's minority population faith. Faith is a fragile thing. As President Reagan has found it difficult, at this writing, to gain the faith of the financial community when he proposes to balance the federal budget while slashing taxes and boosting defense spending, so it is difficult for many minority citizens to have faith in a president who denounces a House-approved (389 to 24) extension of the Voting Rights Act as "pretty extreme," appoints a solitary black and no Hispanics to his Cabinet, appoints mostly whites to the federal bench, announces his opposition to federal affirmative-action guidelines, and cleaves federal programs that assist minorities while keeping intact tobacco subsidies and widening tax "loopholes" for the wealthy. Unavoidably, a symbolic message gets through. By mid-1981, according to the *New York Times*/CBS News poll, white Americans turned increasingly optimistic about their own and the nation's future, largely because of Reagan's take-charge approach to the nation's economy. Black Americans, on the other hand, grew increasingly gloomy. That's another form of trickle-down.

One of the few subjects about which there is a consensus is the need for further research on the underclass. "Despite the growth of the social-research industry, policy is still essentially designed according to gut feelings or the need for a political issue," Garth L. Mangum and Stephen F. Seninger wrote in their 1978 book, *Coming of Age in the Ghetto.* In its final report on the five-year supported-work experiment, the MDRC concluded, "The full exploitation of the findings of this extensive research effort is constrained by the dearth of adequate information from most of the other federally financed manpower programs operated since 1962." An impressive attribute of the MDRC was its commitment to research—to discovering what works and what doesn't, and when and why. The MDRC test-marketed ideas and programs, not slogans. Unlike most program managers, its people sought to determine and assess facts, not collect stray anecdotes.

But there are never enough facts. For example, one area requiring facts is the medical and biological causes of the existence of an underclass—as opposed to the economic, sociological, and psychological causes. A team of scientists at Yale has uncovered evidence that especially violent delinquent boys are more likely than less aggressive delinquents to suffer not just psychological disorders but certain neurological symptoms—blackout spells, falling, and other indications of psychomotor epilepsy. Although one of the authors said that scientific knowledge of delinquency was "primitive," this Yale study —*Violent Juvenile Delinquents,* written in 1979—reported that 81.8 percent of the more violent delinquent youngsters had symptoms of paranoia, as opposed to only 16.7 percent of the less violent boys. The Yale team expressed hope that some of the random violence that seems to distinguish the underclass could be modified with medical treatment: "Programs designed to diminish violence which focus primarily on socioeconomic and psychological factors are likely to be unsuccessful if they ignore the medical problems (e.g., psychotic symptoms, neurological impairment) that contribute so strongly to the expression of violence."

Finally, the MDRC approach to the underclass assumes complexity. "Textbooks don't give you a sense of the complexity of this population," says Charles Knapp, former deputy assistant secretary of labor for employment and training in the Carter administration. "The programs have to be intensive, and we have to be willing to experience a certain failure rate." Lumping all CETA public employment programs together as a failure, the Reagan administration eliminated funding for most of these, including the supported-work program. This action ignores contentions by MDRC officials that in judging programs for the underclass a different definition of success must be applied. "Success is in the eye of the beholder," says William Grinker. "Some people might think that supported work is a success if, for example, the number of people on welfare rolls is reduced by ten percent, and these people work rather than collect welfare. On the other hand, if it costs more to do this, other people will say it is not worth the expense. It's how you define success, and in the end it has to do with values."

A retailer is generally willing to risk failure to achieve modest success. That is a matter of values, but also of judgment. The national demonstrations the MDRC has conducted among the underclass offer ample evidence of how difficult it is to reach those who figuratively reside at the bottom of society's barrel. "There is no pink pill in this business," says Grinker. The MDRC's experiments suggest that progress is not measured by breathtaking touchdown passes, but by grinding out two, three, four yards at a time—Pearl Dawson, William Mason, Mohammed, Susie Haun, Denise Brown, Hope Parker, Timothy Wilson.

Epilogue

On the eve of the 1980 presidential election Marshall D. Shulman, a ranking State Department official, complained to an off-the-record gathering of journalists that campaigns dangerously distort the truth. He observed, for instance, that relations with the Soviet Union were being reduced by all the candidates to bumper-sticker slogans.

"What's wrong with that?" a gentleman in the audience inquired. "Isn't the basic problem with the Carter administration that it has no slogan to deal with the Russians that could fit on a bumper sticker?"

Ridiculous! snapped Shulman. The gentleman persisted, demanding that Shulman explain policy as if it were a bumper sticker.

"How many words am I allowed?" asked the State Department official.

"Two," said the man.

Missing hardly a beat, Shulman said, "My bumper sticker would read, 'Accept Complexity.'"

The one great lesson I learned from my reporting among the underclass and the poor is that generalizations—bumper stickers—are the enemies of understanding. It is perilous to generalize about the "lower class," as conservative Edward Banfield does, or about "victims," as socialist William Ryan does, or about poverty having been "virtually eliminated," as White House domestic policy chief Martin Anderson does, or about government being "the problem," as President Reagan has. From a height of thirty thousand feet, everyone and everything looks like an ant. Banfield overlooked Mohammed, William Mason and Hope Parker of BT-27 when he loftily wrote: "With the exception of the autobiographical accounts of a very few gifted individuals—Frederick Douglass, Malcolm X, and Claude Brown, for example—there is no direct evidence of there ever having been any upward mobility from the lower class." Ryan never saw John Painter, Cecil Breeden, Aubrey Powers, Henry Rivera, or the violent Bolton brothers when he announced that to speak of pathology is to "blame the victim." Anderson's charts don't describe a helpless Willy Joe or the unending poverty and ache inside West Virginia shacks and Harlem tenements. Reagan and the Congress chopped the budget without noticing the success stories federal funding made possible, including people like Pearl Dawson.

On the ground, looking at and listening to the very real people enrolled in the MDRC programs, one is led to the inescapable conclusion that neither the political right nor the political left fully comprehends the changing nature of poverty and the rise of what threatens to become a permanent American underclass. Conservatives have been right over the years to stress the importance of self-reliance, self-help, a work ethic, values. They better understood the perils of dependency. But banishing family planning, sex education, and abortion won't prevent the Jean Madisons of East Harlem from having twenty-nine children; won't provide the love many teenage mothers seek in a child. Preaching parental responsibility or compulsory prayers in all schools won't provide a teenage mother living alone with the day care or other services needed to escape the house, get a job, get off welfare. A child can't receive sex-education from his parents if he has no parents. Ricky Wild, the former president of his high school class in Isola, Mississippi, didn't drop out of school because he lacked "motivation" or concerned parents. He abandoned education because he was the eldest of eight children and his mother was dying of cancer. No free market or tax-free zone will induce a business to hire someone with Henry Rivera's zero skills, with Cecil Breeden and John Hick's attendance or hostile attitudes. People can be "victims"—of bad luck, bad teachers, bad parents, a bad economy, the stigma of being black, Hispanic, an ex-convict, or a "welfare mother."

Liberals have been right when they insist that economic and societal forces can entrap individuals, that few are born monsters. They better understand the alienation and lack of self-confidence felt by many poor people. Many businesses would not hire teenagers from the Youth Entitlement Project because they were black or Hispanic. But the left too rarely understands that compassion and money or a government job are sometimes not enough. Compassion did not prevent Willy Joe from flunking out of BT-27. A guaranteed job did not reduce the drug use of ex-addicts in the supported-work program or induce many eligible mothers on welfare to enroll. Nor did a guaranteed job in the Youth Entitlement Project prevent many youngsters from dropping out of school. Some people have behavioral, as well as income, problems. Some prefer the streets, or the quick rewards from crime. Affirmative action may assist a GS17, but not a black or Hispanic dropout without work experience, skills, or self-esteem. The poor can be "victims" of poor values or uncaring or desperate parents, as well as of "environmental neglect."

Pushing aside the pieties, charts, and stereotypes, one sees that a segment of the poor are sometimes victims of their own bad attitudes, and sometimes victims of social and economic forces. Neither the right's desire to blame individuals, nor the left's to blame the system, addresses the stubborn reality of the underclass. Somewhere between the stale shibboleths, the MDRC experience suggests, lies the truth.

One unavoidable consequence of this truth is that when we strip away ideological bombast and stare at the naked problem, we see that there are rarely any simple or painless cures for the underclass. Those who think there are belong in the bumper-sticker business. Some members of the underclass need help, and some are beyond help. I have no difficulty giving up on violent criminals like the Bolden brothers or street hustlers like Henry Rivera. But knowing how a government helping hand made it possible for Pearl Dawson and William Mason to succeed, would you be willing to write them off? Would you turn your back on Willy Joe?

I wouldn't. And since we can neither eradicate nor walk away from the underclass, for starters perhaps we can at least discuss it. "Silence," Henry Wheeler Shaw once cautioned, "is one of the hardest things to refute."

Bibliography

Readers may be interested in knowing the published sources I used. They are:

Alcaly, Roger E., and David Mermelstein, eds. *The Fiscal Crisis of American Cities.* New York: Vintage Books, 1977.

Andersson, Anne M. Letter to Neal Hirschfeld re Bolden brothers, June 9, 1979.

Appalachian Center, "Changes in the Rural South Appalachian Community." Research Series 7. West Virginia: West Virginia University, Morgantown, W.V.

―――. "Implications of Social Class Differences in Beliefs Concerning Causes of Unemployment." Research Series 2. West Virginia: West Virginia University, Morgantown, W.V., April 1968.

―――. "Poverty in America: The Problem, Anti-Poverty Programs, and a Role for Organized Labor." Information Series 5. West Virginia: Institute for Labor Studies, West Virginia University, Morgantown, W.V., 1967.

―――. "Problems of Community Action in Appalachia." Research Series 4. West Virginia: West Virginia University, Morgantown, W.V., May 1968.

―――. "Social Psychological Factors Associated with Responses to Retraining." Research Series 2. West Virginia: Institute for Labor Studies, West Virginia University, Morgantown, W.V., September 1967.

―――. "Some Facts and a Theory of Migration." Research Series 8. West Virginia: West Virginia University, Morgantown, W.V., December 1968.

Baldwin, James. *Nobody Knows My Name.* New York: Dell, 1961.

Baldwin, Wendy H. "Adolescent Pregnancy and Childbearing—Growing Concerns for Americans." *Population Bulletin,* Vol. 31, No. 2. Population Reference Bureau.

Ball, Joseph. "Implementing Supported Work: Job Creation Strategies During the First Year of the National Demonstration." MDRC, May 1977.

Ball, Joseph, et al. "The Youth Entitlement Demonstration: An Interim Report on Program Implementation." Manpower Development Research Corporation, April 1979.

Banfield, Edward C. *The Unheavenly City: The Nature and Future of Our Urban Crisis.* Boston: Little, Brown, 1968.

Banfield, Edward C., and James Q. Wilson. *City Politics*. New York: Vintage, 1963.

Barclay, Suzanne, et al. "Schooling and Work among Youths from Low-Income Households." A baseline report from the Entitlement Demonstration. MDRC, May 1979.

Bellamy, Carol. Memo to Hugh L. Carey re foster care, March 14, 1980.

———. Release re mental patient discharges. City Hall Council, November 14, 1979.

Bernstein, Blanche. "Do Work Requirements Accomplish Anything?" *Public Welfare*. Spring 1978, pp. 36–45.

———. "An Effort to Improve Welfare Housing—and What Happened to It." *City Almanac*, Vol. 14, No. 3. New School for Social Research, October 1979.

———. "Employability of Welfare Recipients." November 21, 1978.

Bernstein, Blanche, and William Meezan. "The Impact of Welfare on Family Stability." New School for Social Research, Center for New York City Affairs, June 1975.

Bernstein, Blanche, et al. "Obstacles to Employment of Employable Welfare Recipients." New School for Social Research, Center for NYC Affairs, June 1974.

Bernstein, Blanche, and Anne N. Shkuda. "The Young Drug User: Attitudes and Obstacles to Treatment." New School for Social Research, Center for NYC Affairs, June 1974.

Berresford, Susan. Interoffice memorandum: "Black Illegitimacy," Ford Foundation, November 4, 1975.

———. Interoffice memorandum: "Sisterhood of Black Single Mothers Progress Report (#780-0371)," Ford Foundation, July 6, 1979.

Bienstock, Herbert. "Inner City Market Opportunities in the 1980's." U.S. Department of Labor, Bureau of Labor Statistics, November 12, 1979.

———. "Out of Work: Then and Now." U.S. Department of Labor, Bureau of Labor Statistics, October 1979.

———. "Some Facts Relating to Economics and Education." U.S. Department of Labor, Bureau of Labor Statistics, June 1979.

Bishop, Joseph W., Jr. "Criminals and Liberals." *The American Spectator*, July 1979.

Black Enterprise: "A Statistical Profile of Black Economic Development." May 1979, p. 56, and April 1979, p. 72.

Blaustein, Arthur I., and Roger R. Woock et al. *Man Against Poverty: World War III*. New York: Vintage, 1968.

Brecher, Charles, and Raymond D. Horton. *Setting Municipal Priorities, 1982*. New York: Russell Sage Foundation, 1981.

Bright, Clifford. Statement from 47th Precinct, April 5, 1979.

Brown, Claude. *Manchild in the Promised Land*. New York: Signet, 1966.

Brown, Prudence. "The Storefront School Report."

Brown, Prudence, and Martha Beverle. "Promoting Family Competence: A Preventive Practice Model." Report to the Ford Foundation, June 27, 1979.

Bureau of Labor Statistics, "Employment and Earnings April 1980." Vol. 27, No. 4.

———. "Employment and Earnings July 1980." Vol. 27, No. 7.

———. "Job Tenure Declines as Work Force Changes." Special Labor Force Report 235.

———. "Students, Graduates, and Dropouts in the Labor Market, October 1978." Special Labor Force Report 223.

Byrne, Brendan. "Task Force on Unemployment in Atlantic City." June 1980.

Caute, David, ed. *Essential Writings of Karl Marx*. New York: Macmillan, 1967.

Census Bureau. "Characteristics of the Population Below the Poverty Level: 1977." U.S. Department of Commerce, Series P-60, No. 119, March 1979.

———. "Characteristics of the Population Below the Poverty Level: 1978." U.S. Department of Commerce, Series P-60, No. 124, July 1980.

———. "Persons of Spanish Origin in the United States: March 1978." U.S. Department of Commerce, Series P-20, No. 339, June 1979.

———. "Population Profile of the United States: 1977." U.S. Department of Commerce, Series P-20, No. 324, April 1978.

Children's Defense Fund. "America's Children and Their Families." 1979.

———. "What Is CDF? Questions and Answers About the Children's Defense Fund." Washington Research Project, April 1978.

City Planning Commission. Private report by staff member to then-chairman Robert F. Wagner, Jr. "The Development and Growth of a Welfare-Dependent Underclass in New York City: How It Happened and What to Do About It." October 19, 1979.

Clark, B. Kenneth. *Paths of Power*. New York: Harper & Row, 1974.

Clark, B. Kenneth, and Jeannette Hopkins. *A Relevant War Against Poverty: A Study of Community Action Programs and Observable Social Change.* New York: Harper & Row, 1968.

Clark, Ramsey. *Crime in America*. New York: Pocket Books, 1971.

Cleaver, Eldridge. *Soul on Ice*. New York: Dell, 1968.

Community Council of Greater New York, Council Against Poverty. "The Hidden Poor," June 1977.

Cray, Ed. *The Enemy in the Streets*. New York: Doubleday, 1972.

Davidson House Senior Center. Letters: Mario Merola, March 6, 1979; Michael Smith, March 6, 1979; Archie Gorfinkel, March 6, 1979.

DeLone, Richard H. *Small Futures; Children, Inequality and the Limits of Liberal Reform.* New York: Harcourt Brace Jovanovich, 1979.

Diaz, William A., et al. "The Youth Entitlement Demonstration." Second interim report on program implementation, MDRC, March 1980.

Dresner, Morris, and Tortorello Research. Summary of Major Findings: Data Black Study No. 1. Data Black Public Opinion Polls, January 1980.

Eddinger, Lucy, and Janet Forbush. "School Age Pregnancy and Parenthood in the United States." National Alliance Concerned with School-Age Parents, 1977.

Edmonds, Ronald. "Effective Schools for the Urban Poor." *Educational Leadership*, October 1979.

Education Priorities Panel. "Empty Desks at School." May 1980.

Fabricant, Neil. "Behind the Headlines." *Empire State Report*, March 10, 1980.

Faden, Vivian B. "Primary Diagnosis of Discharges from Non-Federal General Hospital Psychiatric Inpatient Units, U.S. 1975." U.S. Department of Health, Education and Welfare, August 1977.

Fairfax, Jean. NAACP Legal Defense Fund private memo re black illegitimacy. December 23, 1975.

Fetterman, John. *Stinking Creek*. New York: Dutton, 1970.

Ford Foundation. Annual Report 1979. October 1978 to September 30, 1979.

Foster, Robert, and Orest Ranum, eds. *Deviants and the Abandoned in French Society; Selections from the Annales,* Vol. IV. Baltimore: Johns Hopkins University Press, 1978.

323

Frumerman, Harry. "Job Vacancy Statistics in the United States." National Commission on Employment and Unemployment Statistics, May 1978.

Furstenberg, Frank F., Jr. "The Social Consequences of Teenage Parenthood." *Family Planning Perspectives,* Vol. 8, No. 4, July/August 1976.

Gans, Herbert J. *The Urban Villagers.* New York: Free Press, 1962.

Gaylin, Willard, Ira Glasser, Steven Marcus, and David Rothman. *Doing Good: The Limits of Benevolence.* Pantheon, 1978.

Gilder, George. *Visible Man: A True Story of Post-Racist America.* New York: Basic Books, 1978.

———. *Wealth and Poverty.* New York: Basic Books, 1981.

Ginzberg, Eli. "Youth Unemployment." *Scientific American,* Vol. 242, No. 5, May 1980.

Gitlin, Todd, and Nanci Hollander. *Uptown: Poor Whites in Chicago.* New York: Harper & Row, 1970.

Glasgow, Douglas G. *The Black Underclass: Poverty, Unemployment, and Entrapment of Ghetto Youth.* Vintage, 1981.

Glazer, Nathan, and Daniel P. Moynihan. *Ethnicity: Theory and Experience.* Cambridge: Harvard University Press, 1975.

———. *Beyond the Melting Pot.* Cambridge: MIT Press, 1963.

Goodman, Emily Jane. "Dreams." Columbia University, Graduate School of Journalism, New York, N.Y., 1980.

Gorham, William, and Nathan Glazer, eds. *The Urban Predicament.* Washington, D.C.: The Urban Institute, 1976.

Grier, William H., and Price M. Cobbs. *Black Rage.* New York: Bantam, 1968.

Griffin, John Howard. *Black Like Me.* New York: New American Library, 1960.

Gwaltney, John Langston. *Drylongso: A Self-Portrait of Black America.* New York: Random House, 1980.

Harlem Youth Opportunities Unlimited, Inc. "Youth in the Ghetto." 1964.

Hand, Learned, O. J. "The Accused Has the Advantage." *U.S. v. Garson,* 291 F. 646 (1923) at 649.

Harrington, Michael. *The Other America: Poverty in the United States.* New York: Penguin Books, 1981.

Harris, Louis, et al. "A Survey of Residents' Perceptions of Neighborhood Services in the Southeast Bronx and Central Harlem." Community Service Society of New York, May 1979.

Hill, Robert B. "The Illusion of Black Progress." National Urban League Research Department, 1978.

Hill, Robert B., et al. "The Widening Economic Gap." National Urban League Research Department, 1979.

Howe, Irving. *World of Our Fathers.* New York: Simon and Schuster, 1976.

Institute for Contemporary Studies. "The Fairmont Papers: Black Alternatives Conference, San Francisco, December 1980." 1981.

Internal Revenue Service. "Estimates of Unreported Income in Individual Tax Returns."

Jackson, Russell, et al. "Project Report 79-03: The Supported Work Demonstration's Research Sample: Characteristics at Enrollment." Mathematica Policy Research/MDRC, October 4, 1978.

Jacobs, Jane. *The Death and Life of Great American Cities.* New York: Random House, 1961.

――――. *The Economy of Cities.* New York: Random House, 1969.

Jordan, Vernon E. Address at the Cleveland Temple. March 3, 1978.

Kemp, Jack. *An American Renaissance.* New York: Harper & Row, 1979.

――――. "The Urban Jobs and Enterprise Zone Act: Some Questions and Answers."

Kilson, Martin. "Black Social Classes and Intergenerational Poverty." *The Public Interest,* Fall 1981.

Koch, Edward I. Personal memo to Herbert I. Sturz re Boldens. June 6, 1979.

――――. Press release re arson. From the Office of the Mayor, February 26, 1980.

――――. Statement on state deinstitutionalization of mentally disabled. July 28, 1980.

Kolan, Nuran. "The West Virginia Supported Work Program: A Case Study." AFL-CIO Appalachian Council/MDRC, October 1979.

Kornblum, William. "Boyash Gypsies: Shantytown Ethnicity." Farnham Reyfisch, ed. *Gypsies, Tinkers and Other Travellers.* New York: Academic Press, 1975.

Kornblum, William, and Paul Lichter. "Urban Gypsies and the Culture of Poverty." *Urban Life and Culture,* Vol. 1, No. 3, October 1972.

Kornblum, William, and Terry Williams. "CUNY Demonstration: Employing Disadvantaged Youth in Community Analysis." Interim Report No. 3, CUNY Graduate School, July 1980.

――――. "Employing Disadvantaged Youth in Community Analysis: A Comparative Demonstration." Graduate School and University Center of the City University of New York.

Kornblum, William, et al. "Interim Report: Employing Disadvantaged Youth in Community Analysis: A Comparative Demonstration." New York: CUNY Graduate School, March 1980.

———. "West 42nd Street: 'The Bright Light Zone.'" Graduate School and University Center of the City University of New York, 1978.

LaBarre, Weston. *They Shall Take Up Serpents.* New York: Schocken, 1969.

Lah, David. "The Cases for and against CETA Targeting." U.S. Department of Labor, February 1980.

———. "Labor Market Theories."

Lasch, Christopher. *The Culture of Narcissism.* New York: Warner, 1979.

Lax, Eric. "Job Placement in Oakland." MDRC, April 1978.

———. "Job Placement in Oakland" (revised) MDRC, February 22, 1980.

Leiman, Joan and Jim Healy. "Supported Work for the Mentally Retarded." MDRC, March 17, 1980.

Leinster, Colin. "Ex-Addicts—1" (draft). MDRC, October 12, 1979.

Leinward, Gerald, ed. *Poverty and the Poor.* New York: Washington Square Press, 1968.

Levine, Alan H., et al. *The Rights of Students.* New York: Avon, 1973.

Levitan, Sar A. and Benjamin H. Johnston. *The Job Corps: A Social Experiment That Works.* Baltimore: Johns Hopkins University Press, 1975.

Levy, Frank. "How Big Is the American Underclass?" University of California, Berkeley, January 1977.

———. "How Big Is the American Underclass?" (working paper). Washington: The Urban Institute, 1977.

———. "The Intergenerational Transfer of Poverty." Final project report (working paper). Washington: The Urban Institute, 1980.

Lewis, Dorothy Otnow, et al. "Violent Juvenile Delinquents." New Haven: Yale University Child Study Center.

Lewis, Oscar. *The Children of Sanchez.* New York: Random House, 1961.

———. *A Death in the Sanchez Family.* New York: Vintage, 1970.

———. *La Vida.* New York: Random House, 1965.

Little Sisters of the Assumption. "Second Interim Report of the Extended Family Program." June 1978.

Machuca, Michael. Statement from 43rd Precinct. January 9, 1979.

Makarenko, A. S. *The Road to Life (An Epic of Education),* Book One. Moscow: Progress Publishers, 1951.

Malcolm X. *The Autobiography of Malcolm X.* New York: Grove Press, 1964.

Mangum, Garth L., and Stephen F. Seninger. *Coming of Age in the Ghetto; A Dilemma of Youth Unemployment.* Baltimore: Johns Hopkins University Press, 1978.

Manpower Demonstration Research Corporation. "Alachua County Participant Discussion Session Report." University of Florida Institute of Black Culture. Manpower Demonstration Research Corporation (MDRC), June 29, 1979.

———. "Albuquerque Participant Discussion Session Report." MDRC, July 11, 1979.

———. "Analysis of Nine-Month Interviews for Supported Work: Results of an Early AFDC Sample." MDRC/Mathematica Policy Research/Institute for Research on Poverty, University of Wisconsin, November 1977 and September 1977.

———. "Basic Conclusions on the Results of the National Tenant Management Demonstration." MDRC Board of Directors, 1980.

———. "Dayton Participant Discussion Session Report." MDRC, August 8, 1979.

———. "First Annual Report on the National Supported Work Demonstration." MDRC, December 1976.

———. "Hillsborough County Discussion Session Report." MDRC, July 19, 1979.

———. "Interviews with Supported Workers." MDRC.

———. "Minutes of the Annual Meeting, October 17, 1975." MDRC.

———. "A Model for Reversing Truancy," a concept paper. MDRC, February 1980.

———. "Monthly Status Report on Youth Incentive Entitlement Pilot Projects, December 1979." MDRC, January 1980.

———. "Monthly Status Report on Youth Incentive Pilot Projects." MDRC, January 1980.

———. "Nature of the National Tenant Management Demonstration." MDRC, April 18, 1980.

———. "1978 Annual Report." MDRC.

———. "Philadelphia Participant Group Discussion Sessions Report: Entitlement Office and Community Health Center." MDRC, July 26, 1979.

———. "Preliminary Research Findings: WIN Research Laboratory Project." MDRC, April 1980.

———. "Project Redirection." A demonstration model for pregnant teenagers and teenage mothers who are on welfare or members of welfare families. MDRC, November 1979.

———. "The Quality of Work Youth Entitlement Demonstration." MDRC, April 11, 1980.

———. "Report on the Field Research to Determine the Effectiveness of the Youth Entitlement Demonstration from the Youth's Point of View." July 14, 1980.

———. "Second Annual Report on the National Supported Work Demonstration." MDRC, April 1978.

———. "Summary and Findings for the National Supported Work Demonstration." MDRC Board of Directors, January 1980.

———. "Summary of the Operating Experience and Statistical Highlights of the Third Year of the National Supported Work Demonstration." MDRC, August 1979.

———. "WIN LABS." MDRC, Spring 1978.

———. "Yiepp Worksite Assessments." MDRC.

Martin, Philip L., and Ellen B. Sehgal. "Illegal Immigration: The Guestworker Option." *Public Policy*, Vol. 8, No. 2, Spring 1980.

Mayhew, Henry. *London Labour and the London Poor*. Vol. I–IV. Door Publications, 1968.

McAnarney, Elizabeth R., and Donald E. Greydanus. "Adolescent Pregnancy—A Multifaceted Problem." *Pediatrics in Review*. Vol. 1, No. 4, October 1979.

McGhee, Dr. James. "Statement on NUL Research Department Report, 'Initial Black Pulse Findings.' " NUL, August 2, 1980.

Medina, Adelita. "Supported Work for Youth: Philadelphia and Jersey City" (draft). MDRC, October 16, 1979.

Mercer, Anthony. Statement from 43rd Precinct. January 25, 1977.

Meyer, Nessa G. "Diagnostic Distribution of Admissions to Inpatient Services of State and County Mental Hospitals, U.S., 1975." U.S. Department of Health, Education and Welfare, August 1977.

Milazzo-Sayre, Laura. "Admission Rates by the Highest Level of Education

Attained—State and County Mental Hospitals, U.S., 1975." U.S. Department of HEW, March 1979.

————. "Admission Rates to State and County Psychiatric Hospitals by Age, Sex, and Marital Status, U.S., 1975." U.S. Department of HEW, November 1977.

————. "Admission Rates to State and County Psychiatric Hospitals by Age, Sex, and Race, U.S., 1975." U.S. Department of HEW, November 1977.

————. "Changes in the Age, Sex, and Diagnostic Composition of Additions to State and County Mental Hospitals, U.S., 1969–1975." U.S. Department of HEW, May 1978.

————. "Changes in the Age, Sex, and Diagnostic Composition of the Resident Population of State and County Mental Hospitals, U.S. 1965–1975." U.S. Department of HEW, March 1978.

————. "State Trends in Resident Patients—State and County Mental Hospital Inpatient Services 1971–1975." U.S. Department of HEW, June 1978.

Miller, Robert W., et al. "Approaches to University Extension Work with the Rural Disadvantaged: Description and Analysis of a Pilot Effort." Morgantown, W.V.: Appalachian Center, West Virginia University, September 1972.

————. "Manpower Development and Job Training in Appalachian States: An Evaluation Study of the AFL-CIO Appalachian Council's 'Operation Manpower.'" Morgantown, W.V.: Appalachian Center, West Virginia University, November 1972.

Mississippi Action for Community Education. "Itinery and Information." Thursday, March 20, 1980.

Morbidity and Mortality Weekly Report. "Teenage Childbearing and Abortion Patterns—U.S., 1977." Vol. 29, No. 14, April 11, 1980.

Morgan, James N. "Individual Behavior, Economic Analysis and Public Policy." The 1977 Wladimir Woytinsky Lecture. Ann Arbor: University of Michigan, 1977.

Morris, Charles R. *The Cost of Good Intentions.* New York: W. W. Norton, 1980.

Moynihan, Daniel P. *Coping: On the Practice of Government.* New York: Random House, 1961.

————. *Maximum Feasible Misunderstanding.* New York: Free Press, 1970.

————. "Patterns of Ethnic Succession: The Rise of Blacks and Hispanics in New York City." First Annual Lecture, Graduate Program in Public Affairs and Administration, Columbia University, New York, November 1978.

————. *The Politics of a Guaranteed Income: The Nixon Administration and the Family Assistance Plan.* New York: Random House, 1973.

————. "The President and the Negro: The Moment Lost." *Commentary,* February 1967.

————. "Rescuing the Family." *America,* July 26, 1980.

Myrdal, Gunnar. *An American Dilemma: The Negro Problem and Modern Democracy.* New York: Harper & Row, 1944.

————. *The Challenge of World Poverty.* New York: Vintage, 1970.

National Association of Counties Research, Inc. "County Employment Reporter." Vol. 7, No. 4, August 1978.

National Association of Elementary School Principals/Institute for Development of Educational Activities. "The Most Significant Minority: One-Parent Children in the Schools." Arlington, July 28, 1980.

National Center for Health Statistics. "Birth Rates and Distribution of Births to Women Under Age 20, According to Age and Race of Mother: U.S. 1966–76." Division of Vital Statistics.

————. "Final Natality Statistics, 1976." *Vital Statistics Report Advance Report.* Vol. 26, No. 12 (Supplement), March 29, 1978.

National Center for Health Statistics. "Health Characteristics of Minority Groups, U.S. 1976." No. 27, April 14, 1978.

————. "Limitation of Activity and Mobility Due to Chronic Conditions: United States 1972."

————. "1976 Summary: National Ambulatory Medical Care Survey." July 13, 1978.

————. "Office Visits to Psychiatrists: National Ambulatory Medical Care Survey, U.S., 1975–76." August 25, 1978.

————. "Trends and Differentials in Births to Unmarried Women: U.S., 1970–76." Series 21, No. 36, May 1980.

————. "Utilization of Short-Stay Hospitals: Annual Summary of the United States, 1977."

National Commission for Manpower Policy. "CETA: An Analysis of the Issues." May 1978.

————. "Manpower and Immigration Policies in the United States." February 1978.

National Puerto Rican Forum, Inc. "Comprehensive Study of Puerto Ricans in the U.S. Mainland." New York, June 1980.

National Urban Coalition. "Restoring Confidence in Public Education: An Agenda for the 1980's." January 24–26, 1979.

———. "Youth Perspectives: Employability Development Programs and the World of Work."

National Urban League. "Interrelationships Between Educational Deficiencies and Delinquency and Crime." August 1980.

———. "The State of Black America 1980." January 1980.

New York City Board of Education. The Dropout Report. New York City Public Schools, Board of Education, October 16, 1979.

———. "Interrupted Education: Students Who Drop Out." Office of Educational Evaluation, September 30, 1979.

New York City Health and Hospitals Corporation. Medical Records—Evelyn Bochino. North Central Bronx Hospital, January 9, 1980.

Newman, Morris J. "A Profile of Hispanics in the U.S. Work Force." *Monthly Labor Review,* December 1978.

North, David S., and Marion F. Houstoun. "The Characteristics and Role of Illegal Aliens in the U.S. Labor Market: An Exploratory Study." Washington, D.C.: Linton and Co., March 1976.

Norton, Eleanor Holmes. "Remarks at 65th Annual Conference of National Urban League." July 30, 1975.

———. Speech at 1979 National Urban League Convention. July 25, 1979.

Novak, Michael. "Race and Truth." *Commentary,* December 1976.

Olsen, Tillie. *Yonnondio.* New York: Delta, 1974.

Parkinson, C. Northcote. *Parkinson's Law.* New York: Ballantine, 1964.

Patterson, James T. *America's Struggle Against Poverty, 1900–1980.* Cambridge: Harvard University Press, 1981.

Pesante, Juan. Statement from 43rd Precinct. August 8, 1977.

Piven, Frances Fox, and Richard A. Cloward. *Poor People's Movements.* New York: Random House, 1979.

———. *Regulating the Poor: The Functions of Public Welfare.* New York: Random House, 1971.

Police Department. "Felony Augmentation Program." New York Police Department, January 9, 1980.

Rainwater, Lee, and William L. Yancey. *The Moynihan Report and the Politics of Controversy.* Cambridge: MIT Press, 1967.

Raskin, Marcus G., ed. *The Federal Budget and Social Reconstruction.* New York: Transaction Books, 1978.

Ravitch, Diane. *The Great School Wars: New York City, 1805–1973.* New York: Basic Books, 1974.

Regier, Darrel A., M.D., et al. "The De Facto U.S. Mental Health Services System." *Archives of General Psychiatry,* Vol. 35, 1978.

Rigby, Robert J., Jr. "Between Sisyphus and a Sliding Pond: A Demonstration in Housing Management and Community Revitalization." Housing Authority of the City of Jersey City, September 1980.

Riis, Jacob A. *How the Other Half Lives.* New York: Dover, 1971.

Ritter, Martha K., and Sandra K. Danziger. "Life After Supported Work for Welfare Mothers: AFDC Follow-Up Interviews" (revised). MDRC, November 25, 1979.

Robison, David. "Training and Jobs Programs in Action: Case Studies in Private-Sector Initiatives for the Hard-to-Employ." Committee for Economic Development, Work in America Institute, May 1978.

Rossi, Alice S., et al. *The Family.* New York: W. W. Norton, 1977.

Rossiter, Clinton. *Conservatism in America: The Thankless Persuasion.* New York: Random House, 1955.

Rutter, Michael, et al. *Fifteen Thousand Hours: Secondary Schools and Their Effects on Children.* Cambridge: Harvard University Press, 1979.

Ryan, William. *Blaming the Victim.* New York: Random House, 1971.

Salins, Peter D. *The Ecology of Housing Destruction.* New York: New York University Press, 1980.

Samuelson, Robert J. "The View from the Battlefield of the War on Poverty." *National Journal,* March 3, 1979.

Sandell, Steven. "Black-White Income Differences in the Seventies" (draft). U.S. Department of Health and Human Services, Washington, D.C., 1980.

Sanger, Bryna Mary. *Welfare of the Poor.* New York: Academic Press, 1979.

Santiago, Tony. "Mississippi Entitlement Visit, February 20–22" (memo). MDRC, February 28, 1980.

Sawhill, Isabell V. "The Economic Status of Women Who Head Families." The Urban Institute, September 1975.

Sawhill, Isabel V., and Maurice MacDonald. "Welfare Policy and the Family" (working paper). The Urban Institute, September 18, 1977.

Sayre, Wallace S., and Herbert Kaufman. *Governing New York City.* New York: W. W. Norton, 1965.

Scheper-Hughes, Nancy. *Saints, Scholars and Schizophrenics: Mental Illness in Rural Ireland.* Berkeley: University of California Press, 1979.

Schrank, Robert. "Evaluating Youth Employment Programs," edited remarks. Reston, Virginia, October 5, 1978.

———. *Ten Thousand Working Days.* Cambridge: MIT Press, 1978.

Schulte, Nancy Fisher. "Illegitimacy Soars, Begets Legacy of Health, Social Hardships." *The Chicago Reporter,* Vol. 9, No. 6, June 1980.

Schweinhart, Lawrence J., and David P. Weikart. "Perry Preschool Effects Nine Years Later: What Do They Mean?" High/Scope Educational Research Foundation, July 1978.

Seeley, David S. "Competence for All Through Collaboration of All." Public Education Association, 1980.

Sehgal, Ellen. "Undocumented Aliens in the United States: Impact of Research on Policy." Office of Research and Development, U.S. Department of Labor, November 9, 1978.

Semo, Vicki A. "Site Visit: January 17 and 18, 1979," West Virginia, memorandum. MDRC, January 23, 1979.

Sennett, Richard, and Jonathan Cobb. *The Hidden Injuries of Class.* New York: Vintage, 1975.

Sexton, Patricia Cayo, and Brendan Sexton. *Blue Collars and Hard Hats.* New York: Vintage, 1972.

Shapiro, Harvey D. "Waiving the Rules." MDRC, June 1978.

Sheehan, Susan. *A Welfare Mother.* Boston: Houghton Mifflin, 1975.

Silberman, Charles E. *Criminal Violence, Criminal Justice.* New York: Random House, 1978.

———. *Crisis in Black and White.* New York: Vintage, 1964.

Smith, M. Estellie, ed. *Those Who Live from the Sea.* New York: West Publishing, 1977.

Southern Regional Council. "Increasing the Options." Task Force on Southern Rural Development, March 1977.

Sowell, Thomas. *Ethnic America.* New York: Basic Books, 1981.

———. *Knowledge and Decisions.* New York: Basic Books, 1980.

———. "Myths About Minorities." *Commentary,* August 1979.

———. *Race and Economics.* New York: Longman, 1975.

———. *Pink and Brown People.* Stanford: Hoover Institute Press, 1981.

Spanier, Graham B. "Outsiders Looking In." *The Wilson Summer Quarterly*, Summer 1980.

Spradley, James P. *You Owe Yourself a Drunk: An Ethnography of Urban Nomads*. Boston: Little, Brown, 1970.

Steinfels, Peter. *The Neo-Conservatives: The Men Who Are Changing America's Politics*. New York: Simon and Schuster, 1979.

Sternlieb, George, and James W. Hughes. *Post-Industrial America: Metropolitan Decline and Inter-Regional Job Shifts*. Center for Urban Policy Research, Rutgers: State University of New Jersey, 1975.

————. "New Dimensions of the Urban Crisis." Center for Urban Policy Research, Rutgers: State University of New Jersey, March 20, 1979.

Strasburg, Paul A. *Violent Delinquents*. New York: Monarch, 1978.

Summers, James C., and Frederick A. Zeller. "Urban 4-H in West Virginia: A Longitudinal Evaluation." Center for Extension and Continuing Education, West Virginia University, July 1977.

Summers, James C., et al. "West Virginia 4-H Community Resource Development Evaluation Report." Center for Extension and Continuing Education, West Virginia University, Morgantown, March 1976.

Sviridoff, Michelle, and James W. Thompson. "Linkages Between Employment and Crime: A Qualitative Study of Rikers Releasees." New York: Vera Institute of Justice, September 10, 1979.

Sviridoff, Mitchell. "Address to the Bay Area Urban League" (San Francisco). Ford Foundation, April 10, 1979.

————. "Human Resources and the Pendulum of Power." Ford Foundation, November 18, 1978.

————. Recommendation for Grand/DAP Action. April 10, 1978.

————. "The Social Pathology of the Ghetto." Conference on Two World Cities: New York and Paris—Urban Policy for Survival, May 24–27, 1978.

Task Force on the New York City Crisis. "Counterbudget '81." Community Council of Greater New York, March 1980.

————. "Social Services Group Predicts State Budget Surplus of $650 Million." January 14, 1980.

Thomas, Piri. *Down These Mean Streets*. New York: New American Library, 1967.

Thompson, Hunter S. *Hell's Angels*. New York: Ballantine, 1966.

Thurow, Lester C. *The Zero-Sum Society*. New York: Penguin, 1981.

Torres, Rafael. Statement from 43rd Precinct. November 9, 1978.

U.S. Department of Commerce. "Money Income and Poverty Status of Families and Persons in the U.S.: 1978, Advance Report." Bureau of the Census, Series P-60, No. 120, November 1979.

————. "The Social and Economic Status of the Black Population in the United States: An Historical View, 1790–1978." *Current Population Reports,* P-23, No. 80.

U.S. Department of Health, Education, and Welfare. "The Measure of Poverty," Technical Paper 5. October 28, 1976.

————. "The Nation's Use of Health Resources 1979."

U.S. Department of Labor. "Completing the Youth Agenda: A Plan for Knowledge Development, Dissemination and Application for Fiscal 1980." Office of Youth Programs, October 1979.

————. "Concepts and Measures of Structural Unemployment." March 1979.

————. "Women Who Head Families: A Socioeconomic Analysis." Bureau of Labor Statistics, 1978.

Valentine, Bettylou. *Hustling and Other Hard Work: Life Styles in the Ghetto.* New York: Free Press, 1978.

Vice President's Task Force on Youth Employment. "A Review of Youth Employment Problems, Programs and Policies." Vol. 2, January 1980.

Walker, Gary C. "Statement for the Record for the Hearings on S.1312, Work and Training Opportunities Act of 1979 of the Subcommittee on Employment, Poverty and Migratory Labor of the Committee on Labor and Human Resources of the United States Senate." MDRC, March 12, 1980.

Warner, Eric. "Violent Juveniles: 17 Case Profiles." Submitted to Mario Merola, January 7, 1980 (Bronx District Attorney's Office).

Washington, Booker T. *Booker T. Washington and His Critics: The Problem of Negro Leadership.* Hugh Hawkins, ed. Boston: D.C. Heath, 1962.

Weisbrod, Jorena Adams. *Family Court Disposition Study.* New York: Vera Institute of Justice, 1981.

West Virginia Department of Employment Security. "Labor Force Statistics in West Virginia Labor Areas." November 1979.

White House Conference on Families. "Delegate Workbook: I. Families and Major Institutions, II. Families: Changes and Responsibilities, III. Families and Human Needs, IV. Families and Economic Well-Being." 1980.

Wright, Richard. *American Hunger.* New York: Harper & Row, 1979.

————. *Black Boy.* New York: Harper & Row, 1969.

————. *Uncle Tom's Children*. New York: Harper & Row, 1936.

Yates, Douglas. *The Ungovernable City*. Cambridge: MIT Press, 1977.

Zeitlin, Irving M. *Marxism: A Re-examination*. New York: Van Nostrand Reinhold, 1967.

Zelnik, Melvin, and John F. Kantner. "First Pregnancies To Women Aged 15–19: 1976 and 1971." *Family Planning Perspectives*, Vol. 10, No. 1, January/February 1978.

Index

About the Author

KEN AULETTA was brought up on Coney Island and attended New York City public schools and the State University of New York at Oswego. He received a master's degree in political science from the Maxwell School of Citizenship and Public Affairs at Syracuse University. He has worked for the federal and city governments. He now reaches two disparate audiences as a writer for *The New Yorker* and a columnist for the *New York Daily News*. His work has also appeared in the *Village Voice*, *New York* magazine, the *New York Review of Books*, and the *New York Times*; he has appeared regularly on television. He is the author of *The Streets Were Paved with Gold*, *Hard Feelings*, and *The Underclass*.

Elijah Anderson